Development with Globa

Can firms and economies utilize global value chains (GVCs) for development? How can they move from low-income to middle-income and even high-income status? This book addresses these questions through a series of case studies examining upgradation and innovation by firms operating in GVCs in Asia. The countries studied are China, India, South Korea, the Philippines and Sri Lanka, with studies of firms operating in varied sectors – aerospace components, apparel, automotive, consumer electronics including mobile phones, telecom equipment, IT software and services, and pharmaceuticals.

In the movement from low-income to middle-income status, the key industrial and firm policies are those of catching-up and learning through reverse engineering, sometimes as part of and sometimes outside GVCs. However, what suppliers actually do to internalize and build upon what they learn through ties with buyers is the crucial factor in effecting upgradation.

In moving beyond catch-up securing rents is important. This can be done through securing process rents. However, higher rents are earned through product innovation, which enable firms and economies to develop as headquarters of value chains and overcome the middle-income trap.

Dev Nathan is Visiting Professor at the Institute for Human Development, New Delhi, India; Research Coordinator of Global Production Network Studies, New Delhi, India; and Visiting Research Fellow at the Duke University GVC Center, Durham, USA.

Meenu Tewari is Associate Professor at the University of North Carolina at Chapel Hill, USA.

Sandip Sarkar is Professor at the Institute for Human Development, New Delhi, India.

Development Trajectories in Global Value Chains

A feature of the current phase of globalization is the outsourcing of production tasks and services across borders, and increasing organization of production and trade through global value chains (GVCs), global commodity chains (GCCs), and global production networks (GPNs). With a large and growing literature on GVCs, GCCs, and GPNs, this series is distinguished by its focus on the implications of these new production systems for economic, social, and regional development.

This series publishes a wide range of theoretical, methodological, and empirical works, both research monographs and edited volumes, dealing with crucial issues of transformation in the global economy. How do GVCs change the ways in which lead and supplier firms shape regional and international economies? How do they affect local and regional development trajectories, and what implications do they have for workers and their communities? How is the organization of value chains changing and how are these emerging forms contested as more traditional structures of North–South trade were complemented and transformed by emerging South–South lead firms, investments and trading links? How does the large-scale entry of women into value chain production impact on gender relations? What opportunities and limits do GVCs create for economic and social upgrading and innovation? In what ways are GVCs changing the nature of work and the role of labour in the global economy? And how might the increasing focus on logistics management, financialization, or social standards and compliance portend important developments in the structure of regional economies?

This series includes contributions from all disciplines and interdisciplinary fields and approaches related to GVC analysis, including GCCs and GPNs, and is particularly focused on theoretically innovative and informed works that are grounded in the empirics of development related to these approaches. Through their focus on the changing organizational forms, governance systems, and production relations, volumes in this series contribute to on-going conversations about theories of development and development policy in the contemporary era of globalization.

Series editors

Stephanie Barrientos is Professor of Global Development at the Global Development Institute, University of Manchester, UK.

Gary Gereffi is Professor of Sociology and Director of the Center on Globalization, Governance and Competitiveness, Duke University, Durham, USA.

Dev Nathan is Visiting Professor at the Institute for Human Development, New Delhi, and Visiting Research Fellow at the Duke University GVC Center Durham, USA.

John Pickles is Earl N. Phillips Distinguished Professor of International Studies at the University of North Carolina at Chapel Hill, USA.

Titles in the Series

- Labour in Global Value Chains in Asia
  Edited by **Dev Nathan, Meenu Tewari and Sandip Sarkar**

- The Sweatshop Regime: Labouring Bodies, Exploitation, and Garments *Made in India*
  Alessandra Mezzadri

- The Intangible Economy: How Services Shape Production and Consumption
  Edited by **Deborah K. Elms, Arian Hassani and Patrick Low**

- Making Cars in the New India: Industry, Precarity and Informality
  Tom Barnes

Forthcoming

- Global Value Chains and Development: Redefining the Contours of 21st Century Capitalism
  Gary Gereffi

Development with Global Value Chains

Upgrading and Innovation in Asia

Edited by

Dev Nathan

Meenu Tewari

Sandip Sarkar

INSTITUTE FOR
HUMAN DEVELOPMENT

CAMBRIDGE
UNIVERSITY PRESS

CAMBRIDGE
UNIVERSITY PRESS

University Printing House, Cambridge CB2 8BS, United Kingdom

One Liberty Plaza, 20th Floor, New York, NY 10006, USA

477 Williamstown Road, Port Melbourne, vic 3207, Australia

314 to 321, 3rd Floor, Plot No.3, Splendor Forum, Jasola District Centre, New Delhi – 110025, India

79 Anson Road, #06–04/06, Singapore 079906

Cambridge University Press is part of the University of Cambridge.

It furthers the University's mission by disseminating knowledge in the pursuit of education, learning and research at the highest international levels of excellence.

www.cambridge.org

Information on this title: www.cambridge.org/9781107104631

First published 2018

Reprint 2020

Printed in India by Thomson Press India Ltd.

A catalogue record for this publication is available from the British Library.

ISBN 978-1-107-10463-1 Hardback

ISBN 978-1-108-73384-7 Paperback

Contents

List of Tables and Figures   *ix*

1. Introduction   1
    Dev Nathan, Meenu Tewari and Sandip Sarkar

2. The Changing Landscape of Contract Manufacturers in the
    Electronics Industry Global Value Chain   20
    Gale Raj-Reichert

3. Gaining Process Rents in the Apparel Industry: Incremental
    Improvements in Labour and Other Management Practices   63
    Dev Nathan and Harsh

4. New Economic Geographies of Manufacturing in China   86
    Shengjun Zhu

5. The Philippines: A Sequential Approach to Upgrading in
    Manufacturing Global Value Chains   107
    Penny Bamber, Jack Daly, Stacey Frederick and Gary Gereffi

6. Learning Sequences in Lower Tiers of
    India's Automotive Value Chain   132
    Meenu Tewari

7. Innovation and Learning of Latecomers: A Case Study of
    Chinese Telecom-Equipment Companies   157
    Peilei Fan

8. From the Phased Manufacturing Programme to
    Frugal Engineering: Some Initial Propositions   176
    Nasir Tyabji

9. Industrial Upgrading in the Apparel Value Chain:
    The Sri Lanka Experience   193
    Prema-chandra Athukorala

10. Strategic Change in Indian IT Majors: A Challenge   229
    Neetu Ahmed

11. Moving from OEM to OBM? Upgrading of the Chinese
    Mobile Phone Industry   247
    Huasheng Zhu, Fan Xu and Qingcan He

12. Indian Pharmaceutical Industry: Policy and Institutional
    Challenges of Moving from Manufacturing Generics to
    Drug Discovery   279
    Dinesh Abrol and Nidhi Singh

13. Revisiting the Miracle: South Korea's Industrial Upgrading
    from a Global Value Chain Perspective   316
    Joonkoo Lee, Sang-Hoon Lee and Gwanho Park

14. Evolutionary Demand, Innovation and Development   349
    Smita Srinivas

15. GVCs and Development Policy: Vertically Specialized
    Industrialization   373
    Dev Nathan

Contributors   409

Index   413

Tables and Figures

Tables

2.1   Revenues and operating margins among ODMs and contract manufacturers   25

2.2   Key characteristics of the top five contract manufacturers in the computer industry   34

2.3   Design and engineering services locations of Flex   48

2.4   Jabil Circuit's design centres   49

2.5   Celestica locations that feature design services   50

3.1   India's ranking in production related problems   71

5.1   Functional upgrades into automotive R&D in the Philippines   117

5.2   The automotive E&E cluster in the Philippines   119

6.1   Aggregate improvements among the participants of UNIDO's team learning initiative, 2002   144

7.1   Global R&D centres of Huawei   165

7.2   Global R&D centres of ZTE   166

9.1   Apparel exports from Sri Lanka, 1970–2012   210

9.2   Apparel manufacturing labour cost in selected Asian countries, circa 2008 (US$/hour)   212

9.3   Composition of Sri Lankan apparel exports, 2003–04 and 2011–12   214

9.4   Composition of apparel exports from Sri Lanka and the major apparel exporting Asian countries, 2014–15 (percentage)   217

10.1   R&D investment by global and Indian IT firms (2015)   234

10.2   Three prongs of dynamic capability building and response of Indian IT firms   236

10.3   Acquisition/partnership of Indian IT firms with start-ups   240

10.4   Some of the biggest acquisitions by Indian IT services companies   242

11.1   Co-operation between multinational companies and Chinese manufacturers   267

11.2   R&D centres of foreign multinational companies in China   268

11.3   Income of Techfaith's main business sections from 2006 to 2011   272

12.1   Pharmaceutical patenting in the United States from the
        Indian pharmaceutical industry, 1992–2013   285

12.2   Investigational new drugs (INDs), 2008–13   291

12.3   Pharmaceutical companies in CRAM activities in India   294

12.4   Pattern of R&D and marketing acquisitions for
        fourteen leading Indian firms, 1999–2011   298

12.5   Types of R&D acquisitions with industries, 1999–2011   299

12.6   Types of R&D alliances, collaborations and
        licensing agreements, 1999–2011   299

12.7   Types of R&D alliances with RI/academia   301

12.8   Pattern of marketing alliances, collaborations and
        licensing agreements, 1999–2011   301

12.9   Domestic pharmaceutical activities of
        commercialized/launched generic compounds   303

12.10   Pattern of coverage of different types of burden of diseases
        in academic collaborations and alliances, 1999–2011   304

12.11   Pattern of coverage of different types of disease burden
        for new chemical entities (NCEs) under development by Indian
        pharmaceutical companies, 1999–2011   305

12.12   Pattern of coverage of different types of burden of
        diseases in industrial collaborations and alliances of
        fourteen leading Indian companies, 1999–2011   306

12.13   Pattern of government funding agencies' programmes/
        schemes-funded burden of diseases by industry, 2005–11   306

12.14   Firm-wise pattern of government funding agencies'
        programmes/schemes-funded burden of diseases by
        industry, 2005–11   307

13.1   Original and contract animation production in
        South Korea, selected years   336

15.1   Comparison of GDP per capita, 1820–1950   385

15.2   GDP per capita in developing and developed countries
        (US$ in current prices and current exchange rates)   385

15.3   Knowledge, rents and development   395

Figures

2.1   Gross profit margin and revenue for Flex   37

2.2   Gross profit margin and revenue for Jabil Circuit   37

2.3   Gross profit margin and revenue for Celestica   38

2.4   Gross profit margin and revenue for HP (Inc.)   38

2.5   Gross profit margin and revenue for Dell   39

2.6   Gross profit margin and revenue for Apple   39

2.7   Flex net sales by market (in percentages)   61

2.8   Jabil Circuit revenue by segment expressed as
       percentage of net revenue   61

2.9   Celestica revenue by end markets (in percentages)   62

9.1   Sri Lanka's share in world apparel exports, 1988–2015   216

9.2   Export similarity index: Sri Lanka versus
       Asian apparel exporting countries, 1995–2015   221

9.3   Volume, unit value and volume indices of apparel
       exports from Sri Lanka, 1985–2015 (1990 = 100)   222

11.1   Changes of the market share of domestic mobile
       phone manufacturers in China from 1999 to 2015   250

11.2   Export volume and the share of Chinese domestic
       MPCs in the international market from 2002 to 2009   251

11.3   Market share of Chinese mobile phone brands in 2006   252

11.4   Market share of Chinese 3G mobile phone brands in 2010   253

11.5   Market share of Chinese mobile phone brands in 2015   253

11.6   Evolution of mobile phone manufacturing value chain
       in China   254

11.7   Business linkages of domestic brand companies with
       EMSs and ODMs   254

11.8   Business linkages of foreign companies with
       EMSs and ODMs   255

11.9   The number of application patents related to
       smartphone technology in China between 2000 and 2010   255

11.10 The number of HCIT patent application of companies
       in the world between 2000 and 2011   256

11.11 The number of HCIT patent applications of companies
       in China between 2000 and 2011   256

12.1   Nature of patents granted to domestic and
       foreign firms in IPO (2005 to March 2013)   287

12.2   Nature of patents granted in IPO (2005 to March 2013)   287

13.1   South Korea's textile and apparel exports   322

13.2   South Korea's automobile production and exports, 1971–2013   328

13.3   South Korean animation exports, 1982–2013   333

14.1   A taxonomy of innovation in developing countries   359

14.2   The evolution of demand   361

1

Introduction

Dev Nathan, Meenu Tewari and Sandip Sarkar

This book is in many ways a follow-up to our earlier edited book (Nathan, Tewari and Sarkar, 2016). While that book dealt with labour conditions and labour issues in global value chains (GVCs) in Asia, this book deals with the manner in which upgrading and innovation have taken/can take place in GVCs; once again, with a focus on the Asian experience.

This 'Introduction' starts out by listing the various dimensions of a GVC; within this, emphasis is placed on the GVC as embodying a division, albeit a changing division, of knowledge and capabilities across geographies. After this, we define the ways in which firms may or may not strategically interact with GVCs. This is followed by listing the different types of upgrading, commonly discussed in the GVC literature. However, different types of upgrading enable the capture of rents, whether process or product rents, which are discussed in the next section. This passage through different types of rents itself depends on the manner in which knowledge is developed, both within and around value chains.

Thus, this introduction stresses upon a scheme where knowledge (which results in both process and product innovations and their corresponding rents) is crucial to development within and around value chains. There are many analyses of innovation, and in the context of many countries having made it from low-income to middle-income status, there is much discussion of the 'middle-income trap'. Some books on the challenges of China's current economic development explicitly place it in the context of overcoming the middle-income trap (for example, Woo *et al.*, 2012; David Shambaugh, 2016; Lewin, Kenney and Murmann, 2016).

Through case studies in Asian countries such as China, India, the Philippines, South Korea, and Sri Lanka, with an examination of diverse industries (electronics, telecom equipment, mobile phones, pharmaceuticals, automobiles, and even garments) this book looks at facets of the processes of industrial catch-up (Nayyar, 2013) and life after catch-up in the context of GVCs. How do firms and economies upgrade and innovate and move from being suppliers to becoming headquarter economies (Baldwin, 2016) or, in GVC-terms, how do firms in these economies becoming lead firms?

The last section of the 'Introduction' briefly highlights some of the contributions of the various chapters.

Dimensions of GVCs

The concept of a GVC has gone through a number of iterations.[1] At its core is the idea of the splintering of production, or outsourcing of production tasks, that results in a product across firms and borders. In an early definition, Gereffi (1994) identified GVCs as having three components: an input–output structure, a territoriality and a governance structure. Other analyses, however, have also introduced two other dimensions of GVC structures. Along with the splintering of production, there is also a division of knowledge between places where different production segments are located (Ernst, 2000; also Nathan and Sarkar, 2014). Furthermore, the GVC structure also results in or influences the distribution of income 'among various nodes of the commodity chain ("economic activities") – each consisting of a combination of different factors of production' (Arrighi and Drangel, 1986, 16; also Nathan and Sarkar, 2011).

The input–output structure is what makes a GVC – outputs in one production segment, such as intermediate electronic components, become inputs in another production segment, that of the assembly of electronic products, which are themselves inputs in marketing. In this input–output structure, what makes the GVC different from any other form of linked production is that the final product, the key output of the GVC, is not necessarily sold on the market by the final producer, or assembler, who sells contracted supplies to the lead firm. Foxconn, which assembles iPhones in China, does not sell the iPhone on the market, nor does a supplier of Nike shoes in Indonesia sell Nike shoes on the market. In some cases, as in automobile production, the final assembler, say, Toyota or Ford, are the companies that carry out the marketing of the final

---

1   For our purposes, in this book we include the concepts of global production networks (GPNs) and global commodity chains (GCCs) within the broader GVC concept. There are differences between all these concepts, but they are not of fundamental importance to the objective of this book or other related analyses. What is important is the splintering of production that informs all GVC-related frameworks.

product. The contractual, rather than the market-based transactions at various stages, is one distinguishing feature of the relations between firms in a GVC.

The outsourcing of production among various firms also requires a manner of coordination of this splintering – all the parts have to be coordinated and then put together in the final product. This coordination of production is what is covered under the term 'governance', which may be understood as the vertical relations within a GVC. Since the different production segments are carried on in different international locations, there is also a territoriality in the relation between production segments. There are local labour market conditions, laws, and other institutional factors that are specific to the territory within which a production segment is located. This territoriality can also be termed as the horizontal or place-based relations within a production segment.

Division of knowledge and capabilities

What, however, is the basis of the spatial division of production segments or tasks between different territories? Any production task or segment (which is a collection of tasks) has a knowledge basis. We can use the GVC literature (see Gereffi, Humphreys and Sturgeon, 2005) to divide the knowledge basis of segments into three categories: codified and easily acquired knowledge, such as the making of garments; codified but not so easily acquired knowledge, such as electronics or automobile manufacture; and relational knowledge, which is created in interaction between different firms, as in IT services.

A somewhat different division of the knowledge basis of tasks is delineated in Autor (2013) and Acemoglu and Autor (2010), who divide tasks into three types – (a) high-skill, analytic and problem-solving tasks, (b) middle-skill, routine or codifiable manual and office tasks and (c) low-skill, in-person service tasks. This division of tasks by high-, medium- and low-skill tasks seems to be well suited to factory production.

In a sense, what the GVC literature identifies as more-easily or less-easily acquired knowledge is conflated into Acemoglu and Autor's 'middle-skill, routine or codifiable manual and office tasks'. These are standard production tasks that can be turned into routines or are codifiable. They are also tasks that are most susceptible to automation and outsourcing. The decision to opt for automation or outsourcing depends on the relative cost of in-house automation against the cost of contracting a firm, with the required capabilities of workers, to carry out that task.

Although both of the types of routine knowledge mentioned here, namely garment manufacture and automobile assembly, are codifiable, there is a difference in the costs of their acquisition. The educational levels of workers that firms require in these sectors (garments and electronics or automobiles) are different. In the case of garments, basic literacy acquired by education up to the middle school level seems adequate, while in electronics and automobiles, firms require a minimum of high school education (Nathan and Sharma, 2016).

Manufacturing a product, however, requires knowledge of different types and levels. What might be described as a less knowledge-intensive product, such as garments, also contains tasks of different knowledge intensities. There is the knowledge of design, which is to a large extent tacit and difficult to acquire, and there is the knowledge of manufacturing or assembling a garment, which is to a large extent explicit and easy to acquire.

Similarly, in the case of knowledge-intensive products such as information technology (IT) services, there is the task of problem/solution identification and the subsequent design of an IT solution and its architecture, all of which involve substantial tacit knowledge. After this phase of difficult-to-acquire tacit knowledge tasks, there are the more routine tasks of programming, testing and maintenance of the IT service.

In distinguishing the knowledge levels of tasks we have to make a necessary distinction between tacit and explicit knowledge. Tacit knowledge is that which is acquired relationally, as in the GVC classification of relational governance; or is high-skill and problem-solving, as in the Acemoglu and Autor classification of tasks. Explicit knowledge, on the other hand, is that which can be codified and expressed in the form of routines.

There are limitations to this analysis. Possession of skills is not necessarily linked to the level of education, as there are many process and product developments that take place on the shop floor – something discussed in Chapter 6 by Meenu Tewari, among others. Furthermore, some handmade products require a high degree of tacit, craft knowledge. A handmade violin requires tacit knowledge of sound and the qualities of wood and shapes far beyond that which is expressed in the form of routines in factory-made violins. High levels of tacit knowledge would obviously mean that outsourcing would be difficult to carry out, as it is difficult to acquire the tacit knowledge. At the same time, many types of formerly tacit knowledge, for example, methods of preparing dough for baking or translation skills, have been successfully turned into routines in bread-making machines and translation programmes.

How will tasks be divided in a GVC? While we have so far talked of knowledge levels and types of tasks, it is necessary to bring in the notion of capability or the competences that a worker requires to perform a task or to utilize a technology in production (modifying Nubler, 2013, 122). Capability is not only a question of having the knowledge required, but also of having the ability to utilize it in production. The costs of acquiring such capabilities would vary between economies of different income levels. The reservation price of workers possessing these capabilities would be more important – they would be higher priced in a high-income country (HIC) than in a low- or middle-income country (LMIC). The relevant cost consideration would be the cost of employing people with the required capabilities.

In an HIC, the cost of employing people with the capabilities to carry out manufacturing or assembly tasks in garments is much higher than the cost of employing people possessing similar capabilities in an LMIC. On the other hand, the differences in costs of employing such persons may not be of the same order for higher-knowledge capabilities, as in high-tech services. In addition, some tacit knowledge related to both the domain of production and that of customer interaction may be virtually impossible to acquire for persons from LMICs, unless they relocate themselves to an HIC.

With such differences in the relative costs of employing people with differing capabilities, it would be expected that HICs would specialize in the performance of high-knowledge tasks and LMICs concentrate on the performance of low- and medium-knowledge tasks. This kind of distribution of knowledge intensities in different segments or nodes of GVC production, however, has implications for the distribution of income within a GVC. Here we are dealing not with the distribution of income between capital and labour, but with the distribution between firms that are linked in a GVC. Before going into an examination of this distribution of income within a GVC, we look further into the dynamics of knowledge distribution – a dynamics that will affect income distribution too.

The dynamics of knowledge distribution

As pointed out earlier, any splintering of production necessarily involves a distribution of knowledge. While the supplier acquires some knowledge, the lead firm may well lose some knowledge of the various segments of production.

For instance, with the manufacture of electronic chips having largely shifted to Asia, the knowledge of running chip-manufacturing factories has also migrated to countries such as Malaysia, which is now a centre of chip production. This migration of knowledge could mean a loss of that knowledge at the original location of the lead firm.

> To the extent that the flagship [the lead firm] has moved to *global sourcing* … this implies an *erosion* of the *collective knowledge* which used to be a characteristic feature of the flagship's home location. In some cases that collective knowledge may have migrated for good to the suppliers' overseas cluster(s). (Ernst, 2000, 17, emphasis in original)

The result was that when problems arose in the production plants in the US, 'We [Texas Instruments] have to send our Malaysian engineers to solve their problems' (ibid., 17).

Supplier firms also make conscious efforts to learn from their work with clients. They receive instructions about specifications and processes, and in the course of carrying out tasks, build up their knowledge of their production segments. Garment factories, for instance, learn about the combinations of specifications, sourcing of materials and different customer requirements, all of which are important in the move from 'cut-make-trim' (CMT) to what is called 'full package supply'. These processes of undertaking new functions go well beyond 'learning by doing'. They involve conscious firm-level efforts to learn both about their interface with input supplies and their own buyers. They also involve attempts to extrapolate from their experiences in serving various clients.

While supplier firms have their own learning strategies, lead firms also have strategies to develop the capabilities of their suppliers – usually to a limited extent so that it does not impinge on the core functions of the lead firms. Levi's, for instance, worked with their supplier factories to develop low-cost methods of treating denim. This lowered their manufacturing costs. Other garment brands have worked with suppliers to enable them to develop sample rooms and be able to move to full package supply, where suppliers carry out all functions after design. From the design received, the suppliers have to work out the sourcing and cutting of fabric. Then, artisanal tailors work on the ways of stitching in what are called sample rooms (see Werner, 2012, for a description of the process of acquiring full-package capabilities in garment manufacture by firms in Latin America).

Even design functions may be handed over to the suppliers – if not individual suppliers, then large intermediaries such as Li and Fung, which prepare whole portfolios of designs from which buyers can choose. Of course, branding and marketing functions are kept away from such functional upgrading. Action may be taken against supplier firms that go too far and try to market their own brand. When the Taiwanese PC and laptop manufacturer began marketing its own Acer brand of computers, its erstwhile buyers quickly cut off manufacturing contracts (Sturgeon and Kawakami, 2012).

Now, there is a two-way flow of knowledge between lead and supplier firms, not just a one-way flow of knowledge from lead to suppler firms, as was seen with regard to chip manufacture in Malaysia and the USA. Both types of GVC firms have their own strategies. Suppliers would try to increase their knowledge and thus the functions they are able to undertake. Lead firms would try to restrict such knowledge acquisition by suppliers to non-core functions. Where the core competence of lead firms is in the supply of equipment and machinery, they may well restrict the knowledge that users acquire of this technology. As Gillian Hart points out, there is a limit to the migration of skills from Japanese equipment suppliers to Malaysian equipment users.

Knowledge acquisition by suppliers through methods such as reverse engineering, however, would change the division of knowledge in the value chain. Such knowledge acquisition also requires adequate and appropriate support from their governments and other development organizations, that is, from the ecosystem within which GVC firms function. At this point, the emphasis is that the terms of interaction between suppliers and lead firms can change in the process of interaction. The relations between these firms can also shift from mutual cooperation to fierce competition.

A clear example of this is the co-evolution in electronics GVCs (Sturgeon and Kawakami, 2012). The buyers retained their core competence (product design and marketing) while outsourcing non-core functions, including the design of chips, to Korean firms. Such chip design capability enabled Korean suppliers such as Samsung which had originally been component suppliers or original equipment manufacturers (OEMs) to become fierce competitors with their own models of smartphones and television sets.

Strategies of interaction

There is an almost unspoken assumption in GVC policies that being part of a GVC is almost the only way to acquire knowledge of the concerned production processes. However, as emphasized by a number of more recent studies, there is both inclusion and exclusion (Bair and Werner, 2011), or, in strategic terms, coupling, de-coupling and re-coupling (Horner, 2014; Coe and Heung, 2015), within GVCs.

One strategy of lead firms to restrict the spread of knowledge is through the use of patents and related forms of intellectual property rights. However, once developing country firms participate as suppliers, they are able to get an idea of at least some part of the production knowledge. Besides, that which is not transferred can be acquired through a deliberate firm-level policy of reverse engineering – taking apart a product to analyse its parts and processes in order to make a copy. Reverse engineering has historically been the method of all late industrializers, whether it was Europe with regard to textile machinery, or, in contemporary fashion, India in automobiles (Chapter 8 by Nasir Tyabji) and pharmaceuticals (Chapter 12 by Dinesh Abrol and Nidhi Singh). The Chinese telecom equipment manufacturers Huawei and ZTE used both reverse engineering and product development to emerge as major players in the telecom equipment sector (Chapter 7 by Peilei Fan).

Reverse engineering has often been carried out under a strategy of de-coupling from GVCs, as with the Indian pharmaceutical and the Chinese telecom equipment industries. It has also been made possible by the localization of product specifications, leading to changes in the product, as in the case of Tata's truck manufacturing collaboration with Mercedes Benz (Chapter 8). As Tyabji points out, when the Tata–Benz collaboration ended there was no truck like the Tata truck in the Benz stable.

Income distribution

Trade relationships in a GVC are contractual relationships. To summarize what is discussed more fully in Nathan, Tewari and Sarkar (2016), the factors that influence GVC bargaining power are: (*a*) the difficulty or ease of producing or acquiring the capability required, (*b*) the number of possible producers of the task and (*c*) the number of alternate buyers for the task.

In the common GVC structure, where there are monopolist lead firms with a competitive suppliers' market, such as in the case of Apple or Nike, the lead firm secures the rent or surplus above the normal profit, while the competing supplier firms merely make the competitive profit required to stay in business (Kaplinsky, 2000; Nathan and Sarkar, 2011). This is the common distribution of GVC surpluses, with the rents being concentrated with firms in the HICs and low levels of competitive profits accruing to firms in the LMICs. This inter-firm distribution of surpluses is a key factor in the inter-country income inequality – firms with rents are concentrated in the HICs, while firms earning competitive profits are concentrated in the LMICs.

Put this way, the question of development in a GVC structure is easily posed as Kaplinsky (2015) does: how can LMIC firms secure rents, rather than just profits? In fact, when this structure of distribution of monopoly rents and competitive profits across firms in GVCs was presented by this author in a seminar at Beijing Normal University, more than one person asked whether this meant that the question of development in a GVC framework required the shifting of Chinese firms from earning competitive profits to securing rents.

That is the central question of this book: how can firms from low- and middle-income countries move from getting competitive profits to securing rents? Following this thread, we also ask: what are the roles of upgrading, which is the process of taking on tasks that capture higher value, and innovation, which is that of making something new, either in a new way as a process innovation, or a new product? Both process and product innovation are types of upgrading, but not all upgrading is innovation. Upgrading is still a part of catch-up, rather than of going ahead, which requires innovation.

Types of upgrading

The GVC literature opines that there are four types of upgrading: function, process, inter-chain and product (Humphrey and Smitz, 2000). Functional upgrading occurs when supplier firms undertake more functions than they did earlier, for example, the move from CMT to 'full package supply' in the case of garments. Process upgrading refers to the change in the method of production or organization of production. As Bhide (2009) points out, most innovations are in fact of the process variety; not the production of a new product, but a change in the method of production.

An important GVC process innovation was that of the global delivery model (GDM) in IT services. Pioneered by the major Indian IT service firms, TCS and Infosys, it involved splitting up a software service into a number of component parts. These parts could then be worked on simultaneously in separate locations differentiated by labour costs. With this, they were able to utilize the global segmentation of the labour market. They could use higher-paid professionals working onshore with the customer for design and related customer interface.

At the same time, lower-paid professionals could work offshore in India on the bulk of the programming and related tasks. In addition, the time difference between these two locations allowed a virtual 24-hour working day. With teams having worked on different components, they could then be put back together and tested for delivery to the client.

This GDM process upgrading reduced costs, since it utilized the segmentation of the global labour force, and also reduced delivery time. The global delivery system was the key process innovation through which Indian IT firms were able to develop as an offshore location for development and delivery of IT software services. However, a characteristic of process innovations is that they cannot be patented and can thus be copied. Consequently, US IT service firms, such as IBM and Accenture, copied the global delivery model and set up offshore locations for programming work in India.

In manufacturing, Chinese firms have carried out numerous process innovations, including the setting up of 'supply chain cities' for different products (Gereffi, 2009). It is these innovations that have allowed Chinese firms to remain competitive despite substantial increases in wage costs. Chinese firms seem to have internalized the doctrine of continuous process improvement in order to remain competitive.

Inter-chain upgrading occurs when a firm shifts from manufacturing in one supply chain to another one. Such a shift would be into a chain that provides a higher margin, possibly one with overall higher margins – such as a shift from the automobile to aircraft supply chains, as discussed in Bamber, Daly, Frederick and Gereffi (Chapter 5).

Product upgrading has been divided into two parts: own design manufacture (ODM) and own brand manufacture (OBM). The former occurs when the supplier firm undertakes the design function, as seen in the example of chip design by Korean suppliers. A supplier may carry out designing duties, but will continue to supply the production on a contractual basis to the OEM and not sell under its own brand name. Brands take time to become established, but when a former supplier is able to sell its own product on the market, then the innovation can be termed own brand manufacture (OBM). The product may not be an entirely new product but merely an incremental improvement on an existing product. However, if the improved product is sold under the former supplier's own brand name, then it would count as OBM. In a sense, OBM signals the end of catch-up industrialization and involves innovation, rather than just imitation. It is also the transformation of suppliers into lead firms, or the setting up of new lead firms in developing countries.

Upgrading and rents

The different types of upgrading – process, function, design and brand – are related to the ways in which income is distributed within a GVC. The distinction between competitive profits and rents can be further refined (as in Davis, Kaplinsky and Morris, 2017). They divide rents into four sets – resource rents, innovation rents, exogenously defined rents and market power rents.

The resource rents are a Ricardian form of rent, where the surplus above marginal cost is due to scarcity – for instance, of high-grade ore. Of greater interest for GVC analysis are innovation rents or Schumpeterian rents created by producers through the application of knowledge in production (Schumpeter, 1992). Davis, Kaplinsky, and Morris include both process innovations (or having better production processes than rivals) and product innovations together under innovation rents. However, there is a difference between the ways in which the two operate in a GVC.

Process rents relate to improved processes of production, where those adopting them are able to reduce costs below that of competitors. However, such a change does not affect the distribution of surplus within the value chain between the lead firms and the suppliers. Such process rents allow some suppliers to get a profit higher than what other suppliers do by reducing costs.

Product rents due to higher quality or new products, however, would enable innovating firms that emerge from former suppliers to move into the category of lead firms and thus compete for rents secured by lead firms. Such an emerging lead firm would then move, at least for that product, from merely securing supplier profits to getting some product rents.

There is also a difference in the knowledge used in process and product rents. In the former, basic knowledge in production does not change; it is only the process that is reorganized through managerial innovations. These managerial innovations are important and can be an important source of rents. However, process innovations are easily copied and cannot get intellectual property protection. Thus, process rents can also be quickly dissipated as utilization of the superior management system diffuses through production units in a GVC avatar of the Prebish-Singer trap (Kaplinsky, 2005; Milberg and Winkler, 2013) from primary commodities to any product that can be commodified.

Similarly, David, Kaplinsky and Morris's category of exogenous rents, those outside of the production system, and due to factors such as publicly provided superior infrastructure, enable some suppliers in some countries to supply at lower costs and thus raise the profits of the producing firms. Such exogenous rents do not affect the distribution of surpluses within the GVC.

The final category of rents identified by Davis, Kaplinsky and Morris is that of monopoly or oligopoly rents due to sheer market power. There can be such rents but they are often also due to products that are superior or perceived to be superior. Sheer market power may exist in undifferentiated products, such as crude oil, but most often market power is related to product differentiation, and generally shored up by intellectual property rights protection.

Market power and its erosion or strengthening do affect the distribution of income within a value chain. The best example is that of the market power of crude oil suppliers manifested through the Organization of Petroleum Exporting Countries (OPEC), which has had substantial effects on the distribution of revenues within the petroleum value chain.

Product rents, however, need to be further divided into sub-types. There can be rents due to small or incremental changes in the product, such as the various iterations of all mobile and smartphones. These incremental product changes are necessary for maintaining market share, but they are not new products. They are, as in the famous example, just better mousetraps.

The second category of product rents is that of a new product itself, such as the invention and commercialization of the TV or the smartphone. These would give far greater benefits to the first movers, as was the case with Sony's Walkman CD-playing music system or Apple's digital music system, the iPod. The product rents from new products will continue until other firms in the industry catch up with the new product.

Within new product rents, it would be useful to further distinguish between consumer and producers' goods. The creation of a technology used in production – a general purpose technology, such as that of electricity or IT – not only creates product rents for the commercial creators of the technology, but is a factor, even a key factor, in establishing not just the firms' dominance in the market, but also the firms' home country's hegemony in the world capitalist system. If iron and steel production and the factory system ensured that the nineteenth century could truly be called Britain's century, electricity and mass production established the 'US century' over the past hundred years. This long twentieth century (Arrighi, 1994) has been extended by the dominance of US firms in the current general purpose information and communication technology (ICT) industries. The creation of a production technology, particularly a general purpose technology, can provide substantial and sustained rents to its developers and producers.

Value chains, knowledge and development

In value chain analysis, the problem of development can be phrased in terms of advancing from low-knowledge segments to high-knowledge segments of production. High-knowledge segments are those that earn high rents. The rents earned have been linked in earlier writings to wages (Nathan and Sarkar, 2011) and the quality of employment (Nathan and Kumar, 2016). In this book, this relationship is further extended between knowledge, firm trajectories and development outcomes as a whole, with development outcomes being summarized in terms of income levels. Thus, what is being argued is that there is a connection between the knowledge bases of production segments, rents earned and employment quality, including wages, and even overall development outcomes.

At the micro-economic or firm level, the argument is that the knowledge base of production is related to the rents earned – (*a*) they are non-existent or just competitive profits are earned when the knowledge base is relatively low, as in the assembly of garments or electronic products, (*b*) there are limited process rents earned by firms that carry out process innovations of the incremental variety or carry out functional upgrading to full package supply and finally (*c*) rents are high where major innovations in products are carried out. The last would be the situation of Schumpetarian rents. Schumpeterian rents are sub-divided into rents from (*i*) incremental changes in products, (*ii*) new products and (*iii*) products that are not only new, but are also the machinery, equipment and services used in production.

From the firm level one needs to proceed to that of the economy. This book deals with the micro-economic or firm level. Only Chapter 13 by Joon Koo Lee, Sng-hoon Lee and Gwanho Park, Chapter 14 by Smita Srinivas and Chapter 15 by Dev Nathan take this analysis to the macro-economic level. This analytic shift can be carried out by aggregating different kinds of firms at the economy or, as done by Coe and Yeung (2015), at the regional level. Here, the hypothesis is that a low-income economy is specialized in terms of having a predominance of assembly-level firms; a middle-income economy is less-specialized in having a dominance of firms carrying out multiple functions as full package suppliers and involved in incremental process improvements; and a high-income economy is again specialized in terms of possessing a preponderance of firms involved in major product and process innovations of the Schumpeterian type and correspondingly earning high rents. Preponderance is in terms of the contributions of different types of firms to national income. This is the structure of what is known as the Smiley curve (Stan Shih, 2010), for which Milberg and Winkler (2013) find some evidence in a cross-country comparison.

Outline of chapters

The chapters in the book deal with the trajectories of changes within firms as they move from access to little or no rent to securing progressively greater rents through process, functional and/or product innovation. Product rents are subdivided into incremental product rents and rents from new products.

Chapter 2 by Gale Raj-Reichert deals with the manner in which contract suppliers in electronics, such as Foxconn, Flex and others, moved beyond solely manufacturing for lead firms in GVCs. They increased their capabilities towards design, innovation and engineering work. As a result, '[t]hey take ideas from branded customers and carry out product design, prototyping, manufacturing innovations, and supply chain management – which brings these ideas to life – *sketch to scale …*' After the initial conception and design of a product, these are methods of joint development of products with lead firms.

Dev Nathan and Harsh (Chapter 3) deal with the management and labour practice improvements that enable some garment firms in India to secure process rents, by reducing costs below those incurred by competitors. Shengun Zhu (Chapter 4) discusses the impact of the rise of wages and the tightening of the labour market in China, and how this led to improvements in factory conditions and movement away from 'sweatshop conditions'.

The Philippines is not much discussed in GVC literature. Penny Bamber, Jack Daly, Stacey Frederick and Gary Gereffi (Chapter 5) deal with upgrading from one chain to another. An upgrading of firms and human capabilities (they use the term 'human capital') enabled Philippine firms that were manufacturing electronic wireless harnesses to move from the manufacture of this part for automobiles to higher-value wireless harnesses for aircraft and also to parts of aircraft interiors. This example shows the importance of developing capabilities in product segments (just wireless harnesses and parts of aircraft interiors), rather than in complete products.

Meenu Tewari (Chapter 6) discusses ways in which firms learn as they undertake forward and backward linkages through collaboration with their clients in a reversal of the direction in which expertise and knowhow flows. The chapter documents the purchase of small-scale design and distribution centres in Europe by their former suppliers. It examines learning and upgrading among automotive component firms in India and their transition through innovative re-combinations of organizational knowledge to multinational corporation (MNC) co-owners and investors in higher-income countries.

The set of chapters listed in the earlier paragraphs are examples of movement of firms from low-profit to rent-earning (even if the rent is minor). The next set of chapters deals with the much more difficult move to develop lead firms from former suppliers.

Peilei Fan (Chapter 7) deals with the growth of telecom equipment manufacturers Huawei and ZTE from China. The Chinese companies moved from reverse engineering telecom equipment to becoming two of the three largest companies in the world in terms of the number of patents acquired. Of course, these patents are likely to be for incremental changes and adaptations, but their rise as two of the largest acquirers of patents points again to the movement from reverse engineering to incremental innovation.

Nasir Tyabji (Chapter 8) looks at the experience of the Tatas in reverse engineering the truck produced in collaboration with Mercedes Benz. Importantly, reverse engineering led to frugal engineering, which is a form of innovation, even if it represents only incremental innovation.

Prema-chandra Athukorala (Chapter 9) presents the case of MAS, well known in Sri Lanka as a supplier of high-quality female inner wear and one of the two largest Sri Lankan suppliers. The company followed the path of upgrading 'package contracting' to developing design capabilities, setting up their ODM. All of these forms of upgrading have enabled Sri Lankan firms earn both functional and process rents with their reputation for flexible and timely delivery.

The Indian IT majors have had to change strategy – from an earlier reliance on their innovation of the GDM for the middle- to lower-end of IT services, they now have to meet clients' changed requirements for end-to-end digital services. Neetu Ahmed (Chapter 10) deals with the challenge of strategic change in the Indian IT majors.

Dealing with the mobile industry, Huasheng Zhu, Fan Xu and Qingcan He (Chapter 11) make the important point that the firms which carried out contract manufacturing for global brands were not the ones that made the jump to developing their own brands. This shows the effect of path dependency, where firms that are established with a particular business model (in this case, being contract suppliers) get locked into it, while other firms develop the strategic capabilities to make new business models based on own-brand manufacture and marketing.

The journey from reverse engineering to own product development, however, is not an easy one. The case study of the Indian pharmaceutical industry by Dinesh Abrol and Nidhi Singh (Chapter 12) examines these problems in close detail. The Indian pharmaceutical industry undertook the reverse engineering of drugs, most famously the anti-retroviral drugs to treat AIDS, to become the 'pharmacy of the developing world'. However, after India amended its patent laws in line with the Agreement on Trade-Related Aspects of Intellectual Property Rights (TRIPS) to provide patent protection for products (and not just processes as earlier), the Indian pharmaceutical industry has made little headway in developing new products based on new knowledge.

Among the cases presented in this book, South Korea is the only country whose firms have successfully made the leap to becoming global lead firms. Chapter 13, by Joonkoo Lee, Sang-Hoon Lee and Gwanho Park, outlines this move. Korean firms began what is now known as triangular trade – taking designs from the USA and managing their production in Chinese factories for supply to US brands. However, what are now global lead firms, such as Hyundai and Samsung, were developed under state-sponsored heavy industry and chemical development policies. They did not begin with a GVC orientation, though they have subsequently utilized GVCs, including the offshoring of design development, while competing as global brands.

Smita Srinivas (Chapter 14) points to the analytical need to place GVCs as part of wider economic development or industrial policies. She points to the inter-linkages between different types of production and innovation systems in an economy.

Is there then something that can be called a GVC development policy? In Chapter 15, Dev Nathan tries to bring together elements of the segment-wise capability approach developed here and presents it in contrast to the product or sectoral approach that typically characterized pre-GVC development policies. Drawing on insights presented in the cases in this book, he argues that GVC-based industrialization can be differentiated from the earlier import-substituting industrialization (ISI) and export-oriented industrialization (EOI), and characterized as vertically specialized industrialization (VSI).

References

Acemoglu, Daron and David Autor. 2010. 'Skills, Tasks and Technologies: Implications for Employment and Earnings.' NBER Working Paper 16082. Accessed 10 September 2015. Available at www.nber.org/papers/w16082.

Arrighi, Giovanni. 1994. *The Long Twentieth Century: Money, Power and the Origins of Our Times*. London: Verso.

Arrighi, Giovanni and Jessica Drangel. 1986. 'The Stratification of the World Economy: An Exploration of the Semi-Peripheral Zone.' *Review* X (1): 9–74.

Autor, David. 2013. 'The Task Approach to Labor Markets: An Overview.' NBER Working Paper 18711. Accessed 1 September 2015. Available at: www.nber.org/papers/w187aa.

Bair, Jennifer and Marion Werner. 2011. 'Guest Editorial: Commodity Chains and the Uneven Geographies of Global Capitalism.' *Environment and Planning A* (43): 988–97.

Baldwin, Richard. 2016. *The Great Convergence: Information Technology and the New Globalization*. Cambridge, MA: The Belknap Press of Harvard University Press.

Bhide, Amar. 2009. *The Venturesome Economy: How Innovation Sustains Prosperity in a More Connected World*. New Haven, NJ: Princeton University Press.

Coe, Neil and Henry Wai-chung Yeung. 2015. *Global Production Networks: Theorizing Economic Development in an Inter-Connected World*. Oxford: Oxford University Press.

Davis, Dennis, Raphael Kaplinsky and Mike Morris. 2017. 'Rents, Power and Governance in Global Value Chains.' PRISM Working Papers No. 2. Cape Town: School of Economics, University of Cape Town. Accessed 26 June 2017. Available at http://www.prism.uct.ac.za/.

Ernst, D. 2000. 'Global Production Networks and the Changing Geography of Innovation Systems: Implications for Developing Countries.' Economic Series Working Paper 9. Honolulu: East-West Centre. Accessed 15 July 2017. Available at http://scholarspace.manoa.hawaii.edu/bitstream/handle/10125/6074/ECONwp009.pdf?sequence=1.

Gereffi, Gary. 1994. 'The Organization of Buyer-driven Global Commodity Chains: How US Retailers Shape Overseas Production Networks.' In *Commodity Chains and Global Capitalism*, edited by G. Gereffi and M. Korzeniewicz, 95–122. Westport, CT: Praeger.

Gereffi, Gary, John Humphreys and Timothy Sturgeon. 2005. 'The Governance of

Global Value Chains: An Introduction.' *Review of International Political Economy* 12 (1): 78–104.

Horner, Rory. 2014. 'Strategic Decoupling, Recoupling and Global Production Networks.'*Journal of Economic Geography* 14 (6): 1117–40.

Humphrey, John and Hubert Schmitz. 2000. '"Governance and Upgrading: Linking Industrial Cluster and Global Value Chain Research.' IDS Working Paper 120. Accessed 26 June 2017. Available at https://www.ids.ac.uk/files/Wp120.pdf.

Kaplinsky, Raphael. 2005. *Globalization, Poverty and Inequality: Between a Rock and a Hard Place*. Cambridge: Polity.

———. 2016. *Inclusive and Sustainable Growth: The SDG Value Chains Nexus*. Geneva: International Centre for Trade and Sustainable Development. Accessed 14 July 2017. Available at http://www.ictsd.org/sites/default/files/research/inclusive_ and_sustainable_growth.pdf.

Lewin, Ariel, Martin Kenney and Johann Peter Murmann, eds. 2016. *China's Innovation Challenge: Overcoming the Middle-Income Trap*. Cambridge: Cambridge University Press.

Milberg, William and Deborah Winkler. 2013. *Outsourcing Economics: Global Value Chains in Capitalist Development*. Cambridge: Cambridge University Press.

Nathan, Dev and Abhishek Kumar. 2016. 'Knowledge, Education and Labour Practices in India.' *Economic and Political Weekly* 51 (36): 37–45.

Nathan, Dev and Sandip Sarkar. 2011. 'Profits, Rents and Wages in Global Production Networks.' *Economic and Political Weekly* 46 (36): 53–57.

———. 2014. 'From Reverse Engineering to Reverse Innovation: GPNs and The Emerging Powers.' In *Globalization and Standards: Issues and Challenges in Indian Business*, edited by Keshab Das, 181–92. Berlin: Springer.

Nathan, Dev, Meenu Tewari and Sandip Sarkar, eds. 2016. *Labour in Global Value Chains in Asia*. Cambridge: Cambridge University Press.

Nayyar, Deepak. 2013. *Catch Up: Developing Countries in the World Economy*. Oxford: Oxford University Press.

Nubler, Irmgaard. 2013. 'A Theory of Capabilities for Productive Transformation: Learning to Catch-Up.' In *Transforming Economies: Making Industrial Policy Work for Growth, Jobs and Development*, edited by Jose M. Salazar-Xirinachs, Irmgard Nubler and Richard Kozul-Wright, 113–149. Geneva: ILO.

Shambaugh, David. 2016. *China's Future?* Cambridge: Polity Press.

Schumpeter, Joseph. 1992. *Capitalism, Socialism and Democracy*. London: Routledge.

Shih, Stan. 2010. *Millennium Transformation: Change Management for New Acer*.Aspire Academy Series. Accessed 4 July 2017. Available at http://www.stanshares.com. tw/StanShares/upload/tbBook/1_20100817144639.pdf.

Sturgeon, Timothy and M. Kawakami. 2012. 'Global Value Chains in the Electronics Industry: Was the Crisis a Window of Opportunity for Developing Countries?' In *Global Value Chains in a Post-Crisis World*, edited by O. Cattaneo, G. Gereffi and C. Staritz, 245–302. New Delhi: World Bank and Academic Foundation.

Werner, Marion. 2012. 'Beyond Upgrading: Gendered Labour and the Restructuring of Firms in the Dominican Republic.' *Economic Geography* 88 (4): 403–22.

Woo, Wing Thye, Ming Lu, Jeffrey Sachs and Zhao Chen, eds. 2012. *A New Growth Engine for China: Escaping the Middle-Income Trap by Not Doing More of the Same*. London: Imperial College Press and Singapore: World Scientific Publishing.

2

The Changing Landscape of Contract Manufacturers in the Electronics Industry Global Value Chain

Gale Raj-Reichert

Introduction

The global electronics industry GVC has experienced significant changes in recent years. Increased competition and restructuring amongst branded firms, technological advancements and opportunities presented in emerging economies have shaped outsourcing, upgrading and transformations in the industry. An important group of supplier firms affected by these changes are contract manufacturers. Contract manufacturers are a small group of first-tier suppliers that carry out most of the manufacturing of electronic products for branded firms in the GVC. According to estimates by the European Commission, branded firms outsourced 80 per cent of their manufacturing to only five contract manufacturers (European Commission, 2012). They are Foxconn, Flex, Jabil Circuit, Celestica and Sanmina-SCI. The majority of these contract manufacturers originated in North America (Jabil Circuit, Flex and Sanmina-SCI in the United States and Celestica in Canada. Foxconn is a Taiwanese firm). Over the past ten years, contract manufacturers have transformed into suppliers with a wide range of capabilities that include design, engineering, technological and manufacturing innovation, alongside diversification strategies that have moved them into higher value-added operations for a variety of industries. In 2015, the contract manufacturing industry was worth US$430 billion (New Venture Research, 2016).

This chapter begins by discussing the changing landscape of contract manufacturing in the electronics industry GVC in light of wider global market dynamics. It aims to update earlier conceptualizations of contract manufacturers in the GVC literature in three ways. First, since the rise of contract manufacturing in the 1990s, these suppliers have moved beyond solely manufacturing for lead firms in GVCs. They have increased their capabilities, both organically and through strategic mergers and acquisitions (M&As), towards design, innovation and engineering work. Second, this increase in their capabilities has occurred in conjunction with diversification into new industries such as the automotive, aerospace, defence and health. Finally, emerging market locations in Asia such as China have opened up further opportunities for expanding design centres. These factors have shaped the upward trajectory of upgrading and growth amongst contract manufacturers. Through these changes, contract manufacturers show a variety of paths to upgrading which challenge earlier descriptions of contract manufacturers in the GVC literature as suppliers with 'generic capabilities' which are interchangeable, easily substitutable and present low switching costs to lead firms (Gereffi, Humphrey and Sturgeon, 2005). The following sections present these findings through a discussion of three key North American contract manufacturers – Flex, Jabil Circuit and Celestica – by chronicling their rise and continuing transformation as global suppliers in the electronics industry GVC.

The primary findings presented throughout the chapter are based on interviews conducted with various representatives from three of the top ten contract manufacturers based on sales in 2016 (*MMI*, 2017), and three of the top branded computer firms – based on sales in 2016 (Gartner, 2017) – in the electronics industry. Contract manufacturers are denoted by CM1, CM2 and CM3 and branded firms as Brand1, Brand2 and Brand3. Interviews were conducted in 2013, 2015 and 2016 in headquarters locations in North America and Europe and manufacturing sites in China, Singapore and Malaysia. Amongst contract manufacturers, interview respondents were engineers of quality control, site managers, directors of human resources and vice presidents in departments overseeing corporate social and environmental responsibility compliance. Amongst branded firms, interviews were conducted with directors of supply chain governance programmes. For all three contract manufacturers, interviews were conducted with a number of different respondents. This will be denoted by D1, D2, and so on, following the firm codes CM1, CM2 and CM3. Secondary data consists of information from the United States Securities and Exchange Commission (SEC) company filings, firm annual reports, firm websites and various media sources.

The changing landscape of contract manufacturing in the electronics industry GVC

Contract manufacturers are a small group of large and highly capable first-tier suppliers that undertake extensive outsourced manufacturing and service functions for branded firms in the electronics industry. These supplier firms originated in the 1960s and 1970s in North America as small firms. They were called 'board stuffers' because they manufactured printed circuit boards (PCBs) that were sold to electronic firms in Silicon Valley. During the 1990s, business strategies amongst branded firms in the electronics industry changed to focus on core competencies such as product design, development, innovation and marketing. At the same time, they started outsourcing other activities such as manufacturing. This led to a boom in outsourcing in the electronics industry, whereby branded firms outsourced a wide range of component manufacturing and final assembly of electronic products to these first-tier suppliers. This activity was called contract manufacturing. Many branded firms such as Hewlett-Packard, Cisco, IBM and Compaq even sold several of their manufacturing facilities to their contract manufacturers.

The business of contract manufacturing took off in the 1990s. Annual growth rates in the contract manufacturing industry averaged from 20 per cent to 25 per cent, which was considerably higher than the 7.5 per cent annual growth rate for the overall electronics industry during the 1990s (Zhai, Shi and Gregory, 2007). From 1996 to 2000, revenues for the eight largest contract manufacturers at the time (Solectron, Flextronics, SCI Systems, Jabil Circuit, Celestica, ACT Manufacturing, Plexus and Sanmina) increased by almost 400 per cent (Lakenan, Boyd and Frey, 2001).

The contract manufacturing model was originally envisioned to consist of expert manufacturers that could easily manage production ramp-ups and changes in production schedule in line with customer demands. However, contract manufacturers quickly went beyond this model and took on additional responsibilities for their customers. Contract manufacturers began providing turnkey services, which handled a gamut of activities to bring a product to market and beyond with the exception of product development. These activities included supply chain management, purchasing and inventory management of components, logistics, after-sales services, and repair (Gereffi *et al.*, 2005; Lakenan *et al.*, 2001; Sturgeon, 1998; Zhai *et al.*, 2007). Contract manufacturers invested heavily in additional capabilities to maintain closer, longer-lasting and cooperative relationships with branded firms (Hamilton and Gereffi, 2009; Luethje *et al.*, 2013; Gereffi, 2014). Over time, contract manufacturers have grown into large multinational corporations (MNCs) in their own right and today have a wide portfolio of activities beyond manufacturing that includes design services, engineering, technological development and innovation in manufacturing. Contract manufacturers have also reduced their dependency on the electronics industry by diversifying into new industries (Raj-Reichert, 2015).

The changing profiles of contract manufacturers may lead to modifications to their conceptualization in the early GVC inter-firm governance framework as set out by Gereffi *et al.* (2005). Contract manufacturers were considered to be in modular value chains whereby specifications for components and product manufacturing are easily codifiable and its technical requirements standardized. Within modular GVCs, the standardization and codification of information exchange reduces the complexity of outsourcing relationships between lead or customer firms and contract manufacturers. Given the relative ease of information exchange combined with the high capabilities of contract manufacturers, this group of suppliers was considered to have generic capabilities that allowed them to supply and cater to a wide pool of lead customer firms. Thus, in the GVC literature, contract manufacturers are considered to be interchangeable and the cost of switching between these suppliers low for lead firms. This translates to a low level of dependency by lead firms on contract manufacturers (Gereffi *et al.*, 2005).

The GVC governance framework, however, also recognized that changes in the industry towards de-codification due to technological change or an increase in supplier activities towards more proprietary functions, such as assisting lead firms with product design, could change the trajectory of contract manufacturers into relational value chains. In relational GVCs, information exchange is complex and proprietary and tends towards a mutual dependence between suppliers and lead firms. Lead firm–supplier relationships tend to be long-term and based on trust and reputation. The higher supplier capabilities drive lead firms to outsource further capabilities and, as a result, the cost of switching suppliers is high (Gereffi *et al.*, 2005). The findings presented in this chapter support and provide evidence for these changes occurring today, which show that contract manufacturers have transformed beyond their original conceptualization as suppliers with 'generic capabilities' in modular GVCs. However, a complete shift into a relational value chain governance model may be constrained by their diversification strategies, new lead firm customers and the commodification of certain types of technology. What is clear is that the contract manufacturing landscape is changing and we may be witnessing the rise of multiple governance structures, not necessarily in a single sector (see Dolan and Humphrey, 2004), but rather within this group of suppliers as they tread into new industry segments with new capabilities.

Related to the changing landscape of contract manufacturers is the discussion of upgrading in the GVC. Upgrading is generally thought to occur through supplier–lead firm relationships which result in learning or knowledge/technology transfer (Humphrey and Schmitz, 2000; Gereffi, 1999). Within modular value chains, contract manufacturers were depicted as having a relatively hands-off relationship with lead firms and less engagement over complex and high value-added parts of the value chain. Therefore, contract manufacturers are considered as firms that face challenges when it comes to upgrading. In these discussions, contract manufacturers tend to be compared with another small group of first-tier suppliers in the electronics industry called original design manufacturers (ODMs). ODMs are (mainly Taiwanese) suppliers who design and manufacture final products, such as laptops, which are sold under other brand name customer firms such as Dell, Hewlett-Packard, Apple and Toshiba. Examples of these ODMs are Quanta, Compal, Inventec and Wistron. ODMs which originally started with lower value-added manufacturing activities were able to upgrade into own product developers due to their close working relationships with multiple brand customers over specifications that required high capabilities in design and technology (Kawakami, 2011). Some previous ODMs, such as Lenovo, ASUS and BenQ, have gone on to become their own brand manufacturers (OBMs). In past years, contract manufacturers, in comparison to ODMs, were considered weak in design and innovation capabilities and stuck in lower value-added segments of the GVC with persistently low margins (Luethje et al., 2013; Sturgeon and Kawakami, 2011). However, falling margins are persistent across both groups of suppliers as consumer products become increasingly commoditized with falling prices (Engardio and Einhorn, 2005). A comparison of recent figures on margins and revenues between the top ODMs and contract manufacturers show a similar picture across suppliers (see Table 2.1; see also Figures A to C of profit margins and revenues of the three contract manufacturers).

Table 2.1 Revenues and operating margins among ODMs and contract manufacturers (in grey)

	2015 revenue (US$ billion)	2015 operating margin (%)
Hon Hai (Foxconn)	136	3.53
Quanta Computer	30.67	2.11
Compal	25.73	1.47
Flex	24.42	1.84
Wistron	18.93	0.67
Jabil Circuit	18.35	2.20
Inventec	12.01	1.63

Source: https://markets.ft.com/, accessed on 19 March 2017.

In the GVC literature, discussions around upgrading amongst contract manufacturers tends to focus on their ability to move up the value chain and become ODMs (and eventually OBMs) in order to capture higher value-added processes (Zhai *et al.*, 2007). While these questions are important for understanding upgrading amongst these suppliers, they inherently limit our thinking about the different pathways and trajectories – in particular in response to marketplace disruptions and increasing competition, technological developments and new markets – that can exist for upgrading in GVCs. Asking whether contract manufacturers will become ODMs assumes a path-dependency to upgrading in the electronics industry GVC. In contrast, this chapter shows how contract manufacturers are making use of different pathways and trajectories to upgrading, which include a combined strategy of (*a*) expanding capabilities into design, engineering, technological and manufacturing innovation, and new product introductions for customer firms, (*b*) diversification into new industries, both of which are being harnessed by them and (*c*) a presence in emerging markets in Asia which presents opportunities for further growth and development.

The pathways and trajectories of upgrading by contract manufacturers are responses to various external drivers. Contract manufacturing is a highly competitive industry. Like most firms in the electronics industry, contract manufacturers face losses in market share to increasingly lower cost competitors and face shareholder pressures to improve revenue growth. There are also other significant changes in the global electronics industry to which contract manufacturers are responding. They are: increased competition, restructuring, supplier consolidation amongst branded customer firms, technological developments, and opportunities in emerging markets, especially in Asia, for expanding economies of scale, design and innovation capabilities, and diversification strategies.

Competition is particularly fierce in the consumer electronics end markets. Prices of consumer electronic products have been on a fast and continual decline since the 1990s. For example, from 1995 to 2010, prices for electronic goods declined by 92.3 per cent and have continued to decline at an annual rate of 16 per cent (MAPI Foundation, 2012). This has also been exacerbated by a fall in sales of personal computers since the late 2000s with the introduction of mobility products such as tablets and smartphones (Murgia, 2017). Without highly innovative products with high levels of technological innovation, many branded firms (with the exception of Apple) have continued to face falling profit margins and declining sales in their commodity hardware products (consumer electronics). This has resulted in profits for most branded firms falling to single digit percentages. For example, the profit margin of Hewlett-Packard's personal computers was 6 per cent in 2011 (Burke and Bandler, 2012).

The falling sales of consumer electronics were exacerbated by disruptions in the marketplace, namely the global recession of 2008, which resulted in further restructuring amongst branded firms. Hewlett-Packard and Dell are key examples. Both firms reassigned their core competencies further away from hardware or commodity products to software and high-margin businesses services such as cloud computing, storage and printers (Cantrell, 2005). Hewlett-Packard, after a couple of years of threatening to sell off its personal computer division, split into two companies in 2015. The first company, Hewlett-Packard, Inc., retained its existing portfolio of hardware products such as personal computers and printers. The second and newly created Hewlett Packard Enterprise, which aimed to rival IBM, began catering to business customers providing software, consulting services, financial services, business incubation projects and technology solutions that include cloud and mobile-ready computing services (SEC 10-K Filing, 2015). Similarly, Dell has moved into storage, software, cloud computing and other business process services since the mid-2000s (SEC 10-K filings, 2010, 2011, 2015). The fast rise of business in data-storage services such as cloud computing by branded firms in the industry (*The Economist*, 2011) provides new outsourcing opportunities to contract manufacturers for manufacturing storage and server units and providing design assistance which can promise higher margins.

Interviews with various contract manufacturers over time show that they are quite aware of the implications of the changing dynamics amongst their branded customers and what it implies for them. In 2013, for example, respondents from contract manufacturers noted:

> The race to be the big player in the market has changed many times. Some [brand] companies had to launch 12 models a year. Customer behaviour has changed as well. Can brands keep up with the technology? Keep up with overhead? Is it a calculative risk for a brand to hand off their designs to trusted partners and managing business administratively and just utilize the brand name? It's about how to balance shareholders with running a business. (CM3D2 Headquarters, 2013)

[and]

> Contract manufacturers have enhanced their development of services and increased their capabilities. The top tier [suppliers] gives complex design solutions to OEM (brand) customers. Some OEMs are not touching products all together, where it is handled from contract manufacturer to consumers directly. Some OEMs don't even design, they only control design quality. Since 5-7 years ago, back-end [services] is as valuable as front-end work. (CM3D1 Headquarters, 2013)

In 2015, recognizing the shift amongst branded computer firms away from manufacturing towards services, a contract manufacturer noted: 'Brands are moving into software because that's where they see the margins are' (CM1 Headquarters, 2015). Similarly, a second contract manufacturer noted the business implications of these shifts for the contract manufacturing industry: 'Some brands are realizing that design is non-core or non-IP specific. Those are things they can outsource. But they need a party who has a vested interest in that design in the long term' (CM2 Headquarters, 2015).

Engaging in design with customer firms is not entirely new for contract manufacturers. From very early on, contract manufacturers designed PCBs for customer firms to avoid disruptive flaws during the manufacturing process. Prior to this, contract manufacturers had to frequently stop production in factories to consult faulty PCB designs with customer firms (Shore, 2001). In the 1990s, contract manufacturers began engaging in a more collaborative model with branded firms during early design phases and new product introductions.

These collaborations were mainly in line with 'design for manufacturing' (Zhai et al., 2007).

From the late 1990s and onwards, branded firms, faced with increasing price competition and pressures to cut costs, began to increasingly engage in 'innovation offshoring' or 'outsourcing innovation', which is the outsourcing of research and development (R&D) to suppliers (Engardio and Einhorn, 2005). Innovation offshoring can be in the form of either intra-firm or inter-firm linkages that create global networks of innovation. Intra-firm linkages are used to tap into a pool of cheap engineers and other higher-skilled workers in lower-cost locations. Inter-firm linkages involve the actual outsourcing of innovation. It can also involve the use of licenses to complement in-house R&D (Ernst, 2006).

Innovation outsourcing has been occurring in other industries such as automobiles, pharmaceuticals and aerospace since as far back as the 1980s. It is a key source of cost savings, risk minimization and higher rates of innovation with greater impacts (Quinn, 2000). In the electronics industry, innovation outsourcing has been important for software development, component innovation and semiconductor development. Take Cisco Systems as an example. Cisco began jointly developing equipment, new technology for its routers and hosting applications with its manufacturing suppliers from the early 1990s onwards (Duffy, 1999; Quinn, 2000). Another example is Dell, which outsourced almost all design, innovation of components, software and non-assembly production since the 1990s (Quinn, 2000). Hewlett-Packard began using suppliers to co-design many of its products, which included servers and printers, in the 2000s. Hewlett-Packard also received help in designing its personal computers from the ODM Quanta and the contract manufacturer Foxconn (Engardio and Einhorn, 2005).

For the electronics industry there is increasing 'modularization' of innovation (Ernst, 2006). Engardio and Einhorn (2005, 2) find that 'the rich West will focus on the highest levels of product creation, and jobs of turning concepts into actual products or services can be shipped out'. According to a former Flex CEO, 'some 80 per cent of what engineers in product development do are tasks that can easily be outsourced – like translating prototypes into workable designs, upgrading mature products, testing quality, writing user manuals, and qualifying parts vendors' (Engardio and Einhorn, 2005, 3). Quoting Daniel H. Pink, the author of *A Whole New Mind*, Engardio and Einhorn (2005, 2) emphasized the regional separations within global networks of innovation as the 'left brain' intellectual tasks that 'are routine, computer-like, and can be boiled down to a spec sheet are migrating to where it is cheaper, thanks to Asia's rising economies and the miracle of cyberspace'. The USA will remain strong in 'right brain' work that entails 'artistry, creativity, and empathy with the customer that requires being physically close to the market'. A key example of commodity design is the personal computer, whose technology became standardized and thus easily outsourced to ODMs (Engardio and Einhorn, 2005). The limit to outsourcing design, however, may be restrictions brand firms make by 'drawing the line' at 'commodity technologies', albeit a moving one, as technology becomes less proprietary. Indeed, the risk would be the rise of new competitors, such as Asian suppliers, who have a better handle on their domestic and regional markets than Western brands.

Because brands have hundreds of products, they welcome the opportunity to purchase designs and products off-the-shelf, which can lower their R&D spending (Engardio and Einhorn, 2005). In fact, R&D budgets across branded firms have fallen as more commodity technology is outsourced (*MMI*, 2015; Luethje *et al.*, 2013). In the early 2000s, Hewlett-Packard's R&D spending went from a long-term 6 per cent (of sales) to 4.4 per cent. Cisco System's R&D budget fell from its average of 17 per cent to 14.5 per cent in the mid-2000s (Engardio and Einhorn, 2005).

The increased opportunities to engage in design work and innovation were reported by all three contract manufacturers interviewed. CM3D2 noted, 'Around 20 per cent of business, contract manufacturers will design and take-over the supply chain' (Headquarters, 2013). According to a representative at a CM3 factory in Penang, extra design services for improving a product were provided for free to win over contracts from competitors (CM3D3 Penang, 2015). Jabil Circuit, for example, is moving into longer-term and more strategic partnerships with customer firms. These inter-firm relationships suggest a movement away from a modular value chain and towards a more relational GVC. According to its CEO, Mondello,

Twenty years ago, contract manufacturing largely involved taking blueprints and instructions from a customer and making the requested product. While some of that still goes on, ... most of Jabil Circuit's relationships with customers 'are quite deep, quite strategic, long-term relationships' ...

Manufacturing, the actual putting together of the parts, is only a portion of what we do. (Minter, 2014, 2)

The increasing capabilities in design and innovation amongst contract manufacturers have also been clear to branded firms. Branded firms no longer consider contract manufacturers as suppliers with generic capabilities. According to one of the computer brands interviewed,

> Outsourcing first began in the 1990s and it was termed 'contract manufacturing'. During this time, Brand 3 did the technical design, built the prototypes in in-house labs and Brand 3 just needed someone to churn it out. They looked for who was the cheapest with the best quality. It was a commodity type relationship, where a contract manufacturer did not have something special. Some were more efficient but they did not bring anything to the table. They did not have anything on intellectual property and nothing to differentiate one from another. Now, the big contract manufacturers, including Foxconn, are bringing technology back to the brands … That is why partnership relationships are created. (Brand3 Headquarters, 2015)

Similarly, a second computer brand noted:

> All of the contract manufacturers have more of this (referring to design capabilities). Inventec, Quanta, Jabil, Flextronics, and Foxconn. Foxconn can now design systems and tell the brands they can do it for them. (Brand1 Headquarters, 2015)

Technological developments also play an important role in the upgrading trajectory for contract manufacturers. For example, developments such as the Internet of Things (IoT) have created new opportunities for innovations by contract manufacturers. The IoT industry, which includes digital wearables and connected devices, is projected to grow to US$4 trillion by 2020 (Manufacturing Market Industry, 2015). It has opened opportunities for innovation linked to smart devices. CM1 noted:

> There are now incubators around the world in the hardware space because devices are still the future. For example, connecting data use in the home, cars, and hospitals. You can collect all this data, but you need gadgets to do something with them. We are hiring as many engineers as we can [to do this work]. We can't attract enough engineers away from other more attractive companies in Silicon Valley. (Interview, 2015)

Another important transformation amongst contract manufacturers is their heavy diversification strategies. This is a mutual response to the increasing use of electronics in industries such as automotive and health and by these industries to use contract manufacturers for the first time in recent years. Contract manufacturers are now able to offer their capabilities to a wider set of industries. CM2D1 described its firm's diversification strategy as a response not only to a 'second wave' of outsourcing by a new set of industries such as aerospace and health but also a recent 'third wave' in the outsourcing of services such as design and engineering by a wide range of industries.

One of the respondents interviewed stated that, 'Manufacturing is a first hurdle that our [first wave] customers go through in outsourcing and once they have gone through that they feel comfortable [to outsource services]' (CM2D1Headquarters, 2015).

Furthermore, according to CM2D1, unlike branded computer firms whose intellectual property rights (IPRs) are increasingly bound up in software, customers in the health industry hold their IPRs in hardware. For example, 'a company like Siemens Healthcare, for their ultrasound product the IP is in the handheld wand. It's not the back-end computer' (CM2D1 Headquarters 2015). For these newer customers, the outsourcing of services is important.

Foxconn is another example. Faced with declining revenues from falling smartphone sales, rising labour costs in China and an over-reliance on Apple's orders, its founder and CEO, Terry Gou, signalled the need for a changing business model at a shareholders' annual meeting in 2014. Mr Gou announced the company's goal to move away from a low value-added and labour-intensive contract manufacturing model into one that included software, hardware and wireless design for a diversified set of industries. In recent years, Foxconn has manufactured displays for the electric car maker Tesla Motors, Inc., become a telecommunication network provider in Taiwan and partnered with Google on robotic operating systems (Luk, 2014a, 2014b, 2014c; Tse and Yip, 2016).

Competitive pressures to reduce manufacturing costs have also led contract manufacturers to introduce efficiencies and innovations to manufacturing such as automation. Foxconn, for example, has developed its own robots, called Foxbots. This has also helped it move into more capital-intensive industries such as automotive and medical equipment (Luk, 2014a). There are reportedly 10,000 Foxbots already in use in a Foxconn factory in China since 2011.

Diversification can lead to upgrading opportunities if it results in higher margins and higher levels of quality, technology and innovation. This can be the case in defence, aerospace and health industries because they have more standards and regulatory requirements. Margins in medical equipment technologies are also higher than for consumer electronics, and the health industry generally can provide more stable contracts, given the longer product life-cycles of its equipment (Tse and Yip, 2016).

Contract manufacturers have also used M&As strategically to obtain capabilities in design and innovation and to diversify into new industries (see Table A in the Appendix). For CM1, for example, acquisitions in past years were made in 'medical and aerospace. Acquisitions are not in the consumer product space' (Interview, 2015). The role of M&As in the growth and development of contract manufacturers becomes quite clear in the next section on Flex, Jabil Circuit and Celestica.

Finally, the various responses to increased competition and technological advancements are occurring in a context of emerging markets, particularly in Asia, which present new opportunities for contract manufacturers to expand not only their economies of scale but also design and innovation capabilities. Indeed, emerging markets in Asia present geographies of future growth in consumer end markets. Moreover, they are also locations with abundant supplies of highly educated engineers at lower costs. This is in conjunction with a general shortage in the supply of knowledge workers and a glut in the pool of engineers in the USA and Europe (Ernst, 2006; Lewin, Massini and Peeters, 2009). All the major contract manufacturers have tapped into this local resource by establishing key design locations in the region (van Liemt, 2007). This reflects the competitive search for talent at a global scale which can be summarized as the 'increased globalisation of human capital' (Lewin *et al.*, 2009, 921). Firms can relocate entire segments of their business functions such as R&D to where the desired human capital is located (Lewin *et al.*, 2009).

Countries in the Asia region such as India and China have become top locations for innovation offshoring (Lundin and Serger, 2007). The creation of a global marketplace for high-skilled knowledge workers plays into the hands of MNCs who are able to source talent and human capital at a lower cost. This translates into lower costs for research and product development (Ernst, 2006). This is in line with an overall push to lower the costs of innovation across industries (Christensen, 1997). Firms like contract manufacturers already engaged in offshore manufacturing in regions with growing access to a highly skilled workforce are well placed to locate or expand R&D activity in these locations. This is more the case when demands for increasing growth and speed to market make it advantageous for doing so. Thus, for the electronics industry, China has become a key location for offshore innovation where firms can locate product development close to manufacturing plants (Lewin *et al.*, 2009).

According to the Organisation for Economic Cooperation and Development (OECD), the reason firms choose to locate R&D in the Asia region

> is not only about competition for (future) market shares, but also competition for the best talent and networks and the R&D activities are therefore a long-term strategic preparation for future market expansion ... This is especially true for the electronics industry ... For instance, as the technology frontier is being moved towards the Asian market and because of the huge demand with specific local characteristics, the R&D investment in the ICT sector is both technology and demand driven. (OECD, 2008, 277)

The growing trend of establishing R&D locations in China by MNCs are also strategic decisions to stay abreast of competitors in the East Asia region. For the electronics industry, the rapid pace of technological development and the search for the next new idea creates a favourable climate for locating R&D in lower-cost locations and sourcing knowledge from outside the home country (Ernst, 2006).

These developments also coincide with the rise of global innovation networks (GINs) in the electronics industry (Ernst, 2006). A new model of innovation for Western corporations in the electronics industry has emerged that involves a global network of players across countries. For example, US chipmakers may work with Taiwanese engineers, Indian software developers and Chinese factories. These global networks are created for efficiency and increased speed in product development and bringing products to end markets (Engardio and Einhorn, 2005). Having access to knowledge or high-skilled workers across the globe also increases the number of working hours – almost the entire 24-hour cycle – spent on research and product development, which meet the ultimate goal of increasing speed to market (Lewin *et al.*, 2009). The location by contract manufacturers of design and engineering services in China and other developing countries in the Asia region no longer coincides with a 'New International Division of Labour' implied by GINs (see Luethje, 2001) where engineering is located in developed countries and high volume manufacturing is located in lower cost locations. Instead, contract manufacturers are co-locating design and engineering in the same geographies of high volume manufacturing due to the rise of a high-skilled workforce in these locations, faster time-to-market efficiencies and for increasing innovation capabilities. Chen considers the attraction of major Chinese cities, such as Beijing, as locations for MNC R&D centres due to their proximity to large local markets, and for the ability to reinvent 'new technology not yet available elsewhere' (Chen, 2008, 627). Large local markets provide incentives for firms to cater to local tastes and needs with new designs and product development (Chen, 2008, 639). The next section explores these various drivers and changes in the contract manufacturing landscape with the case studies of Flex, Jabil Circuit and Celestica.

Case studies: Flex, Jabil Circuit and Celestica

This section presents case studies of three of the five largest contract manufacturers in the electronics industry to discuss the changes and trajectories of upgrading which have transformed these suppliers in the electronics industry GVC. They are Flex, Jabil Circuit and Celestica (see Table 2.2). The discussions of these firms will focus on their expansion into design and engineering services, manufacturing innovations and diversification strategies; the role M&As have played in increasing their capabilities; and the role of Asian locations in the growth and expansion of design.

Table 2.2 Key characteristics of the top five contract manufacturers in the computer industry

Firms	HQ	Revenue ($ million, 2015)	Employees
Foxconn	Taiwan	136,122.773	1.3 million (2015)
Flex	Singapore*	26,147.92	200,000 (2016)
Jabil Circuit	United States	17,899.20	More than 175,000 (2015)
Sanmina-SCI	United States	6,374.54	33,144 (2014)
Celestica	Canada	5,639.20	25,000 (2015)

Sources: http://www.bloomberg.com/markets; www.bloomberg.com/markets; www.google.com/finance.
Note: *Flex originated in California, USA.

All three contract manufacturers originated in North America and started off as contract manufacturers for the electronics industry. Flex was established in Silicon Valley in 1969 as a PCB assembler for firms in the area. In 1980, it was sold to new owners and became a contract manufacturing company. In order to grow as a contract manufacturer of PCBs in those early years, it automated its PCB assembly line to increase its economies of scale in production. It also expanded its services with quality testing of PCBs for its customer firms. By the 1980s, Flex began providing turnkey services to customers. It became a pioneer in establishing offshore manufacturing locations by opening its first offshore factory in Singapore in 1981. In 1990, it re-incorporated itself in Singapore. During the 1990s, Flex faced increasing production orders from customers such as Compaq, Intel and Hewlett-Packard. To meet these additional demands, it built industrial parks in Mexico, Brazil, Hungary, China, Poland and the Czech Republic. These industrial parks housed Flex's own suppliers alongside its factories. Today, Flex has factories in over thirty countries. In Asia alone, it has over 100,000 employees (Perez, 2016). The majority of its manufacturing sites are located in China (company website, accessed 12 June 2015).

Jabil Circuit was established in Michigan (USA) in 1966 as a supplier to Control Data Computers and General Motors (Sturgeon, 1998; van Liemt, 2007). Its early business in the electronics industry was producing PCBs for computer brand firms such as Dell. Jabil grew mainly through greenfield development throughout the 1990s. Today it has over ninety manufacturing sites in twenty-three countries which include India, Malaysia, Vietnam and China (company website, accessed 12 June 2015).

With slightly different origins from the other two contract manufacturers, Celestica was created as an exclusive manufacturing arm of IBM Canada. After seventy-five years of operations, it was spun off in 1994 to become a wholly incorporated subsidiary. Soon after, it began restructuring its business to become an independent firm by widening its customer base globally (Frederick, 2000; Dyck and Halpern, 1999). In the 1990s, most of its activity was specialized in PCB and computer assembly for Hewlett-Packard and Sun Microsystems (Daly, 2015). After being purchased by Onex Corporation in 1996, Celestica expanded its facilities from two (in New York and Toronto) to several manufacturing and design sites in North America, Europe, South America and Asia (Dyck and Halpern, 1999). In 1999 and 2000, Celestica set up greenfield operations in Malaysia, Brazil and Singapore (Frederick, 2000; SEC 20-F Filing, 2000). Today it has forty manufacturing locations in eleven countries (Daly, 2015). Its largest facilities are in China, Thailand and Malaysia (Onex Corporation, 2011).

All the contract manufacturers discussed in this chapter have grown through substantial M&A activity. Flex was one of the earliest contract manufacturers to engage in acquisitions quite aggressively. Between 1993 and 1998, it acquired twelve firms. Some of these included factories from branded customer firms. Jabil Circuit began increasing in size through acquisitions from the early

2000s onwards. After becoming an independent firm in 1996, Celestica also aggressively grew through acquisitions. By the end of 2001, Celestica had made twenty-nine acquisitions, including competitor firms and facilities from branded customers such as Hewlett-Packard, Motorola and NEC (Steinman, 2001; Sturgeon, 2002). The contract manufacturing industry has also had a history of consolidation. One of the largest acquisitions was by two of the top contract manufacturers during the mid-2000s. Flex (then Flextronics) acquired Solectron in 2007 for $4.2 billion in cash and stock, leading to a major consolidation of the contract manufacturing industry (Lipton, 2007; Sturgeon and Kawakami, 2011). Sanmina also acquired SCI in 2001, which moved it into the top three positions amongst contract manufacturers in the industry (Wallack, 2001). Later in this chapter, we will discuss the important role M&As have played in recent years for increasing capabilities in design and for a diversified customer base.

The three subsections that follow discuss the expanding capabilities in design, engineering, and innovation, diversification, and expansion in the Asia region as trajectories of upgrading for Flex, Jabil Circuit and Celestica. These various upgrading activities also beg the question as to whether they have made a difference to profit margins. This is a story of contract manufacturers needing to defend against falling profit margins. Figures 2.1, 2.2 and 2.3 show profit margins and revenues for the three contract manufacturers discussed in this section. All three firms have faced declining profits from the early 2000s onwards, but were able to stop this trajectory and attain a positive growth rate after the global recession of 2008. This is also the time around when branded firms began restructuring their business and core competencies, and when contract manufacturers began increasing their capabilities and diversifying into new industries. Whether branded customer firms are shifting their higher value-added functions to contract manufacturers is something that is not clearly identifiable, but it is clear that they have been facing their fair share of falling profit margins as well. Figures 2.4, 2.5 and 2.6 show declines in recent years for Hewlett-Packard,[1] Dell[2] and Apple. The graphs show trends in the business outcomes for these two groups of firms. The figures help provide a reference point to the following discussions on upgrading and expansion.

---

1 In the fall of 2015, Hewlett-Packard was divided into two companies. The figures for 2015 presented are for HP Inc., which is the company that retained the consumer electronics portfolio such as personal computers and laptops. There is a precipitous fall in profits and revenue from 2015 as a result of the break-up.

2 Dell became a private company in 2014 and no longer reports its company filings to the SEC. The figures presented are up to 2013.

Figure 2.1 Gross profit margin and revenue for Flex

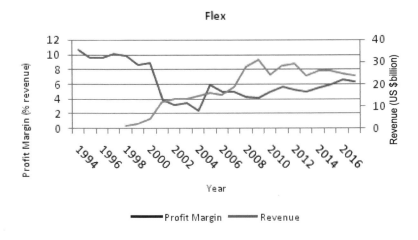

Source: SEC company filings.

Figure 2.2 Gross profit margin and revenue for Jabil Circuit

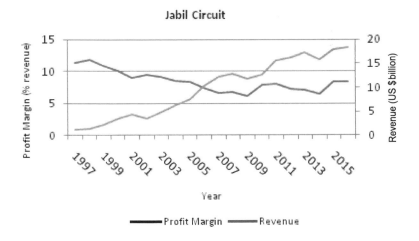

Source: SEC company filings.

38

Figure 2.3 Gross profit margin and revenue for Celestica

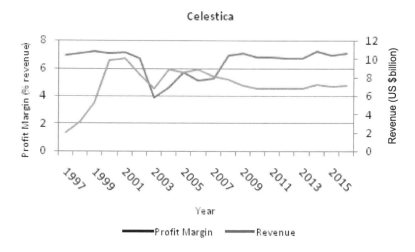

Source: SEC company filings.

Figure 2.4 Gross profit margin and revenue for HP (Inc.)

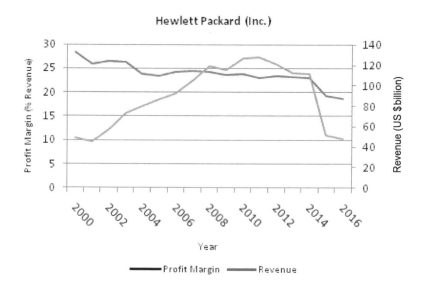

Source: SEC company filings.

Figure 2.5 Gross profit margin and revenue for Dell

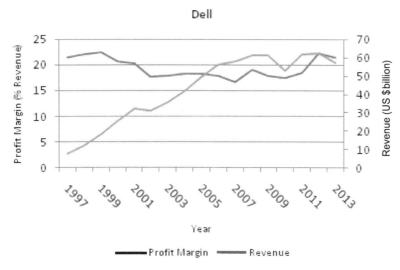

Figure 2.6 Gross profit margin and revenue for Apple

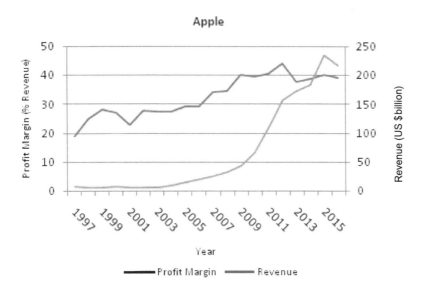

All three contract manufacturers have been engaged in design and engineering services to some degree for many years. While starting at relatively low levels of innovation, in recent years these firms have been suppliers of a set of bundled services – that include product design, prototyping, production innovations, and supply chain management – which have helped branded customers bring product ideas to life.

Flex's early design work involved providing computer-aided design and PCB blueprinting services to customers. In the late 1990s, it firmly established itself as a provider of engineering design services with the establishment of a global network of six Product Introduction Centers (PICs). This is where confidential product ideas were first prototyped and built into physical models and tested, before they were mass-produced for sale to the public (Caulfield, 2012). For example, the Palm Pilot by 3Com and the Microsoft Mouse were designed and built in these centres. In 2007, in its SEC filings, Flex described itself for the first time as a global leading provider of 'vertically-integrated advanced design'. Its *design and engineering services* include selling contract design services on a piece rate system and product-based joint development manufacturing services to customers.

What sets Flex apart from other contract manufacturers in terms of innovation in the industry is its ability to take ideas (from customer firms) and design them, build them physically (including their components), test them and develop the manufacturing technology to mass produce them efficiently. On top of this, Flex handles the logistics and supply chain management of production for its customer firms. Flex trademarked this package of services as *sketch to scale* in 2016. Its growth in this business area is demonstrated by the increasing percentage of revenue from *sketch to scale*, which rose from 7 per cent in 2013 to 21 per cent in 2016 (Flex, 2016).

In the age of the IoT and technological advancements, Flex has also positioned itself through its *sketch to scale* services to assist a diverse set of industries with connected devices (see next subsection). Examples of products which Flex helped produce using its *sketch to scale* services include network products (Palo Alto Networks and FireEye), room cleaners (Bissell), coffee-makers (Kitchen Aid), connected whiteboards (SMART Technologies), handheld glucose testers (Free Style), fitness watches (Pebble), and Chrome Cast video adapters for Google (Weinswig, 2015). In 2016, it was reported Flex had 2,500 designers developing intellectual property for itself and jointly with customer firms (Lashinsky, 2016).

Flex also has a host of centres where innovation takes place. They include Customer Innovation Centers in California and Israel, Innovation Labs, the Collective Innovation Platform, The Interconnect Technology Centre, CloudLabs and Lab IX (SEC 10-K, 2016). Unlike any other contract manufacturer, Flex set up Lab IX as an accelerator programme to support start-ups investing in next generation disruptive technologies. Investments in Lab IX are supported by venture capitalists who are envisioned to become future customers of Flex. Lab IX also helps existing customers gain design technology by exposing them to the start-ups.

Compared to Flex, Jabil Circuit began investing in design capabilities later and to a lesser extent. In 2005, Jabil Circuit described itself as a provider of 'design for manufacturing' (SEC 10-K, 2006). However, its major showcase in the technological innovation space was the opening of its multi-million dollar Blue Sky Center in 2015. Run by design engineers, it showcases the package of services it can provide customers to help them with product ideas, 3D printing, prototyping and design. Jabil Circuit was one of the first to acquire 3D printing technology in the industry (Shinal, 2013). The Blue Sky Center also showcases its Supply Chain Command Center, which manages its supply chain of seven million parts and 17,000 vendors, with real-time data twenty-four hours a day, all year round. It is able to monitor and react immediately to product or component shortages and disruptions in its logistics network – for example, due to environmental or geopolitical reasons. Jabil Circuit has also developed the software *inControl* which allows it to see its entire supply chain down to the component level in minutes. It has been said that Jabil won over $100 million of new business due to its supply chain monitoring ability (*MMI*, 2015).

Part of the competitive advantage of Jabil Circuit is its global footprint of manufacturing locations which is important for customers that need data centres in various locations worldwide. The advantage Jabil Circuit has in this regard is its ability to combine large-scale manufacturing with design assistance for customers. This was summed up by a general manager thus:

> ... we are really aimed at customers who are looking to streamline their IT infrastructure and looking to take advantage of open source software and commodity hardware, but could use help in design, test, and validating and maybe even services and support for these products in their data centres. (Morgan, 2014)

Celestica is also one of the first contract manufacturers to expand early on in design, assembly, testing and repair – including prototyping, distribution and supply chain management services for its customers (Frederick, 2000; van Liemt, 2007). The evolution into design and engineering services is captured well in its 2010 SEC 20-F filing:

> OEMs increasingly rely on EMS [electronics manufacturing service] companies to provide design, engineering support, manufacturing and technological expertise. Through their design and engineering services, and through the knowledge gained from repairing products, EMS companies can assist OEMs in the development of new product concepts, or the re-design of existing products, as well as assist with improvements in the performance, cost and time required to bring products to market. In addition, OEMs gain access to high-quality manufacturing expertise and capabilities in the areas of advanced process, interconnect and test technologies.

Today, Celestica engages in prototyping and new product introduction during the early stages of product development with its customers. This involves Celestica engineers working with customer engineers during the prototyping stages of new products as 'an extension of customers' teams through the product life-cycle'(Reuters Celestica profile, accessed 2 May 2016).

As stated above, M&As have been particularly strategic for the growth and development of these contract manufacturers (see Appendix 2.1). In recent years, M&As have been used to expand the design, engineering, technological and innovation capabilities amongst these contract manufacturers. The acquisition of the Japanese firm Sharp by Foxconn for US$3.5 billion, for example, has assisted the contract manufacturer to expand its manufacturing of flat-panel displays (Inagaki, 2017). Foxconn has also offered a bid to buy the Japanese firm Toshiba NAND which is the semiconductor manufacturing arm of Toshiba, for US$27 billion (Mochizuki 2017).[3] This would help Foxconn enter the semiconductor chip market.

More examples include Flex acquiring nChip, which specialized in semiconductor packaging and multichip modules, in 1994. In 2002, it acquired Palo Alto Products, the designer of the Palm Pilot, including its design team and three factories (Kanellos, 2002). More significantly, after losing out to competition from Taiwanese ODMs in mobile-phone manufacturing in the early 2000s, Flex spent $800 million on acquisitions which created an engineering workforce of 7,000 employees for their software, chip and telecom businesses.

---

3   At the time of writing, the bidding for Toshiba NAND has not been completed and there are competing bidders including the Japanese government.

In 2003 it acquired Microcell, a Finnish mobile phone design firm. One of its largest acquisitions was a $30 million takeover of Frog Design Inc. in 2004 – a firm which helped design Apple Computer Inc.'s original Mac in 1984 (Engardio and Einhorn, 2005).

The acquisition of design houses along with their highly skilled workforce was Flex's preparation for the shift amongst branded customers towards outsourcing R&D. In 2005, Michael Marks, then CEO of Flex, stated, 'Now we will completely restructure design' (Engardio and Einhorn, 2005, 3). This is because core technologies are no longer proprietary and are available to anyone. Marks continued:

> Why should each [brand firm] spend $30 million to develop a new smartphone or $200 million on a cellular base station when they can just buy the hardware designs? ... Some electronics giants will shrink their R&D forces from several thousand to a few hundred, concentrating on proprietary architecture, setting key specifications, and managing global R&D teams ... There is no doubt the product companies are going to have fewer people design stuff ... It's going to get ugly. (Engardio and Einhorn, 2005, 3)

Celestica has also strategically acquired firms for their design capabilities, albeit to a lesser extent. Its acquisition of CoreSim Technology in 2005 was for obtaining advanced design analysis and redesign service capabilities (*EE Times*, 2005), which were used to 'minimize design spins, speed time to market and provide improved manufacturing yields' (SEC 20-F, 2010).

Today, increased capabilities have created a hybrid model of design and innovative manufacturing amongst contract manufacturers. In some ways, it has put contract manufacturers in direct competition with ODMs. Flex, for example, is increasingly discussed in the same realm as ODMs with regard to its design capabilities (Engardio and Einhorn, 2005). It also considers itself to be facing 'particular competition from Asian-based competitors, including Taiwanese Original Design Manufacturing ('ODM') suppliers ... [who] compete in a variety of our end markets and have a substantial share of global information technology hardware production' (SEC 10-K, 2016). Jabil Circuit also conducts joint product development with its customers, for example, in the custom servers and storage market for hyperscale customers. This activity has also put Jabil Circuit in direct competition with the Taiwanese ODM Quanta and even computer brands like Dell (Morgan, 2014). Similarly, Celestica considers itself to be in the business of joint design and manufacturing (JDM). JDM is a combination of OEM and ODM functions. It involves the use of advanced technology design solutions that customers can tailor to their own needs. Its JDM activity is focused on server and communications products, including 'white box' solutions and storage customers. Investments in its global design services and capabilities for JDM continue to increase. Like the other contract manufacturers, this is a space which brings Celestica into direct competition with ODMs. In its SEC filing in 2017, Celestica noted, 'We may face increased competition from ODMs, who also specialize in providing internally designed products and manufacturing services, as well as component and sub-system suppliers, distributors and/or systems integrators' (SEC 20-F, 2017). This points to the increased blurring or demise of the EMS–ODM dichotomy when it comes to capabilities in design, engineering and innovation.

As branded firms such as HP, Dell, Cisco and IBM move more towards cloud computing and reduce their hardware portfolio, it raises questions about the future ownership of commodity-type consumer products. In interviews with branded firms, when asked questions about contract manufacturers becoming future competitors, the responses mentioned the potential threats that mattered, which were in the higher value-added segments such as cloud computing. These concerns are summarized by Brand 2:

> Yes, it is thought about a lot. That is why partnership relationships are created. So we are watching the successes and failures of the contract manufacturers but not on traditional/commodity products. We can allow for new alternative brands to come up for these products. We are happy to give them away. But in the mobility and cloud products, this space is watched closely.

All the three contract manufacturers studied here have clear trajectories in diversifying its end markets and customers into higher value-added business (see Appendices 2.2 and 2.3). From the 2000s onwards, Flex entered a long phase where it started changing its end-product portfolios and diversifying into new markets. The success of this strategy is built on Flex's manufacturing expertise, design and engineering capabilities, and supply chain solutions. Its recent diversification activity corresponds to its 'High Reliability Solutions' (HRS) customers which comprise the medical, digital health, automotive, defence, aerospace and aviation industries. Figure 2.7 in Appendix 2.2 shows growth in the HRS and Industrial and Emerging Industries, which is clearly contrasted by a drop in business in Consumer Technologies. These graphs show a shift towards a more diversified set of customers and business.

Flex has built components for 'Lockheed Martin, Ford Motor Company and more than 1,000 other customers in almost every line of business. There's almost no customer in the electronics chain, and many outside of the electronics chain, that we don't touch … We want to be the supply chain of everything' (Flex CEO Michael McNamara in Simpson, 2013). MacNamara has also stated that 'the industrial energy, automotive, medical [business] in 2010 (they) represented roughly 15 per cent of our overall revenue and today it is like 38 per cent of our overall revenue. So it's actually a huge transition over the course of just 5 years. And especially as people go towards chronic illness, monitor health, [and] continuing monitoring technologies' (*CNBC Mad Money*, 2017).

Based on its SEC 10-K filings, Flex's diversification strategy has been fast-paced. It shifted from focusing on cellular phones, computers, telecommunication and networking in the early to mid-2000s to entering the marine and aerospace industries in 2007 (SEC 10-K, 2005; Markoff, 2012). In 2010, its product portfolio included robotics for the first time, which became a feature in its solar-panel factories (Markoff, 2012).

Technological development has indeed contributed to the higher value-added entry into new industries. McNamara recently discussed how the contract manufacturer is benefitting from the IoT.

> Everything has been connected to the internet for many, many years … and they're intelligent … responding with real-time … you now have new data sources … [and] the actual device itself is now intelligent … There is also connected technologies such as health trackers and autonomous cars where [everything is] connected for example such as light and radar technology … Flex is involved in building the technologies that make the production and manufacturing of such products possible. Flex is also heavily involved in storage systems, which has opened up new business in the automotive industry … And when you think about the autonomous car of the future, the amount of data and the processing of that data is off the chart. And all of a sudden you need servers for cars. (*CNBC Mad Money*, 2017)

A feature of Flex's diversification is its heavy involvement in the automotive industry. In 2013, Ford Motor Company became a top-ten customer (based on net sales) of Flex for the first time. In 2014, its Automotive Group designed, engineered and manufactured lamps, the antenna, parts of the sunroof and various wire harnesses for the Chrysler Jeep (Flextronics, 2014). In 2015, Flex opened a new facility near Detroit, Michigan, to collaborate with the 'Big Three' Detroit automotive firms (Ford, General Motors and Fiat Chrysler) on connected technology development. The facility provides services which 'include product design and development, engineering, validation testing, development garage, prototyping and quality engineering' (Flex Press Release, 14 January 2015).

Another significant new industry for Flex is wearables in the digital health and fitness industry and clothing (Flex, 2015). In 2015, Flex was the sole manufacturer of the Fitbit (Eadicicco, 2015). It also produced the fitness tracker Jawbone in 2016. In 2016, Flex reported that it produced 75 per cent of all such wearables globally. Flex has also obtained patented technology that goes into products such as sensors in textiles that detect and track information on hydration, breathing and stress levels. In this sector, Flex leverages on its automated manufacturing technology (Flex, 2015). For example, Flex began manufacturing shoes for Nike in 2015 using automated technology in the manufacturing process which allowed for custom orders to be processed within days instead of weeks. This was achieved partly through Flex's development of laser cutting technology, which can customize shoes to different sizes automatically and without interruptions (Flex, 2016).

Jabil Circuit has also diversified its portfolio of industries since the mid-2000s. Figure 2.8 in Appendix 2.2 shows a clear increase in its new business portfolio called 'Diversified Manufacturing Services'. This is contrasted with a drop in its traditional EMS business. One of the early drivers of diversification was Jabil Circuit's acquisition of the necessary certifications in its global production sites to manufacture products for the health and automotive industries. The longevity and reliability of customers in these new industries was another driver. The automotive industry, for example, made up 14 per cent of its sales in 2005 (van Liemt, 2007). More significant was the slump in sales of consumer electronics following the global financial crisis in 2008 and the termination of its business with Blackberry after the latter's bankruptcy in 2013 (SEC 10-K, 2016). By 2016, Jabil Circuit was operating in a vast number of industries as part of its Diversified Manufacturing Services. They ranged from wearable technologies, digital homes, defence, aerospace, healthcare, mobility and consumer lifestyles. According to its SEC company filings, Jabil Circuit primarily serves these diversified customers with engineering solutions, with a focus on material sciences and technologies (SEC 10-K, 2005, 2010, 2016).

Celestica has also diversified its markets, business strategies and industry engagements away from consumer electronics such as personal computers and mobile phones. Some of this restructuring is in response to the high level of volatility in the consumer electronics industry. Like Jabil Circuit, one of the most critical events was the cancellation of a large multi-year contract from Blackberry in 2012. Blackberry contracts made up 20 per cent of net revenue for Celestica in 2010. Thereafter, Celestica recovered by diversifying into new sectors such as the aerospace and healthcare industries (Daly, 2015). Today, Celestica has largely moved away from manufacturing low value-added labour intensive products such as mobile phones and gaming consoles to higher value-added products such as storage equipment, servers, semiconductor equipment and providing services such as design and development, engineering, supply chain management and after-sales services. Examples in its diversified portfolio include manufacturing avionics for Boeing and Airbus, high-resolution camera systems, and a pill that can transmit health data via an abdominal patch to doctors' smartphones (McClearn, 2013). Its storage end-market grew from 14 per cent of total revenue in 2013 to 18 per cent in 2015. The portion of revenues from its diversified portfolio grew from 19 per cent in 2012 to around 30 per cent in 2016. Celestica has plans to increase this portion to 50 per cent (Borcard and Metraux, 2015; SEC 20-F, 2017). Figure 2.9 in Appendix 2.2 further shows a clear drop in its consumer and personal computer business and a strong growth in its diversified and storage business.

M&A activity across these three contract manufacturers has also increased capabilities for a diverse set of industries. In 2016, Flex reported that 72 per cent of its M&As were in its diversified HRS division (Flex, 2016). For example, in 2004, it acquired Hughes, a former subsidiary of General Motors, for its extensive capabilities in software development for the automotive industry (Luethje et al., 2013). Jabil Circuit has also used M&As to expand into new industries. A major acquisition was of Nyproin 2013 – a plastics manufacturer in the healthcare industry – which helped turn Jabil Circuit into a major contract manufacturer in the industry. In 2015, it acquired Clothing Plus – a Finnish textile electronics firm for the wearable technology market. Similarly, in 2011 and 2012, Celestica undertook acquisitions to expand its diversified end-market business and specifically the acquisition of semiconductor capital equipment. It also made investments in 2015 to develop solar energy manufacturing capabilities in Asia (SEC 20-F, 2016). Appendix 2.1 provides more examples of strategic acquisitions by these three contract manufacturers and Foxconn.

Expansion into Asia

The role that emerging markets can play in expanding markets and capabilities is an important consideration for contract manufacturers. Indeed, both the historical and the size-wise presence of these contract manufacturers in Asia – China in particular – has embedded them into local supply chains and provided them know-how about business and governmental relationships there. Thus, emerging markets present opportunities for contract manufacturers to expand in scale, focus on domestic markets and build design capabilities.

Take Flex, for example. It has been present in China for many years. In 2010, Flex received its first Chinese customers, Huawei and Lenovo. Today, Lenovo is its largest customer (Perez, 2016). According to its CEO, Mike McNamara, 'China is still the manufacturing centre of the world, but there's no doubt that more and more innovation is coming out of the country at a rapid pace' (Perez, 2016). For example, Flex has seven out of its thirty-two design and engineering service locations in the Asia region (see Table 2.3).

In 2009, Flex expanded its presence in China with a new facility in the Wuzhong Export Processing Zone in Suzhou. It included both a manufacturing site and design centre for computers, laptops and tablets for the Chinese market. While it became Flex's main development centre in the country, it complements already existing computing design centres in Beijing, Shanghai and Wujiang (Flex, 2009). 'You know why innovation is occurring here in China? It's very heavily oriented towards doing very entrepreneurial things and taking risks' (Perez, 2016). McNamara added that the consumption power of China's growing middle class was creating demand for more products. 'They [consumers] get choice. An example is the features [consumers want] on a set-top box. We're now working with a Chinese start-up whose first priority for a set-top box is its karaoke feature' (McNamara in Perez, 2016).

Table 2.3 Design and engineering services locations of Flex

Asia	Americas	Europe
Hong Kong, China	Milipitas, USA	Althofen, Austria
Pudong, China	Farmington Hills, USA	CZ Brno, Czech Republic
Zhuhai, China	Plano, USA	Filderstadt, Germany
Cebu, Philippines	Morrisville, USA	Milan, Italy
Manila, Philippines	Austin, USA	Timisoara, Romania
Kallang, Singapore	Coopersville, USA	
Taipei, Taiwan	Dallas, USA	
Yavne, Israel	Norcross, USA	
Ofakim, Israel	Guadalajara, Mexico	

(Contd.)

(*Contd.*)

Asia	Americas	Europe
Migdal HaEmek, Israel	Juarez, Mexico	Ronneby, Sweden
Haifa, Israel	Burlington, Canada	Stockholm, Sweden
	Ottawa, Canada	
	Toronto, Canada	
	Sorocaba, Brazil	

Source: Flex website.

Jabil Circuit has been responding to the increased outsourcing of product engineering work by branded firms, especially in the data storage equipment sector, by growing its design and engineering workforce on- and offshore. Jabil Circuit has eleven design centres located in Asia (see Table 2.4). Take its compute and storage sector as an example. It has two design centres as part of the sector – one in Colorado and the other in Shanghai. According to the vice-president of the sector, initial design and engineering work starts at the Colorado location and is then completed in Shanghai (Heilman, 2001). Its Shanghai design and engineering centre, which has been growing its design and engineering operations in recent years, specializes in medical equipment such as patient bedside monitoring devices (Delporte, 2011).

Table 2.4 Jabil Circuit's design centres

Asia	North America	Europe
Beijing, China	Colorado Springs, USA	Vienna, Austria
Hong Kong, China	St Petersburg, USA	Bray, Ireland
Shanghai, China	Chicago, USA	Kankaanpää, Finland
Tianjin, China	Clinton, USA	Tampere, Finland
Wuhan, China	Coppell, USA	Hasselt, Belgium
Wuxi, China	Anaheim, California, USA	Jena, Germany
Zhejiang, China	Dublin, California, USA	
Hsinchu, Taiwan	San Jose, California, USA	

(*Contd.*)

(*Contd.*)

Asia	North America	Europe
Taichung City, Taiwan	Ottawa, Canada	
Taipei , Taiwan		
Tampines, Singapore		

Source: Jabil Circuit's annual report, 2015.

Similarly, Celestica has a 300-member design team in Shanghai. This design centre works on cloud servers for customers. According to its website, 'The operation provides full product development with leading technologies, such as product design in blade servers, storage systems, and wired and wireless communication systems' (Celestica, 2017).

Table 2.5 Celestica locations that feature design services

Asia	USA	Europe
Shanghai, China	Portland	Salzburg, Austria
Woodlands, Singapore	San Jose	Leixlip, Ireland
		Valencia, Spain
		Galway, Ireland

Source: https://www.celestica.com/About-us/locations.

In an industry with fierce price competition and low margins, expanding design and innovation capabilities in low-cost locations in Asia as part of the globalization of R&D is logical. It is also strategic as contract manufacturers increasingly produce for the Asian market and the expansion of R&D in regions where they manufacture helps speed up time to market. Co-locating design or R&D centres close to manufacturing can also be crucial for increasing innovation capabilities (Buciuni and Finotto, 2016). The location of design centres in the Asia region, particularly China, is not necessarily to be close to brand customer R&D teams (most of which are still largely located in their home countries). Design centres that work with brand customers, for example Flex's Customer Innovation Centers and Jabil Circuit's Blue Sky Center, are located in California. The design centres in China are located to be close to their own manufacturing facilities. Thus, these are measures to increase efficiency, driven by engineers and designers that are paid lower salaries than in industrially advanced countries, and manufacturing innovations, such as automation. In China, several of the contract manufacturers interviewed had spearheaded automated manufacturing and machinery on their own for increased efficiency and cost-cutting outcomes.

Conclusion

This chapter has shown that contract manufacturers in the electronics industry have upgraded themselves from their earlier positions in the GVC to become providers of design, engineering, technological and manufacturing innovation to a wide set of industries. This chapter has discussed various upgrading trajectories amongst contract manufacturers, all of whom did not necessarily have the end goal of becoming brand firms but, instead, of becoming innovators in manufacturing and product introductions which included design and prototyping services coupled with immense expertise in (real-time) supply chain management. These are innovations that brands have long given up and which have opened up unique niches for contract manufacturers to occupy.

External factors such as restructuring amongst branded firms, increasing price competition in the contract manufacturing industry, technological developments, and opportunities in emerging economies in Asia have been the drivers of these changes. As discussed earlier, the global recession of 2008 was a catalyst for restructuring, especially by brand firms in the electronics industry, which faced falling prices, to further outsource and consolidate their supplier base. Furthermore, as contract manufacturers increasingly gained new capabilities both organically and through M&As, they were able to extend their services to a new set of industries. Indeed, these are pathways towards upgrading which can lead to potential improvements in margins for these suppliers. This is because customer products in the new industries such as aerospace and health tend to be long-term in nature and higher priced.

The case studies show there is a blurring of lines between the original concepts of EMS versus ODM suppliers. This follows earlier discussions by Ernst (2005) on the partial convergence of the EMS and ODM business models in the electronics industry. Today, contract manufacturers are considered 'strategic partners' to many branded firms in the industry (Luethje et al., 2013; Yeung and Coe, 2014). These developments challenge dichotomies in the literature between suppliers that are manufacturers and those which are designers and innovators. Contract manufacturers are serving their customer firms in more sophisticated and efficient ways, which is leading to what is arguably a mutual dependency between the two groups of firms in the GVC (Raj-Reichert, 2015).These dynamics also suggest a potential shift from a modular value chain towards a relational value chain. This may be the case for contract manufacturers that are engaging in strategic and long-term relationships which leverage their higher value-added capacities such as design and innovation with customer firms. However, given how recently they have entered into a variety of new industries, such as health, clothing, aerospace and automobiles, it is yet to be seen if these relationships are indeed relational – that is, whether they are characterized by close collaboration, long-term trust and reputational ties.

There are also limits to a full shift to relational value chains in the contract manufacturing industry. This has to do with the nature of the complexity-versus-standardization of the design and innovation work these suppliers have entered into, which is a topic into which this chapter has not adequately delved. Indeed, innovation in itself is less standardized by nature, and it implies the need for closer relational value chain relationships with customer firms (Dolan and Humphrey, 2004; Gereffi *et al.,* 2005). However, off-the-shelf designs (for example, those based on open software), which are increasingly becoming standardized, and the further commodification of technologies in the industry would maintain a modular value chain relationship with certain customer firms for these contract manufacturers. Thus, contract manufacturers may be entering into a realm of multiple governance relationships across different sets of customers and functions (Dolan and Humphrey, 2004). The differences would be seen across the diversified industries, rather than within one sector, as contract manufacturers are no longer suppliers to the electronics industry GVC alone. We must wait to see whether these relationships change – in particular, whether contract manufacturers enter into longer-term contracts with their traditional brand customers in electronics as they move into storage and cloud computing and/or within the newer diversified industries such as health and automotive, where product life-cycles are longer. Thus, a multi-industry lens must be applied in future research to understand the implications that a variety of value chain governance relationships have on the opportunities and challenges for upgrading for this group of first-tier suppliers.

References

Borcard, S. and N. Metraux. 2015. 'Celestica Inc.' *The Globe and Mail*, 23 June. Accessed 14 March 2017. Available at http://www.theglobeandmail.com/report-on-business/rob-magazine/top-1000/ten-canadian-firms-in-search-of-overseas-success/article25078712/.

Buciuni, G.and V. Finotto. 2016. 'Innovation in Global Value Chains: Co-location of Production and Development in Italian Low-Tech Industries.' *Regional Studies* 50 (12): 2010–23. DOI: http://dx.doi.org/10.1080/00343404.2015.1115010.

Burke, D and J. Bandler. 2012. 'How Hewlett-Packard Lost Its Way.' *Fortune*, 8 May. Accessed 3 April 2017. Available at http://fortune.com/2012/05/08/how-hewlett-packard-lost-its-way/.

Cantrell, A. 2005. 'How Low CanPC Prices Go?' *CNN Money*, 30 August. Accessed 10 April 2017. Available at http://money.cnn.com/2005/08/29/technology/falling_prices/.

Caulfield, B. 2012. 'Made in Silicon Valley.' *Forbes*, 20 June. Accessed 19 April 2017. Available at https://www.forbes.com/global/2012/0716/technology-manufacturing-flextronics-made-in-silicon-valley.html. Celestica. 2017. *www.celestica.com*. Accessed 15 April 2017. Available at https://www.celestica.com/about-us/locations#asia.

Christensen, Clayton M. 1997. *The Innovator's Dilemma: When New Technologies Cause Great Firms to Fail*. Boston: Harvard Business School Press.

CNBC Mad Money. 2017. Interview with Flex CEO Mike McNamara. 14 February. Accessed 3 March 2017. Available at https://s3.amazonaws.com/clips.shadowtv.net/media/request/FLX/1e88d0abbed9430ab503d68c81e93568/index.html.

Daly, J. 2015. 'Ten Canadian Firms Search for Overseas Success.' *The Globe and Mail*, 23 June. Accessed 18 February 2016. Available at http://www.theglobeandmail.com/report-on-business/rob-magazine/top-1000/ten-canadian-firms-in-search-of-overseas-success/article25078712/.

Delporte, C. 2011. 'Jabil Streamlines Design Capabilities in Europe.' *Medical Product Outsourcing*, 17 November. Accessed 14 March 2017. Available at http://www.mpo-mag.com/contents/view_breaking-news/2011-11-17/jabil-streamlines-design-capabilities-in-euro/.

Dixon, Guy. 2000. 'Celestica in $1-billion (U.S.) Deal with Motorola.' *The Globe and Mail*, 7 December. Accessed 26 August 2017. Available at http://www.theglobeandmail.com/report-on-business/celestica-in-1-billion-us-deal-with-motorola/article25575713/.

Dolan, C. S. and J. Humphrey. 2004. 'Changing Governance Patterns in the Trade in Fresh Vegetables between Africa and the United Kingdom.' *Environment and Planning A* 36 (3): 491–509. DOI: https://doi.org/10.1068/a35281.

Duffy, J. 1999. 'Cisco Wants to Help Host Your Applications.' *Network World,* 29 April.

Dyck, R. and N. Halpern. 1999. 'Team Based Organizations Redesign Celestica.' *The Journal for Quality and Participation* 2 (5) (September/October): 36–40.

Eadicicco, L. 2015. 'Fitbit Is Clearly Worried about Apple.' *Business Insider,* 7 May. Accessed 12 December 2016. Available at http://www.businessinsider.com/what-fitbit-thinks-could-hurt-its-business-2015-5?IR=T.

EE Times. 2005. 'Celestica Acquires Design Services Firm CoreSim.' 8 May. Accessed 19 April 2017. Available at http://www.eetimes.com/document.asp?doc_id=1155658.

Engardio, P. and B. Einhorn. 2015. 'Outsourcing Innovation.' *Bloomberg,* 21 March. Accessed 21 March 2017. Available at https://www.bloomberg.com/news/articles/2005-03-20/outsourcing-innovation.

Ernst, D. 2005. 'Limits to Modularity: Reflections on Recent Developments in Chip Design.' *Industry and Innovation* 12 (3): 303–35. DOI: http://dx.doi.org/10.1080/13662710500195918.

———. 2006. 'Innovation Offshoring: Asia's Emerging Role in Global Innovation Networks.' *East-West Center Special Report No. 10.* Honolulu: East-West Center U.S.-Asia Pacific Council.

European Commission. 2012. *ICT Sector Guide on Implementing the UN Guiding Principles on Business and Human Rights.* Brussels: European Commission.

Flex. 2009. 'Flextronics to build Wuzhong, Suzhou, China facility to Support Manufacturing and R&D Capabilities for Computing Products.' Flex Press Release, 15 October. Accessed 20 March 2017. Available at https://investors.flex.com/company-news/press-release-details/2009/Flextronics-to-Build-Wuzhong-Suzhou-China-Facility-to-Support-Manufacturing-and-RD-Capabilities-for-Computing-Products/default.aspx.

———. 2014. 'Supply Chain Solutions, Including Design and Manufacturing Services Provided by Flextronics for All-New Jeep Cherokee.' Accessed 19 April 2017. Available at http://s21.q4cdn.com/490720384/files/doc_news/2014/FLEX_News_2014_4_15_General_Releases.pdf.

———. 2015. 'How Wearables Will Change Everything.' *Intelligence,* Issue One. Accessed 31 December 2016. Available at https://www.theintelligenceofthings.com/article/how-wearables-will-change-everything/.

———. 2016. 'Sketch-to-Scale Solutions: Investor Presentation.' Accessed 25 December 2016. Available at http://www.slideshare.net/maryleeflex/dec2016-irpresentationflex?ref=http://investors.flextronics.com/investor-relations/default.aspx.

Frederick, T. B. 2000. 'Developing Strategies for System Assembly, Flexible Labor, and Inventory in the Electronic Manufacturing Services Industry.' Master's Thesis, Sloan School of Management, MIT.

Gartner. 2017. 'Gartner Says 2016 Marked Fifth Consecutive Year of Worldwide PC Shipment Decline.' *Gartner*, 11 January. Accessed 26 August 2017. Available at https://www.gartner.com/newsroom/id/3568420.

Gereffi, G. 1999. 'International Trade and Industrial Upgrading in the Apparel Commodity Chain.' *Journal of International Economics* 48 (1): 37–70. DOI: https://doi.org/10.1016/S0022-1996(98)00075-0.

―――. 2014. 'Global Value Chains in a Post-Washington Consensus World.' *Review of International Political Economy* 21 (1): 9–37. DOI: http://dx.doi.org/10.1080/09692290.2012.756414.

Gereffi, G., J. Humphrey, and T. Sturgeon. 2005. 'The Governance of Global Value Chains.' *Review of International Political Economy* 12 (1): 78–104. DOI: http://dx.doi.org/10.1080/09692290500049805.

Hamilton, G. and G. Gereffi. 2009. 'Global Commodity Chains, Market Makers, and the Rise of Demand-Responsive Economies.' In *Frontiers of Commodity Chain Research*, edited by Jennifer Bair, 136–61. Stanford, CA: Stanford University Press.

Heilman, W. 2001. 'Jabil Planning to Add 39 Engineers This Year at Springs Design Center.' *The Gazette*, 9 March. Accessed 14 March 2017. Available at http://gazette.com/jabil-planning-to-add-39-engineers-this-year-at-springs-design-center/article/114199.

Humphrey, J. and H. Schmitz. 2000. 'Governance and Upgrading in Global Value Chains.' IDS Working Paper No. 120. Brighton: Institute of Development Studies, University of Sussex.

Inagaki, K. 2017. 'Foxconn's Sharp Acquisition Poses Test for Its Toshiba Plans.' *Financial Times*, 14 March. Accessed 11 July 2017. Available at https://www.ft.com/content/18d4c2c2-0879-11e7-ac5a-903b21361b43?mhq5j=e1.

Kanellos, M. 2002. 'Flextronics Buys Design Firm Palo Alto Products.' www.cnet.com, 2 January. Accessed 14 April 2017. Available at https://www.cnet.com/news/flextronics-buys-design-firm-palo-alto-products/.

Kawakami M. 2011. 'Inter-firm Dynamics in Notebook PC Value Chains and the Rise of Taiwanese Original Design Manufacturing Firms.' In *The Dynamics of Local Learning in Global Value Chains*, edited by M. Kawakami and T. J. Sturgeon, 16–42. London: Palgrave Macmillan.

Lakenan, B, D. Boyd and E. Frey. 2001. 'Why Cisco Fell: Outsourcing and Its Perils.' *Strategy+business*, 1 July. Accessed 1 June 2015. Available at http://www.strategy-business.com/article/19984?gko=e4f2f.

Lashinsky, A. 2015. 'Why Flex Is Going beyond Its Manufacturing Roots.' *Fortune*, 2 October. Accessed 31 December 2016. Available at http://fortune.com/2015/10/02/flex-outsourced-manufacturing-flextronics-international/.

Lewin, A.Y., S. Massini and C. Peeters. 2009. 'Why Are Companies Offshoring Innovation? The Emerging Global Race for Talent.' *Journal of International Business Studies* 40 (6): 901–25.

Lipton, J. 2007. 'Flextronics Muscles In on Solectron.' *Forbes*, 4 June. Accessed 12 July 2017. Available at https://www.forbes.com/2007/06/04/flextronics-solectron-electronics-markets-equity-cx_jl_0604markets06.html.

Luethje, B. 2001. 'Electronics Contract Manufacturing: Transnational Production Networks, the Internet, and Knowledge Diffusion in Low-Cost Locations in Asia and Eastern Europe.' East-West Center Working Paper No. 18. Honolulu: East-West Center U.S.-Asia Pacific Council.

Luethje, B., S. Huertgen, P. Pawlicki and M. Sproll. 2013. *From Silicon Valley to Shenzhen: Global Production and Work in the IT Industry.* Lanham: Rowan & Littlefield.

Luk, L. 2014a. 'Foxconn Is Quietly Working with Google on Robotics.' *Wall Street Journal Blogs*, 11 February. Accessed 26 August 2017. Available at http://blogs.wsj.com/digits/2014/02/11/foxconn-working-with-google-on-robotics/.

———. 2014b. 'Foxconn Sells Communications Technology Patents to Google.' *Wall Street Journal*, 25 April. Accessed 26 August 2017. Available at http://online.wsj.com/news/articles/SB10001424052702304788404579523051086783712.

———. 2014c. 'Foxconn Weighs Plans for a US Plant.' *Wall Street Journal*, 26 January. Accessed 26 August 2017. Available at https://www.wsj.com/articles/foxconn-weighs-plan-for-us-plant-1390725999.

Lundin, N. and S. S. Serger. 2007.'Globalization of R&D and China: Empirical Observations and Policy Implications.' IFN Working Paper 710. Östersund: Swedish Institute for Growth Policy Studies. Accessed 26 August 2017. Available at https://www.researchgate.net/publication/5096351_Globalization_of_RD_and_China_-_Empirical_Observations_and_Policy_Implications.

MMI (*Manufacturing Market Insider*). 2015. 'EMS Innovation Centers Replace Manufacturing R&D for OEMs.' May. Accessed 11 April 2015. Available atv https://mfgmkt.com/wp-content/uploads/2015/06/May-2015.pdf.

———. 2017. 'The MMI Top 50.' Manufacturing Market Insider, 6 April.

MAPI Foundation. 2012. *Facts about Manufacturing*, 9th Edition. Washington, DC: The Manufacturing Institute. Accessed 26 August 2017. Available at http://www.themanufacturinginstitute.org/~/media/1242121E7A4F45D68C2A458654070 3A5/2012_Facts_About_Manufacturing_Full_Version_High_Res.pdf.

Markoff, J. 2012. 'Skilled Work, Without the Worker.' *The New York Times*, 18 August. Accessed 25 July 2016. Available at http://www.nytimes.com/2012/08/19/business/new-wave-of-adept-robots-is-changing-global-industry.html.

McClearn, M. 2013. 'I500: After Losing Its Biggest Customer, Celestica Is Reinventing Itself Yet Again.' *Canadian Business*, 10 May. Accessed 15 April 2017. Available at http://www.canadianbusiness.com/lists-and-rankings/target-transformation/.

Minter, Steve. 2014. '2014 IW 1000: Jabil Circuit – The Manufacturer's Manufacturer.' *Industry Week*, 8 September. Accessed 2 March 2015. Available at http://www.industryweek.com/industryweek-1000/2014-iw-1000-jabil-circuit-manufacturers-manufacturer.

Mochizuki, Takashi. 2017. 'Foxconn Offers up to $27 Billion for Toshiba's Chip Business.' *Wall Street Journal*, 17 April. Accessed 11 August 2017. Available at: https://www.wsj.com/articles/foxconn-could-bid-up-to-27-billion-for-toshibas-chip-business-1491833399.

Morgan, T. P. 2014. 'Contract Manufacturer Jabil Sells Straight into Hypercenter Datacenters.' *Enterprise Tech*, 2 April. Accessed 27 December 2016. Available at http://www.enterprisetech.com/2014/04/02/contract-manufacturer-jabil-sells-straight-hyperscale-datacenters/.

Murgia, M. 2017. 'PC Shipments Drop for Fifth Year in a Row.' *Financial Times*, 12 January. Accessed 10 April 2017. Available at https://www.ft.com/content/1fabbf08-d8cf-11e6-944b-e7eb37a6aa8e.

New Venture Research. 2016. *The Worldwide Electronics Manufacturing Services Market – 2016 Edition*. Nevada City, CA: New Venture Research Corporation.

OECD. 2008. *OECD Reviews of Innovation Policy: CHINA 2008*. Paris: OECD.

Onex Corporation. 2011. *Annual Information Form*. Accessed 1 December 2017. Available at https://www.onex.com/sites/default/files/2017-08/1500087016.pdf.

———. 2012. *Annual Information Form*. Accessed 1 December 2017. Available at https://www.onex.com/sites/default/files/2017-08/1500086947.pdf.

Perez, B. 2016. 'Flex Plans to Launch Technology Accelerator Venture in Mainland China.' *South China Morning Post*, 27 December. Accessed 2 March 2017. Available at http://app.scmp.com/scmp/mobile/index.html#/article/1895081/desktop.

Quinn, J.B. 2000. 'Outsourcing Innovation: The New Engine of Growth.' *Sloan Management Review* 41 (4): 13–29. Accessible via ProQuest.

Raj-Reichert, G. 2015. 'Exercising Power over Labour Governance in the Electronics Industry.' *Geoforum* 67: 89–92. DOI: https://doi.org/10.1016/j.geoforum.2015.10.013.

Shinal, J. 2013. 'New Tech Economy: 3D Printing's Promise in Prosthetics.' *USA Today*, 17 March. Accessed 17 March 2013. Available at http://www.usatoday.com/story/tech/2013/03/17/autodesk-phillipselectronics-3dprinting/1990703/.

Shore, B. 2001. 'Information Sharing in Global Supply Chain Systems.' *Journal of Global Information Technology Management* 4 (3): 27–50. DOI: http://dx.doi.org/1 0.1080/1097198X.2001.10856306.

Steinman, C. 2001. 'Motorola Inc. Announces Alliance with Celestica.' *IT World Canada*,

4 January. Accessed 29 November 2016. Available at http://www.itworldcanada. com/article/motorola-inc-announces-alliance-with-celestica/29309.

Sturgeon, T. 1998. 'Network-led Development and the Rise of Turn-Key Production Networks: Technological Change.' *Global Production and Local Jobs*. Geneva: International Institute for Labour Studies.

———. 2002. 'Modular Production Networks: A New American Model of Industrial Organisation.' *Industrial and Corporate Change* 11 (3): 451–96. DOI: https://doi. org/10.1093/icc/11.3.451.

Sturgeon, T. And M. Kawakami. 2011. 'Global Value Chains in the Electronics Industry: Characteristics, Crisis, and Upgrading Opportunities for Firms from Developing Countries.' *International Journal of Technological Learning, Innovation and Development* 4 (1-3): 120-47. DOI: https://doi.org/10.1504/ IJTLID.2011.041902.

The Economist. 2011. 'Rebooting Their Systems.' 10 March. Accessed 10 April 2017. Available at http://www.economist.com/node/18332916.

Tse, P. and A. Yip. 2016. 'Foxconn: Seeking Diversification beyond Contract Manufacturing.' Case No. 16/003C. Hong Kong: Centennial College Publication.

van Liemt, Gijsbert. 2007. *Subcontracting in Electronics: From Contract Manufacturers to Providers of Electronic Manufacturing Services*. Geneva: International Labour Organisation.

Wallack, T. 2001. 'Sanmina Buys Rival SCI Systems.' *SFGate*, 17 July. Accessed 9 April 2015. Available at http://www.sfgate.com/bayarea/article/Sanmina-buys- rival-SCI-Systems-2899690.php.

Weinswig, D. 2015. '"b." New York: Fung Business Intelligence Centre.' Accessed 19 April 2017. Available at http://www.deborahweinswig.com/wp-content/ uploads/2015/05/FBIC-Global-Retail-Tech-Report-on-Flextronics-Investor- Day_V2.pdf.

Yeung, H. W-C. and N. M. Coe. 2016. *Global Production Networks: Theorizing Economic Development in an Interconnected World*. Oxford: Oxford University Press.

Zhai, E, Y. Shi and M. Gregory. 2007. 'The Growth and Capability Development of Electronics Manufacturing Service (EMS) Companies.' *International Journal of Production Economics* 107 (1): 1–9. DOI: https://doi.org/10.1016/j. ijpe.2006.03.009.

Appendix 2.1

A non-exhaustive list of mergers and acquisitions by Flex, Foxconn and Jabil Circuit

Flex	Foxconn	Celestica	Jabil Circuit
• Late 1990s: Astron Group and FICO Plastics Ltd. (Hong Kong) and Ericsson Business Networks	• 2003: Motorola factory (Mexico) • 2004: Ambit Microsystems & Eimo Oyji (Finland)	• 1997: Design to Distribution (European EMS) • 1998: International Manufacturing Services	• 1999: GET Manufacturing (China) • 2002: Lucent Technologies (China)
• 2000: Casio factory; JIT Holdings Ltd.; Palo Alto Products Inc. (design company); Chatham Technologies; Dii Group	• 2006: Premier Image Technology • 2007: Ennoconn Corporation	• 2000: Bull Electronics Inc. (contract manufacturer)	• 2001: Intel Corporation plant in Malaysia (agreement to be Intel supplier for 3 years)
• 2001: Instrumentation Engineering; 50% Xerox's office equipment; Ericsson facilities	• 2008: Chi Mei Communications • 2012: 50% Sharp Corporation's liquid panel display manufacturing facility (Japan)	• 2001: Omni Industries (Singaporean EMS)	• 2002: Philips Contract Manufacturing Services; Quantum (tape drive manufacturing plant in Penang)
• 2003: Microcell (Finland)	• 2014: Socle Technologies (Taiwan)	• 2004: Manufacturers' Services Limited	
• 2004: Hughes Network Systems, Inc (55% ownership in provider of software and telecom services)	*Mergers*	• 2005: Displaytronix (flat panel display repair services); CoreSim (advanced design and redesign services)	• 2005: Varian, Inc.
• 2005: Nortel Networks' manufacturing division	• 2014: Asia Pacific Telecom Co. (Taiwan) announced		• 2006: Taiwan Green Point Enterprises
• 2006: Iwill (Taiwan)	• 2016: SMART Technologies	• 2010: AlliedPanels (medical engineering and manufacturing service provider);	• 2007: Green Point (manufacturer and service provider for mobility products)
• 2007: Solectron • 2009: SloMedical, a European manufacturer of disposable medical devices	• 2016: Sharp Corporation • 2016: SoftBank Capital		
• 2012: Stellar Microelectronics (provider of microelectronics technologies for aerospace, defence and medical manufacturing); Saturn Electronics and			

(Contd.)

(*Contd.*)

Flex	Foxconn	Celestica	Jabil Circuit
Engineering, Inc. (a supplier of electronics manufacturing services, solenoids and wiring for the automotive, appliance, consumer, energy and industrial markets) • 2013: a manufacturing facility of Motorola Mobility; RIWISA (manufacturing facility for medical, consumer packaging and industrial products in Switzerland) • 2015: Mirror Controls International (manufacturer of glass and powerful mirror actuators in the automotive industry); Alcatel-Lucent's manufacturing facility, equipment, and staff for optical transport equipment in Italy; Farm Design (provider of development and design services for medical device and diagnostic companies); Wink (a smart home platform); NEXTracker (a designer and manufacturer of advanced single-axis photovoltaic trackers) • 2016: Joint venture with RIB Software AG (leading provider of 5D building information modelling big data technology) • 2017: AGM Automotive (announced)		manufacturing operations of semiconductor equipment contract manufacturer) Invec Solutions • 2011: Brooks Automation (manufacturing operations of semiconductor equipment contract manufacturer) • 2012: D+H Manufacturing (manufacturer of components for semiconductor equipment) • 2017: Karel's manufacturing facilities in Mexico and California (metal welding and wire harness assembly for aerospace)	• 2011: Telmar Network Technology, Inc. • 2013: Nypro (plastics manufacturer for healthcare, packaging, and electronics) • 2015: Plasticos Castella (Manufacturer of plastics for food industry and beverage brands); AOC Technologies (Photonics industry); Inala (Energy monitoring services); Shemer (contract manufacturer of capital equipment); Clothing+ (biometric sensor solutions); Kasalis (manufacturer for optics) • 2016: Hanson (metal components manufacturer)

Source: Various news sources and company websites.

Appendix 2.2

Figure 2.7 Flex net sales by market (in percentages)

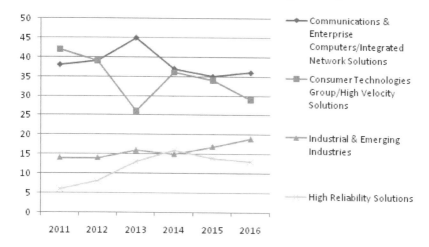

Source: SEC company filings, 10-K report.

Figure 2.8 Jabil Circuit revenue by segment expressed as percentage of net revenue

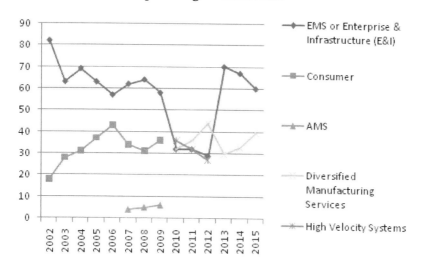

Source: SEC company filings, 10-K report.

Figure 2.9 Celestica revenue by end markets (in percentages)

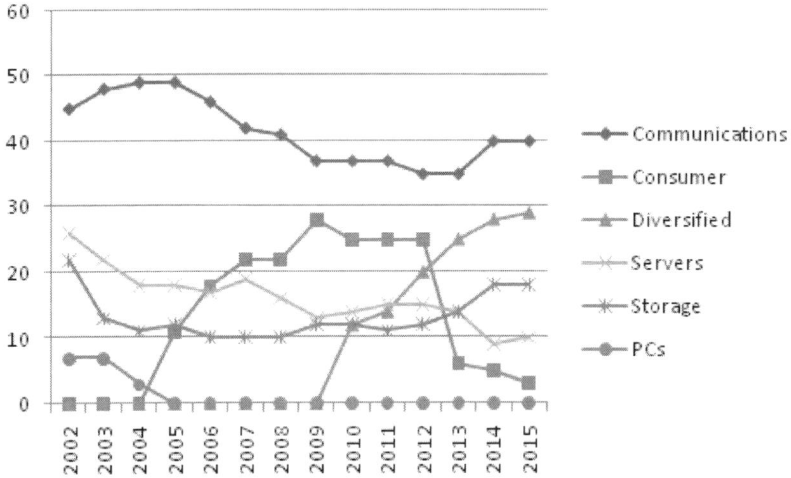

Source: SEC company filings, 20-F report.

3

Gaining Process Rents in the Apparel Industry
Incremental Improvements in Labour and Other Management Practices

Dev Nathan and Harsh

Introduction

Manufacturers in the apparel industry are not price-makers; rather, they are generally price-takers. Entry into the apparel manufacturing global value chain (GVC) segment is relatively easy because there is no requirement for complex technical knowledge, or for a large amount of capital. Apparel manufacture in GVCs is often a country's first entry into modern manufacturing. Thus, there is a high level of competition in the apparel manufacturing GVC segments, both at the national and international levels. This raises the question: is there any scope for apparel manufacturers to increase their returns despite taking prices as given? Obviously, this can happen only if they are able to cheapen the cost of production compared to their competitors, either by reducing the cost of inputs, mainly labour (often called the 'low road'); or by increasing the efficiency of production (the 'high road'). An improvement in the efficiency of production will require some investment, but the investment can pay off in terms of higher returns with respect to the overall investment made.

Increases in returns due to improvements in production processes are called process rents; they are returns on investments which are higher than those secured by competitors who do not carry out such incremental improvements. However, process improvements are easily copied and can spread throughout the industry. If that happens, we get the Prebish-Singer-Kaplinsky (Kaplinsky, 2005) result: the gains of productivity improvement will be captured by the buyers, the brands and big retailers, and not accrue to the producer firms. In order for some firms to secure process rents, the situation would need to be one where some firms undertake the process improvements, but this practice has not spread across the industry as a whole. This spreading of the process improvements would need to be considered not only on a national, but on a global scale, given that lead firms can, over time, switch the location of production.

These process improvements can be called process innovations. Even if they are not new to the industry as a whole, they represent a change or innovation in the functioning of supplier firms. The innovations dealt with fall into the category of incremental innovation. However, it is these incremental innovations that allow some manufacturers to increase their returns even while functioning under the same market conditions as other non-innovative firms.

This chapter draws upon two sources of data. One is that of available literature on better management practices in countries such as Sri Lanka, and countries in the much-studied ILO–IFC Better Work Programme in Cambodia, Vietnam and other countries. The second source of data is a data set gathered by the authors through case studies of some forty apparel manufacturers, spread across many clusters (the National Capital Region around Delhi, Jaipur, Mumbai, South Gujarat, Bangalore and Tirupur) in India. These case studies were conducted under the International Labour Organization (ILO) study conducted for India's Apparel Export Promotion Corporation (AEPC).[1]

In the section after the introduction, we set out the main theoretical analysis of the connections between capabilities and firm performance, followed by summaries of some of the earlier studies of this issue. The results of the ILO–IFC Better Work programme are looked into followed by Sri Lanka's 'Garments Without Guilt'. The section ends with a discussion about whether dealing with abuse and sexual harassment complaints helps increase firm productivity. The next section is the main part of the chapter, dealing with better management in the Indian apparel industry and its reported impact on productivity, enabling on-time delivery and better quality production. In the following section, some improved management practices that lower costs and thus secure process rents are described. Workforce management or labour practices are dealt with in the next section. In particular, there is a discussion of the ways in which the hyper-mobility of precariously employed workers have been dealt with, along with the resulting reported benefits to workers and firms. The section after this then deals

---

1   We would like to thank Sher Verick and Sudipta Bhadra of the ILO's Delhi office and Chandrima Chatterjee of the AEPC for having supported and facilitated this study. We are also grateful to the staff of AEPC's regional offices in Jaipur, Mumbai, Bangalore and Tirupur and to the managers and other senior staff of the visited units who gave their time for discussions. Thanks also to Kanchana Ruwanpura for comments. The usual caveats apply.

with factors that are external to the firm, such as good logistics and providing workers' accommodation in securing process rents. A brief final section sums up firm performance as the result of management and labour practices, the likely resulting lower costs reflecting process rents, and the limitations of this process.

Capabilities and firm performance

Productivity in a firm is largely dependent on the technology used. However, technology has to be used or deployed in production. The way in which technology is used can differ from one firm to another, thus leading to differences in production and productivity. The productivity of technology depends on various management systems and routines, including the manner in which labour is deployed in production.

To give a simple example, inexperienced labour is likely to be able to obtain less out of a machine than experienced labour; this is the famous 'learning by doing' effect of experience on productivity. However, there is much more to overall firm productivity than just the experience and skill of labour. Various management practices affect productivity. For instance, poor inventory management would increase the time taken to secure the parts and supplies needed, thus reducing productivity. Cluttered alleyways between production lines would also increase the time taken to move materials from one section to another, thus affecting productivity by increasing internal logistic time.

These various management practices, including labour practices, together determine what can be called the capabilities of a firm. In using the term 'capabilities', we are referring specifically to production capabilities. Capabilities are the competencies that enable a firm to perform a task or utilize a technology in production (modifying Nubler, 2013, 122).

Capabilities are the result of both the endowments (knowledge and skills) that owners and employees (managers, supervisors and workers) bring to the firm. Along with these endowments, however, there are the management practices and routines that are followed in a firm. The use of the word 'practices', and that too in the plural, is deliberate; this is in order to emphasize that these practices are not given; rather, they are chosen by firms. It is this choice of management practices that is the focus of this chapter. Within management practices, including labour practices, can we identify some practices that result in superior firm performance, as opposed to practices that result in inferior firm performance?

This section primarily depends on material relating to apparel firms in Vietnam, Cambodia and other countries covered in the ILO–IFC Better Work programme. In addition, we refer to studies of Sri Lankan firms (Ruwanpura, 2015; Goger, 2014; Perry, Wood and Fernie, 2014) and of the ILO's Sustaining Competitive and Responsible Enterprises (SCORE) project, besides other secondary sources.

Labour practices or workforce management practices have two aspects. First, they affect the well-being of workers. Second, they affect the firm's performance. One might argue that there is a link between the two as workers whose well-being is improved will be able to work better. For instance, the provision of a nutritious meal during work hours would not only benefit workers, but might also improve their performance. Our concern in this chapter is primarily with this type of relationship between labour practices and firm performance. This is, of course, an instrumental approach to labour practices. However, that is related to the purpose of this chapter, which is to answer the question: do better labour practices enable improved firm performance in securing process rents? This, in turn, is part of the broader question: do management practices matter in firm performance?

Overall assessments of improved management practices

We looked at four overall assessments of the effects of improved management practices in the textiles and garments industry. They are those of Nick Bloom and his co-authors (Bloom *et al.*, 2011); the ILO–IFC Better Work programme for garments; of small scale units in developing countries in the ILO SCORE programme; and the study by McKenzie and Woodruff (2015).

The Bloom study looked at the performance of two sets of textile units in Mumbai. The first set of units was provided consultancy services on improving management practices in the areas of factory operations, quality control, inventory control, machine planning, labour practices (human resource management), and sales and orders. These consultancy services led to the adoption of better practices in these areas. The performance of this set of firms was compared with another set of firms of similar size and product composition that were not provided these consultancy services. The perceived result was that the firms with improved management practices showed a 17 per cent increase in productivity, while the other firms showed no such increase.

The improved practices were relatively simple matters, such as keeping alleyways clear of obstructions, organizing stock rooms so that spares and materials could be easily located, and so on. Yet the overall result was a substantial increase in productivity. Given that both sets of firms (those provided advice and those not provided advice) operated in the same market conditions, one could say that the improved management practices resulted in process rents for the first group of firms.

Do better management practices matter in small units?

Both Bloom (2013) and the Better Work studies are focused on large units. However, do management practices make a difference in small units? Given that a large proportion of Indian garment units are of the small-scale and medium-scale type, this is an important question. The ILO SCORE project works with small units in India and other countries. The project tries to instil better management practices in small units. A summary of the impact of this project in India points out that after the adoption of better management practices, including those that led to cooperative relations between firms and employees, productivity improvements of 15 per cent to 20 per cent have been observed (ILO, 2016). As the study summarizes:

> Studies have shown that better social and environmental conditions enhance company reputations, reduce the costs of doing business and improve competitiveness. SCORE helped the management of Accura Industries Ltd. recognize this and the company has also provided a separate women's toilet and more accessible drinking water. Employee morale and performance has improved, resulting in improvements such as timely cleaning and organizing of workstations, and less lost production time. The women employees can now complete their production targets within a 10-hour working day (inclusive of 2 hours overtime). In three months the company saved 220 sq. ft. (20.4 sq. m.) of space and 50,000 Indian Rupees (US$ 740) by disposing of unwanted materials and obsolete machinery. (ILO, 2016)

A multi-country study of small firms in developing economies also showed that 'owners implementing better business practices have higher sales, profits, labour productivity and total factor productivity' (McKenzie and Woodruff, 2015, 20).

Better work programme in garment factories in South-East Asia

The ILO–IFC Better Work programme began in Cambodia during the Multi-Fibre Arrangement (MFA) regime. The programme linked firm quotas to their compliance with labour standards. Firms that did better received higher quotas and vice versa. Initially, there was a reputation effect as the factories' performance on labour standards was made public. Later, however, even after these factory standards ceased to be made public, the factories did not regress to worse labour standards. As Drusilla Brown *et al.* (2016) argue, the reason there was no regression was because factories gained in productivity and efficiency by maintaining better labour standards. Given the high incidence of factories shutting down in Cambodia, they found that factories with better labour standards had a lower chance of closing down. A study of the same programme in Vietnam found that there was a 5.9 per cent increase in profitability when workers perceived an improvement in working conditions. The fact that there was an increase in productivity and profitability was reinforced by the finding that continued compliance was not the result of pressure from reputation-sensitive buyers, but that of the strategy of instituting better practices in order to increase profits. As the Brown study puts it, 'The path of compliance for firms lacking a reputation sensitive buyer does not diverge from that of firms with a buyer that requires a minimum level of compliance' (Brown *et al.*, 2016, 28).

The studies sum up the factors affecting productivity and leading to an improvement as being: better air quality and factory temperature; safer equipment and fewer accidents; higher-than-minimum wages; greater availability of health services; less in-kind compensation; more accessible grievance mechanisms; more transparent pay and piece rate; less verbal and physical abuse, including sexual abuse; less concern with wage deductions; improved welfare facilities; and less excessive overtime.

The Vietnam study also showed that productivity improves with overall better working conditions – workers reach their targets forty minutes faster than similar workers with worse working conditions (ILO, 2015).

'Garments Without Guilt': Sri Lanka

Sri Lanka is well known as an apparel producer with somewhat better labour and working standards. It produces relatively high-quality products, with a strong position in the production of skill-intensive women's inner wear. This is a different case from those discussed earlier insofar as it shows that improved business processes yield a return in ability to produce a higher quality product rather than increasing productivity in a standard or commoditized product.

There are both national- and firm-level factors in the adoption of better production processes. Labour law in Sri Lanka requires all workers to have direct employment contracts with the factory. This does not allow for the indirectly employed contract labour so ubiquitous in the Indian industry. Along with contracts for indefinite employment, workers must be paid monthly wage payments, eliminating daily or piece-rate payments. The monthly wage is set centrally by a tripartite body.

The requirement of regular contracts for indefinite employment eliminates the possibility of trying to be competitive by reducing wages, or wage competition. In India, firms can try to be competitive by wage-cutting, through the substitution of contract for permanent workers. As pointed out by Piore and Sabel (1994), competition by wage-cutting is inimical to innovation and productivity improvements. The local governments of the Italian fashion districts do not allow wage-cutting and thus force firms to compete on quality and innovation. It could be that there is a similar effect in Sri Lanka, forcing firms to compete on quality and process innovation.

Along with the national factors listed here that encourage improved practices, there is also a range of initiatives that were taken under the 'Garments Without Guilt' programme. This programme was initiated by the industry as the end of the MFA loomed. The Sri Lankan industry decided to try to derive commercial benefits from its better labour practices by branding itself as a destination that provided quality as a way of securing Sri Lanka's global position (Ruwanpura, 2015); in other words, improved labour practices were implemented to provide a process rent in terms of the higher returns from high-quality products.

Factories paid attention to health and safety issues. They also provided transport for workers. In one case, the factory even provided water to the doorsteps of workers' houses, a practice that began after managers found that the reason for workers coming to work tired was due to them having to collect water for the household (Goger, 2014). Factories also provided breakfast to workers. Overall, attention was paid to factory layout and environment, factors that were seen to influence productivity.

Wage costs could not be reduced by substituting insecure contract workers for secure, permanent employment. Individual factories that wanted to retain skilled workers had to take the route of paying above the minimum wage. Higher wages become an incentive to workers; at the same time, they also required firms to use them profitably for higher-value products.

Along with monthly wages, factories do set production quotas. However, there are incentive payments to induce workers to meet and even exceed quotas. Verbal exhortation, which often turned into abuse, was replaced by incentive payments.

While Sri Lankan labour practices are substantially better than those prevailing in India or Bangladesh, there are still problems with these practices. For one, the regular salary, not including overtime and incentive payments, is not a living wage. Thus, in order to earn a living wage, there is a seemingly self-imposed pressure to do overtime work. Further, when production targets have to be met, factories often breach the laws about overtime work (Ruwanpura, 2015, 12–13).

With regard to another improved better practice, one that is part of the ILO's Core Labour Standards, that is, the right to association, it must be noted that Sri Lankan firms discourage workers' unions. Instead, they promote some form of a workers' committee as a way of airing grievances and seeking redress. Of course, as Samanthi Gunawardana (2014) points out, workers also have their own informal (usually unnoticed) day-to-day ways of airing grievances and seeking redress.

With all of these problems remaining to be tackled, we still see that other improved management practices have enabled the Sri Lankan industry to maintain its position as a manufacturer of high-quality products. The difference in the returns from high-quality products compared to those from low-quality products is the rent attributable to the process improvements.

Dealing with abuse and sexual harassment

A major feature of the apparel industry is the high proportion of women employees. About 70 per cent to 90 per cent of the workforce in Bangladesh and Sri Lanka, and about 50 per cent in India, are women. However, this opportunity for women to enter the workforce also seems to go hand-in-hand with a high incidence of abuse and sexual harassment. Abuse is not confined to women; men working in apparel factories in the Indian National Capital Region (NCR) report frequent abuse by supervisors. Additionally, women are subject to sexual harassment, which can vary from normalization of sexual innuendo to inappropriate touching and go up to demanding sexual favours (Society for Labour and Development, 2014).

Do abuse and sexual harassment affect firm performance? Given that the ending of abuse and sexual harassment is a basic goal of human rights legislation, it might seem strange to link sexual harassment with firm performance. However, since our objective in this chapter is to investigate the business case for improved labour practices, we approach it from this instrumental angle, fully recognizing that it is partial.

The ILO–IFC Better Work Programme conducted a study of the connection between both abuse and sexual harassment and firm performance (for a study on abuse in Vietnam, see Rourke, 2014; for a multi-country study on sexual harassment in apparel factories in Haiti, Indonesia, Jordan, Nicaragua and Vietnam, see Lin, Babbitt and Brown, 2014). Verbal exhortation is frequently used as an instrument for securing greater work effort, but this exhortation can often become abusive. Furthermore, the power asymmetry between male supervisors and female workers clearly affects the incidence of sexual harassment (Lin *et al.*, 2014). The addition of production quotas for workers becomes a significant predictor for sexual harassment.

Abuse and sexual harassment both result in a high turnover of workers. This high attrition rate has a negative effect on productivity and on time-to-target production (Lin *et al.*, 2014), which implies that a reduction in abuse and sexual harassment would have a positive impact on productivity.

Operational problems in the Indian apparel industry

While stressing the importance of policy action to overcome structural constraints, there is a lot that can be done by firms to improve their competitive positions. An overview analysis of the Indian garment industry and its major competitors (Bangladesh, Cambodia, China, Indonesia, Turkey and Vietnam) ranked India last in all but one performance category. Table 3.1 contains the relevant data.

Table 3.1 India's ranking in production related problems

Productivity	7th
Worker attrition (monthly – 10.4% to 12.4%)	7th
Customer service	5th
Lead time	7th
Price	7th
Quality	7th
Ease of doing business	7th
Reliability	7th

Source: Birnbaum, Benchmark India Study for AEPC (2014).

The critical operation in the garment industry is that of stitching a garment. This is preceded by cutting and preparing pieces, and followed by checking, finishing and packing. The garment industry calculates production efficiency in terms of standard allowable minutes (SAM) or the amount of time it should take to stitch a particular garment. The total available time in a shift reduced by the time required for toilet and refreshment breaks and divided by SAM gives the number of pieces that can be produced in a shift at 100 per cent efficiency. The Indian industry overall is known for achieving very low efficiency – less than 40 per cent of calculated SAM production. Sri Lanka, on the other hand, achieves more than 75 per cent efficiency, while China is said to manage more than 100 per cent, which is very likely due to the higher level of mechanization.

Since the technology of the sewing machine is fairly standardized, efficiency differences are not due to differences in technology. These differences can be attributed to management weaknesses, which in turn can be divided into problems in managerial routines or processes and problems in the skill levels of the operators. An Indian consultant with decades of experience in the garment industry both in India and abroad estimated that the problem of low efficiency was due in equal part to poor management routines and poor labour practices. Owners, managers and human resources (HR) personnel with whom we had discussions all agreed that poor efficiency is a combination of poor management routines and low worker productivity. In one of the larger firms in the NCR, it was pointed out that while in their Indian units efficiency had been improved from 35 per cent to 40 per cent, in their factories in Jordan, they easily achieved 75 per cent efficiency. Firm strategies and management systems are key factors, working with labour market conditions and institutions, to yield labour practices.

Poor logistics and additional bureaucratic delays add to management routines or poor internal supply chain management, leading to an increase in Indian lead time, which means that they cannot bid for participation in the growing 'fast fashion' segment of the industry. In a World Bank study, several firms reported that they had been downgraded several tiers after they missed deadlines (Jordan, Kamphuis and Setia, 2014, 32). Within this general picture of poor management and functioning in the Indian apparel industry, there are a number of firms that have done somewhat better. Their improved labour and other management practices result in them having lower costs, and thus a process rent greater than the profits earned by poorly managed units.

Three areas of capabilities have been identified as being important to increasing productivity: (*a*) management – to effectively organize internal supply chains, (*b*) supervisors – to maintain production schedules and quality standards and (*c*) tailors – to be multi-skilled in order to sustain production schedules and quality standards.

These problems are not those of capital investment but of developing capabilities. At a policy level, what this means is that the focus of government policies needs to switch from subsidizing capital expenditure to the building of capabilities. As we will see later, there is a connection between management capabilities and labour practices; the latter is not independent of the former. In this part of the study, however, we will deal with the two aspects of managerial routines and labour practices separately. Furthermore, in each area of discussion, we will first take up the problems that have been identified and then bring in the better practices we have observed.

Better practices

In this section, we identify the better practices that can reduce costs and thus lead to process rents. The better practices discussed here are ways in which company production lines can be reorganized so as to reduce wastage of time, use multi-skilled workers, move pieces faster down the line, involve workers in suggesting improvements, and identify and rectify defects early in the production process.

Better practices in assembly-line production

Larger units in Tirupur have carried out backward integration into fabric, dyeing and printing processes to ensure that they have control over the supply chain. A unit in Jaipur that undertakes large-volume production for WalMart stations its executives at the factories carrying out weaving, dyeing and printing to ensure that there is no break in the supply line. A number of factories mentioned that they undertake cutting of fabric at least one day before it is needed for stitching. This ensures that there is no wastage of stitching time.

These methods of backward integration or close monitoring of input suppliers are steps that can be undertaken by large garment manufacturers. However, the proper coordination of activities that are undertaken within a factory is something that even small units can undertake, provided they have the necessary hardware (computers) and software systems. Again, large units can afford computerized management systems more easily than small units. However, a dedicated garment-manufacturing-specific computer software provided through cloud technology could be software provided as a service.

This would considerably reduce the costs of accessing the required computer services and enable even small units to use these services as required. Supporting the development of such cloud-based computer services would be a critical measure in helping small and medium garment units become more efficient, reduce their lead times and be more competitive overall.

To improve efficiency in the assembly line, a number of good practices were observed. Some firms trained their workers to have multiple skills. Each worker's available skills were listed in a skill matrix. This allowed supervisors to allocate workers along the line according to the skills required, making up for deficiencies due to absenteeism. Firm A reported that such multi-skilling and skill matrix allowed them to increase line productivity by 10 per cent to 15 per cent. Firm B pointed out that multi-skilling allowed them to make up for absenteeism and reduce lead time in meeting production targets.

Again, instead of checking only at the end of the line, some factories carried out in-line checking too. Such in-line checking allowed for the quick detection of mistakes and their timely correction, reducing overall rejection rates. Firm A reported that, with in-line checking, the proportion of rejects came down from 5 per cent to 2 per cent or even 1 per cent.

Large units used the hangar system, where pieces were moved on hangars along the assembly line from one tailor to the next. This is a lean production method, which, however, requires higher capital investment and large orders to be economical. However, even small units were able to reduce works in progress by reducing the number of pieces that were bundled together to be passed on from one worker to the next in the assembly line. All the measures listed here reduce operating expenses and, in a sense, provide process rents to those who implement these measures.

Incremental improvements

Remaining competitive in the global economy requires the implementation of incremental improvements in technology utilized. Some large units carry out substantial research and development (R&D) to come up with improvements. Firm C in Bengaluru and Firm D in Tirupur both pointed to their attempts to not just keep up with changes in processes, but also to stay ahead of the curve, carrying out incremental improvements in processes and products.

Some process improvements can be based on suggestions from workers, for example, for reducing lead time. Many factories claim to have Kaizen systems, where workers can send in their suggestions. The one clear example we got of a suggestion that was implemented with great effect, however, was at Firm E in Bengaluru. In its fast-reaction-time 'Made to Measure' (MtM) products, measurements taken at its stores were sent to the factory, where the work order was made out. Moving the work order to the shop floor took time, as workers waited for a number of work orders to be prepared before taking them forward. On a worker's suggestion, a dumb-waiter system was installed so that individual orders could be sent down from the order preparation room to the shop floor just below. Of course, computerization of the work processes and connecting the various departments could eliminate dumb-waiter systems and reduce internal communication time.

Firm A in the NCR has instituted the system of in-line production. In the usual arrangement, cutting, sewing and finishing are all carried out separately. However, in the in-line system, cutting, sewing and finishing are all integrated in one line. In this system there are fewer supervisors and fewer helpers. Problems can be spotted and taken care of much more easily, reducing rejects. This firm reports that there has been a 5 per cent to 6 per cent cost reduction through the adoption of this in-line production system.

Workforce management practices

Hyper-mobility of garment workers

Garment manufacture is usually organized in one of two ways – as an assembly line, with individual tailors carrying out one operation each, or in a modular manner, where a group of tailors stitch a garment together. Tailors in the assembly line carry out one operation each and may often possess the skill for just one type of operation. In the modular system, tailors tend to be multi-skilled and can substitute for each other in the various detailed tasks. The products manufactured in the assembly line method are simpler single-stitch garments, while those manufactured in modular fashion in groups are more complicated lock-stitch garments.

Assembly-line workers are paid on a shift basis, while modular tailors are paid on a piece-rate basis, which they can share among themselves. Shift workers, however, have shift-wise targets to be achieved. Very often (and workers would say usually), the shift targets are set such that they cannot be achieved without doing overtime for a period of two to four hours per shift.

A key feature of labour practices in India is the hyper-mobility of workers. In the Birnbaum (2014) assessment, India ranked last in the list of countries surveyed, as the country with the highest labour mobility, with an attrition rate of 10 per cent to 12.5 per cent per month. This amounts to virtually a complete turnover of the workforce within a year. We found similar levels of attrition common across all the clusters visited. Of course, there are also firms with very little labour attrition – the reasons for which are also necessary to understand.

Why is labour retention low? Basic tailoring skills are based on easily acquired explicit knowledge. These skills are generic and not firm specific. We were told that the specific skill for a particular style could be taught in just one day to a worker who had basic tailoring knowledge. Over the years, a large pool of tailors has developed, making it is easy for factories to recruit tailors as needed.

A large proportion of the tailors are migrants from Uttar Pradesh, Bihar and West Bengal. As some of them explained, they want to maximize the income they earn while they are at work. This leads them to work as many hours of overtime as possible, particularly those who work on piece rates. In addition, these migrants have targets of the amount of money they wish to accumulate – such as ₹ 50,000. Once they have saved this amount they return home after meeting local expenses. Workers may leave at different times of the year, accounting for the monthly attrition rates.

Both firms and workers would have their own reasons for such mobility. Firms in India's cotton fabric apparel sector have a slack period of about three to four months every year. In that period they run at a lower capacity. For this reason, they would prefer not to deal with laying off workers, even if they are contract labourers.

Workers, on their side, seem to be affected by a combination of two factors. The first factor is that they have familial obligations in their villages of origin. The second one is exhaustion, as they almost always work overtime. As one manager in the NCR mentioned, workers regularly ask for glucose drips from the doctors in the area. Any sign of illness or exhaustion becomes an occasion for seeking an energy-boosting drip. For anything more serious, they tend to return to their villages for treatment and care.

To understand why migrant workers work overtime to such an extent, one has to look at the low levels of wages paid to them. The wage ranges from ₹ 8,000 to ₹ 10,000 per month. With overtime, workers are able to earn ₹ 14,000–15,000 per month, which is closer to the living wage of about ₹ 18,000 per month. Furthermore, as workers in one location pointed out, most factories pay around the same wage at the same rates. The few that do pay differently and provide various other services fare very differently with regard to attrition. With wages and the treatment of workers being almost the same in most factories, there is little reason for workers to develop any loyalty to the factory in which they are currently working.

The absence of loyalty is exacerbated by two factors, one specific to migrant workers and the other specific to women. Many migrant workers are recruited through supervisors, who act as labour brokers. Thus, the workers depend on these supervisors for their jobs. If a supervisor leaves a particular firm for some reason, he takes his whole gang of workers with him. The workers' loyalty is thus more towards the supervisor rather than the firm. The factor specific to women is that they also tend to leave a factory when they face sexual harassment.

Some better labour practices that reduce attrition

A number of firms have instituted better labour practices that have made attrition quite negligible: paying more than the minimum wage; paying an additional house rent allowance (HRA) of about ₹ 650 per month; providing medical facilities beyond the statutory provision; providing loans for house construction in the village of origin; vehicle loan, usually for a motor-cycle; subsidized food of good quality in the canteen; provision for railway ticket bookings at the factory; respect and better treatment by managers and supervisors; incentive systems for extra output above target; having a reputation for good working conditions, besides being known to provide work all year round; and air-cooled factories attract workers (Firm H in NCR and Firm I in Jaipur).

A number of benefits were attributed to the resulting greater retention of workers: there was greater retention of artisanal and higher-skilled workers; retraining or re-familiarization was not needed with re-recruitment, thus reducing cost; the firm could operate in higher-value and higher-quality market segments; the firm was more agile in adjusting to style changes and market changes; the proportion of rejects went down; and there were more on-time deliveries. All these benefits are features of process rents that accrue due to a more stable work force.

Incentive payments

Some factories have set up incentive payment systems. Since sudden absenteeism affects production as production lines have insufficient staff, Firm E has incentives to reduce absenteeism – individual attendance incentives. More recently, they have introduced a team incentive; when a team has attendance above a given mark, there is an incentive for all members of the team.

Some others, for example, Firms D and F in Tirupur, report production incentives, payable on reaching and exceeding given targets for the day. Of course, the level at which the targets should be set becomes a matter of negotiation. A container bag manufacturer in south Gujarat also has incentive payments for reaching and exceeding daily targets.

Supervisors

Supervisors play a key role in planning the day's work, assigning workers to tasks and securing work from operators. They also have to ensure that work is of the required quality. Most often they are former tailors who have become highly skilled; they are very often poorly educated.

The poor education of supervisors comes in the way of their handling of quality requirements – it is difficult for them to follow written instructions from buyers. To overcome this limitation, some enterprises like Firm C have recruited local graduates to be quality supervisors, as distinct from the line/ floor supervisors.

In most factories, supervisors play another role: they recruit the workers, making them a combination of contractor and supervisor. This increases their power over workers. It also increases their power vis-à-vis employers, as they can always threaten to walk out of a factory, taking their gang of workers along with them. Their authority vis-à-vis employers was illustrated in an incident in a factory where the owner tried to implement production monitoring for each line but was not able to do it because of opposition from the supervisors.

The key role of supervisors is to get work done. They try to achieve by abusing workers, reinforcing the sweatshop nature of the work. In some factories, we were told by our interviewees that 'abuse is part of the culture' or 'abuse is an old issue'. Abuse in the course of work can be both verbal and physical. Discussions with workers showed that abuse continues to be quite prevalent. It was only a very small number of factories in which we were told that they have taken steps to eliminate abuse, including the dismissal of a production manager in one case. As one manager pointed out, culture is a matter of how it comes down from the top. Abuse will continue only so long as employers condone if not encourage this behaviour. Abuse becomes a way of achieving production targets at low cost, without having to fashion incentives or other ethical systems of encouraging workers to attain targets.

Supervisor behaviour clearly matters and is something that needs to be changed in building work practices suitable for an industry that is world class in all aspects. The problem of the supervisors' behaviour gets exacerbated when there are male supervisors dealing with female workers. This power relationship is easily misused for sexual exploitation. At Firm F we were told that having female supervisors reduces not just sexual exploitation but also leads to better handling of women workers.

Respect for workers is understood to be necessary to promote productivity. This requires measures to eliminate verbal, physical and sexual abuse by supervisors. One manager at Firm G said that respect for workers would reduce attrition by 2–3 per cent. This is borne out by discussions with workers in Bengaluru, who mentioned that abuse, particularly sexual abuse, was usually the reason for women to leave one factory and seek employment in another.

Sexual harassment

In the case of women, leaving a factory is often a response to sexual harassment, most often by supervisors, though not confined to them. Despite the existence of mandated committees, women do not seem to have the confidence that they can take up such matters. Their reaction then is to leave after such sexual harassment. In the terms made famous by Hirschman (1970), in the absence of a voice there is no loyalty and the result is an exit.

We were repeatedly told, wherever we asked the direct question, 'sexual harassment is not a problem in this factory'. However, discussions with female workers in Gurgaon and Bengaluru, as well as a study of newspaper and television reports, point to the high level of sexual harassment. We were assured that there were functioning committees to which women could report any harassment. However, as mentioned earlier, women rarely report such abuse. Workers mentioned that these committees exist only in name.

Of all the factories we visited, only two reported taking any action on sexual harassment. In both cases there were dismissals of the employees committing the offence. In one case, a fairly high-ranking official who was important to the factory's production performance was dismissed. In the absence of such strict action, one would expect that incidences of sexual harassment would be covered up. On the other hand, as mentioned earlier, reducing sexual harassment improves overall working conditions and can contribute to higher productivity.

Women and attrition

We have already mentioned one factor behind the attrition of female workers – that they leave factories after having becoming victims of sexual harassment.

Another factor for leaving is the inability to combine childcare with factory work. This is not something that should occur, but it depends on the presence or absence of crèche facilities. We have seen some factories with good crèches and a high retention of women workers post-childbirth, for example, Firm J in Bengaluru. In addition, women in this factory are tested for anaemia and given iron supplements if they are found to be anaemic. This is claimed to have reduced the incidence of anaemia from 60 per cent to 35 per cent among the female workforce.

Why is this not replicated in other factories? There is a cost involved in maintaining a crèche and larger firms can manage this more easily than smaller ones. One can consider the proposal first put forward by Ester Boserup (1970) that the expense of providing for childcare and other post-maternity benefits can be borne by the state, with firms having to pay a cess based on the number of workers they employed. If the extra cost of employing women was taken over by the state, the present discrimination against employing women after marriage could be considerably reduced, if not ended.

In a meeting with a group of about fifteen female garment workers in Bengaluru, they stressed the importance of the working atmosphere in a factory in determining their choice to work there. Non-abusive behaviour by supervisors and other staff was an essential requirement. Some of them even said that they were willing to accept lower wages (as they did in a factory making leather jackets) in order to work in a good atmosphere.

Firm-external factors in rents

So far we have considered factors internal to firm management, its labour and other management practices, that can result in the capture of some process innovation rents. Reduced costs leading to rents or above-normal profits can also result from factors external to the firm (Davis, Kaplinsky and Morris, 2017). The case of the cost of logistics and China's well-developed logistics chain and 'supply chain cities' (Gereffi, 2009) in comparison to India's poor logistics is well known. It is commonly accepted that India's poor logistics imposes a cost burden of at least 10 per cent (Sarkar, Dev and Mehta, 2012). Turning this around, it means that at the same sale prices that Indian firms get, Chinese firms would get a rent of excess profit of 10 per cent. Besides logistics, paying for or arranging for workers' accommodation can also be a factor in deriving rents.

Workers' accommodation

Providing decent and reasonably priced accommodation may seem to be just a matter of workers' welfare. However, more than one manager in the NCR, where large numbers of workers live in slum-like conditions, told us that factory productivity was negatively affected by poor living conditions. They mentioned that workers in such conditions often fell sick, leading to absenteeism. Of course, they did not see overwork as a factor in sickness. Still, there was substantial concern about poor living conditions. Many managers mentioned that they had raised the issue of providing decent living conditions for workers with the respective state governments, but nothing had been done to provide the necessary accommodation.

Workers' living costs in the Gurgaon area, including the adjacent parts of Delhi, are worsened by the practices of predatory landlords in the region. These landlords have put up buildings in which they provide rooms to workers. They strictly regulate the number of workers who can stay in a room. They force the tenants to buy their food and related provisions from the landlords' own shops, where prices are at least 25 per cent higher than in the market. This effectively reduces the real wages that workers get.

In trying to resolve the accommodation problem, we were told that 50 per cent of factories in Jaipur make some arrangements for workers. In south India, enterprises have come up with dormitory-type residences on their own land. In Tirupur, for example, there is a government-provided dormitory block in which companies can take a set of rooms on rent. The Sumangali system, in which young women workers were only paid at the end of the contract, which was widespread in south Indian spinning mills, has not been replicated in the garment factories. There are dormitories but there is no system of paying regular wages – only a lump sum at the end of the employment period. However, company-owned and supervised dormitories run the risk of putting the workers at the beck and call of the factory, to work whenever and as long as needed, and to be harassed when they do not. Rather than company-provided accommodation, what is needed is a government-provided accommodation or third-party hostel system.

The importance of workers' accommodation in supporting labour-intensive manufacture has been discussed in Nathan (2013). Here, it needs to be pointed out that slum-like living conditions have negative effects on the productivity of workers, and thus reduce profits; conversely, where there are good living conditions firms would get excess profits.

What role do trade unions have in process innovations?

There is a strong anti-union culture in the management of garment firms in India and possibly in many other parts of the world. The legal right of workers to form unions is regularly violated through action taken against anyone trying to form or join a union. On the other hand, while taking up genuine issues affecting workers, unions also need to see that the future of workers lies in better-performing firms. There are few cases of unions working to improve workers' conditions along with firm performance in the garment industry. In Indian manufacturing as a whole, however, incentive payments for workers linked to firm performance have become a standard practice (Venkata Ratnam, 2003). Furthermore, managerial practice in other countries, such as Cambodia, shows that unions in the garment industry are a necessary factor in developing better factories. Monitoring of working conditions is best carried out with the involvement of the workers themselves, either through unions or, at least, functioning workplace committees. Instead of coercing workers into making false statements during audits, it would be better to actually implement the required workplace conditions.

A cooperative workplace is necessary for building capable and competitive factories (ILO, 2016). Both management and unions need to move away from a zero-sum approach to wages and profits and realize that improved working conditions, including living wages, are necessary for building capable and competitive firms that can earn higher profits. There is a co-determination of wages and profits.

Conclusion: Capabilities and the capture of process rents

Firm performance is a result of the management and workers working together. Better performance is possible when there is cooperation between the two. Of course, there will be conflicts between the two. However, a cooperative workplace is essential for improved firm performance. There is a co-determination of employment conditions and firm performance. Poor wages and abusive supervision result in poor firm performance and vice versa.

Better employment conditions promote the development of the capabilities of the workforce, which, along with better management practices, can result in the capture of process rents. Given existing monopsonistic market conditions with suppliers as price-takers, improved firm performance through process innovations can reduce costs, which would increase rents, the increase being the difference between the marginal costs of suppliers and that of process-innovating firm. It could also enable the innovating firm to move on to servicing higher-priced market segments, which is likely to result in increased margins. Of course, a caveat has to be noted: these results are likely for individual firms and even supplier countries. As process innovations can be copied since they cannot be copyrighted as intellectual property, these rents will be eroded as the process innovations spread and the monopsonistic market allows lead firms to capture the benefits of lower costs.

References

Birnbaum, Richard. 2014. 'Enhancing Competitiveness of Indian Garment Industry'. Study for AEPC. Mimeo.

Bloom, Nicholas, Benn Eifert, David McKenzie, Aprajit Mahajan and John Roberts. 2013. 'Does Management Matter? Evidence from India.' *Quarterly Journal of Economics* 128 (1): 1–51.

Boserup, Ester. 1970. *Women's Role in Economic Development*. London: George Allen and Unwin.

Brown, Drusilla, Raymond Robertson, Hongyang Di and Rajeev Dehejia. 2016. 'Working Conditions, Work Outcomes, and Policy in Asian Developing Countries.' Paper presented at ADB Workshop, January. Manila: ADB. Mimeo.

Davis, Dennis, Raphael Kaplinsky and Mike Morris. 2017. 'Rents, Power and Governance in Global Value Chains.' PRISM Working Papers No. 2. Cape Town: School of Economics, University of Cape Town. Accessed 26 June 2017. Available at http://www.prism.uct.ac.za/.

Gereffi, Gary. 2009. 'Development Models and Industrial Upgrading in China and Mexico.' *European Sociological Review* 25 (1): 37–51.

Ghose, Ajit. 2016. *India Employment Report: Manufacturing*. New Delhi: Academic Foundation and Institute for Human Development.

Goger, Anneliese. 2014. 'Ethical Branding in Sri Lanka: A Case Study of "Garments Without Guilt".' In *Workers' Rights and Global Supply Chains: Is Social Branding the Answer?* edited by Jennifer Bair, Marsha Dickinson and Doug Miller, 47–68. New York: Routledge.

Gunawardana, Samanthi. 2014. 'Reframing Employee Voice: A Case Study of Sri Lanka's Export Processing Zones.' *Work, Employment and Society* 28 (3): 452–68.

Hirschman, Albert. 1970. *Exit, Voice and Loyalty: Responses to Decline in Firms, Organizations and States*. Cambridge, MA: Harvard University Press.

ILO. 2016. 'Building Better Morale Boosts Competitiveness.' 1 February. Accessed

27 June 2017. Available at http://www.ilo.org/global/about-the-ilo/newsroom/features/WCMS_444883/lang--en/index.htm.

ILO Better Work. 2015. *Research Brief: Working Conditions, Productivity and Profitability, Evidence from Better Work Vietnam.* ILO: Better Work. Accessed 27 June 2017. Available at http://betterwork.org/blog/portfolio/working-conditions-productivity-and-profitability-evidence-from-better-work-vietnam/.

Jordan, L.S., B. Kamphuis and S. Setia. 2014. *Republic of India Manufacturing Plan Implementation: A New Agenda: Improving the Competitiveness of the Textiles and Apparel Value Chain in India.* World Bank website. February. Accessed 19 January 2017. Available at https://openknowledge.worldbank.org/bitstream/handle/10986/22409/A0new0agenda000value0chain0in0India.pdf?sequence=1&isAllowed=y.

Lin, Xirong, Laura Babbitt and Drusilla Brown. 2014. 'Sexual Harassment in the Workplace: How Does It Affect Firm Performance and Profits.' Better Work Discussion Paper Series No. 16. Accessed 26 June 2017. Available at betterwork.org/global/wp-content/uploads/2014/11/DP16.pdf.

McKenzie, D. and C. Woodruff. 2015. 'Business Practices in Small Firms in Developing Countries.' World Bank Policy Research Working Paper No. 7405. Accessed 26 June 2017. Available at https://www.google.co.in/search?q=World+Bank+Policy+Research+Working+Paper+no.+7405&oq=World+Bank+Policy+Research+Working+Paper+no.+7405+&aqs=chrome..69i57.33815j0j4&sourceid=chrome&ie=UTF-8.

McKinsey and Company. 2016. 'Style That's Sustainable: A New Fast-Fashion Formula.' *www.mckinsey.com.* Accessed 4 December 2016. Available at http://www.mckinsey.com/business-functions/sustainability-and-resource-productivity/our-insights/style-thats-sustainable-a-new-fast-fashion-formula?cid=other-alt-mip-mck-oth-1612.

Nathan, Dev. 2013. '"Public Workers" Housing Helps Labour-intensive Manufacturing.' Economic and Political Weekly 48 (24): 13–16.

Nathan, Dev, Madhuri Saripalle and L. Gurunathan. 2016. 'Labour Practices in India.' ILO Asia-Pacific Working Paper. March. Available at http://www.ilo.org/wcmsp5/groups/public/---asia/---ro-bangkok/---sro-new_delhi/documents/publication/wcms_501117.pdf.

Nubler, Irmgaard. 2013. 'A Theory of Capabilities for Productive Transformation: Learning to Catch-up.' In *Transforming Economies: Making Industrial Policy Work for Growth, Jobs and Development,* edited by J. H. Salazar-Xirinachs, I. Nübler and R Kozul-Wright, ch. 4. Geneva: ILO.

Perry, Patsy, Steve Wood and John Fernie. 2015. 'Corporate Social Responsibility in Garment Sourcing Networks: Factory Management Perspectives on Ethical Trade in Sri Lanka.' *Journal of Business Ethics* 130 (3): 737–52.

Piore, Michael and Charles Sabel. 1994. *The Second Industrial Divide.* New York: Basic Books.

Rourke, Emily L. 2014. 'Is There a Business Case Against Verbal Abuse? Incentive Structure, Verbal Abuse, Productivity and Profits in Garment Factories.' Better Work Discussion Paper Series No. 15. ILO: Better Work, February.

Ruwanpura, Kanchana B. 2016. 'Garments Without Guilt? Uneven Labour Geographies and Ethical Trading – Sri Lankan Labour Perspectives.' *Journal of Economic Geography* 16 (2): 1–24.

Sarkar, Sandip, Dev Nathan and Balwant Mehta. 2012. 'Skills and Manufacturing in India.' New Delhi: IHD and ILO. Mimeo.

Society for Labour and Development (SLD). 2014. *Struggle within the Struggle: Voices of Women Workers.* New Delhi: SLD. Accessed 25 June 2017. Available at https://www.slideshare.net/SLDIndia/struggle-within-the-struggle-voices-of-women-garment-workers.

Tewari, M. and P. Pillai. 2005. 'Global Standards and the Dynamics of Environmental Compliance in India's Leather Industry.' *Oxford Development Studies* 33 (2): 245–67.

Venkata Ratnam, C. S. 2003. *Negotiated Change: Collective Bargaining, Liberalization and Restructuring in India.* New Delhi: Response Books.

World Bank. 2016. *South Asia's Turn: Policies to Boost Competitiveness and Create the Next Export Powerhouse.* Washington, DC: The World Bank.

4

New Economic Geographies of Manufacturing in China

Shengjun Zhu

Introduction

The 'reform and opening-up' policies (*gaige kaifang*) initiated by the Chinese central government in the late 1970s have, on the one hand, enabled the country to achieve remarkable economic development and, on the other hand, fundamentally transformed its economic, political and institutional systems in three ways: (*a*) from a closed or partially closed economy to an open one that becomes increasingly integrated into the global economy and oriented towards export markets (*globalization*), (*b*) from a centrally planned to a decentralized political and fiscal system (*decentralization*) and (*c*) from a state- and collectively owned economy to one with a growing level of market orientation and private ownership (*marketization*) (He, Wei and Xie, 2008; McMillan and Naughton, 1992; Naughton, 1996; Wei, 2000, 2001). These changes have taken place alongside a new wave of economic globalization in which millions of Chinese consumers and workers have become more direct participants in the global economy, a process that has increasingly come to drive China's rapidly changing economic geography (Gereffi, 2009; Henderson and Nadvi, 2011). China's accession to the World Trade Organization (WTO) in 2001 further accelerated these transformations (Zhu and He, 2013). Driven by this export-oriented industrialization model, China's average annual gross domestic product (GDP) growth rate was around 9.8 per cent; exports increased by 12.4 per cent annually in the 1990s, and by more than 20 per cent a year in the early 2000s (National Bureau of Statistics of China, 2011).

There was a boom in some manufacturing sectors in response to internal reforms and international demand for Chinese exports goods (Gereffi, 1999; Lemoine and Ünal-Kesenci, 2004), particularly those dependent on unskilled or semi-skilled low-wage labour and the leveraging of China's domestic advantages, including its large domestic market and the low cost of other input factors, such as land and electricity (Gereffi, 2009). Production and employment in such manufacturing sectors have become heavily concentrated in the coastal regions of east and southeast China, especially in export-processing zones (Fujita and Hu, 2001; He *et al.*, 2008; Wen, 2004). In addition to cheap labour and land, the impressive growth of China's export-oriented production has also been predicated on a flexible business environment, the half-hearted enforcement of labour and environmental regulations and loose inspection of imports and exports (Hsing, 1998; Hsueh, 2011).

However, since the early 2000s, this model of industrialization has begun to experience limits, which are forcing drastic changes in the geography and organization of China's labour-intensive, low-wage, export-oriented production process (Yang, 2012; Zhu and He, 2013; Zhu and Pickles, 2014). First, even though China is often seen as the factory of the world with a seemingly infinite supply of cheap labour, the scenario has changed as Chinese workers are not only quitting low-end and low-wage jobs (generating relative labour shortages, particularly in China's coastal regions) but also requesting higher payments and better working conditions (Li and Fung Research Centre, 2008). In addition to labour shortages and rising labour costs, other factors have also played a critical role in forcing up production costs, including the appreciation of Chinese currency since the mid-2000s and an increase in costs of other input factors (Liao and Chan, 2011; Wang and Mei, 2009; Yang, 2012). The second set of limits derives from policy changes that have an indirect effect on production costs. One notable example is the issuance of a new labour contract law (*Law of the People's Republic of China on Employment Contracts*) in 2008 that has paid more attention to the well-being of labour and has extended labour rights (Lan, Pickles and Zhu, 2015). The increasingly stringent environmental regulation and enforcement, especially in the more developed but heavily polluted coastal region, has also indirectly increased the cost of production (Zhu *et al.*, 2014). Finally, this situation has been compounded by the slackening global demand for Chinese export goods, especially after the 2008 global financial crisis (Zhu and He, 2013).

Since the late 1970s, China's economic transition and institutional change, characterized by the triple process of marketization, decentralization and globalization, has enabled it to become the 'world factory' and transformed its manufacturing industry from a broadly based one towards one that has become increasingly concentrated in China's coastal region (Fan and Scott, 2003; He *et al.*, 2008; Wen, 2004). However, since the early 2000s, this model of export-oriented industrialization has been challenged by internal and external factors in ways that are triggering another round of industrial restructuring and producing new economic geographies of production and employment in China. Consequently, this gave rise to the need to re-examine the geographical and industrial dynamics of China's manufacturing industry as well as its role in global and regional production networks (Liao and Chan, 2011; Yang, 2012; Zhu and Pickles, 2014). With these factors as the backdrop, this paper focuses on the new economic geographies of manufacturing in China and various adaptations Chinese manufacturers are undergoing. I first introduce studies on China's 'old' economic geographies – industrial and spatial shifts during the 1980s and 1990s – and in the next two sections, move on to review more recent works that have adopted various theoretical and analytical frameworks in economic geography, sociology, political economy and international studies to understand the relatively 'new' economic geographies since the early 2000s. The last section summarizes the main findings and provides a future research agenda.

'Old' economic geographies: Economic transition, institutional change and the first round of industrial restructuring

North's (1990) seminal work has pointed out the key role of a region's economic and political institutions in shaping firm activities, economic performance and entrepreneurial activities in the region. Spatial patterns of economic activities in advanced capitalist economies are mainly affected by the market, regional integration and trade liberalization (Hanson, 1998; Sjöberg and Sjöholm, 2004; Storper et al., 2002), while the national and regional institutional contexts where Chinese firms operate are much more dynamic and geographically uneven, which complicate entrepreneurial processes and the subsequent economic geographies of production and employment (He et al., 2008; Wei, 2001, 2002).

Since the late 1970s, China's economic system has been transformed from a command economy, in which the state was the main (if not the only) planner, towards a more market-oriented one, as privatization and market competition were progressively introduced into the economy (McMillan and Naughton 1992). In a command economy, the economic geographies of manufacturing production were conducted largely by state-owned enterprises (SOEs), and thus predicated heavily on the state's social, political and military considerations (Ma and Wei, 1997). Since the early 1980s, the restrictions on business licensing have been gradually lifted and private entrepreneurship has been encouraged in some regions and industries (Chang and MacMillan, 1991). Non-state capital and privately owned firms started to exert an increasingly important effect in economic development. In such a market-oriented economy, firms became more motivated to utilize comparative advantages and more likely to locate close to specialized suppliers and customers in order to reduce not only logistics costs, but also the costs of searching for matched suppliers and customers, which further resulted in industrial clustering. Marketization has unleashed economic vitality, but its effectiveness is quite uneven across regions in China. The coastal region was the first to benefit from the marketization process; many industries have been shifting towards the coast during this time period (Fujita and Hu, 2001; Naughton, 1996). The impact of marketization also varies across industries. In the early stage of reform, the state initially encouraged private enterprises to enter into light and labour-intensive industries, and then lowered the state-owned proportion in other manufacturing industries (Wei, 2001). Up till now, state-owned capital is still dominant in certain industries, such as tobacco processing and petroleum refining.

As the reform policies pushed forward the process of marketization in China's economy, the opening-up policies globalized China's economy and allowed Chinese enterprises to access financial capital, more advanced technologies, knowledge and management skills, and high quality input factors on the international market (He et al., 2008; Wei, 2000). Enterprises benefited from globalization as they learned from foreign firms that started to enter into China since the 1980s on the one hand, and were increasingly encouraged to establish extra-regional linkages with global lead firms in the West by participating in global production networks, on the other hand (Gereffi, 2009; Lin and Wang, 2008). Fujita and Hu (2001) have argued that firms, particularly those in labour-intensive and export-oriented industries, became increasingly concentrated in China's coastal region to better participate in the international market and to reduce logistics costs for export. Foreign direct investments (FDIs) also tended to locate in China's coastal region, particularly in special economic zones (SEZs), to take advantage of agglomeration externalities and gain better market access (He, 2002, 2003; Head and Ries, 1996; Sun, 1999; Wei, 2000).

State-led decentralization policies empowered local governments to get involved in shaping the regional economy as planners, developers and policymakers, some of whom have become heavy-handed actors ever more convinced of the importance of their 'steering' role (He et al., 2008; Wei, 2001; Wei, Li and Wang, 2007). The increasing decentralization affected geographies of production and employment in two ways. On the one hand, local governments in wealthier coastal regions were more capable of providing a variety of subsidies, financial and technological supports, and high-quality infrastructure to attract new entrants and FDIs than their counterparts in less developed inland regions, which reinforced the geographical concentration of footloose and labour-intensive manufacturing industries in the coastal region. On the other hand, political and fiscal decentralization triggered regionalism, local protectionism and fierce inter-regional competition (Bai *et al.*, 2004; Lee, 1998; Poncet, 2005; Zhao and Zhang, 1999). Local governments implemented a variety of measures to protect industries with high tax-profit margins and state-owned proportions under their administrations, since these industries were seen as a base of political power as well as a major source of profits and fiscal revenues (Bai *et al.*, 2004; Zhao and Zhang, 1999). This gave rise to the geographical dispersion of highly protected industries, such as tobacco, medical and pharmaceutical products, and power production.

In short, during the 1980s and 1990s, economic transition and institutional change driven by the reform and opening-up policies transformed China's manufacturing industries, particularly those less protected, export-oriented and labour-intensive ones, from broadly based industries to ones concentrated in China's coastal regions, though a small number of protected and SOEs-led industries (for example, tobacco and petroleum) remained geographically dispersed, partly due to the low level of marketization and/or the high level of local protection of such industries.

'New' economic geographies: Upgrading, relocation and the second round of industrial restructuring

In the mid to late 2000s, this export-oriented, low-wage model started to be challenged by the rising cost of labour and labour shortages in China's coastal region (Wang and Mei, 2009). Alongside the significant and rapidly changing labour market dynamics, other factors have also been important, including labour shortages, the appreciation of China's currency and slackening global demand, especially after the outbreak of the 2008 financial crisis (Yang, 2012). Exogenous shocks such as dwindling international demand and rising production costs led to the rise of the new economic geographies of manufacturing in China.

Zhu and Pickles (2014) have emphasized that since the early 2000s, in response to rising labour wages and intensified competitive pressures, China's national administration has planned to pull out labour-intensive, low-value-added industries from the coastal region so that space and resources can be released to develop high-value-added, high-end industries. This policy would concurrently push forward the economic development of inland China, which is less developed. In particular, they have identified three types of adjustments adopted by Chinese governments and manufacturing firms: upgrading ('Go Up'), regionalization ('Go West') and delocalization ('Go Out'). The 'Go Up' strategy involves encouraging or forcing Chinese manufacturers, particularly those located in the high-wage coastal region, to upgrade from low-value to mid- or high-value production (Butollo, 2015; Liu and Yang, 2013; Yang, 2014b; Zhu and He, 2013, 2015; Zhu et al., 2014). The 'Go West' strategy refers to the relocation of low-wage, labour-intensive production from the coastal region to new lower-cost, lower-wage locations, very often to regions in inland China from which migrant workers have traditionally been drawn (Butollo, 2015; Liao and Chan, 2011; Zhu and He, 2013; Zhu and Pickles, 2015). The 'Go Out' strategy refers to low-value, low-end production being encouraged to outsource or relocate (often from China's coastal region) to low-cost manufacturing bases in South-East Asia, Africa and, in some cases, the Middle East, with the goal of taking advantage of low-wage labour and cheap land in these locations, bypassing trade barriers and obtaining local market access (Azmeh, 2015; Azmeh and Nadvi, 2013; Henderson et al., 2013; Henderson and Nadvi, 2011; Zhu and He, 2013).

On the one hand, the relocation and upgrading of production have long been central aspects of manufacturing industries involving the fragmentation of tasks and the division of labour across geographical space, usually with the relocation of labour-intensive elements of the production process to lower-cost locations, while core competencies, like research and development (R&D), design and brand ownership, are considered to be less spatially flexible, being tied more closely with human capital resources and knowledge networks (Evans and Smith, 2006; Scott, 2006). For instance, the last few decades have witnessed a significant relocation of labour-intensive, low-end manufacturing production away from producing regions in Europe and North America, through Japan, Taiwan, South Korea, Hong Kong and Singapore, to coastal China (Evans and Smith, 2006). Now we have seen a similar round of relocation in China's coastal regions as labour wage and production costs rise (Zhu and Pickles, 2014).

On the other hand, the new round of relocation of labour-intensive production from China's coastal regions is a much more complex process, as the economic geography of manufacturing in China is rapidly changing from one mainly driven by low-end, low-tech, low-value and labour-intensive production for export markets towards one integrated into far more complicated global and regional production networks. In analysing the rise of China in global value chains (GVCs), it is important, therefore, to not only show how these processes of upgrading and relocation structure the complex geographies of competitiveness and cost regionally, but also to assess how these processes are at work in China's own production networks. While the processes of 'Go Up' and 'Go Out' resemble previous rounds of relocation from South Korea, Taiwan and Hong Kong to coastal China, 'Go West' and the subsequent restructuring of the country's global, national and regional production works can be seen only in the case of China, a country with a vast territory and an enormous domestic market. These have given rise to a new international and regional division of labour where Chinese manufacturers in the coastal region outsource to suppliers in inland China or other low-cost, low-wage locations outside China and deliver the finished products to international and (more recently) domestic markets (Butollo, 2015; Zhu and He, 2013). Furthermore, the capacity of Chinese manufacturing firms to relocate and upgrade has been shaped by local institutional contexts in which inter-firm learning, social networks, government policies, the labour market and conventions create a dynamic field of opportunities and constraints (Pickles *et al.*, 2006; Storper, 1997). In other words, industrial upgrading, relocation and the new economic geographies of manufacturing in China must be examined through various lenses. It is to this we now turn.

Globalization, regionalization and localization

One primary analytical framework for understanding China's changing economic geographies and industrial restructuring – the GVC and the global production network (GPN) – has paid particular attention to how Chinese regions have been integrated into globally organized value chains, and, more importantly, has considered the implications of industrial upgrading (Bathelt and Li, 2014; Chen, 2014; Gereffi, 2009; Liu and Yang, 2013; Wei, 2009, 2010, 2011, Wei, Lu and Chen, 2009; Zhu and He, 2013; Zhu and Pickles, 2015). The upgrading process has been attributed to the acquiring of new capabilities and increasing competencies through participating in particular GVCs, a process that generates knowledge and causes information to flow from lead firms to their suppliers (Gereffi, 1999, 2009; Gereffi, Humphrey and Sturgeon, 2005); or, as suggested by GPN scholars, to a process of strategic coupling between local actors and their counterparts in the global economy (Coe, 2011; Coe, Dicken and Hess, 2008). It is an increasingly important element in shaping the new economic geographies of production in China, as Chinese manufacturers, especially those based in the coastal region, strive to maintain or increase their competitiveness by shedding low-value activities and the social and economic problems they can generate in favour of higher-value activities, particularly during the 2000s, when labour costs rose and competitive pressure intensified (Yang, 2012; Zhu and Pickles, 2014). Here, the primary focus has been on the mechanisms through which firms and industries engineer various types of upgrading within GVCs to capture additional, higher value-added functions in supply chains (Chen, 2014; Wei, 2010; Zhu and He, 2013; Zhu and Pickles, 2015).

In addition to upgrading, globalization also has had an effect on industrial relocation in China. Many Chinese suppliers are integrated into captive GVCs where the actions and motivations of global lead firms are the key causal forces in the organization of global contracting systems. Access to global markets in the West is controlled by lead firms who have increasingly required Chinese suppliers to 'race to the lower bottom' and forced the latter to outsource or relocate to lower-cost locations, as labour costs in China increased (Zhu and He, 2013; Zhu and Pickles, 2015). Having large manufacturing bases in low-wage inland China or other low-cost countries is becoming a pre-requisite for some Chinese suppliers to receive orders from global lead firms.

However, globalization has not wiped out the importance of localities, which remain critical sites for learning and innovation (Cammett, 2006). Although integration into the global economy can be a feasible way for upgrading, this tends to overlooks the fact that industrial clustering at the local level is still important due to local sources of competitiveness driven by local economic agents and their vertical and horizontal relationships, which generate collective efficiency and knowledge spillovers (Marshall, [1890] 1920), institutional thickness (Amin and Thrift, 1994), embeddedness (Granovetter, 1985), and traded and untraded interdependencies (Scott, 1988; Storper, 1997). The capacity of Chinese manufacturers to upgrade is also seen as dependent on local institutional contexts (Chen, 2014; Lin, Li, et al., 2011; Wei, 2009, 2011; Yang, 2014b; Zhu and He, 2015; Zhu and Pickles, 2015). The local dimension becomes more important in this case, as China's manufacturing industry often exists in the form of clusters with local characteristics (Wang, 2014; Wei, 2011; Wei et al., 2007, 2009). Manufacturing production and employment has heavily concentrated in the coastal region of east and southeast China in general, and in a series of industrial clusters in coastal provinces in particular (Fujita and Hu, 2001; He *et al.*, 2008; Wen, 2004).

The Chinese firms' embeddedness in local clusters also explains why complete relocation has been rare since the early 2000s. In other words, manufacturers are deeply embedded in their original locations as they benefit from labour pools, knowledge spillover and inter-firm synergies that have been cultivated over time. These advantages, generated by local social networks, have counteracted the negative impact of rising labour costs on manufacturers to some extent on the one hand, and alleviated the urgency for complete relocation on the other hand (Zhu and He, 2013, 2015; Zhu *et al.*, 2014; Zhu and Pickles, 2015). What has often been seen in China's manufacturing industry since the early 2000s is partial relocation where firms upgrade and retain high-value production (for example, R&D and headquarters) in the coastal region while simultaneously outsourcing or relocating their low-cost, labour-intensive production (for example, assembly) to low-cost manufacturing bases in inland China or South-East Asian countries. Such partial relocation allows firms to take advantage of not only vertical and horizontal linkages within local clusters in China's coastal region (Li, 2014; Li, Bathelt and Wang, 2012), but also cheap labour and less stringent labour regulations outside China's coastal region (Azmeh and Nadvi, 2013; Butollo, 2014, 2015).

Geographical proximity matters, not only due to the benefits derived from local social networks, inter-firm linkages and institutional contexts, but also to the so-called modern factors at the regional level proposed by Abernathy, Volpe and Weil (2006), further developed by Pickles *et al.* (2006) and Tokatli (2008), in their interpretation of the emergence of regional production networks. The emergence of new considerations in sourcing such as the importance of 'short-cycle replenishment' and short turnaround times in the procurement of time-sensitive items has added further stickiness to the process of firm (re)location, which further reinforces the importance of geographical proximity (Smith *et al.*, 2014; Tewari, 2006). In this view, the relocation of Chinese manufacturers from the coastal region fuels the need for regionalized production systems to achieve flexibility, quick response and 'lean production' in the face of uncertain market demand. Empirical studies have pointed out that Chinese manufacturers tend to relocate or outsource to low-cost locations in neighbouring provinces to shorten their supply chain and reduce related logistics cost (Butollo, 2015; Yang, 2013, 2014a). Even though some firms did relocate or outsource to geographically remote areas (for example, South-East Asian countries), they still needed to balance the advantages derived from cheap labour, new market access, and lax labour and environmental regulations in those locations on the one hand, and the disadvantages associated with a long supply chain (for example, high logistics cost, insufficient supporting facilities and backward infrastructure) on the other hand (Zhu and He, 2013; Zhu and Pickles, 2015).

Recent studies on the new economic geographies of manufacturing in China often focused on one or more of the three processes of globalization, regionalization and localization. For example, studies by Wei (2010, 2011) have emphasized that industrial restructuring in China's manufacturing industry is a complex process, which should be understood through a lens that scales up from the new regionalism perspective and scales down the GPN/GVC perspective on regional development. Similarly, Zhu and He (2013, 2015) have also formulated a new analytical framework to examine the articulation between globalization, regionalization and localization and how these processes have co-shaped the ways in which and the extents to which Chinese manufacturers upgrade and relocate, producing diverse geographies of production and various regional development trajectories.

Evolutionary economic geography

Some recent empirical studies seek to understand the rise and fall of regional economies and the restructuring of industrial areas in China through an evolutionary economic geography (EEG) model (Guo and He, 2015; Li *et al.*, 2012; Yang, 2009, 2012, 2013, 2014a). This model argues that an economic landscape inherits the legacy of its own past economic and industrial development, and its history affects its own future development (Grabher, 1993; Martin and Sunley, 2006). This interpretation further argues that the past strengths of a region (for example, its industrial atmosphere, highly developed and specialized infrastructure, the close inter-firm linkages, and strong political support by regional institutions) may turn into stubborn obstacles to innovation, resulting in increasing fixity or rigidities in the patterns of industrial activity, and restrict ongoing regional development, particularly during the process of industrial restructuring (Grabher, 1993; Hassink and Shin, 2005; Henning, Stam and Wenting, 2013; Martin and Sunley, 2006; Schamp, 2005). Martin and Sunley (2006) have summarized five possible strategies to escape such a negative lock-in, including technological development, innovation, upgrading and relocation. In this sense, EEG models are useful complements to existing analytical frameworks based on local clusters and global and regional production networks, particularly in the ways in which they conceive of the spatial evolution of industrial clusters (MacKinnon, 2012; MacKinnon *et al.*, 2009).

Guo and He (2015) have pointed out that regional industrial evolution in China is a path-dependent process that has been affected by the pre-existing industrial structure of the region. However, their findings also show that some regions in China have managed to transcend the path-dependence process and move from low-productivity to high-productivity activities through industrial upgrading. Li *et al.* (2012) have predicated their empirical study at the interface between EEG and the clustering theory, and emphasized that the evolution of clusters in China is shaped by the aggregated action of local agents, as well as the unintended consequences of this action. Following Mackinnon's (2012) recent attempts to forge links between EEG and GPN/GVC approach, Yang (2013) has postulated a new analytical framework based on an idea of evolutionary strategic coupling, as well as recoupling and decoupling to study GPN restructuring and regional evolution in China. The main argument is that regions have the capacity to enhance their position within GPNs/GVCs through processes of upgrading and relocation, based on the decoupling and recoupling of regional assets and lead firms. This work has portrayed the ways in which Hong Kong- and Taiwan-based transnational corporations (TNCs) have decoupled from source regions in China's coastal provinces and recoupled with inland China in the post-crisis world economy.

Application to China's manufacturing industry

Recent studies on the new economic geographies of manufacturing in China have also pointed out the need to take into account some other factors that often neglected in traditional analyses based on local clusters, regional and global production networks, and industrial evolution. First, they have highlighted the significant role that the state plays through national economic regulations and policies in shaping patterns of industrial upgrading and relocation in China (Liu and Dicken, 2006; Wei *et al.*, 2009; Zhu and Pickles, 2014). In this process, a reconsideration of the role of national industrial policies, trade policies and labour regulations in the process of industrial restructuring is emerging (Lan *et al.*, 2015; Yang, 2014b). This is particularly the case in China, where, despite the apparent retreat of the state since its market-oriented reforms, the state has continued to be an active participant not only in strategically critical industries such as the manufacture of transport equipment and electronics (Hsueh, 2011; Liu and Dicken, 2006; Yang, 2014b), but also in the 'most globalized' and least protected industries such as apparel (Zhu and Pickles, 2014). For instance, Zhu and Pickles (2014) have argued that after a period of globalization, marketization and decentralization, during which the direct role of the state in shaping industrial locational and organizational decisions was diminished, government strategies are still key drivers of industrial upgrading in China's coastal region and crucial drivers of the relocation of labour-intensive, low value-added segments of the manufacturing industry to other regions and countries, through three broad state policies: the 'Go Up', 'Go West' and 'Go Out' policies. Subnational localities are also important units of economic political authority, since state-led decentralization policies empowered local governments to become involved in shaping the regional economy, as planners, developers and policymakers (Wei, 2010). Clear vision, objectives and appropriate cluster policies could be set up beforehand by local public authorities to stimulate regional development, foster innovation and enhance entrepreneurship (Zhu and He, 2015; Zhu et al., 2014).

The key role of Chinese governments in the second round of industrial and geographical restructuring can be also seen in Zhu and He's (2015) research that closely examines two industrial clusters in China – Ningbo's apparel cluster and Yongkang's hardware cluster. Both are leading clusters in China. The traditional Ningbo and Yongkang models are similar, both based on a production system dominated by family workshops and embedded in dense, historically rooted, local institutions. Despite these similarities, their development paths diverged since the 1980s. Ningbo is a prefecture-level city and one of China's largest manufacturing bases. Its apparel industry has not received much financial, technological and political support from the local government, since its output only accounts for 4 per cent of the city's total output. Ningbo's firms had to upgrade through learning from global buyers, resulting in strong global governance. However, once they started to encroach on the core competencies of global buyers, upgrading barriers were constantly set by their partners – the global buyers. As production costs in China's coastal region increased, Ningbo's apparel firms, as captive suppliers, had to comply with imperatives from global buyers, relocating some of their production to lower-cost locations, which weakened the domestic firms' local embeddedness. In contrast, Yongkang is a small, county-level city. The hardware industry is its key industry, accounting for more than 50 per cent of its output. The local government has been actively providing various financial and technological supports for its most important industry, allowing local firms to learn with government support and target mainly the domestic market. As competitive pressures increased in the 2000s, firms tended to upgrade *in situ* or relocate to adjacent areas, as they have been deeply embedded in the nurturing environment created by vertical local governance.

Second, recent studies have also stressed the rise of the domestic market and domestic-market-oriented production networks in China since the early 2000s, as well as their impact on industrial upgrading and relocation (Butollo, 2015; Yang, 2013, 2014a; Zhu and He, 2013; Zhu and Pickles, 2015). As Chinese manufacturers transformed from firms supplying export markets to producers for domestic markets, they managed to expand their role and upgrade from low-value assembly production to high-value marketing, designing, retailing and branding activities (Butollo, 2015; Zhu and Pickles, 2015). In contrast, some export-oriented firms in China failed to upgrade and became locked into the traditional processing trade regime, because they did not actively decouple from external markets and recouple with the domestic market (Yang, 2014a). The formation of domestic-market-oriented production networks has also encouraged manufacturers to relocate, as they sought to tap into new markets in inland China (Zhu and He, 2013). Finally, the strategic intent and autonomy of Chinese manufacturers should never be underestimated (Zhu and Pickles, 2015). Li *et al.* (2012) has demonstrated the ways in which new cluster paths and development trajectories can be created through the collective mobilization of local agents in a low-tech industry, while Wang, Lin and Li (2010) and Lin *et al.* (2011) have focused on the high-tech ICT industry and concluded that in China's main ICT industrial clusters, most manufacturers obtained their core technology largely through internal R&D activities.

The importance of the domestic market, domestic-market-oriented production networks and the strategic intent and autonomy of Chinese manufacturers has been stressed in Zhu and Pickles' (2015) work. Using a detailed case study of one former state-owned domestically oriented Chinese apparel producer – Seduno – they have shown that the initial advantages as a large low-cost exporters have, with increased costs and competition from South-East Asia, led to deepened relations with, and learning from, its Turkish partners to develop a cost-competitive export profile, which in turn has been leveraged into new domestic end markets in China, a process they (and the firm) call 'Turkishization'. There are three ways in which Seduno has learned from Turkish firms. First, Seduno became 'fast' enough, though still 'slower' than its Turkish teacher, to meet the requirement of some design-intensive but slightly less quick-response product categories. Second, Seduno learned the value of expanding its role as a supplier to fast-fashion domestic retailers and global retailers in domestic markets. Third, it benefitted from developing its own brand in the domestic market. Seduno's upgrading and relocation, on the one hand, could be attributed to its strategic intent and a group of young, aggressive high-level managers who believed such a strategy to be necessary for long-term development. On the other hand, it is due largely to Seduno's capability to develop other sources and learn, not only from neighbouring predecessors in the same cluster, but also successful, sometimes remote, precursors elsewhere.

Conclusion

This chapter has provided a review of existing research on economic transition, institutional change and industrial restructuring in China's manufacturing industry by paying particular attention to two strands of literature – one on China's 'old' economic geographies during the 1980s and 1990s and the other on more recent industrial dynamics and geographical shifts in China's manufacturing industry since the early 2000s. Examining these literatures primarily from an economic geographer's perspective, the overarching aim is to explicate how a wide range of methods and analytical frameworks from economic sociology, political economy, international studies and economic geography have been adopted by economic geographers to interpret China's changing economic, political and institutional landscape.

Literature on the first round of spatial restructuring and the old economic geographies of China's manufacturing tends to emphasize the role of economic transition and institutional change triggered by the reform and opening-up policies in the late 1970s, and argues that China's institutional context has been co-shaped by a triple process of marketization, globalization and decentralization, resulting in enormous spatial and temporal variation in the economic and institutional landscape. More recent studies have pointed out that the 'race to the bottom' that typified the 'China price' and the rapid rise of China as a global supplier, particularly of the low-end, labour-intensive manufacturing industries, over the past few decades is now changing in ways that are having profound effects on the industrial organization and spatial structure of production and employment, and will change the ways in which we understand China's role in global and regional production networks in the coming years. These studies not only build on recent insights in economic geography on industrial clusters, global and regional production networks, upgrading, relocation, and national and regional industrial evolution, but also take into account the role of state actions and institutional contexts, the rise of China's domestic market, the role of local agents and other factors that have been often overlooked in traditional industrial restructuring analyses. They seek to understand what the new government policies and firm strategies were and how these emerging strategies have affected the spatial patterns, organizational structure and value segments of China's manufacturing industry after labour costs increased and competitive pressure intensified.

Finally, I see great future research potential along these avenues, linking a variety of theories and methods together, and formulating new analytical frameworks by paying attention to the interface between GVC, GPN, EEG and industrial clustering approaches. I also see great value in testing these theories and concepts in the context of China, where non-traditional factors may come into focus, such as the role of national and local governments, the balance between domestic and export markets, the harmonies and disharmonies between firms and governments, and the role of SOEs, foreign firms and local entrepreneurs in industrial restructuring, which may enable us to challenge and/or broaden the explanatory power of the GVC/GPN, EEG and industrial clustering paradigms.

References

Abernathy, F. H., A. Volpe and D. Weil. 2006. 'The Future of the Apparel and Textile Industries: Prospects and Choices for Public and Private Actors.' *Environment and Planning A* 38 (12): 2207–32. DOI: 10.1068/a38114.

Amin, A. and N. Thrift, eds.1994. *Globalization, Institutions, and Regional Development in Europe*. Oxford: Oxford University Press.

Azmeh, S. 2015. 'Transient Global Value Chains and Preferential Trade Agreements: Rules of Origin in US Trade Agreements with Jordan and Egypt.' *Cambridge Journal of Regions, Economy and Society* 8 (3): 475–90. DOI: 10.1093/cjres/rsv017.

Azmeh, S. and K. Nadvi. 2013. '"Greater Chinese" Global Production Networks in the Middle East: The Rise of the Jordanian Garment Industry.' *Development and Change* 44 (6): 1317–40. DOI: 10.1111/dech.12065.

Bai, C.E., Y. Du, Z. Tao and S. Y. Tong. 2004. 'Local Protectionism and Regional Specialization: Evidence from China's Industries.' *Journal of International Economics* 63 (2): 397–417. DOI:10.1016/S0022-1996(03)00070-9.

Bathelt, H. and P. F. Li. 2014. 'Global Cluster Networks: Foreign Direct Investment Flows from Canada to China.' *Journal of Economic Geography* 14 (1): 45–71. DOI: 10.1093/jeg/lbt005.

Butollo, F. 2014. *The End of Cheap Labour? Industrial Transformation and "Social Upgrading" in China.* Frankfurt am Main: Campus.

———. 2015. 'Growing against the Odds: Government Agency and Strategic Recoupling as Sources of Competitiveness in the Garment Industry of the Pearl River Delta.' *Cambridge Journal of Regions, Economy and Society* 8 (3): 521–36. DOI: 10.1093/cjres/rsv020.

Cammett, M. 2006. 'Development and the Changing Dynamics of Global Production: Global Value Chains and Local Clusters in Apparel Manufacturing.' *Competition and Change* 10 (1): 23–48. DOI: 10.1179/102452906X91993.

Chang, W. and I. C. MacMillan. 1991. 'A Review of Entrepreneurial Development in the People's Republic of China.' *Journal of Business Venturing* 6 (6): 375–9. DOI:10.1016/0883-9026(91)90026-A.

Chen, L. 2014. 'Varieties of Global Capital and the Paradox of Local Upgrading in China.' *Politics and Society* 42 (2): 223–52. DOI: 10.1177/0032329213519422.

Coe, N. M. 2011. 'Geographies of Production II: A Global Production Network A–Z.' *Progress In Human Geography* 36 (3): 389–402. DOI: 10.1177/0309132511402784.

Coe, N. M., P. Dicken and M. Hess. 2008. 'Global Production Networks: Realizing the Potential.' *Journal of Economic Geography* 8 (3): 271–95. DOI: 10.1093/jeg/lbn002.

Evans, Y. and A. Smith. 2006. 'Surviving at the Margins? Deindustrialisation, the Creative Industries, and Upgrading in London's Garment Sector.' *Environment and Planning A* 38 (12): 2253–69. DOI:10.1068/a38285.

Fan, C. C. and A. J. Scott. 2003. 'Industrial Agglomeration and Development: A Survey of Spatial Economic Issues in East Asia and a Statistical Analysis of Chinese Regions.' *Economic Geography* 79 (3): 295–319. DOI: 10.1111/j.1944-8287.2003.tb00213.x.

Fujita, M. and D. Hu. 2001. 'Regional Disparity in China 1985–1994: The Effects of Globalization and Economic Liberalization.' *The Annals of Regional Science* 35 (1): 3–37. DOI:10.1007/s001680000020.

Gereffi, G. 1999. 'International Trade and Industrial Upgrading in the Apparel Commodity Chain.' *Journal of International Economics* 48 (1): 37–70. DOI:10.1016/S0022-1996(98)00075-0.

———. 2009. 'Development Models and Industrial Upgrading in China and Mexico.' *European Sociological Review* 25 (1): 37–51.DOI: 10.1093/esr/jcn034.

Gereffi, G., J. Humphrey and T. Sturgeon. 2005. 'The Governance of Global Value Chains.' *Review of International Political Economy* 12 (1): 78–104. DOI:10.1080/09692290500049805.

Grabher, G. 1993. 'The Weakness of Strong Ties: The Lock-in of Regional Development in the Ruhr Area.' In *The Embedded Firm: On the Socioeconomics of Industrial Networks*, edited by G. Grabher, 255–77. London: Routledge.

Granovetter, M. 1985. 'Economic Action and Social Structure: The Problem of Embeddedness.'*American Journal of Sociology* 91 (3):481–510.DOI:10.1086/228311.

Guo, Q. and C. He. 2015. 'Production Space and Regional Industrial Evolution in China.' *Geo Journal* 80 (6): 1–18. DOI:10.1007/s10708-015-9689-4.

Hanson, G. 1998. 'North American Economic Integration and Industry Location.' *Oxford Review of Economic Policy* 14 (2): 30–44. DOI: 10.1093/oxrep/14.2.30.

Hassink, R. and D. H. Shin. 2005. 'The Restructuring of Old Industrial Areas in Europe and Asia.' *Environment and Planning A* 37 (4): 571–80. DOI: 10.1068/a36273.

He, C. 2002. 'Information Costs, Agglomeration Economies and the Location of Foreign Direct Investment in China.' *Regional Studies* 36 (9): 1029–36. DOI:10.1080/0034340022000022530.

———. 2003. 'Location of Foreign Manufacturers in China: Agglomeration Economies and Country of Origin Effects.' *Papers in Regional Science* 82 (3): 351–72. DOI: 10.1007/s10110-003-0168-9.

He, C., Y. H. D. Wei and X. Xie. 2008. 'Globalization, Institutional Change, and Industrial Location: Economic Transition and Industrial Concentration in China.' *Regional Studies* 42 (7): 923–45. DOI:10.1080/00343400701543272.

Head, K. and J. Ries. 1996. 'Inter-City Competition for Foreign Investment: Static and Dynamic Effects of China's Incentive Areas.' *Journal of Urban Economics* 40 (1) 38–60. DOI:10.1006/juec.1996.0022.

Henderson, J. and K. Nadvi. 2011. 'Greater China, the Challenges of Global Production Networks and the Dynamics of Transformation.' *Global Networks* 11 (3): 285–97. DOI:10.1111/j.1471-0374.2011.00326.x.

Henderson, J., R. P. Appelbaum and S. Y. Ho. 2013. 'Globalization with Chinese Characteristics: Externalization, Dynamics and Transformations.' *Development and Change* 44 (6): 1221–53. DOI: 10.1111/dech.12066.

Henning, M., E. Stam and R. Wenting. 2013. 'Path Dependence Research in Regional Economic Development: Cacophony or Knowledge Accumulation?' *Regional Studies* 47 (8): 1348–62. DOI:10.1080/00343404.2012.750422.

Hsing, Y. T. 1998. *Making Capitalism in China: The Taiwan Connection.* New York: Oxford University Press.

Hsueh, R. 2011. *China's Regulatory State: A New Strategy for Globalization.* Ithaca, N. Y.: Cornell University Press.

Lan, T., J. Pickles and S. Zhu. 2015. 'State Regulation, Economic Reform and Worker Rights: The Contingent Effects of China's Labour Contract Law.' *Journal of Contemporary Asia* 45 (2): 266–93. DOI:10.1080/00472336.2014.940592.

Lee, P. K. 1998. 'Local Economic Protectionism in China's Economic Reform.' *Development Policy Review* 16 (3): 281–303. DOI: 10.1111/1467-7679.00065.

Lemoine, F. and D. Ünal-Kesenci. 2004. 'Assembly Trade and Technology Transfer: The Case of China.' *World Development* 32 (5): 829–50. DOI:10.1016/j. worlddev.2004.01.001.

Li and Fung Research Centre. 2008. 'China's Industry Relocation and Upgrading Trends: Implications for Sourcing Business.' *China Distribution and Trading* (56): 1–16. Accessed 25 June 2017. Available at http://www.funggroup.com/eng/ knowledge/research/china_dis_issue56.pdf.

Li, P. F. 2014. 'Horizontal Versus Vertical Learning: Divergence and Diversification of Lead Firms in the Hangji Toothbrush Cluster, China.' *Regional Studies* 48 (7): 1227–41. DOI: 10.1080/00343404.2012.709610.

Li, P. F., H. Bathelt and J. Wang. 2012. 'Network Dynamics and Cluster Evolution: Changing Trajectories of the Aluminium Extrusion Industry in Dali, China.' *Journal of Economic Geography* 12 (1): 127–55. DOI: 10.1093/jeg/lbr024.

Liao, H. and R. K. Chan. 2011. 'Industrial Relocation of Hong Kong Manufacturing Firms: Towards an Expanding Industrial Space Beyond the Pearl River Delta.' *Geo Journal* 76 (6): 623–39. DOI:10.1007/s10708-009-9316-3.

Lin, G. C. S., C. C. Wang, Y. Zhou, Y. Sun and Y. H. D. Wei. 2011. 'Placing Technological Innovation in Globalising China: Production Linkage, Knowledge Exchange and Innovative Performance of the ICT Industry in a Developing Economy.' *Urban Studies* 48 (14): 2999–3018. DOI: 10.1177/0042098010396232.

Lin, H. L., H. Y. Li and C. H. Yang. 2011. 'Agglomeration and Productivity: Firm-Level Evidence from China's Textile Industry.' *China Economic Review* 22 (3): 313–29. DOI:10.1016/j.chieco.2011.03.003.

Lin, J. Y. and Y. Wang. 2008. 'China's Integration with the World Development as a Process of Learning and Industrial Upgrading.' Policy Research Working Paper no. WPS 4799. Washington, DC: World Bank.

Liu, W. and P. Dicken. 2006. 'Transnational Corporations and "Obligated Embeddedness": Foreign Direct Investment in China's Automobile Industry.' *Environment and Planning A* 38 (7): 1229–47. DOI: 10.1068/a37206.

Liu, Y. and C. Yang. 2013. 'Strategic Coupling of Local Firms in Global Production Networks: The Rise of the Home Appliance Industry in Shunde, China.' *Eurasian Geography and Economics* 54 (4): 444–63. DOI:10.1080/15387216.2014.883286.

Ma, L.J.C. and Y. Wei. 1997. 'Determinants of State Investment in China, 1953–1990.' *Tijdschrift Voor Economische en Sociale Geografie* 88 (3): 211–25. DOI: 10.1111/ j.1467-9663.1997.tb01599.x.

MacKinnon, D. 2012. 'Beyond Strategic Coupling: Reassessing the Firm-Region Nexus in Global Production Networks.' *Journal of Economic Geography* 12 (1): 227–45. DOI: 10.1093/jeg/lbr009.

MacKinnon, D., A. Cumbers, A. Pike, K. Birch and R. McMaster. 2009. 'Evolution in Economic Geography: Institutions, Political Economy, and Adaptation.' *Economic Geography* 85 (2): 129–50. DOI: 10.1111/j.1944-8287.2009.01017.x.

Marshall, A. 1890/1920. *Principles of Economics*, 8th Edition. London: Macmillan.

Martin, R. and P. Sunley. 2006. 'Path Dependence and Regional Economic Evolution.' *Journal of Economic Geography* 6 (4): 395–437. DOI: 10.1093/jeg/lbl012.

McMillan, J. and B. Naughton. 1992. 'How to Reform a Planned Economy: Lessons from China.' *Oxford Review of Economic Policy* 8 (1): 130–43. DOI:10.1093/oxrep/8.1.130.

National Bureau of Statistics of China. 2011. *China Statistical Yearbook 2011*. Beijing: China Statistics Press.

Naughton, B. 1996. *Growing out of the Plan: Chinese Economic Reform, 1978–1993.* Cambridge: Cambridge University Press.

North, D. C. 1990. *Institutions, Institutional Change and Economic Performance.* Cambridge: Cambridge University Press.

Pickles, J., A. Smith, M. Buček, P. Roukova and R. Begg. 2006. 'Upgrading, Changing Competitive Pressures, and Diverse Practices in the East and Central European Apparel Industry.' *Environment and Planning A* 38 (12): 2305–24. DOI: 10.1068/a38259.

Poncet, S. 2005. 'A Fragmented China: Measure and Determinants of Chinese Domestic Market Disintegration.' *Review of International Economics* 13 (3): 409–30. DOI: 10.1111/j.1467-9396.2005.00514.x.

Schamp, E. W. 2005. 'Decline of the District, Renewal of Firms: An Evolutionary Approach to Footwear Production in the Pirmasens Area, Germany.' *Environment and Planning A* 37 (4): 617–34. DOI:10.1068/a36275.

Scott, A. 1988. *Metropolis: From the Division of Labor to Urban Form.* Berkeley: University of California Press.

———. 2006. 'The Changing Global Geography of Low-Technology, Labour-Intensive Industry: Clothing, Footwear, and Furniture.' *World Development* 34 (9): 1517–36. DOI:10.1016/j.worlddev.2006.01.003.

Sjöberg, Ö. and F. Sjöholm. 2004. 'Trade Liberalization and the Geography of Production: Agglomeration, Concentration, and Dispersal in Indonesia's Manufacturing Industry.' *Economic Geography* 80 (3): 287–310. DOI: 10.1111/j.1944-8287.2004.tb00236.x.

Smith, A., J. Pickles, M. Buček, R. Pástor and B. Begg. 2014. 'The Political Economy of Global Production Networks: Regional Industrial Change and Differential Upgrading in the East European Clothing Industry.' *Journal of Economic Geography* 14 (6): 1023–51. DOI: 10.1093/jeg/lbt039.

Storper, M. 1997. *The Regional World: Territorial Development in a Global Economy.* New York: Guilford Press.

Storper, M., Y. C. Chen and F. De Paolis. 2002. 'Trade and the Location of Industries in the OECD and European Union.' *Journal of Economic Geography* 2 (1): 73–107. DOI: 10.1093/jeg/2.1.73.

Sun, H. 1999. 'DFI, Foreign Trade and Transfer Pricing.' *Journal of Contemporary Asia* 29 (3): 362–82. DOI:10.1080/00472339980000181.

Tewari, M. 2006. 'Adjustment in India's Textile and Apparel Industry: Reworking Historical Legacies in a Post-MFA World.' *Environment and Planning A* 38 (12): 2325–44. DOI: 10.1068/a38279.

Tokatli, N. 2008. 'Global Sourcing: Insights from the Global Clothing Industry – the Case of Zara, a Fast Fashion Retailer.' *Journal of Economic Geography* 8 (1): 21–38. DOI: 10.1093/jeg/lbm035.

Wang, C., G. C. S. Lin and G. Li. 2010. 'Industrial Clustering and Technological Innovation in China: New Evidence from the ICT Industry in Shenzhen.' *Environment and Planning A* 42 (8): 1987–2010. DOI: 10.1068/a4356.

Wang, J. 2014. *Institutional Change and the Development of Industrial Clusters in China: Case Studies from Textile and Clothing Industry.* Singapore: World Scientific.

Wang, J. and L. Mei. 2009. *Dynamics of Labour-Intensive Clusters in China: Relying on Low Labour Costs or Cultivating Innovation?* Geneva: ILO.

Wei, Y. D. 2002. 'Multiscale and Multimechanisms of Regional Inequality in China: Implications for Regional Policy.' *Journal of Contemporary China* 11 (30): 109–24. DOI:10.1080/10670560120091165.

Wei, Y. H. D. 2000. *Regional Development in China: States, Globalization, and Inequality.* London: Routledge.

———. 2001. 'Decentralization, Marketization, and Globalization: The Triple Processes Underlying Regional Development in China.' *Asian Geographer* 20 (1–2): 7–23. DOI:10.1080/10225706.2001.9684073.

———. 2009. 'China's Shoe Manufacturing and the Wenzhou Model: Perspectives on the World's Leading Producer and Exporter of Footwear.' *Eurasian Geography and Economics* 50 (6): 720–39. DOI:10.2747/1539-7216.50.6.720.

———. 2010. 'Beyond New Regionalism, Beyond Global Production Networks: Remaking the Sunan Model, China.' *Environment and Planning C: Government and Policy* 28 (1): 72–96. DOI: 10.1068/c0934r.

———. 2011. 'Beyond the GPN–New Regionalism Divide in China: Restructuring the Clothing Industry, Remaking the Wenzhou Model.' *Geografiska Annaler: Series B, Human Geography* 93 (3): 237–51. DOI: 10.1111/j.1468-0467.2011.00375.x.

Wei, Y. H. D., W. Li and C. Wang. 2007. 'Restructuring Industrial Districts, Scaling up Regional Development: A Study of the Wenzhou Model, China.' *Economic Geography* 83 (4): 421–44. DOI:10.1111/j.1944-8287.2007.tb00381.x.

Wei, Y. H. D., Y. Lu and W. Chen. 2009. 'Globalizing Regional Development in Sunan, China: Does Suzhou Industrial Park Fit a Neo-Marshallian District Model?' *Regional Studies* 43 (3): 409–27. DOI:10.1080/00343400802662617.

Wen, M. 2004. 'Relocation and Agglomeration of Chinese Industry.' *Journal of Development Economics* 73 (1): 329–47. DOI:10.1016/j.jdeveco.2003.04.001.

Yang, C. 2009. 'Strategic Coupling of Regional Development in Global Production Networks: Redistribution of Taiwanese Personal Computer Investment from the Pearl River Delta to the Yangtze River Delta, China.' *Regional Studies* 43 (3): 385–407. DOI:10.1080/00343400802508836.

———. 2012. 'Restructuring the Export-Oriented Industrialization in the Pearl River Delta, China: Institutional Evolution and Emerging Tension.' *Applied Geography* 32 (1): 143–57. DOI:10.1016/j.apgeog.2010.10.013.

———. 2013. 'From Strategic Coupling to Recoupling and Decoupling: Restructuring Global Production Networks and Regional Evolution in China.' *European Planning Studies* 21 (7): 1046–63. DOI:10.1080/09654313.2013.733852.

———. 2014a. 'Market Rebalancing of Global Production Networks in the Post-Washington Consensus Globalizing Era: Transformation of Export-Oriented Development in China.' *Review of International Political Economy* 21 (1): 130–56. DOI:10.1080/09692290.2013.776616.

———. 2014b. 'State-Led Technological Innovation of Domestic Firms in Shenzhen, China: Evidence from Liquid Crystal Display (LCD) Industry.' *Cities* 38 (June): 1–10. DOI:10.1016/j.cities.2013.12.005.

Zhao, X. B. and L. Zhang. 1999. 'Decentralization Reforms and Regionalism in China: A Review.' *International Regional Science Review* 22 (3): 251–81. DOI: 10.1177/016001799761012424.

Zhu, S. and C. He. 2013. 'Geographical Dynamics and Industrial Relocation: Spatial Strategies of Apparel Firms in Ningbo, China.' *Eurasian Geography and Economics* 54 (3): 342–62. DOI:10.1080/15387216.2013.849402.

———. 2015. 'Global and Local Governance, Industrial and Geographical Dynamics: A Tale of Two Clusters.' *Environment and Planning C: Politics and Space* 34 (8): 1453–73. DOI: 10.1177/0263774X15621760.

Zhu, S., C. He and Y. Liu. 2014. 'Going Green or Going Away: Environmental Regulation, Economic Geography and Firms' Strategies in China's Pollution-Intensive Industries.' *Geoforum* 55 (August): 53–65. DOI:10.1016/j.geoforum.2014.05.004.

Zhu, S. and J. Pickles. 2014. 'Bring In, Go Up, Go West, Go Out: Upgrading, Regionalisation and Delocalisation in China's Apparel Production Networks.' *Journal of Contemporary Asia* 44 (1): 36–63. DOI:10.1080/00472336.2013.801166.

———. 2015. 'Turkishization of a Chinese Apparel Firm: Fast Fashion, Regionalisation and the Shift from Global Supplier to New End Markets.' *Cambridge Journal of Regions, Economy and Society* 8 (3): 537–53. DOI: 10.1093/cjres/rsv009.

5

The Philippines
A Sequential Approach to Upgrading in Manufacturing Global Value Chains

Penny Bamber, Jack Daly, Stacey Frederick and Gary Gereffi

The Philippines in manufacturing GVCs: An overview

After decades of stagnant growth, in the 2010s, the Philippines emerged to become one of the fastest-growing economies globally, with an average annual gross domestic product (GDP) growth of 5.4 per cent between 2005 and 2015 (World Bank, 2016a). The country's economic development was driven by an expanding population, improvements in trade and investment conditions, and strong human capital. In 2014, total exports reached US$87 billion, while foreign investment increased five-fold between 2010 and 2014, accounting for approximately 2.5 per cent of the country's GDP that year (UNCTAD, 2016; World Bank, 2016b). These trends helped foster strong job creation, a key agenda for governments of the period, which placed a premium on an inclusive economic growth agenda (NEDA, 2011).

Export-led growth and the entry and upgrading of the Philippines in a variety of global value chains (GVCs) were important elements of the country's development. While services exports contributed significantly to growth, the Philippines also entered new manufacturing value chains and expanded both global and regional trade in niche product categories.[1] Although the country was still a relatively small and low-value player in manufacturing GVCs compared to its regional peers in Asia, by the middle of the decade, it began to diversify, upgrade and innovate in a few select chains.

While electronics has been the country's largest global industry, the automotive electronics and aerospace industries were two sectors where the Philippines' emergence and upgrading has been most visible. In addition to

---

1   The Philippines' services exports accounted for approximately 28.5 per cent of GDP in 2014 and quadrupled since 2005 to reach US$25 billion (UNCTAD, 2016b).

becoming a hub for wire harness production, the Philippines increased its exports of automotive electronics and began manufacturing and assembling flight controls and aircraft interiors for the sophisticated aerospace industry. This upgrading boosted both the quality and quantity of jobs in the country – the assembly of wire harnesses is labour-intensive, and entry into the aerospace industry provided an opportunity for large numbers of engineers.

Involvement in these manufacturing GVCs was predicated on several factors, including: (*a*) strong human capital associated with a growing population, (*b*) favourable investment regimes and (*c*) exploitation of similar strengths across related value chains. The Philippines' population – young and educated – topped 100 million in 2013, and the size of the labour force was 39 million in 2015. Literacy rates were high and English-speaking workers with strong soft skills were considered an asset by companies operating across industries (Bamber, Frederick and Gereffi, 2016, 11–15).[2]

Human capital advantages made the Philippines particularly appealing to American and Japanese firms. The number of foreign investors in the Philippines increased by an impressive 89 per cent from 2011 to 2014, and foreign direct investment (FDI) amounted to US$6.2 billion at the end of that period (UNCTAD, 2016b; World Bank, 2016b). The investment regimes associated with export processing zones (EPZs) played a key role in this expansion through the provision of a variety of incentives, including income tax holidays, tax and duty free imports, reduced bureaucracy such as simplified import and export procedures, and access to special non-immigrant visas for employees. These investment schemes were oriented to drive export-oriented manufacturing in general rather than prioritizing industries.

Finally, firms in the Philippines engaged in inter-sectoral upgrading by adapting and exploring niches where they could compete despite entrenched weaknesses. Across diverse sectors such as automotive, electronics and aerospace, firms in the country focused on low-volume, high-value products that leveraged the country's workforce and favourable value-to-weight ratio, which meant the goods could be shipped by air.

In 2012, based on this early upgrading, the Aquino administration launched an ambitious industry development plan – the Manufacturing Resurgence Plan – with the explicit goal of integrating the manufacturing sector into global

---

2   While the literacy rate improved from 92.3 per cent in 2000 to 97.5 per cent in 2010 (PSA, 2016), the government also invested heavily in education through the Philippine Development Plan 2011–16.

value chains. While the Philippines had a long history of trying to support the automotive sector as well as implementing specific measures to improve its EPZ operations, broad attention to manufacturing sectors had been less widespread – little of the upgrading that was detected in the industries studied could be attributed to strategic intent.

There has been further evolution in more recent years. In 2012, the Department of Trade and Industry-Board of Investments (DTI-BOI) launched an ambitious Industrial Development Program, the first stage of which was the Industry Roadmap Initiative. The DTI-BOI, in association with the Chamber of Commerce, tried to identify industrial policy needs for a wide range of different industries in the Philippines economy. By 2015, industry roadmaps had been completed for thirty-two sectors, and twenty-two more industries had indicated interest in participating in the project. Manufacturing was a key element of this programme: the DTI-BOI formulated the Manufacturing Resurgence Program to revitalize the manufacturing sector.[3]

A key outcome was to cultivate stronger private sector industry associations as well as to strengthen public–private coordination. In general, the private sector assumed a proactive stance vis-à-vis industry development, and the new coordination mechanisms opened up channels of communication between industry players and the government. In addition, by 2015, efforts were underway to improve interdepartmental coordination to ensure that policies could be effectively implemented with an inter-agency council. The Industrial Development Council led by the Secretary of the DTI was tasked with bringing together working groups at the government level (DTI, 2016a; DTI, SPK and BOI, 2014). This information was obtained during an interview conducted by Penny Bamber, Stacey Frederick and Jack Daly in November (2015), January and February (2016).

While these efforts partly contributed to the ongoing upgrading in automotive electronics and aerospace sectors, with GVC analysis being used to inform policy decisions in these sectors, constraints continue to threaten the Philippines' potential for deeper integration into GVCs. Infrastructure and related services are key determinants of competitiveness in global industries, primarily affecting

---

3 The initiative included an extensive range of programmes and initiatives to gather information to more fully understand the scope of activities in the country, develop incentive structures to support and prioritize industries for growth, and to attract investment. Its specific goal was to increase manufacturing's contribution to the economy to 30 per cent of total value added (up from 22.8 per cent) and to generate 15 per cent of the country's total employment by 2025 compared to 10 per cent in 2013 (DTI, 2016b).

transportation/logistics and energy (Bamber *et al.*, 2013, 11, 33; Kowalski, 2014, 43–45; Taglioni and Winkler, 2016, 117–43). This is heightened in archipelago countries where domestic shipping plays an important role.

Poor infrastructure plagued the Philippines even as the country made economic gains. In 2015, serious deficits persisted with respect to the number and capacity of ports, city congestion and resistance to liberalizing domestic shipping channels (DTI, 2016c). Estimates suggested that the economic cost of congestion in metropolitan Manila alone was about US$27 billion each year (JICA, 2014, 2–41; KPMG, 2015). This meant that companies had to hold higher inventories of required raw materials and use more expensive shipping methods (for example, air freight) to meet customer schedules. At the same time, the separation of the administration of the ports (under the Department of Public Works and Highways [DPWH]) and road infrastructure development and management (under the Department of Transportation and Communication [DOTC]) impeded the implementation of improvements.

While transportation infrastructure remained one of the more entrenched challenges associated with the development of the Philippines' manufacturing sectors, inadequate energy supplies and a poor reputation for protecting intellectual property were other concerns. With respect to energy, a lack of investment in new technologies and capacity undermined the country's ability to meet growing demand for power (*EIU*, 2015; *Enerdata*, 2014).[4] In 2014, manufacturers faced rolling blackouts and had to invest inexpensive back-up generators to provide sufficient energy to ensure that their manufacturing capacity remained as close to 100 per cent as possible. Intellectual property protection has also been weak. The Philippines was on the US Special 301 Watchlist continuously for 22 years up until 2014, and it ranked 100 out of 140 countries in 2011 in the World Economic Forum's Global Competitiveness Ranking for IP protection (United States Trade Representative, 2014; World Economic Forum, 2016).

Given these constraints and the complexities of competing with low-cost, experienced Asian peers in regional manufacturing, further upgrading by the Philippines on a national scale is not assured. Some of the country's advantages –

---

4   In 2014, the government estimated that it needed to add around 1,000 MW of new capacity every year to avert a repeat of the energy crisis of 2013 (*Enerdata*, 2014). Electricity demand in the Philippines is projected to grow at 5.7 per cent per year on average between 2015 and 2020 and 4.6 per cent annually over the next twenty years (*EIU*, 2015; IEA, 2013, 58).

a large, educated young population, for example – can also be observed in nations such as Vietnam that are also in closer proximity to important regional trading partners such as China. In order to maximize future opportunities, the Philippines will benefit from leveraging its strengths rather than focusing on the low-cost labour strategy that supported the entry into GVCs for so many developing countries around the world.

This chapter explores the Philippines' entry into manufacturing GVCs in the early decades of the twenty-first century and its subsequent upgrading by looking at three sectors. First, it examines the past role of the Philippines in manufacturing GVCs, which was based on the electronics industry. Second, it discusses the emergence of the country as a player in the automotive electronics and electrical sectors, focusing on upgrading and innovation that has already occurred. Finally, the chapter explores how this experience has helped launch the Philippines into the more competitive and sophisticated aerospace sector. The chapter draws on field research carried out between September 2015 and May 2016. Sixty-nine individuals were interviewed at twenty-nine firms (the majority of the interviewees were in senior management positions), six industry associations, and eight public and educational institutions.

Semiconductors: A foundation for manufacturing GVCs

The backbone of the Philippines' participation in manufacturing GVCs was the electronics and electrical (E&E) equipment industry.[5] A booming global industry with close to US$3 trillion in trade in 2014, these products form the foundation of the country's export basket. At the turn of the century, E&E equipment accounted for 74 per cent of Philippine merchandise exports (UNComtrade, 2015); by 2014, they still generated US$28.8 billion in exports, although their share of exports had fallen to 51 per cent. Indeed, E&E equipment has played an important role in the Philippine economy since the 1970s as a result of investments from large multinational corporations (MNCs) including several of the world's largest integrated circuit companies, such as Intel, Texas Instruments, STMicroelctronics, NXP, ON Semiconductor, Analog Devices and Maxim, among others (Frederick and Gereffi, 2016, 36–44).

The presence of these firms helped to establish the Philippines as a leading global semiconductor supplier, complemented by a strong cluster of electronics component exporters. By 2014, with semiconductor exports valued at US$12

---

5   As defined by the Harmonized System (HS) Commodity Classification codes 84 and 85.

billion, the Philippines was the ninth largest global exporter, accounting for 2.8 per cent of world semiconductor trade. Firm-level export data registered approximately 258 companies with over US$1 million in 2014 in the electronic and electrical-related product category exports (PSA, 2007–14). In general, investments in the sector were highly 'sticky' with a low exit rate. With the exception of Intel, which moved its operations to Vietnam in 2009, firms that set up operations in the Philippines remained and continued to upgrade their facilities to maintain operating efficiency (Frederick and Gereffi, 2016, 46–47). Several operations, such as Texas Instruments, had a company history in the country that dated back to the late 1970s and 1980s.

The electronics sector helped facilitate social mobility (that is, social upgrading) by attracting both men and women to a range of diverse positions. In 1976, the industry employed just 5,000 people, but it quickly jumped to 47,000 in the next decade. By 2014, sectoral employment had reached close to 345,000 workers, representing approximately one-fifth of the manufacturing labour force. Electronics firms were large and labour-intensive, and employed a considerable number of workers at each firm (an average of 769 employees per establishment). It also attracted a significant number of women – female employees accounted for 70 per cent of the electronics workforce, compared to 46 per cent in the broader manufacturing sector. Furthermore, wages in electronics components for the GVC were 29 per cent on average higher than in the manufacturing sector as a whole (Philippines NSO, 2013).

While E&E was an important economic driver domestically, the Philippines was a relatively small contributor to the global industry, accounting for just 1 per cent of global exports in 2014. However, by the end of the 2000s, it became clear that the potential for the Philippines to harness the sector for innovation and upgrading was limited. There had been relatively minimal export diversification or movement into new products and technologies. Although the number of products with electronic content in the global market was rising, the majority of Philippine exports comprised computer-related office equipment and hard disk drives, which were considered 'sunset products' with less room to grow (World Bank, 2015, 78). Thus, the export value in the Philippines declined between 2007 and 2014; the country had a negative compounded annual growth rate (CAGR) (-3.7 per cent) compared to a global growth rate of 3.9 per cent.

There was stiff regional competition from peers that did not share the Philippines' infrastructure constraints. Intel's 2009 relocation to Vietnam is illustrative of this trend. Although Vietnam only entered the sector in the mid-2000s, the country had surpassed the Philippines in E&E exports by

2013. Vietnam benefited from equally low labour costs as the Philippines, but it possessed greater proximity to China. In that same year, Malaysia's E&E exports (US$83 billion) were three times as large as the Philippines', even though the two countries entered the industry around the same time in the 1970s and 1980s. Malaysia benefitted from its diversification into a broader range of components and products.

The Philippines' stagnation was partially due to the continued focus of foreign subsidiaries on assembly and testing (A&T) in the country, leveraging its low-cost labour and cost-effective and efficient EPZs, but failing to build backward linkages to domestic businesses. Foreign ownership dominated in E&E firms compared to manufacturing as a whole – 72 per cent for electronics and 30 per cent for electrical, compared to 18 per cent for manufacturing (Frederick and Gereffi, 2016, 38). From the beginning, E&E had been driven primarily by foreign subsidiaries of semiconductor firms (Lohr, 1984). Early investments made by leading semiconductor firms from the United States (US) and Europe in A&T sites were accompanied by contract A&T manufacturers as well. In the 1990s and early 2000s, these trends shifted. Japanese, and to a lesser extent Korean, FDI began to dominate. By 2014, Japanese investors accounted for 43 per cent of all FDI in electronics, followed by Koreans at 10 per cent (Philippines NSO, 2013).

Although plants expanded and continued to improve production technology, little functional upgrading had taken place despite four decades of engagement in the industry. Corporate strategies kept higher-value activities at company headquarters or closer to key markets and raw materials suppliers. Furthermore, although the Philippines had a strong entry-level manufacturing workforce, there was a limited supply of industry-specific technicians and engineers required to move into new product areas, end markets and more skill-intensive functions. Finally, the sector suffered from weak backward linkages. Inputs tended to be imported, and domestically purchased components came primarily from foreign-owned firms. Domestic firms only fulfilled relatively low value-added roles in packaging provision. Clearly, growth in GVCs would need to be driven by other sectors.

Automotive wire harnesses: A foothold for functional upgrading into automotive electronics

The automotive sector, surprisingly, emerged through an organic, but strategic, growth trajectory. Generally, the automotive GVC is difficult for emerging nations to enter. There is pressure to produce automobiles in markets where they are sold, especially in large countries such as China and the USA. Production tends to be organized regionally or nationally in large countries, with bulky and model-specific parts concentrated close to final assembly plants. Because many automotive parts tend to be heavy and firms employ just-in-time delivery to reduce costs, parts production and final assembly tend to be clustered. As a result, regional parts production operations feed final assembly plants, which concentrate on national or regional markets. Because of deep investments in capital equipment and skills, local automotive clusters usually are very long-lived once established (Sturgeon *et al.*, 2016, 1–3).

Throughout most of the late twentieth century, the Philippines attempted to integrate itself into automotive GVCs through a variety of industrial policies that encouraged the establishment of manufacturing plants. There were different explanations as to why the industry failed to gain traction depending on the period; however, the most prominent reasons in the twenty-first century included low relative demand for vehicles in the Philippine market, insufficient economies of scale for domestic suppliers and, importantly, competition from locations such as Thailand that developed as regional hubs. Local firms saw their competitiveness erode, particularly as intra-ASEAN trade picked up.

Despite these industry headwinds, automotive firms saw opportunity in the Philippines for many of the same reasons that electronics companies originally did – low-cost labour as well as effective EPZs. Over time, a cluster of firms emerged as the Philippines proved to be competitive in manufacturing operations that generated smaller, lighter products that did not incur excessive transport costs, but that nonetheless required technical knowledge and cost-competitive labour to assemble. With respect to the automotive sector, these strengths manifested themselves in two key product lines:

1. **Wire harnesses:** Low labour costs and relatively close geographic proximity to important markets such as Japan and Thailand caused the Philippines to become a global supplier of wire harnesses. As the automotive industry evolved and became more electronic, the importance and sophistication of wire harnesses and the potential for upgrading within the sub-sector opened opportunities for firms to undertake product upgrading.

2. **Automotive electronics:** Wire harness production served as a springboard for functional upgrading into research and design as well as an expansion into automotive electronics. Many Japanese companies that located operations in the Philippines to manufacture wire harnesses have subsequently added

engineering capabilities. Other foreign firms that were first attracted to the Philippines by low labour costs have similarly upgraded their facilities and expanded their product lines for more intricate automotive electronics products. Meanwhile, domestic electronic companies have had success concentrating on automotive sectors because of product specifications that aligned with accrued skills.

Wire harnesses

While the global automotive industry is often characterized by regional or national clusters of production, lighter and more generic parts are an exception to the rule. Wire harnesses, which help distribute and control the flow of electronic power and impulses throughout the vehicle, are a promising area for developing countries, which can use their cost advantages to attract foreign investment.

More than just bundles of wires with connectors, wire harnesses include many high-cost electronic control modules and once completely integrated tend to be one of the more expensive components in an automobile. The importance of the sub-system grew as the electronics content of vehicles increased – global exports jumped by 53 per cent in the time period from 2007 to 2014, from US$21 billion to a little more than US$32 billion (UNComtrade, 2015). There are also opportunities for innovation and upgrading within the sub-sector as electronic devices became increasingly common in vehicles and weight requirements become stricter for electric and hybrid cars.

The Philippines has had success against this global backdrop. With exports growing by 129 per cent between 2007 and 2014, the country quickly became the fourth-largest wire harness exporter behind Mexico, China and Romania. The country's global market share increased from 4.2 per cent in 2007 to 6.3 per cent in 2014. During that period, wire harnesses' share in the country's total automotive exports jumped from 29.8 per cent to 51.2 per cent, with some US$2 billion in exports in 2014.

The location of the Philippines helped it integrate into Japanese, North American and Asian regional production networks. The three largest export destinations – Japan, USA and Canada – accounted for almost 84 per cent of the country's total exports in 2014. Thailand, a hub for Toyota's regional production network, also emerged as an important destination in the early 2010s. The Philippines' wire harness exports to Thailand increased from US$400,000 in 2007 to US$75 million in 2014, boosting Thailand's overall share of total global wire harness exports from 0 per cent to 3.7 per cent (UNComtrade, 2015).

Inside the country, the Philippines' growth was generated by a relatively small number of firms. There were fifteen to twenty wire harness manufacturers operating in the country in 2015, most of which were Japanese owned. While six of these companies were among the country's largest ten exporters of automotive products, the largest five businesses within the sub-sector accounted for 80 per cent of all sales (PSA, 2007–14). Two of the segment's leading firms – Yazaki and Sumitomo – had long-standing investments stretching back to 1974 and 1988, respectively. Those companies were joined by major suppliers Lear (2002) and Furukawa (2012), giving the Philippines four of the world's largest suppliers.

Wire harness capabilities contributed significantly to job creation. Although wire harness production is primarily a low value-added activity, its high labour intensity – it takes as many as 400–500 minutes to complete a single unit – provided opportunity for high school graduates in predominantly rural areas, such as Tarlac. Employment growth was rapid as a result. Firms added as many as 1,000 workers on an annual basis, and by 2014, there were close to 30,000 employees in the sector. Many of these were line workers with either a high school education or vocational training. As in export-oriented electronics, wire harness assembly also provided important opportunities for women, with companies using female employees in high numbers. In 2010, 68 per cent of the hours worked in the sub-sector were worked by female employees (DTI, 2014), who were prized for their 'manual dexterity'.

Automotive electronics

The Philippines' position as a wire harness production hub helped facilitate the development of its nascent automotive electronics sector. In some respects, the expansion of both sectors was interrelated. Systems that were once controlled in motor vehicles through mechanical systems – instrumentation, acceleration, seat adjustment, window and brake actuation – are now controlled electronically by electrical impulses running through the wire harnesses. Automotive electronics expanded into a growing number of systems; by 2015, they were present not just in navigation and entertainment, but also in critical systems such as engine control units, vehicle stability control, automated transmissions, as well as a range of safety and warning systems such as airbag igniters, cameras, sensors, speed alerts and collision warning systems, amongst others.

With the growing number of devices in cars, wire harness companies have focused on improving their processes to serve new emerging models;

several set up research centres close to their manufacturing operations in the Philippines to improve their products. This helped to attract higher-value and more knowledge-oriented jobs to the Philippines. A series of key investments were made by 'wire harness' companies, which supported functional upgrading in the country. In 2010, Furukawa Automotive Systems Design set up the Lima Technology Center in Batangas, a research centre that would engage in the design and development of criteria for wire harnesses and parts using computer-aided design (CAD). In 2008, Denso, a diversified Japanese producer of automotive electronics and electrical systems (including wire harnesses), set up a software development operation in the Philippines for electronic engine controls. Sumitomo also began investing in design and engineering functions in the country (PEZA, 2015). Similarly, the Japanese engineering company Chiyoda expanded its wire harness assembly operations to include engineering design services. Table 5.1 lists some of the sector's notable research and development investments since 2007.

Table 5.1 Functional upgrades into automotive R&D in the Philippines

Company	Original investment	Activity
Flextronics	2007	• Electronic hardware/software design of automotive control modules • Mechanical design and flexible circuit assembly (FCA) of all these automotive mechanical components
F. Tech R&D	2008	• To engage in research and development (R&D) of automotive products
Denso	2008	• To engage in embedded software development
Chiyoda	2009	• To engage in engineering design and IT-enabled engineering services
Furukawa Automotive Systems Design	2010	• To engage in the business of design and development of criteria for wire harness and parts using computer-aided design (CAD)
Philippine Auto Components	2012	• To engage in the design and testing of instrument clusters and other auto parts for original equipment manufacturer (OEM) car assemblers

(Contd.)

(Contd.)

Company	Original investment	Activity
Philippine EDS Techno-Service	2012	• To provide technical services for Yazaki Corporation's automotive electrical distribution systems (EDS) development centres around the world • To engage in electronics and instrumentation design and development
International Wiring Systems (Phils.) Corp. (Sumitomo)	2012	• To include design engineering function

Source: PEZA (2015).

While wire harness suppliers in the Philippines adapted to increasing electronics content in vehicles, local electronics firms moved into the automotive sphere, taking advantage of specialized niches created by GVC lead firms and first-tier suppliers. Domestic companies such as IMI and Ionics had initially competed in the traditional consumer electronics fields. Consolidation and changing industry dynamics undermined their competitiveness, and these firms began to look at emerging electronics markets in automotive, aerospace and defence, along with industrial and medical device manufacturing, where products had longer lifecycles and orders were smaller, more complex and subject to higher regulations. These market segments favoured nimble firms that could respond and adapt to client needs. IMI, in particular, found success. By 2015, automotive electronics accounted for 43 per cent of its output, the company ranked seventh globally amongst electronic suppliers for the automotive sector, and counted key auto manufacturers such as Volvo amongst its customers. IMI employed 4,500 people in the Philippines by 2015 with a further 10,000 abroad at its fifteen global locations (Frederick and Gereffi, 2016, 18).

Successful examples of foreign investment can also be found in the sector. Notably, diversified foreign automotive firms with operations in electronics as well as foreign electronics firms serving the automotive sector that were initially attracted to the Philippines by low labour costs began to upgrade their facilities and expand their product base to include increasingly sophisticated products. Two examples are Continental Temic and Flextronics. Continental Temic set up operations in 2004, but by 2015 they had expanded or added new products and functions at least nine times. Likewise, Flextronics set up operations for electronic hardware and software design of automotive control units in 2007 (PEZA, 2015). Together, these activities all contributed to a dynamic automotive electronics cluster. Table 5.2 provides details about the firms active in the Philippines.

Table 5.2 The automotive E&E cluster in the Philippines

Segment	Global market value (US$ billions)	Segment	Philippines Manufacturing	Design/ R&D	Global Manufacturing
Electrical	32	Wire harnesses	Yazaki, Sumitomo, Furukawa, Lear	Sumitomo, Furukawa	Denso, Leoni, Delphi, Fujikura
	N/A	Lithium-ion batteries for EVs	Talino EV, Pangea Motors, Acbel Polytech Philippines		LG Chem, SK Innovation, E-one Moli Energy, Toshiba, Xalt, Samsung SDI, Panasonic Energy
Electronic *Types of semiconductors* Discrete power, analog, microcontrollers, *Sensors* Three areas: Powertrain/ chassis, infotainment, safety	22	Semiconductors	Analog Devices, NXP, STM, TI, On Semi, Maxim, Fairchild, Micosemi		Infineon, Renesas, Agilent, Xilinx, Freescale, Siemens, Toshiba, Bosch, Rohm
	23	EMS	IMI, Ionics, SIIX	Flextronics, F. Tech R&D	Jabil, Flextronics, Compal, Sanmina-SCI
	164	Tier 1	Fujitsu Ten, Continental Temic	Denso	Bosch, Denso, Aisin, Valeo, Delphi, Panasonic

Source: Frederick and Gereffi (2016).

Automotive and electronics success paves the way for entry into the aerospace GVC

As the automotive electronics cluster consolidated, momentum was also gathering for Philippine participation in the aerospace GVC. Although host to a major flight controls manufacturer – Moog – since 1985, the industry only began to expand after 2008. During the subsequent period (2008–14), the Philippines ramped up its aerospace manufacturing exports, reaching US$604 million in 2014 – 1 per cent of the country's total goods exports – and more than tripled employment to reach 6,000. Production was oriented to the manufacture of flight controls, aircraft interiors such as galley equipment, and electronics. By 2014, although the Philippines was still a very small player and relative newcomer to the growing global aerospace industry, accounting for less than 0.15 per cent of its global capacity, the incipient growth was promising.

The Philippines entered the aerospace GVC at a pivotal time. Increased global air travel and more fuel-efficient planes had boosted demand for new aircraft models such as the 787 Dreamliner and the A350, while growth in regional travel was sustaining staple models such as the 737 and A320. In 2015, Boeing forecast that total commercial jet deliveries over the next twenty years would reach 39,000, almost double the size of the global fleet that year (Airbus, 2016; Boeing, 2016; S&P Capital IQ, 2015). The unprecedented demand, together with the cost of new, more sophisticated planes, forced Airbus, Boeing and other integrators to restructure their supply chains, industrializing production in order to meet critical delivery schedules. Integrators shifted increasing degrees of design and production responsibility and financing down the chain to their leading 'Tier 1' suppliers in what are known as 'risk-sharing' relationships. In turn, these suppliers – limited in their ability to bear the risk and production demands to conduct all manufacturing in-house – began to outsource more activity to a smaller set of Tier 2 and 3 suppliers (Bamber *et al.*, 2016, 10, 16–18).

Strong global demand ushered in a period of increased globalization and incorporation of new manufacturing locations into what had been a rather consolidated industry based in just a few countries. Global trade increased by 56 per cent during 2007–14, from US$271 billion to US$423 billion (UN Comtrade. 2015).[6]Although the sector remained fairly consolidated with the top twenty supplier countries continuing to account for over 90 per cent in most product categories, several developing countries including Mexico, India and Poland benefitted from this expansion; each of these countries' aerospace

---

6   Statistics are difficult to track as two major players in the industry, the USA and the UK, stopped reporting disaggregated trade statistics for the sector during this time. All US aerospace exports are now included under the HS-88 code. This is probably due to the sensitive nature of the industry, given its role as a technology driver and its overlap with the defence sector.

exports grew by 50 per cent or more during the 2007–14 period (Bamber *et al.*, 2016, 12–13).

The Philippines leveraged Moog's long-term presence in the country, as well as its low-cost engineers and the manufacturing capabilities in the automotive and electronics industries, to enter the industry. The slow early development between 1985 and 2008, when Moog, mostly in isolation, expanded its product lines and capabilities with sporadic engagement of local suppliers, was followed by greater expansion momentum between 2008 and 2015.[7] This latter period involved a larger subset of firms. By 2014, the total number of firms in the sector, though still small, was growing; that year, ten firms registered exports over US$500,000. Three leading global supplier firms, including B/E Aerospace (USA), JAMCO (Japan), and Surface Technology International (UK), had joined Moog Controls in the country. These firms transferred existing product lines, but, more importantly, a significant share of their production was oriented towards the production of new models and products, thus establishing the Philippines as a primary manufacturing site.

Evolution of the anchor-firm model in the aerospace sector

MNC firms were influenced by the changes underway in the global industry. These companies established operations with high levels of outsourcing. However, as an emerging cluster, there was an absence of co-located global Tier 2 and Tier 3 suppliers, and the local supply base had virtually no experience in the industry. This led to an 'anchor firm' approach to entering the GVC. This model – seen in earlier years in Bombardier's expansion into Mexico's Queretaro region (Niosi and Zhegu, 2010) – involves attracting investments by larger GVC players which in turn contract and train an expanding set of smaller local suppliers, simultaneously demanding and helping these suppliers increase their capabilities to meet industry standards.

Distinct from lead firms, which control the GVCs, anchor firms may simply

---

7   Moog Controls Corporations is the oldest aerospace firm in the country, having established operations near Texas Instruments in Baguio in 1985. The firm began operations with just 24 employees – mostly engineers manufacturing two simple components. By 2015, it had 1,300 employees and manufactured over 2,000 distinct components. The company initially identified as an electronics firm supplying the automotive and aerospace industry. This evolved at the global level as the firm developed, and the operations in the Philippines became increasingly concentrated on serving the aerospace sector.

be large firms (foreign or domestic) that generate sufficient economies of scale and scope to support the entrance of new local suppliers and generate backward linkages.[8] In some countries, the government or aid agencies provide incentives to these firms to engage with smaller suppliers through tax holidays, subsidies or other benefits. In the case of Queretaro, the Queretaro Secretariat for Sustainable Development directly engaged with Bombardier to encourage backward linkage development with local suppliers who had previously worked in the automotive sector, while providing financial support for these smaller firms to obtain the specific certifications required by Bombardier (Bamber and Gereffi, 2013, 28–31). The relationships required close interaction between Bombardier and its local suppliers, to whom an increasing range of activities including machining and finishing operations for components were outsourced.

In the Philippines, although there were no specific initiatives or programmes to encourage these relationships, their emergence – led initially by Moog – was key to process and functional upgrading among these local firms, and the development of relatively strong backward linkages. In the short term, this model can limit functional upgrading for local suppliers for operations required to serve the anchor firm's function. For example, the dominance of this governance structure is reflected in the evolution of the Philippines' exports with product groups limited to the final products or components produced by the four Tier 1 firms (Bamber et al., 2016). The leading aerospace exports for much of the 1990s and 2000s were related to flight control systems, including servo valves and servo actuators sold by Moog.[9] After 2008, exports became more varied as new Tier 1 firms entered the industry, with some consolidation in the production of components and sub-assemblies for interiors systems. Interior products include machined seat parts, galley inserts (for example, coffee makers, ovens, and so forth), galley structures and lavatories for a range of commercial jets, particularly for the high-selling aircraft models of Airbus (A320, A350) and Boeing (737, 787), which justify large-scale industrial operations. However, in the medium term, if local suppliers have access to other financial resources and entrepreneurial skills, they may leverage their capability base to engage with

---

8   Anchor firms can also be GVC lead firms; their categorization as an 'anchor' is based on their development role with respect to the particular geographic location in which they establish operations.

9   These include hydraulic or electrohydraulic actuators and include high-lift and gear-type actuators. They come in various sizes and the largest one can weigh up to 200 pounds. For a single Boeing 787, Moog supplies over 200 separate servo actuators (APEC Policy Support Unit, 2015, 61).

a wider range of buyers. The functional upgrading discussion below indicates how several Philippine suppliers did this.

Social upgrading in the aerospace sector

The sector also drove social upgrading through job creation for higher knowledge work. Three thousand full-time and three thousand part-time jobs were generated by 2015. Employment creation was largely oriented towards engineers – particularly electrical, mechanical and industrial engineers, who account for close to half of the total number of employees in the sector. Generally speaking, the more complex and critical the products being manufactured by firms, the higher the percentage of engineers in their workforce. The quality of employment was considered to be much higher than in other sectors such as the automotive industry, offering more challenging and engaging roles rather than routine operations (Bamber *et al.*, 2016, 44). The industry also provided important opportunities for female workers, with men and women each comprising approximately half the workforce.

Workers were typically provided full-time contracts, due to the significant training required for their participation in the sector. The low-volume, high-mix production model requires employees to perform multiple functions such as operating multiple tools, machines, understanding materials' characteristics and following detailed schematics, among other things. It could take a machinist three to five years to reach full proficiency. As a result, developing employees was/is very costly and retention is key to competitive success and upgrading (Bamber *et al.*, 2016, 44).

Although the country's engagement in the industry was still relatively recent in 2015 and limited to a small number of operations, the Philippines made important strides in expanding local capabilities at the process, product and functional levels, illustrating its rapid capacity to learn and upgrade. This was largely the result of the availability of human capital as well as past experiences in the automotive and electronics fields. This occurred at both the foreign and local firms. Three examples of early upgrading trajectories are discussed below.

1. **Process and product:** At the product level, all Tier 1 firms at least doubled their production operations since opening and expanded beyond their first product line. Moog, for example, began operations with just 24 employees, most of whom were engineers manufacturing two simple components. By 2015, the company had 1,300 full time employees, fabricated and serviced over 2,000 distinct components and smaller sub-assemblies for aerospace

flight controls systems, and the facility's products could be found in all the new plane families: the 787, A380 and A350. The Philippines also became the firm's key manufacturing hub across its global production network, producing directly for Airbus, Boeing, Bombardier and Embraer, but also for other Tier 1 firms such as Liebherr and Goodrich (APEC Policy Support Unit, 2015, 59–62; Estoque, 2015).

Supplier firms expanded their product portfolios to keep abreast. Product upgrading was facilitated by the development of additional processing capabilities. Machining, sandblasting, buffing, painting and anodizing processes were soon all carried out locally. Supplier firms invested heavily in new computer numerically controlled (CNC) machines dedicated exclusively to their production for the aerospace sector. In addition, between 2009 and 2016, in order to meet the requirements of global firms, nine manufacturing firms achieved their AS9100 certifications, including several local suppliers (International Aerospace Quality Group, 2016). A newly emerging industry association and its entrepreneurial members provided informal support to peer firms in the process. At the same time, some local machine shops, realizing that their capacity to meet all requirements would take time, forged alliances with suppliers in neighbouring countries, allowing them to offer complementary services, while at the same time broadening their market base.

2. **Functional upgrading:** While production occurred primarily in the components manufacturing and assembly segments of the chain, it drew on the engineering talent in the country. Many of these engineers had worked in the automotive manufacturing sector, were skilled in terms of interpreting engineering designs, developing manufacturing engineering plans and, most importantly, accustomed to working under the lean manufacturing principles of Japanese MNC firms. This experience facilitated the rapid expansion of the operations in the country from following detailed engineering instructions provided from headquarters to locally producing production plans and programming machinery (Bamber *et al.*, 2016, 42–43).

Compared to aerospace production sites based in the USA or the European Union, this engineering talent was very inexpensive. Due to the relative shortage of opportunities in high-tech industries in the Philippines, which did not generally participate in these more sophisticated sectors, engineers were willing to take production line positions to work in the aerospace sector. Firms were thus able to rapidly build up engineering talent with shop floor experience. This provided a significant edge in readjusting production plans and programming to increase efficiency.

In addition, a handful of local suppliers, which initially worked with the locally based Tier 1 firms, began to deal with additional buyers via direct exports. By 2015, firms in the industry reported serving a wide range of customers at the Prime and Tier 1 levels, including Airbus, Boeing and Mitsubishi Heavy Industries, amongst others (Bamber *et al.*, 2016, 41–43; Estoque, 2015). Local firms had to upgrade their capabilities, not only in marketing and sales functions, but also in procurement operations, forecasting and financial management, in order to manage inventory risk for raw materials. To achieve this, suppliers drew on the growing business administration talent in the country, while also tapping into foreign expertise by recruiting experienced personnel from abroad. At the same time, this required the upgrading of enterprise resource planning systems and software to improve traceability, including the implementation of barcoding of inventory, and establishing quality management and performance improvement systems in line with the market demands.

3. **Chain upgrading**: An important element for local firms for establishing themselves as aerospace suppliers was their previous experience in the automotive segment. At least three of the supplier firms had served that industry before venturing into aerospace. Ongoing supply work in the automotive GVC helped to procure the significant investments required to upgrade into aerospace (Bamber *et al.*, 2016, 41–46). One firm, Famous Secret Precision Machining, entered manufacturing by providing parts for the bicycle industry. As India and China entered the market, however, the firm was forced to upgrade in order to cater to the motorcycle industry, and then enter various automotive market segments in order to remain competitive. With each shift, the company increased its product complexity, investing in new and increasingly sophisticated equipment, before eventually moving into the aerospace sector.

This upgrading required a major shift of operations for these suppliers. The automotive sector is a high-volume, low-mix production operation, and orders can include half a million or more pieces for less than ten product parts, with low regulatory control. Comparatively, when serving the aerospace sector, the model shifts to a significantly larger variation of products with much smaller order sizes – for example,1,000 product numbers with ten pieces per unit – under much greater regulatory control. As firms gained these capabilities, there were increased opportunities for the Philippines to diversify and upgrade in high-tech manufacturing.

Accounting for upgrading success

The Philippines has successfully upgraded in manufacturing value chains despite considerable obstacles. Traditional drivers of competitiveness in the manufacturing sector such as large domestic markets, easy access to foreign consumers, availability of raw materials, low energy costs, and strong regulatory frameworks for R&D and innovation did not favour the country. Similarly, there was no history of engagement or a supportive industrial policy for key sectors such as automotive electronics or aerospace.[10]

Why, then, did the Philippines enter and undertake upgrades to stay in these three value chains? What explains the innovations that could be detected in 2015? Also, what could the government learn from these experiences to continue to drive growth in the face of the strong competition from regional peers such as Vietnam and China? GVC analysis suggests there were three critical elements associated with the upgrading of the Philippines' manufacturing industries.

The first is human capital. Foreign investors almost unanimously identified the Philippine workforce as the leading reason for establishing operations in the country (Bamber *et al.*, 2016, 44; Frederick and Gereffi, 2016, 45; Sturgeon *et al.*, 2016, 36–37). Several characteristics of the workforce made it attractive, providing both short-term and long-term advantages, including the following:

1. **The large/growing number of engineers:** In Philippines, the annual numbers for graduated engineers and technology majors was 63,500 in 2013–14, which was up by 30 per cent from 2005–06 numbers. There was also room for future growth, especially in the number of engineers – graduation rates by 2014 were still relatively low, with only 18 per cent of students completing their studies.

2. **Low wages:** In 2013, average wages in the Philippines were only marginally higher than in Vietnam, one-third of those in China and Malaysia, and less than 10 per cent of those in Japan (ILO, 2014, 2). This cheap and easily available workforce was a major draw for the automotive wire harness manufacturers, which are labour-intensive. The largest wire harness company in 2015 had some 13,700 employees in the Philippines, making it the largest single employer in the automotive sector and one of the largest in the country. While wages will probably rise as the country

---

10 The Philippine Department of Trade and Industry (DTI) began to engage with manufacturing industry in 2012. Prior to that, these sectors had moved ahead with little direct government support.

becomes more developed, this short-term advantage is complemented by the fact the workforce also speaks English and has a cultural affinity with the USA, Spain and Latin America. This is also considered an asset by many employers as it reduces the amount of resources needed for translation and cultural considerations. This was a major advantage in the aerospace industry, where production remains less automated and more reliant on problem-solving and communication skills.

3. **Workplace loyalty:** Most wire harness manufacturing firms operating in the Philippines reported annual turnover rates of less than 5 per cent. In the aerospace sector, that dropped to 2–4 per cent. Companies regularly cited the challenges of labour retention in China and Vietnam in comparison. As a result of the aggressive growth patterns in both these countries, workers have a wide range of opportunities there, contributing to increased militancy and attrition, as they can easily find other jobs. In this sense, while workplace culture played an important role, the Philippines' upgrading success could also be viewed as a positive outcome of its late industrialization compared to its regional peers, where workers did not have many other options.

The second factor associated with the Philippines' entry and upgrading within the E&E and aerospace value chains was a combination of favourable investment regimes and effective EPZs operated by the Philippines Export Processing Zone Authority (PEZA).

Together, these features helped level the playing field with regional competitors. PEZA has a strong reputation for efficient and effective operations, with four-to-six year tax holidays followed by a competitive 5 per cent long-term tax rate, and a 70 per cent output export threshold that allowed firms to serve the domestic market. PEZA's institutional leadership also helped provide the necessary political stability in the face of the country's six-year presidential cycles. A General Seheme of Preferences (GSP) and GSP+ then provided duty-free access to the US and EU markets respectively. With the majority of foreign investment oriented to EPZs, these characteristics helped the country attract investors despite its relatively weak position in global competitiveness rankings compared to regional peers.[11]

Finally, the Philippines' particular evolutionary trajectory in these sectors

---

11 In 2015, even though improvements had been made, the country still ranked 95th out of 167 in Transparency International's Corruption Perception Index (Transparency International, 2015). In 2016, the World Bank Doing Business report ranked the country 103 out of 189 economies. This placed it well below the regional average, including below potential regional competitors like Vietnam, Thailand and Malaysia.

offers insights into its past success and future possibilities. Firms and human capital alike have followed a clear path of inter-sectoral upgrading, constantly being forced to adapt and seek out niche areas where they could compete. The stability of the A&T semiconductor sites in electronics instilled confidence in Japanese investors to establish wire harness operations in the country. As domestic electronics firms sought to diversify into more stable end-market niches that were too small and customized for the Philippines' regional competitors, the wire harness manufacturing experience illuminated potential strengths in the automotive sector. The dive into automotive electronics that followed opens up the possibility for an integrated industry that can export increasingly sophisticated wire harnesses across sectors; Mexico followed a similar trajectory with considerable success. The country's entry into aerospace – largely supported by its human capital and experience in the automotive industry – also has wide scope for upgrading. Companies are eager to protect their technology from Chinese firms, making the Philippines an attractive low-cost location in the region. Building on its focus on aerospace interiors and automotive wire harnesses, a natural upgrading path – also followed by Mexico – would be into the wire harness segments for aircraft.

To summarize, the Philippines' experience in these industries is an example of a country upgrading in manufacturing GVCs despite entrenched challenges. Where the country has succeeded, it used its advantages and experiences to reinforce its development across multiple sectors, positioning it to become a prominent player in specialized niches. From an institutional perspective, early growth prior to 2012 can largely be attributed to the natural comparative and competitive advantages of low-cost labour, combined with proactive approaches by PEZA to increase export-oriented manufacturing and bypass many of the challenges faced by the country. Subsequent efforts by DTI have helped to tap into the momentum generated by PEZA's early work; however, continued targeted strategies are required to build on this growth in the future.

References

Airbus. 2016. 'Orders & Deliveries.' *www.airbus.com*. Accessed 22 February 2016. Available at http://www.airbus.com/company/market/orders-deliveries/.

APEC Policy Support Unit. 2015. 'Manufacturing of Aircraft Control Systems in the Philippines.' In *Services in Global Value Chains: Manufacturing-Related Services*, 41–65. Singapore: Asia-Pacific Economic Cooperation.

Bamber, Penny and Gary Gereffi. 2013. *Costa Rica in the Aerospace Global Value Chain:*

Opportunities for Entry and Upgrading. Durham, N.C.: Center on Globalization, Governance and Competitiveness. Commissioned by the Costa Rican Ministry of Foreign Trade. Accessed 15 April 2017. Available at http://www.cggc.duke.edu/pdfs/2013_08_20_Ch4_Aerospace.pdf.

Bamber, Penny, Karina Fernandez-Stark, Gary Gereffi and Andrew Guinn. 2013. *Connecting Local Producers in Developing Countries to Regional and Global Value Chains.* Paris: Organisation for Economic Co-operation and Development. DOI: 10.1787/18166873.

Bamber, Penny, Stacey Frederick and Gary Gereffi. 2016. *The Philippines in the Aerospace Global Value Chain: Opportunities for Upgrading.* Durham, N.C.: Center on Globalization, Governance and Competitiveness. Commissioned by USAID and the Philippine Department of Trade and Industry. Accessed 15 April 2017. Available at http://www.cggc.duke.edu/pdfs/2016_Philippines_Aerospace_Global_Value_Chain.pdf.

Boeing. 2016. 'Orders & Deliveries.' Accessed 22 February 2016. Available at http://www.boeing.com/commercial/index.page - /orders-deliveries.

DTI. 2016a. 'Industry Development Council.' Accessed 10 March 2016. Available at http://industry.gov.ph/industry-development-council/.

———. 2016b. 'Manufacturing Resurgence Program.' Accessed 10 March 2016. Available at http://industry.gov.ph/manufacturing-resurgence-program/.

———. 2016c. *National Logistics Master Plan.* Manila: Department of Trade and Industry.

DTI, SPIK and BOI. 2014. *Philippine Chemicals Industry Roadmap.* Manila: Philippine Department of Trade and Investment. October.

EIU (The Economist Intelligence Unit). 'Power Sector Woes.' Accessed 14 May 2016. Available at http://www.eiu.com/industry/article/1173164301/power-sector-woes/2015-05-14.

Enerdata. 2014. 'Philippines High Electricity Price Is Keeping Foreign Investors Away.' 6 March. Accessed 10 March 2016. Available at http://www.enerdata.net/enerdatauk/press-and-publication/energy-news-001/philippines-high-electricity-price-keeping-foreign investors-away_26287.html.

Estoque, Willy. 2015. 'Moog Controls Corporation.' Paper presented at conference: Global Value Chains, Industrial Policy, and SME Integration in GVCs: Transformation Strategies for More Inclusive and Sustainable Growth, Makati City, 23 November.

Frederick, Stacey and Gary Gereffi. 2016. *The Philippines in the Electronics and Electrical Equipment Global Value Chain: Opportunities for Upgrading.* Durham, N.C.: Center on Globalization, Governance and Competitiveness. Commissioned by USAID and the Philippine Department of Trade and Industry. Available at http://www.

cggc.duke.edu/pdfs/2016_Philippines_Electronics_Electrical_Global_Value_
Chain.pdf.

IEA. 2013. *Southeast Asia Energy Outlook: World Energy Outlook Special Report.*
Paris: International Energy Agency and the Economic Research Institute for
ASEAN. September. Accessed 30 May 2016. Available at https://www.iea.
org/publications/freepublications/publication/SoutheastAsiaEnergyOutlook_
WEO2013SpecialReport.pdf.

ILO. 2014. *Wages in Asia and the Pacific: Dynamic but Uneven Progress.* Bangkok: ILO
Regional Office for Asia and the Pacific. Accessed 30 May 2016. Available at http://
www.ilo.org/wcmsp5/groups/public/---asia/---ro-bangkok/---sro-bangkok/
documents/publication/wcms_325219.pdf.

International Aerospace Quality Group. 2016. 'Online Aerospace Supplier Information
System.' Accessed 20 February 2016. Available at https://www.sae.org/?PORTAL_
CODE=IAQG.

JICA. 2014. *Roadmap for Transport Infrastructure Development for Metro Manila and its
Surrounding Areas.* Japan International Cooperation Agency (JICA) and National
Economic Development Authority (NEDA). Acccessed 30 May2016. Available at
http://www.jica.go.jp/english/news/field/2014/140925_03.html.

Kowalski, Przemyslaw, Javier Lopez Gonzalez, Alexandros Ragoussis and Cristian
Ugarte. 2015. *Participation of Developing Countries in Global Value Chains:
Implications for Trade and Trade-Related Policies.* Paris: OECD. December. DOI:
http://dx.doi.org/10.1787/5js33lfw0xxn-en.

KPMG. 2015. 'Infrastructure In-depth: Philippines.' Accessed 30 May 2016. Available
at https://home.kpmg.com/content/dam/kpmg/ph/pdf/InvestmentGuide/2015P
HInvestmentGuideInfrastructureIn-depthPhilippines.pdf.

Lohr, Steve 1984. 'A Rare Success in Philippines.' *The New York Times*, 13 August.
Accessed 8 December 2015. Available at http://www.nytimes.com/1984/08/13/
business/a-rare-success-in-philippines.html.

NEDA. 2011. *The Philippines Development Plan 2011-2016.* Manila: National
Economic Development Agency. Accessed 30 May 2016. Available at http://www.
neda.gov.ph/2013/10/21/philippine-development-plan-2011-2016/.

Niosi, Jorge and Majlinda Zhegu. 2010. 'Multinational Corporations, Value Chains
and Knowledge Spillover in the Global Aircraft Industry.' *International Journal of
Institutions and Economies* 2 (2): 109–41.

Niosi, Jorge and Majlinda Zhegu. 2005. 'Aerospace Clusters: Local or Global
Knowledge Spillovers?' *Industry and Innovation* 12 (1): 5–29.

PEZA. 2015. *Firm-Level PEZA Investment Data (through November).* Manila:
Philippine Economic Zone Authority (PEZA). Accessed 30 November 2016.
Available at http://www.peza.gov.ph/index.php/pezadownloads/27-downloads/
enterprise.

Philippines NSO. 2013. 2010 *Annual Survey of Philippine Business and Industry*

(ASPBI) - *Manufacturing Sector: Final Results.* Manila, Philippines. Accessed 27 November 2015. Available at https://psa.gov.ph/content/2010-annual-survey-philippine-business-and-industry-aspbi-manufacturing-sector-final-results.

PSA. 2007–2014. *Firm-Level Customs Trade Data.* Manila: Philippines Statistics Authority (PSA).Unpublished raw data provided on electronic drive.

————. 2016. *NSO's 2010 Census of Population and Housing (CPH).* Accessed 15 March 2016. Available at http://www.psa.gov.ph.

S&P Capital IQ. 2015. *Aerospace and Defense.* McGraw Hill Financial.

Sturgeon, Timothy, Jack Daly, Penny Bamber, Stacey Frederick and Gary Gereffi. 2016. *The Philippines in the Automotive Global Value Chain: Opportunities for Upgrading.* Durham, N.C.: Center on Globalization, Governance and Competitiveness. Commissioned by USAID and the Philippine Department of Trade and Industry. Accessed 15 April 2017. Available at http://www.cggc.duke.edu/pdfs/2016_Philippines_Automotive_Global_Value_Chain.pdf.

Taglioni, Daria and Deborah Winkler. 2016. *Making Global Value Chains Work for Development.* Washington, D.C.: World Bank.

UNComtrade. 2015. *United Nations Comtrade Database: Philippines Exports by All Partners, 2005–2014.* New York: United Nations Statistics Division (UNSD). Accessed 31 October 2015. Available at https://comtrade.un.org.

UNCTAD. 2016. 'UNCTAD STAT: "General Profile: Philippines".' Accessed 30 March 2017. Available at http://unctadstat.unctad.org/CountryProfile/GeneralProfile/en-GB/608/index.html.

United States Trade Representative. 2014. 'US Removes the Philippines from the Special 301 Watchlist.' April. Accessed May 2016. Available at https://ustr.gov/about-us/policy-offices/press-office/press-releases/2014/April/US-Removes-the-Philippines-from-the-Special-301-Watch-List.

World Bank. 2015. *Philippine Economic Update: Making Growth Work for the Poor.* Accessed May 2016. Available at http://www-wds.worldbank.org/external/default/WDSContentServer/WDSP/IB/2015/08/10/090224b082c25bc6/1_0/Rendered/PDF/Philippine0eco0th0work0for0the0poor.pdf.

————. 2016a. *World Development Indicators.* Accessed 30 May 2016. Available at http://data.worldbank.org/data-catalog/world-development-indicators.

————. 2016b. 'Foreign Direct Investment, Net Inflows (BoP, current US$).' Accessed 30 May 2016. Available at http://data.worldbank.org/indicator/BX.KLT.DINV.CD.WD.

World Economic Forum. 2016. 'Global Competitiveness Report: Philippines.' Accessed 30 March 2017. Available at http://reports.weforum.org/global-competitiveness-report-2015-2016/economies#economy=PHL.

6

Learning Sequences in Lower Tiers of India's Automotive Value Chain

Meenu Tewari

Introduction

With the rise of global value chains (Gvcs) and the tiered, internationally dispersed organization of production associated with Gvcs, important questions have arisen about the conditions under which small suppliers and dependent contractors in supplier countries can create value and rise up from their position at the bottom of these chains (Carré, 2017; Bair and Gereffi, 2001; Gereffi 1999). A vast literature has arisen on the processes and prospects of upgrading within Gvcs and production networks (Humphrey and Schmitz, 2002; Sturgeon *et al.*, 2008; see Pipkin and Fuentes, 2017, for an excellent review). A vexing puzzle, however, persists about the substantial variation in the upgrading and learning outcomes among similarly situated firms located in the region, the same policy environment and even in the same sector. For example, I interviewed over forty component suppliers in the Indian automotive industry between 2000 and 2013, following about fifteen of them longitudinally through repeated interviews over time. During this period – a time of immense churn and growth in the Indian automotive sector with the arrival of many global auto-manufacturers and their suppliers into the country – some of the smallest suppliers in my sample thrived while others of similar size and in similar locations stagnated or went out of business.

Why do some firms succeed in upgrading and growing while other similarly situated firms are unable to do so? How and under what conditions can small suppliers in the lower reaches of Gvcs and production networks learn to upgrade and improve their position within these value chains and networks?

This chapter contributes to the literature on upgrading among small producers in lower tiers of competitive Gvcs. It explores the learning sequences associated with the upgrading pathways of suppliers that are usually regarded to be at risk of being trapped at the bottom of fast-moving GVCs (Barnes and Kaplinsky, 2000), or vulnerable to being displaced by more powerful, sophisticated and better connected top-tier suppliers of global original equipment manufacturers (OEMs) (Humphrey, 2003). The question of learning and upgrading among small suppliers is important because the vitality of an economy's manufacturing sector and its ability to compete and innovate in the face of global competition is shaped in part by the depth, quality and robustness of its locally rooted supply base. The quality of a sector's lowest-tier suppliers provides a benchmark for the quality of this supply base. Upgrading the capabilities of the lowest-tier suppliers can lift up the entire sector by a notch. However, how do firms learn? Who can make it up the upgrading ladder and how do collective actors and the state assure that learning opportunities and 'resources go to the weakest actors who need to learn the most about learning' (Sabel and Reddy, 2003; Tendler, 2001)?

Drawing on interviews with fifteen Indian auto-component suppliers that I followed longitudinally between 2000 and 2013, and in particular case histories of three firms (ADM Auto Components, AF Autos and SF Ltd.), I explore the upgrading pathways of lower- and mid-tier suppliers in the Indian automotive sector. To do so, I examine the choices firms make as they embark on their upgrading path, including how they navigate their relationships with buyers and suppliers in the value chain, make choices about technology and business strategy, and when, whether and how these decisions induce learning. I also examine factors outside the firm – linkages with sectoral institutions and business associations as well as the state and external policy environments – to analyse when and under what conditions these relationships might trigger learning.

The firms I report on are based in Chennai, Pune and the National Capital Region (NCR). They are all currently second- or first-tier suppliers to global automotive OEMs that have located production facilities in India. They produce a variety of parts (sheet metal parts, rubber mountings, linings, precision tooling, high tensile fasteners, gear shifters, components of brake systems, and so on). Most of the firms currently employ 150–300 workers in a unit, though many of them began with less than 10 workers at the time of origin. Some of the suppliers have spun off several units and became part of a group or cluster of companies, all small, focusing on different components for different clients. I also draw on interviews conducted in other mid-tech manufacturing sectors in the same locations as the auto-component firms to draw out some contrasts.

My central finding is that two conditions seem to cut across the cases where learning and successful upgrading occurred relative to cases where it did not. The first was the presence of implicit or explicit performance standards that induced learning behaviour in the firms that had moved up the chain. The performance standards (or performance pressures) took varied forms and could occur at or be tied to any stage of the production process; they could stem from internal managerial decisions made by the firm or result from the nature of their interactions with their buyers, or be imposed by outside market or policy circumstances (such as by government programmes or judicial decisions linked to environmental standards as in the cases I report on). More importantly, the firms that learned the fastest did not just meet the imposed performance standard, but invested in integrating and internalizing the learning by applying it to other contexts and processes, thus deepening their grasp on it. The second pattern was that the successful firms had access to institutional support or supportive policies that helped diffuse the learning and adjustment – interestingly not only to the firm itself, but more widely among linked producers in the firm's network. In many cases these institutional supports involved mechanisms of group learning.

The rest of the chapter is organized as follows: after a brief description of the current state of the automotive industry in India, the following section examines learning sequences of small suppliers that succeeded in moving up the automotive value chain by drawing ethnographically on two case studies. It examines decisions and learning impulses from inside the firms, as well as those stemming from their outside institutional and policy environment. The next section examines cases in related sectors where the lack of performance standards has led to stalled growth and missed opportunities. The following section examines the case of larger suppliers and how some of them learned to build a global footprint. This section draws on the surprising case of a firm that upgraded by seeming to downgrade first for a period of time. The final section concludes the discussion.

Learning sequences among small auto-component suppliers

India's automotive industry has made rapid strides over the past forty years. The data suggests that it is transitioning from a high-cost, low-volume sector to a vibrant industry with cost-competitive production and rapidly growing exports

(Veeramani and Atukhorala, 2017). Between 1999 and 2016, India's share in the global production of passenger cars rose from 1.3 per cent to 5.1 per cent in terms of volume, and its rank among automobile producing countries increased from 16 to 6 during the same period. Passenger car production crossed the 1 million mark in 2004 and stands just under 4 million in 2017, and the sector attracted US$15.79 billion in foreign direct investment between 2000 and 2016, from US$195 million in 2000.[1] Many credit this growth to the arrival of world-class global automotive assemblers and their lead suppliers, and to India's growing insertion into automotive GPNs and export value chains. In this view, learning from global buyers, capability formation through participation in demanding global networks, technology diffusion through partnerships and joint ventures, and spill-overs of organizational and managerial knowledge through a variety of alliances have helped Indian auto producers progressively upgrade, modernize and grow (Sutton, 2004; Humphrey, 2003; Veeramani and Atukhorala, 2017; Kumaraswamy *et al.*, 2012).

However, as the vast literature on upgrading has pointed out, gains from insertion in global production networks are not automatic or even enduring (for the auto sector see McDermott and Carredoira, 2010; Humphrey, 2003; Kumaraswamy *et al.*, 2012; Tewari, 2001). The fact that many firms fail to capture value despite insertion in these networks and partnerships shows that there are difficulties inherent to learning and in creating value through participation in GPNs or other alliances (for a similar argument in the context of alliances and networks see Anand and Khanna, 2000; Gulati, Nohria and Zaheer, 2000). There are a large number of accounts of the disruption, takeover and displacement of existing suppliers, especially the smallest ones (see Kumaraswamy *et al.*, 2012; Humphrey and Memedovic, 2003; McDermott and Corredoira, 2010; Fluery, 2000; Barnes and Kaplinsky, 2000).

If upgrading sequences associated with participation in GVCs are not

---

1   Veeramani and Atukhorala (2017) report these striking numbers. They found that, between 1999 and 2016, India's share in the global production of passenger cars rose from 1.3 per cent to 5.1 per cent in terms of numbers, and domestically the share of passenger car production in total production increased from 56 per cent in 1985 to 82 per cent in 2015. The strong domestic market focus of the industry has begun to shift towards increasingly robust exports and India has emerged as an important hub for the production and export of small and compact cars. Between 2000 and 2015, India's global market share of compact car exports rose from barely 0.01 per cent in 2000 to 3.7 per cent in 2015, and for small cars, exports increased from 0.9 per cent to 5.3 per cent during the same period (Veeramani and Atukhorala, 2017). Clearly, the industry stands transformed.

automatic, then how does learning occur when firms do move up – especially smaller firms lower down the value chain? In this section, I draw on the upgrading trajectory of a small supplier, ADM Autos, based in Chennai, but now with factories near Delhi as well to explore the decisions it made as it moved up the value chain.

The story of ADM Autos: A view from inside the firm

ADM Auto Components was a small no-tier brake-shoe manufacturer for the domestic Indian aftermarket in 1993.[2] Seventeen years later, when I interviewed the firm in 2010, it had grown from no-tier status to being a valued, SQ certified supplier for Hyundai's top brake manufacturers and for several other OEM suppliers.[3] AF Auto Components, another small supplier which produced exhaust, engine and gearbox mountings, similarly rose from the bottom tier of the aftermarket in 2000 to the status of an upper-tier supplier and exporter ten years later when I interviewed them. Yet, during the same period (2000–13), several other similarly sized firms had stagnated and some had gone out of business.

In this section we analyse the trajectory of ADM Auto Components (ADM from now on), its key turning points and its learning sequences.

Modest origins, building a reputation and staged learning processes

ADM's history illustrates a business strategy that was common among several of the small suppliers that had succeeded in capturing value as they moved up the supply chain. These firms started small with a single focus on simple products for the domestic aftermarket. But what distinguished them from others that remained stuck in these downmarket niches was that the better performers used their time in the replacement market to build skills, learn strategically to produce at progressively better quality, and to build a reputation. It was often this reputation that brought them their first major order from larger buyers higher up in the value chain. This breakthrough order, in turn, became a turning point in their growth trajectory.

ADM started out as an artisanal parts maker in 1993, focusing on simple components for automotive brake systems for the aftermarket. In the beginning, ADM did not have its own factory but shared space with a sister concern that

2   The names of firms that requested anonymity have been changed or abbreviated.
3   Supplier Quality (SQ) certification provided by the Hyundai group.

produced sheet metal parts. Even though the products they manufactured were for the replacement market, ADM focused on one thing at a time and sought to learn everything they could about the product. They cultivated distributors in the market who would give them the space to make mistakes and learn, and who would also give them feedback. This feedback and relationship-intensive phase of the local aftermarket, where one is engaged with distributors with whom one shares social ties and spatial embeddedness, is not new and has been noted by many scholars in this field (Nadvi, 1999; Tewari, 1999; Schmitz and Knorringa, 2000; Humphrey and Schmitz, 2002). ADM said their attitude was to use their ties with distributors to build a 'strong reputation' and become known for quality, willingness to learn and reliability.[4] They were very open to anything that could help them with that goal: taking a loss on errors, not cutting corners, listening to their buyers. This openness and focus on quality became crucial later on in their dealings with OEM suppliers.

It was their reputation that brought them their first major contact with an OEM's supply chain. A vendor development agent from Allied Nippon, which supplied brake systems to various Japanese OEMs, visited their factory (the one ADM shared with the sheet metal business) with five brake system components to ask if ADM would be interested in developing them (developing here means that while the specifications come from the buyer, the supplier figures out the process of producing them, and that in turn determines the quality and reliability of the output; the cost of developing the prototype is also borne by the supplier with no guarantee of an order). ADM agreed to develop the parts and their prior investment in their capabilities helped them to successfully develop the components not only to the quality required but at a speed and cost that was better than what Allied Nippon expected. ADM received their first major order from Allied Nippon. As the orders grew, ADM spun off a separate factory dedicated to producing brake system related components – brake shoes, brake pads and others. ADM saw the investment in an independent factory as essential: 'It focuses the attention of the operator on precision and quality [if you have] dedicated lines and technologies for a dedicated product' (ADM interview, 2010).

As their link with Allied Nippon became consolidated, their reputation grew. They then reached out to other Tier 2 suppliers and were approached by other OEM brake suppliers as well (Rane, Roland Brakes, Sundaram Brake Linings, SBL and Continental). ADM gradually began producing for a number of Tier 2 suppliers. Once they had produced for several Tier 2 suppliers, they

---

4   Interview with ADM Auto conducted by the author in 2010, National Capital Region.

were approached by one of Hyundai's Tier 1 suppliers. Eventually they now produce for several Tier 1 OEM suppliers – Nissan Brakes, Hyundai Brakes India, Bosch and Mando Brakes, among others.

ADM's supply strategy was interesting. It traced a path of strategic diversification of its customer base. As the firm learned how to meet the demands of suppliers belonging to one level, they moved up to suppliers belonging to the next (higher) level, with more stringent demands. From the single focus with which they began, they had now learned to cross-pollinate their learning and draw lessons from the standards that different OEMs held, and applied that learning to their own production strategy. Gaining experience by working with firms across platforms, they credit the development of their skills to having first-hand knowledge of what it took to satisfy different kinds of customers. 'We started with one company – second-tier [Allied Nippon], learned from them, and then supplied to all second tiers. Then we supplied to one first tier, learned from them, and now we supply to almost all companies making brake systems for OEMs. We started with loose components and now we are moving into sub-assemblies for direct OEM suppliers and exports to South Korea' (ADM interview, 2010).

Hyundai and Maruti Suzuki are its major customers today. In 2006, ADM received an award from Hyundai for being a 'most valued group supplier' for their zero-defect performance and timely delivery. They also completed the assessment for and successfully received an SQ certification from Hyundai. By 2013, they had a plant in NCR to supply sub-assemblies (on behalf of their first-tier buyer) directly to the OEM Maruti Suzuki, and a second one in Chennai to supply Mando Brakes and Hyundai Brakes India, direct suppliers for Hyundai (ADM interview, 2010).

This trajectory of upgrading illustrates how ADM intentionally or unintentionally crafted a staged and sequenced learning process. Starting with the goal of learning and building its reputation during the 'easier' phase in the replacement market, ADM progressively shifted its sights higher as it learned to deal with the demands at each stage fully before adapting to the demands of the next higher tier of buyers. Eventually it moved from components to sub-assemblies through a strategy of learning the requirements of each stage of work well. It did not 'expand upwards too quickly', remaining focused on 'maintaining our reputation' for 'quality and delivery' at each stage (interview, ADM Components, 2010).

Auditors as frontline disseminators of standards and tacit knowledge

The company's search for ways to learn and build up its capacities reveals an important difference between how small, lower-tier suppliers such as ADM learn and how larger suppliers that have direct access to OEMs learn. In contrast to the reciprocal access that the latter have to OEMs' engineering and vendor development departments, the ADM case showed that buyer audits and auditors can potentially become important sources of learning for smaller tier suppliers provided the supplier cultivates an openness to these ties.

In its early days in the replacement market, ADM had been very focused on its distributors for feedback and suggestions that it then implemented on the shop floor. As it moved to OEM-driven value chains, distributors became substituted by third-party auditors as interlocutors. Entering, and then rising within OEM-linked chains required submitting to audits initially by upper tier suppliers ADM did business with (Mando Brakes, Hyundai Brakes India, Continental, and so on) and then to the OEM's own supplier quality certifications. These audits can become a farce, a superficial accounting exercise and much has been written about the shallowness or incompleteness of third-party audits (with respect to labour outcomes see O'Rourke, 2000). But ADM reported treating them as a resource. When the various auditors arrived, '…We did not hide defects or pretended that we knew everything. We asked for suggestions and what we could do to improve. The auditors appreciated our openness and shared a lot of information with us about good practices, the approach of other firms, especially the Korean firms they audited' (ADM interview, 2010).

This was especially evident in the assessments they went through to obtain Hyundai's SQ certification in 2005–06. They benefited greatly from this knowledge sharing and reported how it was central for not only achieving the standards for Hyundai's certification, but also making other improvements that helped them improve their performance across the board. The three areas that they singled out for improvement were: ways to achieve zero-defect compliance, processes they could adopt to improve delivery times and, most importantly for the company, information about technology upgrades that have been crucial to increasing quality, improving productivity and cutting costs. By contrast, ADM reported how another supplier of Hyundai's first tier in the same industrial area was much less open with the auditors, which led to a tense and strained relationship with the company. This supplier was eventually cut out of the supply chain (ADM interview, 2010).

These audits and certification processes also stimulated a more inclusive learning process. This inclusive learning impulse came from Hyundai. After ADM completed the SQ certification, Hyundai asked it to train other Tier 1 and Tier 2 suppliers with the knowledge that it had gained through the SQ mark.[5] ADM trained 25–26 firms, some of whom were its own customers as well as potential customers. Interestingly, while Hyundai had earmarked funds for this downward diffusion process, ADM chose to bear most of the cost of this additional training. It was a way to cultivate goodwill and build social capital within its network. ADM saw the sharing of knowledge as a way to give back and 'gain status and improve its image' in the eyes of their peers. The image it sought to cultivate was of a company associated with good quality production and good performance; but it was also an image of a company that believed not just in competition, but also co-operation (ADM interview, 2010). ADM explained how this helped them build a wider network they could outsource to and cultivate new reciprocal relationships, and better absorb the practices and standards themselves by teaching them to their others in their circle.

Under some conditions then, auditors can become front-line agents in the diffusion of tacit knowledge to small suppliers – sharing knowledge about good production practices, technologies, market knowledge, and insights into technical and organizational trouble-shooting. Audits – and certification processes – can thus impose performance standards that carry an important learning impulse for the firm, and this learning impulse can spill over into other linked firms in the network beyond the company that was formally certified.

Calibrating work-processes to an internal performance standard

For a company that started out as a no-tier replacement market supplier with a handful of workers, and now employing 150 workers, ADM has come a long way. However, what is more important for their learning strategy was what the company did with the knowledge it gained from exposure to the processes followed by the various tiers of customers it supplied. While it responded to each buyer's requirements based on the different specifications and drawings

---

5   Indeed, in my interviews with first and second tier suppliers of Honda and Toyota there is a similar expectation by the OEM to have training passed down by suppliers they trained to others in the chain. ADM also insisted that even before earning the SQ mark it had a practice of sharing the knowledge it had gained from auditors not only with its own suppliers and collaborators, but also laterally with other firms with whom it had social (not business) ties (ADM interview, 2010).

that the buyers provided, ADM internalized the tacit knowledge it gained by listening, comparing, learning and then adapting these lessons to upgrade its own capacities and production processes.

It also involves listening to various *less formal* and tacit demands of buyers, navigating and figuring out what to prioritize in order to meet diverse demands. Despite individual variation among buyers, ADM said there is an unsurprising common thread to all: 'Cost, quality, delivery time.' Of these, what do you prioritize? Reading between the lines, ADM said it had learned that it is critical to prioritize quality first – 'For ADM quality is #1.' This is not only because the products they manufacture are precision brake systems – hence, safety is a crucial non-negotiable feature. But for ADM the real insight was that a focus on quality would have a disciplining effect that could bring all other demands in line. The question to them was how to attain quality while keeping costs down and delivering on time. This has led to a focus on three things: (*a*) partnerships, (*b*) training and (*c*) technology.

In practice, partnership meant that they have moved from trying to do everything in-house to building networks they can outsource to. The diffusing of training (such as in the SQ experience above) to others in their supply chain allowed them to outsource without compromising on quality. They also built ties with intermediaries with specialized skills that they themselves did not possess. For example, ADM's tool-and-die-making processes now includes sophisticated technology partners who have global alliances of their own and can access high quality know-how, including partners who work with (or supply to) Korean and German tool and die companies. They have also learned that technology and strategic automation can increase quality and precision while cutting costs and production time and raising productivity and output.

Indeed, a pattern that stood out across many small suppliers such as ADM was one of an aggressive absorption of technology and strategic automation of production processes. The impetus for technical change of this sort came from a diversity of sources – buyers, their auditors and vendor development agents – but the reasons for technology adoption by suppliers were productivity gains and cost-cutting, a euphemism for reducing the number of their employees. For example, ADM stated that 'We always advance with our customers' with respect to technology. One of their auditors had told them about an automatic '8 for 1' machine from Japan that would allow them to complete most operations in a single stage instead of eight different steps, leading to a drastic reduction in time and requiring a smaller workforce. With the new machines that ADM was in the process of installing, they would need only five machines instead of fifty-two, and could cut down their workforce from ten to two per station for the same amount of work. The Poka Yoke system they were implementing also meant that they could work with shop-floor workers with lower-level skills, in comparison to the older system where skilled workers were essential on the shop floor.[6]

Ironically, this new system has led not just to a reduction of the workforce, but to a segmentation of the workforce that remains. The 'top level' workers – engineers, research and development (R&D) personnel, managers, unit heads, skilled operators and marketing executives – were retained with enlarged jobs, higher wages and benefits, and clear career paths for improved retention. By contrast the shop-floor workforce was cut drastically and replaced by younger, less-skilled workers, many of them on contract (ADM interview, 2010). This pattern was common across many better-performing small firms in my sample. Some suppliers had even agreed to shop-floor unionization in return for a revised staffing structure and new wage rates (higher wages for fewer people) against the backdrop of automation. What was good for the firm was not necessarily good for (all) its workers. While the labour strategies (and outcomes) of the upgrading process of small firms in GVCs is a subject that deserves a separate discussion, it is clear that economic upgrading, even in the lower tiers of the supply chain where the social distance between owners and their workers is not very vast, does not necessarily result in social benefits for all.

Institutional supports outside the firm

A second broad pattern associated with the ability of small suppliers to learn and upgrade their position in the automotive supply chain was related to the presence of institutional supports outside the firm that aided their adoption of improved production practices. In this section, we discuss the group learning initiative that firms like ADM Autos, AF Autos and a half dozen other small auto-component suppliers that I have tracked over time have had access to.

---

6   On the face of it, it might seem surprising that in a low-wage, labour-surplus country where interest rates are especially high, even small firms are rushing to invest in capital-intensive processes and very high levels of automation. My colleague Professor Sandip Sarkar, however, made an astute observation. He clarified that the perverse outcome of increasing capital intensity among small firms in India is the result of policies in India that make capital 'cheap'. This is because India allows annual depreciation rates of 20–25 per cent (compared to not more than 10 per cent in most other countries). This enables firms to write off their capital investments and equipment purchases quickly and not worry about machine productivity. I thank Professor Sarkar for this insight.

This programme was originally piloted by the United Nation's Industrial Development Organization (UNIDO) in partnership with the government (Ministry of Industry) and the Indian Automotive Component Manufacturers Association (ACMA), among others, in 1999 as a way to mentor and help small suppliers improve their competitiveness by adopting high-performance work practices, particularly those associated with the Toyota production system.

The Indian automotive industry was at a critical turning point in the late 1990s and faced intensified global competition after liberalization and exposure to newly arrived global assemblers in the sector. Suzuki, Ford, Hyundai, Mitsubishi, Fiat and others had set up joint ventures in the country and brought in many of their own global suppliers. Amidst the ongoing churn and restructuring in the sector UNIDO's experiment in collaboration with sector associations and the government was one institutional effort to stabilize and improve the performance of local suppliers. Once the pilot ended in 2000, it was adopted and offered by the Automotive Component Manufacturers Association (ACMA) with financial and technical support from UNIDO and the Ministry of Industry. We will also see how other changes in the institutional environment of the auto sector in that period (1999–2000) such as the indirect effects of judicial rulings on emissions standards also triggered learning through the imposition of higher standards in the Indian automotive sector, and reinforced the importance of training programmes such as UNIDO and ACMA's in helping small firms adapt.

A group learning and mentoring model

The group learning programme is centred around a mentoring model. Industry associations (ACMA) and UNIDO convene small and medium auto-component producers in groups of twenty and bring them together with a few top tier suppliers for focused shop-floor centred learning.

UNIDO's original pilot was initiated in 1999 in collaboration with a private industry sponsor (FIAT), Indian industry associations such as ACMA, Automotive Research Association of India (ARAI), the Ministry of Industry and two European academic partners (INSEAD and the Prince of Wales Business Leaders Forum). The programme's objective was to diffuse practices associated with the Toyota production system among small and medium auto-component firms to upgrade their capacities and help them compete in a globalized industry.[7] The pilot was based in Pune, India, and brought together

---

7   See Samii *et al.* (2002) for details of this early experiment.

twenty small and medium component producers with higher-tier (first tier) suppliers (such as Bharat Forge and others) to engage in an eight-month-long programme of group learning and mentoring focused on the factory floor. The activities involved a ten-day shop-floor immersion programme where mentors provided step by step assistance to small suppliers on incorporating elements of the Toyota System into their current work organization. It also involved some classroom training and two study tours to award-winning factories in India (for example, Deming prize winners). The pilot also included international exposure through a visit by the group to an international automotive fair in Europe where they could engage in bilateral discussions with potential overseas partners. Finally, it included in-house training by UNIDO experts on enterprise resource planning (ERP) and financial planning software (see Samii *et al.*, 2002).

The pilot was popular (interview with ACMA, 2003). Many credited it with productivity improvements on the shop floor, and data from UNIDO and ACMA appear to support these claims (see Table 6.1). But the initial programme was also expensive and relied on one global sponsor, FIAT, that was contributing to general purpose upgrading of suppliers who were not part of its own supply network. FIAT exited after the pilot. But the auto-component association, ACMA, took over implementation of a modified programme with the support from UNIDO and the Ministry of Industry.

Table 6.1 Aggregate improvements among the participants of UNIDO's team learning initiative, 2002

(n = 20)	
Average reduction in lead time	52%
Increase in shop-floor training	0–238 /month
Drop in absenteeism	39%
Introduction of standard operating procedures	54%
Space saving	25%

Source: UNIDO (1999); also see Samii *et al.* (2002, 1001).

The modified version of the programme which continues till today is similar to the original but has no overseas tours. It runs for two years instead of eight months, and participants now pay to enter the programme. Several of the participants whom I interviewed had paid a fee of ₹ 70,000 or about US$1,100 per year. Each group of twenty small and medium suppliers meets with their higher-tier mentors on the shop floors of the participants by turn. Together with their mentors and ACMA officials, they problem-solve specific issues and learn about adopting high-performance work practices (the Toyota system as in the original pilot). They discuss concrete upgrading strategies and learn about relevant technologies. Factory-based learning is supplemented by instruction on the adoption of ERP technologies and financial planning. The firms also still tour the factories of award-winning top-tier suppliers.

Firms like ADM Autos and others who have succeeded in upgrading their position in the value chain reported several benefits of participation in the networked learning programme. These included finding customized solutions from their peers in the mentoring group to specific problems about quality, learning about new technologies, gaining an understanding of how some firms achieved continuous improvement, experiencing the importance of collaboration and, in general, coming away with 'a changed mind set'. AF Auto components, a small supplier of exhaust, engine and gearbox mountings that had participated in the programme in 2005–06, reported how it 'changed ... the thinking of people in his factory'. It also embedded the firm in networks that they had been able to draw upon later – even after the programme ended (interview with AF Auto Components, 2010).

Interestingly, some of the firms that had not yet participated in the programme said they were in the process of improving and upgrading some of their production processes *in order to* be ready to participate in the cluster learning programme and be able to absorb its lessons. The learning and upgrading effects of the programme were thus apparent even before suppliers participated in it (interview with AST Auto Components, 2010). The presence of supports in the institutional environment of small suppliers that can aid their adoption of progressively higher production processes and quality standards can shape the ability of small suppliers to move up to higher or more stable positions in their production network in important ways.

When policy induces learning (and when it does not)

It is also noteworthy that the general milieu in which programmes such as those described above have been designed and offered to small suppliers in the automotive industry has been one where important judicial decisions and policy shifts have pushed the Indian automotive industry to adopt progressively higher emission standards in the domestic market. While mass emission norms were first introduced in India in 1991 (for petrol cars and 1992 for diesel cars) immediately after the opening up of the economy to trade and foreign direct investment (FDI), more stringent standards based on international norms (European mostly) were first introduced in 2000–01 when standards based on Euro I and II norms were introduced in many parts of the country. Since then stricter standards have been introduced at regular intervals with Bharat Stage IV (Euro IV) norms introduced in 2010 and enforced across the country in mid-2017, and BS VI (Euro VI) set to be adopted by 2020.[8] This environment of continuous upgrading of emission-related environmental standards has also created continuous pressures for adaptation by auto manufacturers, pushing firms to change the way they do business. These regulations have imposed performance standards on firms and brought upgrading pressures not just on the final assemblers, but also on their component suppliers down the chain.

Though most of the regulatory changes have been planned, and firms have had time adjust, there was an important moment of unexpected pressure to upgrade in 1999–2000 just when the group learning pilot was being adopted by ACMA, with the active support of the Ministry and UNIDO. This pressure came from an unforeseen ruling by the judiciary on environmental and emissions matters, and made it more likely that the group training initiative aimed at helping small firms upgrade was carried forward with government and industry support.

In 1998, a New Delhi-based non-profit organization, the Centre for Science and Environment (CSE), filed a public interest litigation in the Indian Supreme Court arguing that the proliferation of vehicles not compliant with Euro I and Euro II standards on Delhi roads was causing extensive damage to public health, especially the health of children. The Indian motor vehicle industry had already settled on a timetable to meet Euro I by mid-2000 (and then Euro II five years later). However, the litigation changed all that. In a ruling in favour of the NGO, the 'green bench' of the Supreme Court advanced the dates of enforcement of Euro I standards for both petrol and diesel cars to June 1999, earlier scheduled for April 2000, and advanced compliance with Euro II norms by five years, to April 2000 (*Down to Earth*, 1999). This ruling applied to New Delhi, and was later extended to other Indian metropolitan cities as well.

As a reporter present in the court room on the day of the judgment noted, 'The mood at ... Court number 1-A was anything but jubilant. The

---

8   See Society of Indian Automobile Manufacturer's account of the history of emission norms in India: http://www.siamindia.com/technical-regulation.aspx?mpgid=31&pgidtrail=33, accessed 25 November 2017.

judges [presided over by the Chief Justice of India] came down heavily on the government and the automobile manufacturers, who asked for "breathing space and time". "Shall we give you breathing space to comply with regulations, or shall we worry about those who have to breathe with the help of cortisone?'" (Malik, 1999).[9] The Supreme Court also noted that while automobile manufacturers in India supplied European customers with cars compliant with Euro II standards, similar cars had not been introduced in the Indian market (Malik, 1999). The ruling created a dilemma for the Ministry of Industry and the auto assemblers. The ministry, which was allied with the auto industry and its associations in appealing against the Supreme Court's timeline (and later won a little reprieve in terms of time), had at the same time to oversee the implementation of the certification standard, over which there was considerable confusion.

An indirect outcome of this new environmental ruling was that it triggered a long period of adjustment, cooperation and collective action between the sector's auto assemblers, associations the government, and other private and quasi-public sector institutions that led to the upgrading of many small suppliers involved in the manufacture of engine-related components. Technologically, the issue of meeting the more stringent Euro I standards was not very complex. As the president of the Society of Indian Automobile Manufacturers (SIAM) said,

> Fortunately, we [the Indian industry] had the technology to meet the new standards. It was a matter of substituting one type of component for another. The problem was to get the funding that was needed to carry out the changes in a short time, and all at once. (Interview with SIAM 2005)

The real challenge was to also 'train and transmit the changes to small suppliers' of engine-components lower down the supply chain and get them to be compliant with the revised norms in a timely manner. Although the court eventually relented and gave the industry a small extension, the ruling and the foreshortened timeline for compliance pushed various automotive industry associations – there was an urgency and interest on the part of the auto-manufacturers association (SIAM), the component manufacturers association (ACMA) and the government to join hands to support compliance across the sector (interview with SIAM 2005; *Indian Express*, 1999).

The presence and continuation of the hands-on, group learning, cluster development experiment that UNIDO had just pioneered in 1999 thus makes

---

9   The three-judge bench was comprised of Chief Justice A. S. Anand, Justice M. J. Rao and Justice Santosh N. Hegde.

sense in light of these outer pressures that helped embed a programme now ACMA and the government support. The environmental ruling on emissions by the Supreme Court continued to bring higher performance standards to bear on small suppliers and there was now a related programme that helped some firms learn and upgrade their production processes. The emission policy had an upgrading effect. This can be contrasted with other kinds of policies that might protect producers from competition or subsidize small producers but may not trigger learning or upgrading. In analysing how and under what conditions firms learn, the foregoing example shows that policies that induce learning are those that directly or indirectly help raise performance standards. By contrast, other policies, notably protectionist policies, protect without inducing learning.

When the lack of performance standards stalls growth

In this section, I draw upon a few interviews from outside the automotive sector (specifically the power sector) to illustrate how the lack of standards can trap production chains in low quality equilibria.

The low quality trap

Like many public sector companies, public utilities in India award projects though a tender system and applicants are judged at two levels. First, they are required to meet a set of technical standards, which, according to the respondents, are quite basic – adequate but rudimentary. Once a bidder qualifies on technical grounds they are evaluated on their financial offer, with the contract going to the lowest bidder. Therefore, even if a company comes up with a technically better product or an innovative technical process, they run the risk of being out-bid on price. The main objective of bidders is to somehow meet the basic technical parameters rather than to propose new things or new ways of doing things. This 'least-common-denominator' approach to technical standards eliminates incentive on the part of supplier firms to innovate or move towards the industry frontier. 'If [the government's] technical standards are higher and the norms more stringent, then better products will come up' (IEEMA interview, 2013).

A second key issue that reinforces this low-level equilibrium trap is India's electric power subsidies. On the face of it, the utilities' use of a no-frills bidding process to keep prices down is not unusual – it happens around the world. However, steep power sector subsidies create an added negative feedback loop that further retards the sector's technical growth (IEEMA interview, 2013). The politics around power prices is well known. Electricity prices are kept artificially low, which has a ripple effect throughout the value chain from generation to transmission to distribution. Since power companies have to provide electricity at a low price, they have to produce it at an even lower price. This leads to 'cutting down project costs by the use of cheap products, or inferior quality equipment', which eventually traps the system in a low-technology, low-efficiency, low-productivity cycle (IEEMA interview, 2013).

When asked about cutting costs through upgrading or innovation, the response was that most generation and distribution companies had very low profit margins, and given the unsustainably low prices at which they had to deliver power, and the losses they had to deal with, many were in the red and 'there is no money to make new investments and [firms] are not interested in upgrading' (IEEMA interview, 2013). As a consequence, the price pressures that cascade down the chain have an adverse effect on innovation and R&D, creating long-term sector-wide weaknesses that saddle the industry with obsolete and lagging technology.

The irony is that in reality, the purported cost-saving obtained through unrealistic price-setting and imposing barely acceptable minimal technical standards at the front end proves illusory and only ends up hurting the sector. They add to costs rather than saving them, first, by discouraging modernization that keeps high-cost system-wide inefficiencies locked in and, second, because of low technical standards to which the sector is held and the 'fixes' adopted by firms to cut costs, there may be frequent breakdowns, work stoppages and productivity losses, which end up adding to costs over time. In contrast, a life-cycle view of costs – unit costs and efficiencies over time – would reveal that fostering continuous innovation, learning and upgrading within the sector by incrementally pushing up standards in gradual congruence with global norms would lead to greater cost savings from the better performance of the equipment and the higher productivity of the system as a whole. These benefits could then be passed on to the consumer or invested in R&D. Some policymakers and government officials are beginning to look at life-cycle costs and are of the view that if a product is priced higher but has a longer and trouble-free life cycle, it should be preferred over the lowest-cost model (IEEMA and Das interviews, 2013).

Thus, a product's primary end-users can significantly shape the prospects of upgradation of the suppliers. In this case, where public parastatals and power companies dominate, the government could leverage its presence strategically as a demanding buyer to foster innovation and help raise standards in the industry, instead of keeping them down.

Downgrading to upgrade

After having looked at the various ways in which performance standards can aid learning sequences that support upgrading, especially for small firms, I examine a case of upgrading in a larger, upper-tier supplier where learning came from deliberately choosing to downshift to a simpler product and to produce it in larger volumes.

We generally associate upgrading with moving from lower to progressively higher-value nodes in a chain, or from low to high-value activities. However, as I try to show in this section, sometimes the skills and knowledge a firm needs to gain in order to move up or capture a larger share of value in the supply chain may come from downshifting rather than upshifting. SF, a US$470 million company, is a top-tier supplier of all kinds of high tensile fasteners, power metallurgy, pumps and assemblies, power train components, hot and cold forged parts and other components (SF Annual Report, 2016). Founded in 1962, it is part of a storied automotive components conglomerate based in southern India. In its sixty-five-year history, SF has moved steadily to produce higher-value, more technologically sophisticated and more complex components for OEMs.

In 1991, SF decided to bid for – and won – a contract to produce high tensile radiator caps (oil filler caps and petrol filler caps) for General Motors's (GM) global platform. The component was simple, standardized and had a modest unit value of US$0.86. Once it had the order, SF bought out a UK radiator cap making plant and used that equipment and technology to set up a dedicated plant for GM's product, setting up a just-in-time supply chain for GM's US plant. Eventually, it came to supply 80 per cent of GM's requirement of radiator caps (at one time becoming the sole supplier) and won GM's 'Supplier of the Year' award five times in a row.

Although the radiator cap was a simple and standardized component with little room for design or upgrading in itself, it was very significant that this contract made SF one of the first Indian auto-component suppliers to successfully penetrate a leading manufacturer's global supply platform (and become a sole supplier) that produced according to the scale, quality and delivery times of one of the world's leading OEMs (G. P. interview, 2013). As a manager at SF explained, this taught them extremely valuable skills – producing and managing the delivery of a product of world-class quality on a scale at which they could not have produced with a focus on the domestic market alone. It gave them skills in quality management and, more importantly, in logistics. Eventually they built a dedicated business around logistics which has served them well as global competition – within and outside India – has intensified in the auto industry, where timeliness and delivery are critical assets. Even if the product was simple, tremendous learning had taken place, which spilled over widely in the overall management of their business.

However, things changed with the radiator cap business with GM in 2011. Just as SF was negotiating with GM to revise the price of the caps they produced to US$1.03, given rising input and production costs, they were outbid by a global competitor who was able to supply the same part to GM for US$0.43, or 60 per cent less than the cost SF was quoting. By the end of 2011, SF's orders from GM for the radiator cap fell to less than one-third of previous levels (G.P. interview, 2013).

The surprise was that SF was outbid on price not by a lower-cost manufacturer from an emerging or low-income market (China, Vietnam or some other emerging economy), but by an Austrian firm. The Austrian company, which entered the radiator cap business in 2010 in the wake of the recession in Europe, was able to supply the caps at less than half the cost of SF because it had opted for a fully automated production process. This generated a lower cost product of greater precision, more consistent quality and shorter turn-around times (G. P. interview, 2013; Tewari and Veeramani, 2016).

On the face of it, this experience might illustrate the kind of dangers faced by suppliers after being inserted onto major global platforms of leading automakers and their value chains. A twenty-year-old relationship seemed to have soured over a small monetary difference. Underneath the surface, however, things are more complex. GM and SF still have a strong relationship and SF still supplies a third of GM's radiator caps. Moreover, when it became clear that under present manufacturing conditions in India, cutting costs by the order of magnitude GM required was not possible for SF, GM shifted the order to the lower bidder, but at the same time gave SF orders for an alternative, higher-value product: a US$6 shifter that could better absorb the new cost structures. SF thus diversified and moved up the value chain by a notch. Meanwhile, other global buyers (Ford) approached SF to supply radiator caps to them, and SF's radiator business is still running at near-full capacity.

The important point, therefore, is that although there were fluctuations in its business with GM, the skills SF gained through the twenty years of close association (which continues at a different level) were important to its overall growth trajectory. SF's logistics business and experience has become a significant separate venture in its own right, operating on both domestic and global platforms. Its reputation with GM helped build a network inside and outside GM that led to new orders and higher-value business later on. In the wake of the crisis described here, industrial upgrading did take place, albeit through a non-linear pathway, and was accompanied by a deepening of the firm's place within global networks – not a withdrawal.

Conclusions

In this chapter, I have examined the question of how learning can be induced among small, lower-tier suppliers at the bottom of GVCs. Drawing on field work and grounded evidence from the Indian auto-components sector, the chapter explores why some firms can rise up from no-tier status to much higher and stable positions in the value chain while others in the same sector and location are not able to similarly upgrade. To understand this variation, I examined how suppliers lower down the value chain built up their capacities, how they improved their position within these chains, and what the characteristics were of the learning sequences associated with the upgrading trajectories of small suppliers who succeeded in moving up the value chain. The picture that emerged was one of 'everyday forms of learning' that set better performing firms apart from others, and also conditioned how they engaged with and across other firms in their network. Such firms made everyday strategic decisions in ways that put pressure on them to catch mistakes early, learn and make constant adjustments for improvements. In a world where the demand is constantly to lower costs, deliver on time and supply good quality output, good performing firms chose to prioritize clear goals that carried with them built-in inducements for continuous learning – such as prioritizing reputation for quality on time as in the case of ADM autos – and then learning from every single interaction with their collaborators, buyers and distributors how they could stick to their goal. This generated multiple learning opportunities and other related qualities (low cost, innovation, and so on) which then became outcomes or by-products of this single-minded focus on one key goal of quality. Better performers were also open with their buyers and interlocutors about what they did not know, and opened themselves up to learning and intense feedback. As ADM moved from supplying to the replacement market to supplying sub-assemblies to

OEMs such as Hyundai and Maruti Suzuki via their first-tier suppliers, it first learned everything it could at each stage it was at before moving up. After it supplied to one second-tier firm, it first tried to supply to all other second-tier firms, before moving to a first-tier supplier. It was striking to find out the better performers even used auditors as sources for comparison and learning about good practices of higher-tier firms. Such firms also diffused laterally and downwards to their own suppliers the learning that they themselves had gained, thus creating excellence in their entire sourcing network – an important way to ensure consistent quality in a networked world. In sum then, for firms that succeeded in moving up their chains, successful learning was an 'everyday process'– it was embedded in all that the firm did, in the strategic decisions it made within the firm as well as how it engaged with its relationships outside the firm. At times this was aided by the presence of supporting associations and institutions in response to positive pressures from the prevailing policy environment. The common thread was the presence of self-induced or outwardly induced (buyer or policy induced) performance standards, often implicit, that generated learning sequences.

In some cases these strategic decisions of the better performers included seeming downgrading, in order to learn skills or capacities (producing at large volumes as in the SF case) that eventually allowed them to upgrade with greater effectiveness.

To conclude, my argument in this chapter, based on the examples and ethnographies of suppliers that succeeded in improving their positions in their value chains, is: for firms in late developing countries that are competing in global production networks from positions well within the knowledge and technology frontiers, learning often takes place in quite ordinary or even downmarket forms or spaces (or at least begins there). Among others, two factors seem to set apart the learning sequences of those who do succeed in upgrading themselves. These are the presence of the discipline of implicit or explicit, self-induced or other-induced performance standards in the upgrading pathways, or in policy regimes that impinge on firms from outside. Whether directly or (more often) indirectly, when firms put pressure on themselves to respond to such standards, they learn and act in upgrading-inducing ways. The second factor that seems to matter is whether there are institutional supports available in the firm's broader production network, or policy environment that can aid this type of performance-based learning and build new capabilities to improve their position within their supply networks. Not all government policies, programmes or associational supports are learning inducing. It was striking that the programmes that induced clear learning were those that also embodied implicit or explicit performance standards. The grounded, factory-based team-based group learning initiative of ACMA with the support of the government and UNIDO was an example of this process, as were judicial decisions about the adoption of higher emissions standards that induced sector associations, larger assemblers and government to collaborate around the group-learning initiative that helped many small suppliers upgrade. Policies that induce learning are those that directly or indirectly help raise performance standards, as opposed to policies that simply protect or subsidize without inducing learning.

References

Anand, B. and T. Khanna. 2000. 'Do Firms Learn to Create Value: The Case of Alliances.' *Strategic Management Journal* 21 (3): 295–315.

Bair, J. and G. Gereffi. 2001. 'Local Clusters in Global Chains: The Causes and Consequences of Export Dynamism in Torreon's Blue Jeans Industry.' *World Development* 29 (11): 1885–1903.

Barnes and R. Kaplinsky. 2000. 'Globalization and the Death of the Local Firm? The Automobile Components Sector in South Africa.' *Regional Studies* 34 (9): 797–812.

Carré, F. 2017. 'Application of Informal Employment Definition to Developed Countries.' Mimeo. Prepared for the WIEGO Research Conference, Harvard University, 10–12 November 2017.

D'Costa, A. P. 2004. 'Flexible Practices for Mass Production Goals: Economic Governance in the Indian Automobile Industry.' *Industrial and Corporate Change* 13 (2): 335–367.

Down to Earth. 1999. 'Applying the Brakes.' 31 May. Accessed on 25 November 2017. Available at http://www.downtoearth.org.in/news/applying-the-brakes-19863.

Fluery, A. 2000. 'Upgrading in Global Value Chains: The Case of Brazil's Manufacturing Sector.' Presentation at the Rockefeller Global Value Chains Workshop, Bellagio, Italy. October.

Gereffi, G. 1999. 'International Trade and Industrial Upgrading in the Apparel Commodity Chain.' *Journal of International Economics* 48 (1): 37–70.

Gulati, R., N. Nohria and A. Zaheer. 2000. 'Strategic Networks.' *Strategic Management Journal* 21 (3): 203–215.

Humphrey, J. 2003. 'Globalization and Supply Chain Networks: The Auto Industry in Brazil and India.' *Global Networks* 3 (2): 121–141.

Humphrey, J. and H. Schmitz. 2002. 'How Does Insertion in Global Value Chains Affect Upgrading in Industrial Clusters?' *Regional Studies* 36 (9): 1017–1027.

Humphrey, J. and O. Memedovic. 2003. *The Global Automotive Industry Value Chain: What Prospects for Upgrading by Developing Countries*. UNIDO Sectoral Studies Series. Vienna: UNIDO.

Kumaraswamy, A., R. Mudambi and H. Saranga. 2012. 'Catch-Up Strategies in the Indian Auto-Components Industry: Domestic Firms' Responses to Market Liberalization.' *Journal of International Business Studies* 43 (4): 368–395.

McDermott, G. A. and R. A. Corredoira. 2010. 'Network Composition, Collaborative Ties, and Upgrading in Emerging-Market Firms: Lessons from the Argentine Autoparts Ssector.' *Journal of International Business Studies* 41 (2): 308–329.

Malik, V. 1999. 'Car Chaos Continues in Delhi; SC Directives May Be Extended Gradually to Rest of India.' Accessed on 22 October 2017. Available at http://www.rediff.com/business/1999/may/21emit.htm.

———. 1999. 'Supreme Court Denies Breathing Time to Cars That Suffocate.' Accessed on 22 October 2017. Available at http://www.rediff.com/business/1999/may/13emit1.htm.

Nadvi, K. 1999. 'Collective Efficiency and Collective Failure: The Response of the Sialkot Surgical Instruments Cluster to Global Quality Pressures.' *World Development* 27 (9): 1605–1626.

O'Rourke, D. 2000. 'Monitoring the Monitors: A Critique of PricewaterhouseCoopers (PwC) Labor Monitoring.' Mimeo. Cambridge, MA: Massachusetts Institute of Technology. Accessed on 22 October 2017. Available at http://web.mit.edu/dorourke/www/PDF/pwc.pdf.

Pipkin, S. and A. Fuentes. 2017. 'Spurred to Upgrade: A Review of Triggers and Consequences of Industrial Upgrading in the Global Value Chain Literature.' *World Development* 98: 536–554.

Rediffusion. 1999. 'Ford India Not Happy with SC's Car Pollution Order.' Accessed on 22 October 2017. Availabel at http://www.rediff.com/business/1999/may/03ford.htm/.

Sabel, Charles and Sanjay Reddy. 2003. 'Learning to Learn: Undoing the Gordian Knot of Development Today.' Columbia Law and Economics Working Paper 308.

Samii, R., L. N. V. Wassenhove and S. Bhattacharya. 2002. 'An Innovative Public-Private Partnership: New Approach to Development.' *World Development* 30 (6): 991–1008.

Schmitz, H. and P. Knorringa. 2000. 'Learning from Global Buyers.' *Journal of Development Studies* 37 (2): 177–205.

Society of Indian Automobile Manufacturers (SIAM). 2017. 'Emissions Norms.' Accessed on 25 November 2017. Available at http://www.siamindia.com/technical-regulation.aspx?mpgid=31&pgidtrail=33.

Sturgeon, T., J. V. Biesebroeack and G. Gereffi. 2008. 'Value Chains, Networks and Clusters: Reframing the Global Automotive Industry.' *Journal of Economic Geography* 8 (3): 297–321.

Sundaram Fasteners. 2016. *Annual Report.* Accessed on 20 October 2017. Available at http://www.sundram.com/pdf/InvestorInformation/Financials/AnnualReport/sflar2016.pdf.

Sutton, J. 2004. 'The Auto-Component Supply Chain in China and India: A Benchmarking Study.' Mimeo. London: London School of Economics.

Tendler, J. 2001. Comments on 'Governance and Upgrading', paper for Workshop on 'Local Upgrading of Global Chains.' Mimeo, Cambridge, MA: Massachusetts Institute of Technology, 7 February 2001.

Tewari, M. 1999. 'Successful Adjustment in Indian Industry: The Case of Ludhiana's Woollen Knitwear Cluster.' *World Development* 27 (9): 1651–1671.

———. 2001. 'Engaging the New Global Interlocutors: Foreign Direct Investment and the Transformation of Tamil Nadu's Automotive Supply Base.' Mimeo. Cambridge, MA: Harvard University, Centre for International Development.

Tewari, M. and C. Veeramani. 2016. 'Network Trade and Development.' *Global Economy Journal* 16 (2): 349–388.

Veeramani, C. and P. Atukhorala. 2017. 'From Import Substitution to Integration into Global Production Networks: The Case of the Indian Automobile Industry.' Draft. *Management and Organization Review* (under review).

7

Innovation and Learning of Latecomers

A Case Study of Chinese Telecom-Equipment Companies

Peilei Fan

Introduction

'In ten years, only three telecom-equipment companies will dominate the world: Siemens, Alcatel, and *Huawei*.' This was how Ren Zhengfei, the CEO of Huawei, expressed his ambition for his company in 1994 (Fan, 2010). At that time, Huawei, a small local producer, just developed its first large-scale switching equipment, C&C08, and together with other domestic companies, such as Great Dragon Corporation, ZTE and Datang, it was on its way to start catching up with the multinational corporations (MNCs) in China's telecom-equipment industry. Huawei, ZTE and other domestic companies were fighting hard against the large MNCs in China to gain a share in the domestic market. Two decades later, the landscape of the global telecommunication industry dramatically changed. Ren's prediction about Siemens and Huawei as two of the top three became true, though. Following the lead of Siemens, Ericsson, Huawei, Alcatel-Lucent, Nokia Siemens Networks and ZTE are considered the global telecom companies that 'dominated the world' (listed here in decreasing order of their revenue in 2011). Huawei and ZTE, two Chinese telecom-equipment MNCs, have not only emerged into the scene, but also become the crucial players in the global market, thriving in emerging markets such as Africa, Asia and South America as well as in the developed markets of North America and western Europe.

In the early 1980s, China relied almost completely on imports to satisfy its demand for telecom equipment (Zhang, 2000). Within less than three decades, Chinese companies not only achieved remarkable success in the domestic market, but also competed directly with global giants in the mainstream markets mentioned earlier. Leading domestic companies set up networks of sales offices on almost every continent, built manufacturing facilities in key markets and established research and development (R&D) centres in global innovation centres such as Silicon Valley, Stockholm and Bangalore. In terms of innovation capability, some, such as Shanghai Bell, initially relied on technology transfer through joint ventures, whereas others, such as Huawei, ZTE, Great Dragon Technology (GDT) and Datang, developed their own capability from the beginning and made considerable technological catch-up (Fan, 2006a, 2006b; Shen, 1999) due to their knowledge of their own market and production sites, their focus on incremental and architectural innovation rather than radical innovation, and their integration with global knowledge networks (Ernst, 2006). Huawei and ZTE are widely acknowledged for their innovation capability and technological strength. Both were granted the largest number of invention patents in mainland China in 2012. Furthermore, in 2011, ZTE and Huawei were ranked as the first and third among WIPO-administered Patent Cooperation Treaty (PCT) applicants, with Panasonic, Sharp and Bosch the second, fourth and fifth, respectively.

How have Chinese telecom companies transformed themselves from local producers to global giants in a short period of two decades? Using Huawei and ZTE, two leading Chinese firms in the telecom industry, as the principal case studies, this chapter traces the development and catching up of Chinese telecom-equipment companies, with a focus on how they caught up in terms of learning and developing innovation capability as latecomers in a globalized economy. Established in the middle of the1980s in Shenzhen, both firms started reverse engineering a mature technology (switch technology) of advanced countries. After their initial success, they repeated the process of reverse engineering and improved other higher-level technologies from advanced countries, such as access systems and SDH transmission systems. Technological learning contributed to their rapid growth and success in domestic and international markets. They are both top-ranking domestic firms with a combined domestic market share of over 25 per cent in 2005. With more than 50 per cent of their sales revenue from the overseas market, they have developed into major global players in almost all subsectors of the telecom industry, especially in optical transmission, DSL, router and mobile equipment. Advancing into established markets such as western Europe and North America, Huawei and ZTE became two of the main suppliers to global service providers such as British Telecom and Vodafone in the mid-2000s. Along with market expansion, they established global R&D centres in various parts of the world, including the USA, France, Sweden and South Korea, as well as emerging economies such as India and Russia.

The rest of the chapter is organized as follows. The next section will introduce the innovation strategies of Huawei and ZTE as latecomers, and the section after that explains how innovation has been considered as a dynamic process. The succeeding section highlights the strategy of R&D globalization from a latecomer's perspective. The following section reveals the external factors that have affected decisions on and the formation of innovation capability. The final section concludes this study.

Innovation strategies as latecomers[1]

Latecomers, in comparison with first movers, suffer from latecomer disadvantages, such as the technological leadership of incumbent firms, pre-emption of assets and high buyer switching costs (Kardes and Kalyanaram, 1992; Lieberman and Montgomery, 1988, 1998), but are also blessed with advantages because enhanced information and the free-rider effects can save them costs and time due to information spillover and learning from the experiences of first movers. Further, changes in market or consumer tastes and technological regimes, in combination with the resources, manpower and organization committed by first movers to meet earlier market and technology requirements, can put first movers at a disadvantage and offer opportunities for latecomers to catch up (Cho *et al.*, 1998; Lieberman and Montgomery, 1998; Richardson, 1996).

How did Chinese companies use the latecomer advantages and overcome latecomer disadvantages to develop their innovation capability? Do the existence of latecomer advantages imply that latecomers can provide less investment in R&D and innovation capability and rely on the free-rider effects to focus on manufacturing capacity? Furthermore, is innovation for latecomers easier in the telecom-equipment sector compared to other sectors, and if so, why?

The development of Huawei and ZTE indicates that in-house R&D has been the most important factor for them to improve their innovation capability, because both companies have invested a large amount of capital and devoted a large percentage of their workforce to R&D activity. The amount of investment and the size of the assigned workforce are much greater than most of the other domestic electronics companies in China as well as the multinational corporations in the telecom-equipment industry there. First, both firms invested heavily in R&D: Huawei and ZTE have invested from 10 per cent to 20 per cent of their revenues in R&D annually since the 1990s. In 2002, together

---

1   Most of this section is revised based on material from Fan (2006a).

with Datang, another domestic telecom firm, they were listed as the top three in terms of 'R&D spending as percentage of revenue' of 'China's 100 largest electronics companies' (MII, 2003). It is comparable to leading MNCs, whose average R&D spending was 15 per cent of their revenue in 2002. As the leader in innovation capability and the industry, Huawei was listed as the seventh largest electronics company in China by revenue, but its R&D expenditure topped all other companies listed in 'China's 100 largest electronics companies' in 2002. Furthermore, in the same year, the percentage of the workforce leading domestic telecom-equipment companies (ZTE, Huawei, Datang and GDT) devoted to R&D were 42 per cent, 46 per cent, 30 per cent and 54 per cent, respectively. It is significantly higher than most MNCs' operations in China. For instance, the number of employees working in R&D in Lucent, Motorola, Nokia and Nortel were 16 per cent, 10 per cent, 6 per cent and 4 per cent, respectively.

An examination of the workforce's education level indicates that Huawei and ZTE probably have the most highly educated workforce in China. Both companies have a workforce of over 70–80 per cent educated up to the bachelor's degree level and 20–60 per cent educated up to the master's degree level or higher. For instance, among Huawei's 22,000 employees, more than 85 per cent have bachelor's or higher degrees, and about 60 per cent hold a master's or PhD degree.

It is worth mentioning that, with the committed R&D resources, the Chinese latecomers have used the 'intense focus' strategy that effectively concentrates resources on one particular area and exploits the latecomer advantages. This strategy involves identifying a potential growth area first and then devoting almost all available resources into the development of this area. This is illustrated by Huawei's shifting R&D focus in its development history. In 1993, five years after the establishment of Huawei, it devoted all the resources it had accumulated since its establishment to the R&D of its large-scale public digital switch system (PDSS), C&C08. Later, when C&C08 reached the market successfully, Huawei transferred its energy and concentrated its effort in the R&D of synchronous digital hierarchy (SDH) of optical fibre networks. When its SDH products were in a good position in the market, Huawei shifted its focus to data network equipment (Fan, 2010).

Domestic Chinese companies have also utilized some specific latecomer advantages of R&D in the local market vis-à-vis the MNCs. This was revealed in the course of some of our interviews with managers. One interviewee (a ZTE manager) considered that MNCs have two disadvantages in R&D in

China, which implies that domestic firms have two advantages. First, unlike major domestic companies such as ZTE and Huawei, foreign firms (joint ventures or wholly owned subsidiaries) do not have high-level R&D staff in China. Instead, they are mostly staffed with marketing and local R&D people for simple customization. The reason could be that MNCs worry about the leakage of their tangible knowledge, especially in a country that has issues with the enforcement of intellectual property. However, in another sense, it echoes the general trend of R&D resource deployment of MNCs where higher-level R&D, that is, exploratory and advanced development, is located close to production centres or markets (Amsden, Tschang and Goto, 2000). Second, while foreign firms suffer from the separation of their marketing staff from the core R&D staff in their home country, domestic firms have their marketing divisions closely connected with their R&D staff. Thus, once domestic firms grasp the needs of service providers through marketing analyses (and sometimes even through the R&D staff), their R&D departments can develop solutions to provide the desired products and services in a timely fashion. The disadvantages faced by MNCs imply that domestic firms could focus on exploratory and advanced development and then gradually ramp up their innovation capability through backward linkage.

Finally, the catch-up of Chinese companies has benefited from the trend of the telecom-equipment industry of moving towards configuration technologies, as it has made innovation in specific areas possible and faster for Chinese domestic producers. Configuration technologies refer to those technologies matching the complexity of systems technologies, but which are designed to allow great flexibility in development and application (Shen, 1999). Information and communication technologies have increasingly taken the form of configuration technologies due to modular design and the use of open standards (William, 1997). The industry has been moving towards the separation of component manufacturing from system provisioning. Huawei and ZTE, as system providers, have been able to focus on building their key technologies and acquiring other parts from suppliers. This particular way of participating in the global value chain (GVC) of the telecom-equipment industry has been effective for the rapid growth of system providers. One R&D manager from ZTE explained that this strategy, which allows the company to concentrate on developing its own 'core technologies' and purchase the rest from suppliers, can satisfy customers' 'comprehensive solutions' requests (Smith-Gillespie, 2001).

Innovation as a dynamic process[2]

There are extensive literatures concerning catching-up and the technology upgrading strategies of latecomers (for example, Hobday, 1995; Leonard-Barton, 1995). For instance, in her influential book *Wellsprings of Knowledge: Building and Sustaining the Sources of Innovation*, Leonard-Barton (1995) described a 'technological capability ladder' to characterize the formation of the product-development capability in developing countries (Austin 1990) which include (*a*) assembly or turnkey operations, (*b*) adaptation and localization of components, (*c*) product redesign and (*d*) independent design of products. Kim (1997) also observed that the technological trajectories of catching-up countries are in the opposite direction to those of advanced countries, that is, they begin with imitation, acquiring, assimilating and improving mature technologies from advanced countries, then they repeat the process with higher-level technology in the consolidation stage in advanced countries and, finally, if successful, they may eventually accumulate indigenous capability to innovate, that is, generate emerging technologies.

Huawei and ZTE have followed the general pathway of technological learning of latecomers as described by Kim because they initially imitated mature foreign technology for large-scale switching, then repeated the same process for higher-level technologies in the consolidation stage in more advanced countries. After they caught up with their MNC rivals in several key subsectors such as access systems, optical transport, data communication and mobile communications, both firms transformed themselves from imitators to innovators, generating emerging technologies such as the third-generation and fourth-generation CDMA2000, WCDMA and TD-SCDMA mobile communication technologies (Fan, 2011).

It should be noted that, in addition to this sequence of catching up, there is also a dynamic process of developing the innovation capability, which involves knowing when and how to use externally developed technologies. At first glance, collaboration with multinational corporations or technology transfers through joint ventures or acquisitions seem to be shortcuts for obtaining advanced technology. However, due to financial resource constraints and lack of interest from the MNCs, Chinese domestic firms have relied mainly on internal development and domestic resources at the early stage of their catching up in the 1980s and 1990s. Only after they developed their own capability did they

---

2   Most of this section is revised based on material from Fan (2011) (general pathway of learning and R&D globalization).

start meaningful collaborations with established partners as a complementary approach to internal development for developing innovation capabilities. For instance, ZTE was commissioned by the internet service provider Aircell to collaborate with Qualcomm in developing Gogo technology because of ZTE's unique strength in CDMA EV-DO Rev. A networking equipment manufacturer, 3Com, collaborated with Huawei because of Huawei's strength in data communication, which is comparable to 3Com's long-term rival Cisco. This finding echoes with Hu *et al.* (2003), who pointed out that the contribution of technology transfers was found to be conditional on its interaction with in-house R&D for large- and medium-size Chinese enterprises.

The case of the joint venture between Huawei and 3Com has indicated that latecomers do not necessary play a subordinate role regarding collaboration with incumbent firms in the GVC. Common wisdom states that latecomers who participate in the GVC can obtain crucial knowledge or technology from collaborating or being a contract manufacturer of leading global companies. However, H3C, the joint venture set up by Huawei and 3Com in 2003 and headquartered in Hong Kong, was majority-owned by Huawei and its knowledge and technology came mainly from Huawei. Instead of serving as contract manufacturers, that is, supplying designated equipment tooled to 3Com designs and specifications, Huawei played the role of an equal or even a superior in the joint venture in terms of knowledge and technology. Huawei contributed its product portfolio of low-end and middle-range routers and LAN switches and their licenses as its intellectual property to the joint venture, whereas 3Com contributed $160 million cash, mobilized its existing operations in China and Japan, and shared licenses for some of its intellectual property. Furthermore, most of the 1,500 initial employees of H3C were sourced from Huawei. Both parties acknowledge that the partnership was established mainly to reduce the costs for expansion into the respective new markets for both companies (Huawei, 2013). The H3C collaboration illustrates that Huawei has surged ahead to become a leading global company, thus playing a major role in the GVC vis-à-vis other major players.

The experiences of Chinese telecom producers support Mathews' view that to gain the most benefit from R&D collaboration, latecomers should have their own unique ownership advantages (technological strength in certain specialized areas). Furthermore, latecomers should also focus on the advantages that can be accessed externally by establishing links with established firms so that resources can be leveraged (Mathews, 2002).

Finally, a latecomer's innovation capability is closely associated with market strategies, as is illustrated by the experiences of both companies. When Huawei and ZTE initially entered the sector, they focused on China's countryside market for small-scale switch equipment, avoiding head-to-head competition with the MNCs. However, once both developed their own large-scale switch equipment, they started to compete with incumbent MNCs in China's domestic market. Later, their venture into the global market followed the same pathway: both first entered markets in developing countries and transitional economies to test the waters. Huawei and ZTE eventually entered the mainstream markets in North America and western Europe after they further improved their innovation capability to match the higher standards of telecom operators in these markets, such as British Telecom (Fan, 2010).

R&D globalization[3]

It should be noted that R&D globalization has become an increasingly important strategy for firms from advanced countries as well as those from catching-up countries. Examining the locations, purposes and patterns of R&G globalization can add important insights about the technological learning of latecomers. What are the locations, motivations and development patterns of global R&D units for Chinese firms? How has their status as latecomers with lower levels of resources and capabilities (Niosi and Tschang, 2009) affected their R&D globalization? In this section, I briefly examine the locations, purposes and development patterns of R&D globalization of the Chinese firms.

R&D globalization has been considered a crucial strategy for firms from technologically advanced countries (Cantwell and Janne, 1999; Kuemmerle, 1999a, 1999b; Niosi, 1999). Latecomers from emerging countries, such as Huawei and ZTE, have also used R&D globalization to build their innovation capability (Reddy, 2000, 2005; UNTCAD, 2005). Since the 1990s, in order to tap into global R&D resources in telecom research, Huawei and ZTE have set up strategic global R&D units, which can be classified into home-base-augmenting (HBA) units and home-base-exploiting (HBE) units, based on their purpose and function. In general, HBA units are established 'to augment firm-specific capabilities if this mode of augmenting firms' knowledge base offers higher payoffs than licensing in' (Kuemmerle, 1999a, 184) and almost entirely clustered in just five regions of the world – the north-eastern USA,

---

3   Most of this section is revised based on material from Fan (2011).

California, the United Kingdom, western Europe and South Asia. They are also close to universities and government research laboratories. In contrast, HBE units are set up to 'exploit firm-specific capabilities if this mode of exploitation offers higher pay-off than licensing out' (Kuemmerle, 1999a, 184); these are dispersed across a much wider range of regions and are close to markets and manufacturing facilities (Kuemmerle, 1999b). For Huawei and ZTE, their HBA units are located in carefully selected global innovation centres of telecom technology, whereas their HBE units are closely integrated with manufacturing and marketing needs and dispersed in different regions (Tables 7.1 and 7.2).

Table 7.1 Global R&D centres of Huawei

R&D institutes	Date of establishment	Location	Type of unit	Purpose
Chip R&D institute	1993	Silicon Valley	Home-base-augmenting	Monitoring and developing chip technology
Telecommunication R&D institute	1999	Dallas	Home-base-augmenting	Monitoring and developing ASIC, CDMA, NGN
India R&D institute	1999	Bangalore	Home-base-augmenting	Software development, cutting development costs, increasing development efficiency, and using local IT resources
Russia R&D institute	1999	Moscow	Home-base-exploiting	Adapting to the local market and supporting local subsidiaries

(Contd.)

(Contd.)

R&D institutes	Date of establishment	Location	Type of unit	Purpose
Sweden R&D institute	2001	Stockholm	Home-base-augmenting	Monitoring and developing CDMA technology and standardization work, radio frequency technology and algorithms

Source: Fan (2011, Table 3).

Table 7.2 Global R&D centres of ZTE

R&D institutes	Date of establishment	Location	Type of unit	Purpose
US R&D institute (1)	1998	New Jersey	Home-base-augmenting	R&D on VoIP Soft switch and NGN
US R&D institute (2)	1998	San Diego	Home-base-augmenting	Monitoring and exchanging the latest development of CDMA and WiMax technology
US R&D institute (3)	1998	Dallas	Home-base-augmenting	R&D on optical transmission
Korea R&D institute	2000	Seoul	Home-base-augmenting	R&D on CDMA terminal products
Sweden R&D institute	2003	Stockholm	Home-base-augmenting	Monitoring the development on WCDMA and 4G

(Contd.)

(Contd.)

R&D institutes	Date of establishment	Location	Type of unit	Purpose
France R&D institute	2005	France	Home-base-exploiting	Serving as the training centre for western Europe and Africa (especially French-speaking ones) and supporting markets of the regions
India R&D centre	2005	Bangalore	Home-base-exploiting	Adapting to the Indian and South Asian markets and supporting Indian subsidiaries
Pakistan R&D centre	2005	Islamabad	Home-base-exploiting	Adapting to the Pakistan market and supporting local subsidiaries

Source: Fan (2011, Table 4).

Huawei and ZTE set up their R&D units mainly to gain strategic assets or access to markets. To enhance their innovation capability, they located their HBA units in Silicon Valley, Dallas, Kista, Seoul and Bangalore, despite the fact that R&D costs are usually higher than in the home country. These HBA units can access strategic asset-concentrated R&D talents with specific technological skills. In addition, resource-tapping units, a type of HBA unit, are located in cities of emerging countries such as India (the city being Bangalore), and are specifically targeted at gaining strategic assets in software development which are not available in China and can reduce overall R&D costs. Meanwhile, HBE units, dispersed in different regions of Europe and Asia, have helped Huawei and ZTE serve local markets.

For latecomers, it is extremely important to identify emerging technology that has high market potential. Placing R&D units in global knowledge centres has ensured the integration of Huawei and ZTE with special knowledge clusters so that they can benefit from spillover effects and localized learning via geographic and relational proximities, although they need to overcome cultural and institutional differences. For instance, both Huawei and ZTE set up their HBA R&D units focusing on mobile communication technology in the 'global wireless and mobile valley' of Kista, Sweden, because they can access its pool of talent and experienced consultants here, while enjoying the overall low research costs and high standard of living in Sweden (Stockholm Business Region, 2009). In addition, whereas HBA units focus on embedding into the local research community, HBE units concentrate on embedding with the general local community, consisting of local agents, service providers and host governments, similar to manufacturing and market subsidiaries (author's interview note, 2009).

Second, the order of development and the pace of R&D globalization of Chinese firms have not followed the evolution path of global foreign R&D, exemplified by firms originally from developed countries. The internationalization process (IP) theory (Johanson and Vahlue, 1977) suggests that R&D internationalization will follow market and production internationalization where firms expand internationally according to geographic and psychic distances; that is, firms begin to internationalize operations in locations which are geographically and psychologically close to their home countries. In contrast to the IP theory, Huawei and ZTE's R&D globalization has progressed simultaneously with, and sometimes even ahead of, their foray into global markets and manufacturing. Furthermore, both firms set up HBA units first, followed by HBE units, unlike MNCs from industrialized countries. Moreover, geographical and cultural distances do not seem to matter in their R&D globalization process. For instance, Huawei set up its Silicon Valley R&D unit in 1993, when it just started to rise in the domestic market in China and did not even export to any foreign markets. Similarly, ZTE set up three of its US-based R&D units in 1998, seven years before its entry to the US market in 2005. Although advanced markets may pose fierce competition and high production costs for latecomers' marketing and manufacturing units, they may serve as cost-effective locations for HBA R&D units due to the agglomeration effects of global innovation centres. In addition to serving as HBA units for both firms, the US and Swedish R&D units went on to function as bases for research collaborations with other global players in the USA and Sweden, and as anchor points for Huawei and ZTE to enter these markets.

These differences confirm that the R&D globalization of latecomers is not so much about exploiting the existing 'ownership' advantages suggested by the eclectic 'ownership-location-internalization' (OLI) theory (Dunning, 1981, 1988), as the established multinationals do, but, rather, to tap into resources and markets that would otherwise be unavailable (Buckley *et al.*, 2007; Li, 2007; Luo and Tung, 2007; Niosi and Tshang, 2009). Furthermore, as these units are particularly attractive to local skilled personnel who originally came from China, the global R&D units of latecomers may contribute to skills circulation without the individuals physically returning to China.

Innovation and external factors[4]

External factors, such as government intervention and the global environment for technology transfer, may have significant effect on industrial development and improvement in innovation capability, because domestic firms in late-industrializing countries are usually weak and not competitive vis-à-vis the MNCs. In contrast to the neoclassical view, some scholars have emphasized the directive role of governments in the industrialization of East Asia, especially Japan and South Korea. They argue that the governments in Japan, South Korea and Taiwan have pursued a vigorous industrial policy and have guided the market towards planned structural change (Singh, 1992, 1994). The seminal work of Amsden (1989) advocated the role of government in industrialization and documented in detail how South Korea's government has pursued a vigorous policy in its domestic industrial development and imposed strict performance standards on those industries and firms that it aids. A large number of academic studies have observed that governments in newly industrialized economies (NIEs) have been actively involved in helping firms in high-tech sectors advance their innovation capabilities through investment in education and infrastructure support, as well as by setting up large government-funded institutes, such as the prestigious Korea Institute of Science and Technology (KIST) and the Industrial Technology Research Institute (ITRI) in Taiwan, to carry out R&D, train engineers and researchers, and transfer technology to local firms. In addition, other external factors have also affected the choices of domestic companies. Constraints from the international market, such as the unavailability or the high cost of key technology, have driven domestic companies to vie for building their own innovation capability (Fan *et al.*, 2007).

The development of China's telecom-equipment industry provides an excellent opportunity to study the impact of external factors, such as government

---

4   Most of this section is revised based on material from Fan (2006b) (government intervention) and Fan (2007) (barrier for technology transfer).

intervention and export controls imposed by international organizations, on domestic innovation.

By using different intensities and forms of intervention, government intervention has greatly facilitated the development of innovative Chinese firms, especially at the early stages. The Chinese government has intervened differently at different stages. In the early and middle 1990s, after Great Dragon Technology (GDT), a major domestic company at the time, developed China's first public digital switch system, the HJD04, several domestic firms also started to make their own switch equipment. The government started to offer direct support in the finance, marketing and export components of these domestic producers. This heavy intervention had the desired effect: several domestic firms that developed their own switch equipment achieved fast growth during this period. For instance, Huawei, ZTE, GDT and Datang saw rapid increases in revenue growth rate from 40 per cent to 100 per cent annually during the period. In the mid- and late-1990s, domestic firms dominated China's switch equipment market and started to expand their product range to other sub-sectors of telecommunications, such as optical transmission and access systems. Responding to the changing situation, the government intervened less and offered technical support indirectly through selecting capable domestic firms for national science and technology programmes. In the last decade, especially after a series of reforms of the telecom service sector, the government completely withdrew direct financial aid for domestic firms and focused on supporting the development of cutting-edge technologies and standards. TD-SCDMA, the indigenous 3G standard developed by Datang, is a case in point (Gao and Liu, 2012).

It is worth mentioning that government intervention has been strategic as it has been guided by the development level of domestic firms and aimed at nurturing innovative domestic firms with self-priority technologies. First, it is primarily the development level of domestic firms that has guided the forms and intensity of government intervention. At the beginning of the catching-up period, when foreign imports dominated markets and few domestic firms existed, the government focused on encouraging research into the development of domestic switch equipment. Later, when a number of firms were able to produce large public digital switch equipment, the government provided the much-needed financial resources and market access to domestic firms. Finally, after the domestic firms became mature and could compete with MNCs on an equal footing, the government withdrew most of its intervention and only focused on R&D projects of strategic national importance such as the new-generation mobile communication standard.

Second, the government's intervention ensured that those firms with the greatest innovation capability received the most benefits. Financial assistance targeted firms which had developed technologies and needed to improve them further. Market access and loans helped those who had already developed their own self-proprietary technologies. National science and technology (S&T) programmes benefitted those who already had a strong R&D base and were committed to R&D development. All these interventions facilitated the rapid growth of firms with a strong innovation capability and the financial success of these firms further promoted their heavy investment in R&D.

Other external factors, especially the export controls imposed by international organizations, have also affected the effort of domestic firms in developing self-proprietary technologies. This can be illustrated by the influence of the Coordinating Committee for Multilateral Export Control (COCOM). Growing out of the Cold War and rooted in the North Atlantic Treaty Organization (NATO), COCOM had a total of seventeen members (almost all of them advanced nations) in 1989. Formed to protect the West by preventing the export of technology to the East (including China) that might be put to military use, COCOM is considered to have a pervasive impact on China's economic and technology development. Telecommunication technologies that China was interested in for technology transfer were usually on COCOM's list of prohibited items. Under COCOM's regulations, companies belonging to its member countries either could not obtain export licenses or had to wait several years to get a license application. These regulations created significant difficulties for China in acquiring foreign telecom technology and equipment. Unlike South Korean firms who enjoyed access to foreign technology and technology transfer while developing their high-tech industry – an example would be the earlier access to semiconductors (Kim, 1997) – COCOM's export controls forced Chinese telecom equipment companies to develop their own technologies. Although COCOM was replaced in 1994 by another organization with far less power over its members in terms of export controls, COCOM and its successor have a profound influence on China's choice of technology strategies (Tan, 1997).

Conclusion

The experiences of Chinese firms demonstrate that in-house R&D, indicated by the amount of R&D investment and in-house R&D staff, has turned out to be the most important factor for Huawei and ZTE for improving their innovation capability. Furthermore, effective strategies for latecomers include the 'intense focus' strategy that concentrates resources on one particular area, as well as the strategy of focusing on exploratory and advanced development that requires close integration of R&D and marketing functions, which is where MNCs are at a disadvantage in China. It should be noted that the catch-up of Chinese companies has benefited from the trend of the telecom-equipment industry moving towards configuration technologies, which has made innovation in specific areas possible and faster for Chinese domestic producers.

Other than the general methods of catching up by climbing up the ladder and going through the process from 'imitation' to 'innovation', Chinese companies have collaborated with established partners as a complementary approach to internal development only after they developed their technological strength in specialized areas. In addition, R&D globalization has been implemented as an important technological strategy to gain strategic assets or access to markets, with its own distinct development pattern, which is different from similar activity by multinational corporations of advanced countries.

It should be highlighted that external factors have affected domestic Chinese firms' development of innovation capability. In particular, based on the level of development of domestic firms, government intervention has effectively nurtured technologically advanced domestic firms in China's telecom-equipment industry. Furthermore, although export control created barriers for technology transfer, it has motivated indigenous innovation by Chinese companies.

References

Amsden, A. H., T. Tschang and A. Goto. 2000. 'New Classification of R&D for International Comparisons (With a Singapore Case Study).' Working Paper for the Asian Development Bank (ADB) 2000. Manila: Asian Development Bank.

Amsden, Alice. 1989. *Asia's Next Giant: South Korea and Late Industrialization*. Oxford: Oxford University Press.

Austin, James E. 1990. *Managing in Developing Countries: Strategic Analysis and Operating Techniques*. New York: Free Press.

Buckley, P. J., L. J. Clegg, A. R. Cross, X. Liu, H. Voss and P. Zheng. 2007. 'The Determinants of Chinese Outward Foreign Investment.' *Journal of International Business Studies* 38 (4): 499–518.

Cantwell, Johnand Odille Janne. 1999. 'Technological Globalization and Innovative Centers: The Role of Corporate Technological Leadership and Locational Hierarchy.' *Research Policy* 28 (2–3): 119–44.

Cho, D. S., D. J. Kim and D. K. Rhee. 1998. 'Latecomer Strategies: Evidence from the Semiconductor Industry in Japan and Korea.' *Organization Science* 9 (4): 489–505.

Dunning, J. H. 1981. *International Production and the Multinational Enterprise.* London: Allen and Unwin.

———. 1988. 'The Eclectic Paradigm of International Production: A Restatement and Some Possible Extensions.' *Journal of International Business Studies* 19 (1): 1–31.

Ernst, Dieter. 2006. 'Innovation Offshoring: Asia's Emerging Role in Global Innovation Networks.' *East-West Center Special Report No. 10.* July. Honolulu, Hawaii: East-West Center.

Fan, Peilei. 2006a. 'Catching Up through Developing Innovation Capability: Evidence from China's Telecom-Equipment Industry.' *Technovation* 26 (3): 359–68.

———. 2006b. 'Promoting Indigenous Capability: The Chinese Government and the Catching-up of Domestic Telecom-Equipment Firms.' *China Review* 6 (1): 9–35.

———. 2010. 'From a Latecomer to a Global Telecom Giant: The Development Path of Huawei.' *International Journal of Business System Research* 4 (5/6): 691–719.

———. 2011. 'Innovation, Globalization, and Catch-up of Latecomers: Cases of Chinese Telecom Firms.' *Environment and Planning A* 43(4): 830–49.

Fan, Peilei, Xudong Gao and Kazuo Watanabe. 2007. 'Technology Strategies of Innovative Chinese Domestic Companies.' *International Journal of Technology and Globalization* 3 (4): 344–63.

Gao, Xudong and Jianxin Liu. 2012. 'Catching Up through the Development of Technology Standard: The Case of TD-SCDMA in China.' *Telecommunications Policy* 36 (7): 531–45.

Hobday, Michael. 1995. *Innovation in East Asia: The Challenge to Japan.* Cheltenham, Glos: Edward Elgar.

Hu, G. Z., G. H. Jefferson and J. Qian. 2003. 'R&D and Technology Transfer: Firm-Level Evidence from Chinese Industry.' William Davidson Institute Working Paper No. 582. Michigan: Ann Arbor, MI: William Davidson Institute, University of Michigan.

Huawei. 2013. Company Website. http://www.huawei.com.

Johanson, J. and J. E. Vahlne. 1977. 'The Internationalization Process of the Firm: A Model of Knowledge Development and Increasing Foreign Market Commitments.' *Journal of International Business Studies* 8 (1): 23–32.

Kardes, F. R. and G. Kalyanaram. 1992. 'Order-of-Entry Effects on Consumer Memory and Judgment: An Information Integration Perspective.' *Journal of Marketing Research* 29 (3): 343–57.

Kim, Linsu. 1997. *From Imitation to Innovation: Dynamics of Korea's Technological Learning.* Cambridge, MA: Harvard Business School Press.

Kuemmerle, W. 1997. 'Building Effective R&D Capabilities Abroad.' *Harvard Business Review* (Jan–Feb): 61–70.

———. 1999a. 'Foreign Direct Investment in Industrial Research in the Pharmaceutical and Electronics Industries: Results from a Survey of Multinational Firms.' *Research Policy* 28 (2–3):179–93.

———. 1999b. 'The Drivers of Foreign Direct Investment into Research and Development: An Empirical Investigation.' *Journal of International Business Studies* 30 (1): 1–24.

Leonard-Barton, Dorothy. 1995. *Wellspring of Knowledge: Building and Sustaining the Sources of Innovation*. Cambridge, MA: Harvard Business School Press.

Li, P. P. 2007. 'Toward an Integrated Theory of Multinational Evolution: the Evidence of Chinese Multinational Enterprises as Latecomers.' *Journal of International Management* 13 (3): 296–318.

Lieberman, M. B. and D. B. Montgomery. 1988. 'First-Mover Advantages.' *Strategic Management Journal* 9 (Summer Special Issue): 41–58.

———. 1998. 'First-Mover (Dis)Advantages: Retrospective and Link with the Resource-Based View.' *Strategic Management Journal* 19 (12):1111–25.

Luo, Y. and R. L. Tung. 2007. 'International Expansion of Emerging Market Enterprises: A Springboard Perspective.' *Journal of International Business Studies* 38 (4): 481–98.

Mathews, J. A. 2002. *Dragon Multinational*. New York: Oxford University Press.

Ministry of Information Industry (MII). 2003. http://www.mii.gov.cn.

Niosi, J. 1999. 'Introduction: The Internationalization of Industrial R&D from Technology Transfer to the Learning Organization.' *Research Policy* 28 (2–3): 107–11.

Niosi, J. and F. T. Tschang. 2009. 'The Strategies of Chinese and Indian Software Multinationals: Implications for Internationalization Theory.' *Industrial and Corporate Change* 18 (2): 269–94.

Reddy, P. 2000. *Globalization of Corporate R&D: Implications for Innovation Systems in Host Countries*. London: Routledge.

Reddy, P. 2005. 'R&D Related FDI in Developing Countries: Implications for Host Countries.' In *Globalization of R&D and Developing Countries, Proceedings of the Expert Meeting*, Geneva, 24–26 January 2005, 89–105. New York: United Nations.

Richardson, J. 1996. 'Vertical Integration and Rapid Response in Fashion Appeal.' *Organization Science* 7 (4): 400–12.

Shen, Xiaobai. 1999. *The Chinese Road to High Technology: A Study of Telecommunication Switching Technology in the Economic Transition*. London: Macmillan Press Ltd.

Singh, Ajit. 1992. 'The Actual Crisis of Economic Development in the 1980s: An Alternative Policy Perspective for the Future.' In *New Directions in Development*

Economics, edited by A. K. Dutt and K. Jameson, 81–116. Aldershot, UK: Edward Elgar.

———. 1994. 'State Intervention and the "Market-Friendly" Approach to Development: A Critical Analysis of the World Bank Theses.' In *The State, Markets and Development—Beyond the Neoclassical Dichotomy*, edited by A. K. Dutt, Kwan S. Kim and Ajit Singh, 38–61.Cheltenham, UK: Edward Elgar.

Smith-Gillespie, Aleyn. 2001. 'Building China's High-Tech Telecom Equipment Industry: A Study of Strategies in Technology Acquisition for Competitive Advantage.' Masters Thesis, MIT.

Stockholm Business Region. 2009. 'Chinese Huawei Focuses on R&D in Sweden.' Accessed 10 October 2010. Available at http://www.stockholmbusinessregion.se/ templates/page 39127.aspx?epslanguage=EN.

Tan, Z. A. 1997. 'The Impact of Foreign Linkages on Telecommunications and Development in China.' In *Telecommunications and Development in China*, edited by S. N. L. Paul, 263–80. Cresskill, NJ: Hampton Press.

United Nations Conference on Trade and Development (UNCTAD). 2005. *World Investment Report: Transnational Corporations and the Internationalization of R&D*. New York: United Nations.

Williams, Robin. 1997. 'The Social Shaping of Information and Communications Technologies.' In *The Social Shaping of Information Superhighways*, edited by H. Kubicek, W. Dutton and R. Williams. Frankfurt: Campus Verlag.

Zhang, Q. 2000. *Zhong Guo Zhi Zhao, Pu Tian Ji Tuan (Made in China, Pu Tian Enterprise Group)*. Beijing: China Yanshi Publishing.

8

From the Phased Manufacturing Programme to Frugal Engineering

Some Initial Propositions[1]

Nasir Tyabji

Frugal engineering as the latest managerial fad?

'Frugal engineering' predates the term 'frugal innovation'. It describes (in the same way that 'reverse engineering' describes itself) the norms of engineering practice in Indian companies designed to lower the cost of product development and manufacturing.[2] Carlos Ghosn, the Chief Executive Officer of Nissan and Renault, is usually attributed with the first use of the term (Radjou *et al.*, 2012). In mainstream management circles, frugal engineering was highlighted by *The Economist* (2010a, 2010b).

Frugal innovation has arisen not from the writings of academics or experts but out of management responses to unique economic, social and competitive challenges faced by firms in developing countries. There are no generally accepted guidelines or simple rules that can be universally followed in order to materialize any perceived or promised results. Frugal innovation, as it stands, seems to be complex, multifaceted and can be interpreted and applied in a number of ways in different firms (Kar, 2012).

---

1 This chapter was originally a paper presented at the National Conference on 'India's Industrialisation: How to Overcome Stagnation?' held at the Institute for Studies in Industrial Development, New Delhi, during 19–21 December 2013. A version of this chapter was published in the *Economic and Political Weekly of India*, vol. L, no. 14 (4 April 2015): 45–50. The author would like to thank Ashok Desai for suggesting a critical link which galvanized the writing of this paper.

2 It has been claimed by Ryans (2008, quoted in Bhatti and Ventresca, 2012, 7) that in the pharmaceutical industry, transnational corporations 'over-engineer' the research and development (R&D) process and that even such firms which focus so closely on performance should include the costs of innovation in their strategies.

While it was in the management practitioners' literature that the concept of frugal innovation was originally defined, this has been followed by the research concerns of the academic community. The practitioners' conception may continue to remain dominant but for organizations to imitate effectively or to adopt frugal innovation strategies, academic research is needed to help define its full potential as well as to understand its limitations. Towards the end of the twentieth century, 'lean' processes based on eliminating waste (for example, lean engineering and just-in-time manufacturing) originating in Japan's Toyota Production System (TPS) was widely adopted by other firms.

The legacy of lean practices

Lean manufacturing is emerging as the dominant paradigm for the design and operation of current manufacturing facilities. The term 'lean' is usually understood to be associated with the operational aspect of a manufacturing enterprise, including processes associated with the supply of materials, component production, the delivery of products and customer service. However, lean thinking can also be applied outside manufacturing operations, although examples of this (such as applications in service-based enterprises) are relatively rare.

Knowledge-based activities such as design, new product introduction (NPI), engineering and product development (PD) are areas within an enterprise where the potential benefits from the adoption of lean engineering principles may be significant.

Western companies tend to focus on lean engineering through its practical application in tools and techniques, whereas their Japanese counterparts treat it as a philosophy or culture. The philosophical perspective is a multidimensional approach affecting the entire organization in every one of its functions. It encompasses a wide variety of management practices, including just-in-time, quality systems, work teams, cellular manufacturing and supplier management, all conceived as components of an integrated system. Whatever the perspective, the elimination of waste is the principle that has traditionally been at the heart of the lean approach

In the case of Toyota, the PD system has been key to its success. Toyota's lean manufacturing system is actually an extension of their product development philosophy and not the reverse. However, most firms are focusing their lean initiatives on manufacturing operations alone, with far fewer attempts to adopt lean management for design-related processes.

There are a wide variety of examples where the principles of lean manufacturing have been applied such as software, construction and aerospace. In software, the consideration of the waste principle addresses the shortening of long information feedback loops – the existence of which is cited as the reason why over 50 per cent of all newly developed software is seldom (if ever) reused. The result of shortening feedback loops allows an increased flow of information which improves the speed and the quality of project implementation. This, in turn, reduces costs and adds value to the final product. The major implementation issue here was the requirement for deep changes in the way organizations were managed. Within the construction industry, the lean principle of waste elimination in the design process is conceptualized as a flow of information, which lends itself to waste reduction through minimizing the amount of time before information is used. Value generation arises from capturing the customer's requirements and transmitting these accurately in the overall design process. In later work, the analogy between the role of information in the PD value stream and the role of material in manufacturing has been noted.

The first principle of lean management is to 'specify value'. This value can be specified as the 'capability provided to a customer at the right time at an appropriate price, as defined in each case by the customer' (Womack and Jones, [1996] 2010, 353). However, when these principles are applied to PD, it is recognized that waste is much more difficult to identify than in a manufacturing environment. In manufacturing, excess inventory or work-in-progress (WIP), which are considered forms of waste, is physically and financially visible. However, in PD, the WIP inventory is generally in the form of information. As a result of work carried out as part of the United States Lean Aerospace Initiative, it was argued that the usual definitions of value did not provide the necessary precision when applied to identifying the root causes of the waste that is present in most PD processes. Value is added in PD when useful information is produced. The value of this information can increase certainty or reduce risk. Value in the PD process can be created by adding and taking away activities.

Set-based concurrent engineering (or set-based design), as practised by Toyota, is suggested as the preferred approach to lean PD (Baines *et al.*, 2006, 1544). Set-based design imposes agreed constraints across different functions to ensure that a final subsystem solution chosen from a set of alternatives from a particular function (such as power transmission or engine management) will work with convergent solutions from all other functions. During the design process, as each alternative is evaluated, trade-offs are made, weaker solutions are eliminated and new ones are created, often by combining components in new ways. Redundancy is built into the system, radically reducing risk. Instead of being designed from in a top-down manner, the actual system configuration evolves from creative combinations of multiple solution sets.

The generation, use and reuse of knowledge and information are key to a successful adoption of lean management principles in PD (Baines *et al.*, 2006, 1545). Standardized concurrent engineering techniques are effective in sharing and reusing knowledge and information at the detail design phase. This sharing of design (and manufacturing) knowledge across the product introduction process is viewed as a knowledge management problem. The challenge is to ensure that the information is structured in such a way that it is easily communicable between different systems. Systems for controlling documents, central databases, knowledge-based systems, project management systems, computer-aided design, manufacture and engineering (CAD/CAM/CAE) systems, product data management (PDM) systems, and web-based data-sharing and communication tools can all be used to implement lean manufacturing.

TELCO's technological ascendance

The Tata Engineering and Locomotive Company (TELCO) was incorporated in September 1945 at Jamshedpur following Tata Sons' takeover of the Singhbhum Shops from East India Railways in June 1945. Started with the objective of producing locomotives and general engineering equipment, TELCO's first locomotive was produced in 1952 (Bowonder, 1998, 646–47). Subsequently, it collaborated with Daimler-Benz AG for the manufacture of trucks and buses. It was permitted to manufacture 3 to 5-tonne diesel vehicles under the phased manufacturing programme (PMP). This programme, which envisaged, over a defined time period, a systematic increase in the proportion of components manufactured indigenously, was an essential part of all foreign technological collaboration agreements. Under the TELCO PMP, it was planned that the engine would be manufactured at the end of the last stage, in 1959, well within the Second Five Year Plan period (1956–61). The foreign exchange component of the project was financed by a 10 per cent equity stake in TELCO that Daimler-Benz was allocated.

As there was need for an expansion in manufacturing capacity, TELCO built a new motor vehicle manufacturing unit in Pune, which became operational in 1965. To establish a technological base for indigenous innovation capability in the manufacturing processes of both existing and new products it acquired the long-established Investa Machine Tool Company. This unit supplied the machine tools needed by TELCO. The creation of a design centre in 1967 by TELCO in a field when no other major Indian firm had any research and development (R&D) activity illustrates the importance given to design and new product development by TELCO (Bowonder,1998, 649). In fact, according to TELCO's philosophy (as well as that of Daimler-Benz), a truck or an automobile was regarded as a high-grade technical product possessing commercial content, not a piece of merchandise that incidentally possessed technical content (TELCO, 1969, 1243–44). This remarkable statement of manufacturing philosophy was made by Sumant Moolgaokar (1906–89), who was the Chairman of TELCO at that point in time. Equally remarkable was his assertion, made as early as 1953, that the government was the only agency through which the productive efficiency of the manufacturing sector could be increased (Moolgaokar, 1953). Moolgaokar was an engineer trained at the City and Guilds Institute and Imperial College, London. In the pre-independence period, he had worked in the cement industry and helped develop the manufacturing of cement-manufacturing machinery during the Second World War. After the formation of TELCO in 1945, he was closely associated with its development until his death. He played an active role as a consultant in planning the development of the heavy engineering industry in India, notably through the conducting of a benchmark survey of existing engineering capacity in the country in the mid-1950s (Government of India, 1954).

For some years before the end of the collaboration agreement the process of adaptation had begun. Various modifications and improvements were incorporated into the Tata Mercedes-Benz (TMB) vehicles to make them suitable for the difficult road conditions and operating environment in the country. By this process, the Indian vehicles had already been incorporated into a design trajectory distinct to that of Daimler-Benz vehicles. By the time the fifteen-year agreement between TELCO and Daimler-Benz expired in March 1969, the Press Tool Division at Pune was in full production; the complex tools and dies produced there eliminated dependence on imports for current operations and also provided a base for future tool manufacturing (TELCO, 1969, 1243–44). As a result of an agreement with Rheinstahl Henschel AG of West Germany, the facilities of the machine tool division in Pune enabled TELCO to produce indigenously the large number of special-purpose machine tools needed for replacing and modernizing the equipment of the automobile division in Jamshedpur, much of which had been operating continuously for many years (TELCO, 1968, 1189–91).

The manufacture of steam locomotives at Jamshedpur, which began in January 1952, ceased in June 1970 on the termination of TELCO's contract with the railways. The company had implemented plans for the utilization of the workers and plant facilities released by the cessation of locomotive manufacture (TELCO, 1970, 1309–11). New products, including tippers, forklifts and dumper placers, developed by the company's research and development engineers were being produced in the shops previously engaged in locomotive manufacture.

Many industrial plants in the country had been allowed to deteriorate through neglect, overworked for quick profits or badly maintained, resulting in not only their capability to incorporate technical change being depleted, but even their existing productive capacity decreasing. In TELCO, it was recognized that the size of the assets of a company did not determine the company's capabilities of production, especially on a continuing basis (TELCO, 1973, 1258–60). Great attention was paid to the maintenance of equipment, the reconditioning of old equipment and the replacement of worn-out machines. Large workshops in Jamshedpur and Pune, along with the machine tool division (also located in Pune) were active, meeting a significant part of the company's requirement of replacement machines which were usually imported in earlier times. The import of machine tools had become increasingly difficult and very costly, while indigenous manufacturers were not able to meet requirements fully, especially for the more sophisticated special-purpose machines.

It was not only through new models that the benefit of design and development efforts led to technological developments. Existing models were being continuously upgraded to attain higher standards of performance, leading to the development of fuel-efficient, rugged, abuse-proof products with low life-cycle costs (TELCO, 1982, 1276–77). Moreover, engineering developments in TELCO were not merely restricted to improvements in products. The automotive industry drew upon a multitude of complex, fast-changing technologies where know-how was being developed at an ever-increasing rate. Superficially, it would appear attractive to acquire such know-how merely through repeated foreign technological collaborations, but this was not the path best suited for long-term needs (TELCO 1984, 1180-81). The longer and harder route of training workers who were capable of absorbing the latest technology, along with giving them the facilities needed for their development, would ensure that the upgradation of technology become an inevitable component of growth in general. Such an approach did not exclude the import of existing technology or even that of component knocked-down (CKD) packs to start with. TELCO was encouraged by the Government of India to adopt this model.

Upgrading their manufacturing facilities had been a major element of TELCO's strategy. Along with the introduction of new manufacturing technologies, testing facilities were upgraded (Bowonder, 1998, 663). The focus was on the continuous improvement of productivity, quality and manufacturability through automation. In order to produce the 407 series of light commercial vehicles (LCVs) within a targeted time-frame, TELCO installed a number of computer numerically controlled (CNC) milling machines. A new electronic centre was established in Pune to support the manufacture and maintenance of CNC machines. These measures contributed to the establishment of a base for a higher level of flexibility.

Once the 407 series of LCV production started, the development of the heavier 608 series began. The manufacture of CNC machines with collaboration started during the 1986–87 financial year (Bowonder, 1998, 663). The collaboration was with two Japanese firms, Niigata Engineering Co. Ltd for NC/CNC horizontal machining centres and Nachi-Fujikoshi Corp. for NC/CNC in-line machining centres and flexible manufacturing systems (Dynamic Levels, n.d.). TELCO started retrofitting sophisticated control systems on older machines as part of its reconditioning and modernization programme. In 1987–88, a machine reconditioning programme was started as a part of the continuous plant rejuvenation efforts. After initiating steps for introducing the 608 LCV series, the next major effort was to develop production facilities for the 206 series pickup vehicles.

Because of the entry of larger transnational corporations into the automobile manufacturing sector in India, TELCO found it necessary to increase the level of automation in their factories. In 1994–95, for the first time in the country, TELCO produced three basic robots in collaboration with Nachi–Fujikoshi Corp. of Japan (Bowonder, 1998, 663). These were a spot-welding robot, a sealant application robot and an arc-welding robot. The continuous improvement of manufacturing systems, increased automation and retrofitting of older equipment were major initiatives to improve the company's manufacturing capabilities. The product development efforts and manufacturing technology improvements were implemented in a uniform manner to ensure that productivity never lagged.

The pool of technical talent engaged in various manufacturing activities constantly interacted with vehicle designers. A vehicle concept was thus developed by the vehicle design engineers through an intensive cross-flow of information from the marketing, testing, engineering, production and service functions (TELCO, 1988, 1672–73). It was this simultaneous collaboration that permitted the introduction of new vehicles to be speeded up. The traditional sequential procedure would have added years to the product introduction cycle. The best ideas available internationally (from engineers, suppliers and customers) contributed to the final design.

TELCO devised a strategy which used indigenous competence along with the acquisition of technology from abroad (Bowonder, 1998, 657). Most of these collaborations had been in the area of manufacturing process technology. The transfer of manufacturing process technology and rapid learning of competencies for new product engineering helped TELCO to become technologically competitive.

TELCO/Tata Motors' resource acquisition strategy in passenger cars

After a longer period of organic and incremental growth, TELCO was hit by a cyclical 40 per cent shrinkage of the Indian commercial vehicle (CV) market in 2000–01 which triggered a transformative phase of restructuring, process improvements and the rejuvenation of its management, preparing the ground for bolder strategic initiatives in the future (Bruche, 2010, 6). While TELCO's high degree of vertical integration was a boon in better times, this very factor was responsible for the company's underperformance in trying times. While it reaped the benefits of producing virtually all its components in-house, that advantage turned into its Achilles heel when the going became difficult, with the adverse situation magnifying itself all along the value chain (*Economic and Political Weekly*, 1999, 2284). In an attempt to deal with the cyclical demand patterns in the commercial vehicle industry, the company planned to apply a strategy to transform itself from a domestic commercial-vehicle maker to an automotive company. TELCO also adopted outsourcing and moved away from high levels of vertical integration (*Economic and Political Weekly*, 1999, 2284).

The focus of competitiveness had shifted from manufacturing capability to product development. Supply chains were increasingly driving manufacturing activity, with efficient assembling as the focus of attention (Bowonder, 2004,

292). This meant that product variety, product platforms, product development flexibility and product development cycle time were becoming the crucial differentiating elements in competition. With the growth of the commercial vehicle market slowing down, global competition had essentially focused on the passenger car market – the medium- and low-end markets.

The entry of Tata Motors – the renamed version of TELCO – into the passenger car market, its ascent as a relevant domestic player and its recent internationalization of sales and manufacturing in the passenger car segment have been underpinned by an intricate asset acquisition, accumulation and organizational learning process (Bruche, 2010, 7). In hindsight, four overlapping phases of this process can be discerned. Some phases were triggered by external events and usually involved the in-house implementation of strategic initiatives or projects. The phases were not results of a grand strategy, but rather the outcome of a strong intent to overcome a disadvantageous situation, coupled with an evolutionary search within a changing institutional context and internal resource conditions. When the management of Tata Motors decided to enter and compete in the passenger car segment, it relied to a considerable extent on strategic assets and capabilities built during its history as a commercial-vehicle only manufacturer. Long before Tata Motors entered the passenger car segment in the early 1990s, the company had taken some steps to extend its technological base and upgrade its capabilities in automobile design and manufacturing (TELCO, 1969, 1243). The establishment of an engineering research centre at Pune in 1967 facilitated the creation of an internal engineering force which would increase Tata Motors' absorptive capacity for external technologies and create a basis for indigenous product development. A more immediate facilitating condition was the development and manufacture of LCVs in the period immediately preceding Tata Motors' decision to enter the passenger car segment (the 407 model launched in 1986, followed by the Tata Mobile pickup in 1988), which provided a platform, engine technology, manufacturing capabilities and tooling capabilities (TELCO, 1989, 1824).

The initial entry of Tata Motors into passenger car manufacturing relied on an incremental extension or resource leverage from its LCV manufacturing framework, as both the Sierra (launched in 1991) and the Estate (launched in 1992) were built on the platform of the pickup (Bruche, 2010, 8). As B. Bowonder, the former Director of the Tata Management Training Centre, writes in his account of the Tata Motors' small car development project, 'the learning needed for making a car essentially started with the pickup vehicle

207' (Bowonder, 2004, 300). While the initial entry was focused on the large car segment, it had become increasingly clear that the Indian passenger car market would, for the foreseeable future, be a small car market. After market analyses and feasibility studies, in 1994, Tata Motors started its attempt to develop the first Indian small car for the domestic market – the Indica (*Economic and Political Weekly*, 1997, 2572). The car was to be positioned as a competitor to the Maruti 800, the market leader in this segment (which was manufactured by the Japanese carmaker Suzuki). As Bowonder put it, in terms of its principal approach in the Indica project, Tata Motors

> adopted the philosophy that all components critical to the car business were not to be sourced but should be produced internally. Specialised products were to be procured, especially those available in the market. Products for which suppliers had to make substantial investments would be done through joint ventures. Finally, generic components would be procured from good suppliers in India. With this in mind, critical capabilities needed from a long-term perspective were identified. Potential partners were identified for all critical components not available. This was done keeping in mind that the alliance relationship should give Tata Motors some inherent learning value. (Bowonder 2004, 310)

The development process involved some 700 engineers and cost (including tooling and the setting up of production facilities) $400 million, in comparison to the approximately $2 billion such a process would cost in a developed country (Bruche, 2010, 9). Tata Motors also set up a new organizational structure for tiered supplier management and entrusted the Tata Group affiliate Tata Automobile Components (TACO), newly formed in 1995, with this task. In only four years, Tata Motors significantly improved its capability to manage automobile development projects, and used the significant learning opportunities to expand its organizational as well as staff-level skill sets. The physical proximity of R&D, tooling and production in one place (Pune) were an advantage in building the complex concurrent engineering capabilities needed in automotive development projects (*Financial Express*, 2005; Bruche, 2010, 9).

The Nano project

Tata Motors was weak in technological capability, especially in product development capability. In 2003, when a project was started as an advanced engineering project, the objective was to develop a car that would be 'ultra cheap'

(Lim *et al.*, 2009, 16). The commercial project for the car was initiated in 2005. The team was given a base model product, the target price of $2,500, and the minimum performance requirements. This investigative process was guided by three parameters: acceptable cost ($2,500 price level), acceptable performance and regulatory compliance (safety and environmental regulation). The concept of PD was broadened to include the consideration of manufacturing costs. Thus, the design efficiency of each of the assemblies was examined through an exercise, the design for manufacturing and assembling; also, though the car's overall design was integral, some of the car's components were designed to be modular, so that the car could be built after assemblies were shipped to different locations where they would be integrated (Lim *et al.*, 2013, 18).

Tata engineers played a key role in the design of particular components as well as that of overall design. According to the Nano Project Head, the conventional approach towards motor vehicle design required the one-time specification in detail of the design, with targets for subsystems. The quality displayed in the execution of the entire project was the benchmark of success. With the Nano Project, on the other hand, emphasis was placed on iterations in design, the redefinition of targets and working closely with suppliers through the redesign process. The iterations in design were coordinated through daily sessions of the concerned groups, where prevailing assumptions could be challenged, failures and delays in execution be explicitly recognized, successes equally be celebrated and, above all, decisions on necessary design changes could be taken quickly.

The lean design principle was further extended to vendor management. Around 85 per cent of the value of the car was outsourced, of which about 70 per cent came from indigenous sources while the balance was imported. The suppliers participated in developing components with lower costs from an early stage of product development.

Although a new organization was created, drawing primarily from laterally hired recruits rather than internal Tata Motors personnel, the project team continued to make use of expertise from within Tata Motors. Assistance from the commercial vehicle arm was sought to identify ways to lay alternate fuel lines, make better use of plastics or build better lamps (Palepu *et al.*, 2011, 5–9).

Tata Motors extensively utilized three-dimensional CAD to support the PD process. This made it possible to build prototypes digitally, perform certain tests with simulation exercises and perform evaluations. According to an engineer from a consulting company that had advised Tata Motors on the use of digital technology, the design process for the Nano was an advance on that for the Indica in terms of computer-aided design, the use of digital mock-ups, digital validation for final assembly, digital validation for the body and digital factory modelling (Lim, 2009, 22). This investigative process was guided by three parameters: (*a*) acceptable cost (a \$2,500 price level), (*b*) acceptable performance and (*c*) regulatory compliance (safety and environmental regulations). The project was to be based on the Maruti 800 with an investigation of the assumptions underlying its design, the materials used in its manufacture and the actual manufacturing process. Thus, in this case, the lean product development (LPD) process initially involved a process of reverse engineering, of exploring a given product concept to achieve a drastic reduction in cost while adhering to the design parameters.

Transfer of frugal engineering expertise

One of the major foreign component suppliers for the Nano was the Bosch Automotive Group, a German automotive ancillary known for engineering excellence. Dr Bernd Bohr, Chairman of the Automotive Group, described the project environment inside Bosch:

> Tata did not come to us with large rulebooks or specifications. They simply told us what the weight of the car would be, that it would have a two-cylinder engine, and would need to achieve Euro IV emission regulation. In addition, it needs to drive, of course. And that was the major difference from other auto projects or customers.

> Early in the process, one could already see that our teams were coming up with new ideas that created a kind of self-momentum. Where usually one would say that cost reduction is not so exciting for an engineer, here we really had teams having fun. For example, typically each cylinder has an injection valve on an engine; here, our engineers came up with the idea of saying, let us have one injection valve for two cylinders and give two spray holes so that it takes care of two cylinders. On the software side, a typical electronic control unit (or ECU) for a middle-class car in Europe would have 5,500 parameter groups; for the Nano we have 1,700. With that complexity out of the system one can have a smaller processor, less power consumption, and so on. Similarly, the idle speed control, which keeps the engine at the same rest when you are idling, has over 100 parameters you can adjust in a typical car. The Nano has seven. Maybe in some cases the RPMs would vary by 10 or 20 RPM, the engine will still not stall, and 99 per cent of drivers would not notice. But that's the kind of 'perfection' that has accumulated in control systems over the years.

Questioning things we have taken for granted is useful. We are now using low-price vehicles as a training and learning ground to do things simpler. In terms of technical innovation itself, I would probably put this project at a five or six. There were some things like pushing diesel injection from 2,000 to 2,500 bar, coming up with new materials and new laser machining processes, where it would be an eight or nine. However, the major challenge was getting across the cost barrier while doing all this. That would be a 10. (Palepu *et al.*, 2011, 7)

Bohr emphasized that while Bosch would not 'buy' itself into this market segment and the margins that they expected were similar to that on large-volume European projects, they anticipated a learning experience. This would later be transferred to products for their European, American and Japanese customers. He claimed that there were already early success stories of this transfer. It was for the first time that Bosch was proud of having designed cost reduction techniques (Palepu *et al.*, 2011, 8).

The Nano development project was also achieved in close cooperation with Tata Technologies Limited (TTL). INCAT is an operating company of TTL. INCAT was a British-owned engineering company until 2005, when it was acquired by the Tata group (*Business Line*, 2005). INCAT's services include product design, analysis and production engineering, and product-centric information technology (IT) services including IT services for the digital tools supporting product development. It has a cooperative relationship with Dassault Systems, UGS and Autodesk – companies that provide PD digital technology. It has around 3,000 employees globally, with engineering centres in North America, Europe, India and Thailand. INCAT has been involved with the development of the Nano from the start and has worked with 'a significant number' of Nano's suppliers.

Conclusions

The organization of R&D in TELCO from 1965, the formation of Tata Technologies in 1989 as part of TELCO, its separation as a subsidiary in 1994 and the acquisition of INCAT in 2005 are all identifiable stages in the organic and acquired growth of technological capability within TELCO/Tata Motors, and within the Tata Group as a whole. The movement of innovative capabilities in manufacturing processes which preoccupied TELCO during the 1970s and 1980s found fruition in the product development expertise exemplified by the introduction of the Indica, Ace and Nano (Palepu and Srinivasan, 2008). Although the Nano project was considerably aided by the expertise embodied in INCAT, what is of note is the absorption of lean design capabilities within Tata Technologies and its transfer to consultancy projects in advanced manufacturing projects and even to its sub-systems suppliers (Simhan, 2013; Baggonkar, 2010).

This chapter has concentrated on the evolution of technological competence in TELCO/Tata Motors and Tata Technologies. This is largely because of the greater attention paid to developments in these firms in management literature, if not yet in the academic field. However, there are indications that other Indian firms in the automotive sector share these attributes (Kar, 2012). This allows us to conclude that not only is there a generic competence embodied in what has been termed frugal innovation, but that the application of the import substitution initiative and the phased manufacturing programme did indeed provide the basis for this now internationally accepted achievement (KPMG, 2011; Bound and Thornton, 2012).

References

Al-Ashaab, Ahmed *et al*. 2013. 'The Transformation of Product Development Process into Lean Environment Using Set-Based Concurrent Engineering: A Case Study from an Aerospace Industry.' *Concurrent Engineering* 21 (4): 268–85.

Baggonkar, Swaraj. 2010. 'Our Indian Operations Are Helping Us Better the Technology. Interview with Bernd Bohr, Chairman, Automotive Group, Bosch.' *Business Standard*, 5 January. Accessed 12 December 2013. Available at http://www.business-standard.com/article/companies/-our-indian-operations-are-helping-us-better-the-technology-110010500065_1.html.

Baines, T. *et al*. 2006. 'State-of-the-art in Lean Design Engineering: A Literature Review on White Collar Lean.' *Proceedings of the Institution of Mechanical Engineers, Part B: Journal of Engineering Manufacture* 220 (9): 1539–47.

Bhatti, Yasser Ahmad and Marc Ventresca. 2012. 'The Emerging Market for Frugal Innovation: Fad, Fashion, or Fit?' Accessed 11 December 2013. DOI: http://dx.doi.org/10.2139/ssrn.2005983.

Bound, Kirsten and Ian Thornton. 2012. 'Our Frugal Future: Lessons from India's Innovation System.' Accessed 1 November 2013. Available at http://www.nesta.org.uk/publications/our-frugal-future-lessons-india%C2%92s-innovation-system.

Bowonder, B. 1998. 'Competitive and Technology Management Strategy: A Case Study of TELCO.' *International Journal of Technology Management* 15 (6/7): 646–89.

————. 2004. 'Concurrent Engineering in an Indian Automobile Firm: The Experience of Tata Motors.' *International Journal of Manufacturing Technology and Management* 6 (3/4): 291–314.

Bruche, Gert. 2010. 'Tata Motor's Transformational Resource Acquisition Path: A Case Study of Latecomer Catch-Up in a Business Group Context.' Working Papers of the Institute of Management Berlin at the Berlin School of Economics and Law (HWR Berlin), No. 55. Accessed 27 November 2013. Available at http://hdl.handle.net/10419/74359.

Business Line. 2005. 'Tatas to Acquire UK Co Incat for ₹416 Cr.' 18 August. Accessed 27 December 2013. Available at http://www.thehindubusinessline.com/todays-paper/tp-corporate/tatas-to-acquire-uk-co-incat-for-rs-416-cr/article2186808.ece.

Chase, Jim. 2000. 'Measuring Value in Product Development.' Massachusetts Institute of Technology, The Lean Aerospace Initiative Working Paper Series WP00-05. Stab Accessed 24 December 2013. Available at http://dspace.mit.edu/bitstream/handle/1721.1/7330/Measuring%20Value%20in%20Product%20Development.pdf?sequence=1.

Dynamic Levels. n.d. *Tata Motors Company History - Dynamic Levels.* Accessed 11 June 2017. Available at https://www.dynamiclevels.com/en/tata-motors-company-history.

Economic and Political Weekly. 1997. 'Large Investment Programme.' 32 (41): 2572.

————. 1999. 'Mixed Performance.' 34 (33): 2284.

The Economist. 2010a. 'First Break All the Rules: The Charms of Frugal Innovation.' 15 April. Accessed 1 November 2013. Available at http://www.economist.com/node/15879359.

————. 2010b. 'The World Turned Upside Down.' 15 April. Accessed 1 November 2013. Available at http://www.economist.com/node/15879369.

Financial Express. 2005. 'Pune Sets the Pace in Industrial Design.' 17 June. Accessed 27 December 2013. Available at http://www.financialexpress.com/news/pune-sets-the-pace-in-industrial-design/142561/0.

Government of India. 1954. *Report of the Engineering Capacity Survey Committee.* New Delhi: Ministry of Commerce and Industry Manager of Publications.

Haque, B. 2003. 'Lean Engineering in the Aerospace Industry.' *Proceedings of the Institution of Mechanical Engineers, Part B: Journal of Engineering Manufacture* 217: 1409–20.

Kar, Sayantani. 2012. 'Frugal Engineering Is Not At All about Cost-Cutting: Pawan Goenka. Interview with President, Automotive and Farm Division, M&M.' *Business Standard,* 8 October. Accessed 8 October 2012. Available at http://www.business-standard.com/article/management/frugal-engineering-is-not-at-all-about-cost-cutting-pawan-goenka-112100800030_1.html.

KPMG. 2011. 'The Irresistible Rise of Frugal Engineering.' Accessed 1 November 2013.

Available at http://www.kpmg.com/uk/en/issuesandinsights/articlespublications/pages/the-irresistible-rise-of-frugal-engineering.aspx.

Li, Zejian. 2012. 'Market Life-Cycle and Products Strategies for Emerging Markets: Toward a New Age of Indian Automotive Market.' MMRC Discussion Paper Series No. 387. Accessed 6 December 2013. Available at http://merc.e.u-tokyo.ac.jp/mmrc/dp/pdf/MMRC387_2012.pdf.

Lim, Chaisung. *et al.* 2009. 'Low-Cost Disruptive Innovation by an Indian Automobile Manufacturer.' MMRC Discussion Paper Series No. 280. Accessed 6 December 2013. Available at http://merc.e.u-tokyo.ac.jp/mmrc/dp/pdf/MMRC280_2009.pdf.

Miles, Walton. 1999. 'Strategies for Lean Product Development.' Massachusetts Institute of Technology, The Lean Aerospace Initiative Working Paper Series WP99-01-91. Accessed 11 December 2013. Available at   http://dspace.mit.edu/bitstream/handle/1721.1/7519/Strategies%20for%20Lean%20Product%20Development.pdf.

Moolgaokar, Sumant. 1953. 'Letter to T. T. Krishnamachari'. 5 October. TTK Papers. Correspondence with S. Moolgaokar File, 1-2. Nehru Memorial Museum and Library, New Delhi.

Palepu, Krishna G. and Vishnu Srinivasan. 2008. 'Tata Motors: The Tata Ace.' Harvard Business School Case No 108-011. Obtainable by e-mail.

Palepu, Krishna G., Bharat N. Anand and Rachna Tahilyani. 2011. 'Tata Nano – The People's Car.' Harvard Business School Case No. 710-420. Obtainable by e-mail.

Radjou, Navi, Jaideep Prabhu and Simone Ahuja. 2012. 'Frugal Innovation: Lessons from Carlos Ghosn, CEO, Renault-Nissan.' *Harvard Business Review*, 2 July. Accessed 3 December 2013. Available at http://blogs.hbr.org/2012/07/frugal-innovation-lessons-from/.

Ryans, A. 2008. *Beating Low Cost Competition: How Premium Brands Can Respond to Cut-Price Rivals.* Chichester: Wiley.

Sarkar, Prasanta and Debarsish Hazarika. 2011. 'Engine Management on a Budget.' *Automotive Engineering International* 119 (2): 28–30.

Simhan, T. E. Raja. 2013. 'Tata Tech Comes Out of Parent Firm's Shadows to Boost Revenues.' *Business Line*, 30 July. Accessed 7 November 2013. Available at http://www.thehindubusinessline.com/industry-and-economy/info-tech/tata-tech-comes-out-of-parent-firms-shadows-to-boost-revenues/article4970785.ece.

TELCO. 1968. 'Tata Engineering and Locomotive Co Ltd: Statement of the Chairman, Mr J. R. D. Tata.' *Economic and Political Weekly* 3 (30): 1189–91.

———. 1969. 'Tata Engineering and Locomotive Co Ltd: Statement of the Chairman, Mr J. R. D. Tata.' *Economic and Political Weekly* 4 (28–30): 1243–44.

————. 1970. 'Tata Engineering and Locomotive Co Ltd: Statement of the Chairman, Mr J. R. D. Tata.' *Economic and Political Weekly* 5 (29–31): 1309–11.

————. 1973. 'Tata Engineering and Locomotive Company Limited: Statement of the Chairman, Mr. S. Moolgaokar.' *Economic and Political Weekly* 8 (28): 1258–60.

————. 1982. 'The Tata Engineering & Locomotive Company Limited: Statement of the Chairman, Mr. S. Moolgaokar.' *Economic and Political Weekly* 17 (32): 1276–77.

————. 1984. 'The Tata Engineering & Locomotive Company Limited: Statement of the Chairman, Mr. S. Moolgaokar.' *Economic and Political Weekly* 19 (30): 1180–81.

————. 1988. 'The Tata Engineering & Locomotive Company Limited: Statement of the Chairman, Mr. S. Moolgaokar.' *Economic and Political Weekly* 23 (33): 1672–73.

————. 1989. 'The Tata Engineering & Locomotive Company Limited: Statement of the Chairman, Mr. Ratan N. Tata, for the year 1988–89.' *Economic and Political Weekly* 24 (32): 1824–25.

Womack, James P. and Daniel T. Jones. 1996/2010. *Lean Thinking: Banish Waste and Create Wealth in Your Corporation*, Second edition. New York: Free Press.

9

Industrial Upgrading in the Apparel Value Chain

The Sri Lanka Experience

Prema-chandra Athukorala

Introduction

The global landscape of the apparel industry is being profoundly transformed following the termination of the Multi-Fibre Arrangement (MFA) on 1 January 2005. International buyers are now free to source apparel from any country, subject only to the system of tariffs. Since they are no longer constrained by country-specific quotas, buyers can demand many more attributes of products from suppliers in addition to price. These would include things like product variety, quality and timely delivery. They have also started to aggressively restructure their sourcing patterns to procure from fewer efficient suppliers worldwide and to develop long-term strategic partnerships with core suppliers by setting up local sourcing offices, bypassing their erstwhile sourcing agents (Fung, Fung and Wind, 2007; USITC, 2012). The importance of these non-price factors in export success in the post-MFA era has been further elevated by the ongoing process of 'lean retailing', a business strategy that has become widespread in the apparel trade in developed countries since the mid-1990s (Abernathy *et al.*, 1999, 2006; Evens and Harrigan, 2005; Harrigan and Barrows, 2009). Lean retailing involves replenishing the range of apparel on offer on the shop floor in very short cycles (rather than seasonally, as was traditionally done), while defraying the inventory risk by holding low stocks. In the process of lean retailing, 'suppliers' warehouses and distribution centres act in many ways as virtual warehouses and distribution centres for the retailer (Abernathy *et al.*, 1999, 16). The buyers also increasingly require suppliers to undertake tasks such as labelling, packaging and barcoding, which were traditionally done in the buyer's warehouses or distribution centres (Abernathy *et al.*, 2006; Fung *et al.*, 2007).

In this context, the export success of apparel manufactures depend crucially on industrial upgrading, the ability to 'climb the value chain from basic assembly activities to full-package supply and integrated manufacturing' (Gereffi and Fernandez-Stark, 2016, 5). Understanding the processes and drivers of industrial upgrading is vital for crafting national policies for facilitating the required industrial adjustment. Much has been written about the impact of MFA on global trade patterns and the governance of the global apparel value chain, especially about the way in which lead firms organize their supply chain on a global scale. There is, however, a dearth of studies of the experiences of exporting countries in repositioning in the apparel value chain in the post-MFA era. This chapter aims to contribute towards filling this gap by examining structural adjustment in the apparel industry in Sri Lanka, a country that provides an interesting case study of this subject. For over three decades, Sri Lanka's apparel industry has remained deeply embedded within the global apparel supply chain. The industry has managed to maintain its world market share, in spite of the disappearance of assured market access provided by export quotas under the MFA and significant increases in manufacturing wages relative to the other low-wage countries in the regions. A number of large Sri Lankan firms have consolidated their position in the world apparel trade as credible suppliers to leading brand name owners.

The study is based on data pieced together from secondary sources and information gathered from field research. The secondary sources include unpublished investment approval and monitoring records of the Sri Lanka Board of Investment; unpublished exporter-level customs data disaggregated by commodity, destination and the mode of shipment; the UN Comtrade database; the news clipping collection at the Institute of Policy Studies, Colombo; and company websites. As part of the field research, face-to-face interviews were conducted during June-July in 2016 and July-August 2016 with top executives of thirteen apparel exporting firms of varying sizes, and senior officials of the Joint Apparel Association Forum (JAAF), the Ceylon Chamber of Commerce, the Sri Lanka Export Development Board, the Institute of Policy Studies, and the Ministry of Industry and Commerce.

The chapter is structured as follows. The next section introduces the conceptual framework that underpins the ensuing empirical analysis. The succeeding section provides an overview of the initial conditions and policy reforms that provided a setting for the expansion of the export-oriented apparel industry in Sri Lanka. The following section is an analytical narrative of the evolution of Sri Lanka's engagement in the apparel value chain, focussing specifically on the role of international buyers and the role of specific socio-economic factors which shaped the relationship between international buyers and domestic apparel producers. The section before the final one examines Sri Lanka's performance in apparel exports, paying particular attention to the emerging trends and patterns following MFA abolition. The key findings and inferences are summarized in the final section.

Analytical framework

The analytical framework of this study is a pragmatic mixture of the global value chain (GVC) approach and mainstream economics of patterns and determinants of manufacturing exports from developing countries. In order to understand the drivers of export performance and industrial upgrading of a given country within a demand-responsive industry such as apparel, it is necessary to go beyond the standard economic analysis and examine its experience in the context of changing governance patterns of the global apparel value chain.[1] For this purpose, we draw on the GVC framework developed by Gereffi (1994, 1999) and elaborated by many others (Gereffi *et al.*, 2005; Bair and Peters, 2006; Neidik and Gereffi, 2006; Gereffi and Frederick, 2010; Humphrey and Schmitz, 2002). The prime focus of the GVC approach is on inter-firm networks by which developing country producers, through foreign buyers, access international markets. In order to capture the full picture of a country's engagement in the value chain of a given industry, it is necessary to incorporate the GVC approach in a more general economic analysis of export-oriented industrialization, paying attention to both relevant country-specific characteristics and the policy context.

The GVC framework is built around the role of the international buyer (the lead firms) as the key driver in the formation and shaping of the global value chain in demand-responsive industries. It postulates that the mediated linkages between the lead firms and sellers shape international production and trade patterns. The success of a developing country's firms entering export markets and achieving industrial upgrading – movement from low-value to increasingly high-value activities in the GVC – depends crucially on the links they forge with lead firms.

---

1   A demand-response industry is one that is economically organized 'backward' in direct response to the demand from global buyers of the final product (the 'lead firms'); using information on final demand collected through point-of-sales information or other means such as focus group surveys, the lead firm locates manufacturers that can produce the goods at quality and quantity levels required by the consumers (Feenstra and Hamilton, 2006).

In its application to the global apparel industry, the GVC framework specifies four sequential phases in the process of industrial upgrading: cut, make, and trim (CMT) (simple assembly) activities; original equipment manufacture (OEM) (package contracting); original design manufacturing (ODM) (full-packaging); and original brand manufacturing (OBM) (Gereffi, 1999; Gereffi and Frederick, 2010). Moving from CMT to OEM status involves acquiring an expanded set of capabilities in filling orders placed by the lead firms, which includes making samples; procuring or manufacturing the needed inputs; meeting international standards in terms of price and quality and delivery; and packing and shipping the finish goods. The full-package role requires manufacturers to coordinate the entire manufacturing process, including the procurement of fabric and other inputs. In addition to the experience gained and the strong links developed with buyers through OEM, there are two strategies that would help a firm obtain ODM status. The first strategy is to integrate the production process vertically (the creation of backward linkages) to gain a competitive edge involving improved quality, timely delivery of fabric and other ancillary inputs. Since fabric is the most important input in the clothing chain, virtually all countries that want to develop full-package capabilities need to develop a strong textile industry. The second strategy is the creation of cross-border triangular manufacturing arrangement by setting up production bases in other countries to gain competitive advantages from differences in the cost of production (mainly the labour cost) in order to reap relative cost advantages and preferential market access. The OBM status, which entails the firm developing its own brands, is the most advanced stage of industrial upgrading. It requires design and marketing capabilities in addition to the preconditions required for achieving ODM status. A transition from ODM to OBM status is difficult because of complex barriers to entry into developed country markets. For many firms in developing countries, the viable strategy for achieving OBM would be to begin with brand development for the domestic market or markets in neighbouring developing countries (Neidik and Gereffi, 2006).

The way the relationship between the lead firm and the manufacturing firm (the supplier) shapes the industrial upgrading of the latter depends on the nature of activities the former performs within the GVC. To understand the nature of this relationship, the GVC framework comes up with a four-way typology of lead firms: mass retailers (for example, Walmart, K-mart, Sears, Dillards, C&A), speciality retailers (L Brands,[2] Gap, Marks and Spencer, Mango,

---

2   Formerly known as Limited Brands Inc. and The Limited Inc.

Abercrombie), brand marketers (Nike, Polo, Hugo Boss, Gucci, Victoria's Secret, Ralph Lauren, Inditex [Zara], Hennes & Mauritz [H&M]) and brand manufacturers (Wrangler, Levi's, Van Heusen, VF). Mass retailers normally do not directly deal with the manufacturers (do not undertake direct sourcing); they predominantly source through value-chain intermediaries (alternatively knows as sourcing agents, international buyers, sourcing companies, jobbers and packagers). The other three types use a mix of direct sourcing and reliance on value-chain intermediaries, with brand marketers and brand manufacturers generally placing greater weight on direct sourcing compared to speciality retailers. Compared to sourcing through intermediaries, direct sourcing presumably involves greater transmission of capabilities from the lead firm to the manufacturer, facilitating industrial upgrading.

'Participation in global value chains is a necessary step for industrial updating because it puts firms and economies on potentially dynamic learning curves' (Gereffi, 1999, 59). However, in order to understand the process of industrial upgrading in a given economy it is important to pay attention to the buyer–producer interaction within the broader international and national institutional and policy contexts (Bair and Peters, 2006; Feenstra and Hamilton, 2006). On the international front, global trade policy regimes (the MFA phase-out being a classic example) and regional or global trade preference schemes are an integral part of the operational environment within which the buyers operate. On the domestic front both country-specific (non-policy) and policy-related factors play an important role in determining the nature of the buyer–producer international and the upgrading outcome. Country-specific factors include country-size measured by population, historical legacies such as colonial links, and geographic location. Openness to trade and foreign investment, labour market flexibility, the availability of trainable labour and the quality of trade-related infrastructure figure prominently among the policy-related factors.

Initial conditions and policy reforms

In the 1960s, when the 'retail revolution' in developed countries propelled the global spread of apparel production (Feenstra and Hamilton, 2006, 352),and well into the late 1970s, the Sri Lanka economy remained virtually delinked from the global economy with a highly interventionist trade and industrial policy regime (Lal and Rajapatirana, 1989; Athukorala and Rajapatirana, 2000). From the late 1960s, when the state-led import-substitution industrialization was in severe crisis because of foreign exchange scarcity, there was policy emphasis on promoting manufacturing exports and encouraging export-oriented foreign direct investment (FDI) through selective incentives. However, these attempts largely failed, because the overall business climate of the country continued to be characterized by a significant 'anti-export' bias. Moreover, during the period from 1970 to 1977, widespread nationalization of private properties and businesses, coupled with various economic controls, effectively marginalized the private sector in the economy. International buyers and the 'quota-hopping' apparel firms in East Asia, therefore, bypassed Sri Lanka, notwithstanding its specific advantages, such as its strategic location, the availability of cheap and trainable labour, trade links forged during the colonial era and trade-related infrastructure of reasonable quality.[3]

The expansion of export-oriented apparel production in Sri Lanka began only after liberalization reforms were initiated in 1977. The first round of reforms carried out during 1977–79 included the elimination of quantitative import restrictions, a significant reduction of import tariffs, revamping the foreign investment approval and monitoring process, and the setting up of the Greater Colombo Economic Commission (GCEC) in 1978 with wide-ranging powers to establish and operate export processing zones (EPZs) with an internationally competitive incentive package.[4] As an important part of the FDI policy, steps were also taken to enter into investment protection agreements and double taxation relief agreements with the major investing countries. A guarantee against nationalization of foreign assets without compensation was provided under Article 157 of the new Constitution of Sri Lanka adopted in 1978. Wide-ranging export promotion schemes, including

---

3   Sri Lanka's missed opportunities are vividly illustrated in a comparison with Mauritius, the remote Indian Ocean island state which had far fewer favourable initial conditions for joining the apparel value chain. A free trade zone set up in 1969, which effectively insulated the export sector from trade restrictions and labour-market rigidities in the rest of the economy, provided the setting for the expansion of clothing exports from Mauritius. A thriving export-oriented apparel industry had developed in the country by the mid-1970s, with the involvement of investors from Hong Kong who came there following colonial trade roots to circumvent MFA quotas (Subramanian and Roy, 2003).

4   The first EPZ, at Katunayaka near the Colombo International Airport (henceforth KEPZ), was opened in 1978. The remarkable success of the KEPZ paved the way for the setting up of a second EPZ in Biyagama (a northern suburb of Colombo) (BEPZ) in 1982 and a third in Koggala (KGEPZ) on the southern coast in June 1991. Five other mini EPZs were opened in regional cities (Mirigama, Wathupitiwala, Pallekele, Seethawaka and Hambantota) during the ensuing years. Katunayaka and Biayagama zones have remained fully occupied for the past ten years.

an all-encompassing duty rebate scheme with flexible operational procedures and a manufacturing-in-bond scheme, were introduced for export-oriented firms located outside free-trade zones (FTZs) under a newly established Export Development Board (EDB).

As part of a 'second wave' liberalization reform package introduced in the early 1990s, most of the restrictions on the ownership structures of joint-venture projects located outside EPZs were abolished, and free-trade-zone privileges were extended to export-oriented ventures in all parts of the country (in addition to the ones located in the area demarcated by the original GCEC Act). The GCEC was reconstituted in 1991 with the new name of the Board of Investment (BOI), and further liberalization of foreign trade ensued. In 1992, the BOI introduced a new incentive scheme ('The 200 Garment Factory Programme') to entice the apparel industry to move to rural areas. Under this scheme, firms which set up factories in rural area were offered attractive tax incentives, access to bank credit and also priority in allocation of export quotas under the MFA. Import duties on textiles and yarn were abolished in 1998 to relieve apparel producers of administrative costs involved in using the duty rebate and bonded warehouse schemes. This was followed by the introduction of a Temporary Import for Export Processing (TIEP) scheme (as an alternative to the existing duty rebate and bonded warehouse schemes) to facilitate duty free access to other imported intermediate goods. Under this scheme, exporting firms were able to import inputs against a bank guarantee without paying tariffs and other fiscal levies and without requiring customs inspection of warehouses.

There has been some backsliding in liberalization reforms from around 2005, in particular after the end of the separatist war in May 2009 (Athukorala, 2012). The foreign investment regime has become increasingly opaque/interventionist. There has also been some reversal in trade liberalization with a range of new import taxes introduced in order to defray the costs of specific government services and/or to promote import-substituting domestic production. However, export-oriented firms have continued to remain insulated from the distortion in the overall trade regime because of the EPZ and TIEP schemes, which provide exporters with access to imported inputs at international prices.

The organized labour market in Sri Lanka has long been characterized by significant rigidities, in particular with costly processes involved in resolving labour disputes and retrenchment, as well as trade union activism (World Bank, 2005). The liberalization reforms package of 1977 included sweeping labour market reforms to achieve greater labour market flexibility, but the government was forced to abandon the proposed reforms in the face of widespread opposition by trade unions. However, the government managed to abolish the ban on night-work for women in FTZ enterprises under the GCEC Act. Firms located within FTZs were also cushioned against labour-market rigidities in the rest of the economy by enabling these enterprises to recruit workers from applicants who were registered with the GCEC after prior police screening for trade union involvement, and through a tight inspection process for monitoring the daily entry of workers to EPZs.

The available data suggest that production disruption caused by trade union action continued to remain far less in apparel factories located outside FTZs compared to the other industries. Employment conditions, particularly in large firms, have improved significantly, leaving little room for trade union action. Moreover, the dominance of female workers in the work force is an important source of industrial peace.[5] The 'masculinist orientation' of political trade unionism in Sri Lanka hindered women from participation in trade unions. Also, female workers do not have any compelling reason for joining unions because of the short-term nature of their employment; they typically remain in the labour force or a period of about five years before returning to their villages to move onto other forms of employment and getting married (Gunawardana, 2007).

Expansion of apparel industry

The 'quota-hopping' apparel producing firms in East Asia, in particular from Hong Kong, the major developing-country exporter of apparel at the time, responded swiftly to liberalization reforms in Sri Lanka. By the mid-1980s, there were over fifty foreign invested enterprises (FIEs) operating in the Sri Lankan apparel industry. When apparel exports from Sri Lanka began to come under MFA quotas in 1983, the BOI started considering the ability to produce non-quota products as a key criterion in approving new investment projects. Consequently, from the early 1990s, the arrival of new East Asian firms (whose entry was driven primarily by the quota-jumping motive) virtually stopped and a number of such firms phased out operations in Sri Lanka. However, there was no decline in the number of FIEs because of a notable increase in the arrival of new investors from developed countries, in particular the UK, Italy and Germany. There was also a clear pattern of 'localization' of

---

5   Young women drawn from the rural poor make up approximately 85 per cent of all
    workers in the garment industry (Nordås, 2003).

the export-oriented apparel industry. The number of completely locally owned firms set up with the approval of the BOI increased from 14 (18 per cent of all BOI-approved firms) in 1994 to 108 (44 per cent of all BOI firms) in 2015. With increased localization, there was a shift in the ownership structure of FIEs from full foreign ownership to joint ventures with local investors. In 2015, only 8 per cent of all BOI-approved apparel firms in operation (10 out of 120) were fully foreign owned, compared to 80 per cent (12 out of 16) in 1982.[6]

At the formative stage, the Sri Lankan apparel industry was very much an integral part of the 'triangular apparel network' centred on East Asia (Gereffi, 1994) in which the East Asian firms shifted some of the orders to affiliated factories in Sri Lanka and shipped finished products directly to the foreign buyer under the quota issued to Sri Lanka by the importing country. The newly emerged Sri Lankan (local) apparel assembly firms were predominantly subcontractors to the subsidiaries of East Asian companies.

From around the mid-1980s, the importance of triangular trade began to diminish owing to three important developments. First, as the volume of exports expanded, many international buyers began to set up buying offices in Sri Lanka. These buying offices soon began to play a crucial role in linking local firms to international markets. Second, the developed-country (mostly European) firms which set up production plants in Sri Lanka came with already established direct market links with retailers and brand marketers in their countries of origin. Third, more recently a number of large local firms began to deal directly with lead firms based on market links established with the help of joint-venture operations with foreign firms. Some of these firms have set up their own sales offices in major importing countries and in Hong Kong.

The apparel industry in Sri Lanka, as in other second-tier exporting countries, started with 'cut, make and trim' (CMT) operations: simple 'contract manufacturing' for international buyers, using designs and all intermediate inputs (fabrics and accessories) provided by the buyer. At the time, the industry was often referred to as a 'glorified tailor shop'. However, from the late 1990s, an increasing number of firms embarked on package contracting (original equipment manufacturing, OEM): producing apparel according to customer specifications, but sourcing fabrics and other inputs from foreign suppliers designated by the buyers. A number of these firms have now become full-package

---

6 The data provided in this paragraph is based on unpublished official records of the Sri Lankan Board of Investment.

manufacturers (or original design manufacturers [ODMs]). They offer a full range of services to customers encompassing product development, pattern making, finishing, sourcing, manufacturing and delivery. ODM firms now account for about 60 per cent of total exports (by value), with the rest coming from package contractors. CMT activity has virtually become a relic of the past. There are also a few reported cases of Sri Lankan firms gaining 'original brand manufacturing' (OBM) status (JAAF, 2012). So far there has been only one successful case of a Sri Lankan firm (MAS Holdings, the largest firm in Sri Lanka) launching its own brand (a sign of graduating to OBM status), but the new lingerie brand still accounts for only a tiny share of its total exports (Athukorala and Ekanayake, 2016, Appendix 2).

By the late the 1990s, the Sri Lankan apparel industry had a well-developed customer base including well-known brand names such as Victoria's Secret, Marks and Spencer, Sainsbury's, Tesco, Hunkemöller, Abercrombie and Fitch, GAP, Liz Claiborne, Nike, Pierre Cardin, Ralph Lauren and Tommy Hilfiger. Large apparel firms (at least the top ten companies in terms of export value in 2013) had established their own design centres which worked closely with design teams of brand owners. Most large companies (in particular the top ten) have invested in computer-aided designing (CAD) and computer-aided manufacturing (CAM) and electronic fitting ('e-fitting'), which enable design decisions by visualizing the garment digitally, skipping the standard fit-on session with a model.

The type of international buyers who came to the country had a significant impact on the evolution and industrial upgradation of the Sri Lankan apparel industry. Before exports from Sri Lanka came under MFA quotas, the major buyers of apparel produced in Sri Lanka were mass retailers who procured products from East Asian intermediaries under triangular exporting arrangements. However, the attractiveness of the country for mass retailers rapidly diminished as the country began to come under MFA quota allocation systems. The quota for a given product was not adequate for achieving the scale economies needed to be a competitive supplier.[7] So, from the mid-1980s, Sri Lankan exports were predominantly to speciality retailers and

---

7   For instance, Epic, a Hong Kong-based large-scale supplier of trousers to mass retailers, came to Sri Lanka in the early 1990s but soon left for Bangladesh because, under the 'the complex web of quotas that dominated international trade in garments [it] could not get enough quota allocation to make one product [trousers] … in the tiny country' (Jacob, 2013). However, the failed Sri Lankan operation gave Epic access to a pool of excellent managers; many of Epic's managers in its Bangladesh operations are from Sri Lanka.

brand marketers, who sought greater variety and smaller orders that suited the small-scale operations of Sri Lankan firms. Moreover, these buyers, unlike the buyers for mass retailers, often worked closely with local manufacturers, imparting technical, managerial and marketing know-how required for product improvement. Close links with brand marketers were accompanied by a shift in the product mix from mass-market products to niche products, particularly women's underwear and brassières, and knitted intimate apparel and active wear.

Some buyers of brand marketers made an even greater impact on the upgradation of local firms by becoming joint-venture partners in manufacturing. Among them, the role of Mast Industries, the overseas buying arm of The Limited, deserves particular attention (Brandix Lanka Limited, 2015). In the mid-1980s, Mast set up joint ventures with two small local companies in Sri Lanka to produce inner wear (pantyhose and brassières) and casual wear. With marketing and technical know-how obtained from this vital initial link, these two apparel firms (later renamed MAS Holdings and Brandix) have grown to become not only the two largest apparel exporters in the country, but also important players in these product lines at the world stage (Athukorala and Ekanayake, 2014, Appendix 2). They have also become multinationals in their own right, with production operations in a number of other countries. They have been instrumental in making Sri Lanka a design hub in South Asia.

In the mid-1990s, a number of Sri Lankan apparel companies set up production plants in countries like the Maldives, Madagascar, Bangladesh, Mauritius and Kenya in order to circumvent MFA quota restrictions on their operations in Sri Lanka. These ventures employed Sri Lankan technicians and managers and, in some cases, Sri Lankan machinists. Some of these 'quota-hopping' production bases were shifted back to Sri Lanka after MFA's abolition; only those located in countries which continue to assure profitability due to tariff preferences and/or relatively low wages compared to Sri Lanka have continued to remain in operation. Following the MFA's abolition, the three largest Sri Lankan firms have set up plants in Vietnam, Bangladesh and India. Recently, a medium-sized Sri Lankan firm set up a manufacturing plant in Jordan as a direct response to its US buyers, whose sourcing calculations has been changed because of a free-trade agreement between Jordan and the USA. These firms are coordinating production in these countries to meet orders from their strategic buyers, reminiscent of the triangular manufacturing practices of the East Asian firms during the MFA era.

Backward linkages

A key determinant of a firm's success in flexible manufacturing is the domestic availability of high quality fabric at competitive prices. This enhances the international competitiveness of firms by avoiding the transport costs of inputs, time delays and the time required by management to coordinate the fragmented supply chain.

In many countries, the expansion of the export-oriented apparel industry was aided by a well-established textile base developed during the import-substitution industrialization phase (Feenstra and Hamilton, 2006; Tokatli and Kizilgun, 2008; Tewari, 2008a). However, the expansion of apparel exports from Sri Lanka began without a strong domestic textile base. The government-owned textile factories were closed down following liberalization reforms as they failed to face the new competitive market conditions. At the initial stage of the expansion of apparel exports, presumably 'triangular trade' discouraged the early emergence of textile factories. The East Asian firms operating in Sri Lanka found it more profitable to supply yarn and textiles from their established procurement sources in their home countries than to attempt to produce them in Sri Lanka. For these reasons, the domestic content of apparel exports was basically equivalent to the labour context (about 20 per cent) and the low level of backward integration was a major concern of policymakers (Kelegama and Foley, 1999).

From the mid-1990s, the three largest firms (MAS Holdings, Brandix and Hidramani) began to set up a number of yarn, textile and ancillary inputs manufacturing units (hangers, bra moulding, packaging material, labels and buttons to be used mostly in their own apparel factories but also to meet the requirements of others), as part of their strategy to prepare themselves for the abolition of MFA quotas. By this time, the volume of exports had also reached levels that could provide scale economies for fabric (in particular knitted fabric) production. In most cases, these factories were joint ventures with foreign firms which had been established suppliers for many years. The most prominent cases included Ocean Lanka, a joint venture of Bandix, Hidramani and Fountain Set of Hong Kong (the largest manufacturer of weft-knitted fabric in the world); Textured Jersey, a joint venture between MAS Holdings, Brandix and Textured Jersey (UK) (automated dye dispensing system); MAS Fabric Plant (weft-knitted fabric producers), a US$30 million warp-knit factory, a joint venture of MAS, Dogi International Fabrics of Spain and Elastic Fabrics of America; Stretchline Lanka, a joint venture of MAS Holdings and Stretchline UK (elastics and a range of high-quality yarn for the production of lingerie and inner wear). A number of independent fabric and embroidery manufacturing firms have also emerged to serve apparel producing firms. Among them, the largest is Hayleys MGT Knitting Mills (denim producer), a joint venture between a local conglomerate, the Hayleys Group, and MGT Knitting Mills of Australia.

Among these firms, Stretchline Lanka, which is engaged in the production of elastic, has played a pivotal role in strengthening Sri Lanka's position in the world apparel industry as a significant producer of upmarket lingerie and inner wear.[8] With an annual turnover of over US$170 million, it is now the world's largest producer of elastic. In addition to meeting the input requirements of Sri Lankan apparel producers, it now operates highly profitable production plants in China, Indonesia, Mexico and Honduras. It has sales offices in the UK, the USA and Hong Kong; a research lab in the UK; and has set up a subsidiary in the British Cayman Islands to manage royalty income from five products it has invested in and patented in the UK and the USA.[9]

Currently about 60 per cent of fabric used in apparel production in Sri Lanka is produced domestically: about 80 per cent of fabric used in knitted apparel and about 20 per cent of that in woven apparel.[10] The bulk of the ancillary inputs (embroidery, hangers, labels, buttons, and so on) are also produced domestically. The difference in the local content of fabric used between knitted and woven apparel can be explained by different investment requirements for establishing production plants for the two fabric types. The investment requirement for establishing a similar sized woven textile mill is about ten times the investment required for a knit fabric mill (Abernathy *et al.*, 1999; Staritz, 2011).[11]

Corporate social responsibility

A recent development in the world apparel trade, which has significant implications for lead firms' sourcing decisions in a quota-free apparel trade, is the NGO-led campaign in developed countries for imposing corporate social

8   See the discussion below on the composition of apparel exports from Sri Lanka.

9   This paragraph is based on information from the company website (http://www.stretchline.com/index.php and interviews).

10 Tentative estimates provided by JAAF.

11 According to available estimates for Bangladesh, a knit fabric mill including a dyeing and finishing unit of a viable economic size requires an investment of at least US$3.5 million whereas the investment requirement for a similar factory in woven fabric amount to at least US$35 million. For this reason, in Bangladesh, as in Sri Lanka, the domestic fabric content of knitted apparel is almost four times of that of woven apparels (Staritz, 2011, 146).

responsibility (CSR) norms (internationally accepted labour standards, taking care of the well-being of employees and meeting environmental standards) on developing-country exporters. The apparel industry has been at the forefront of the implementation of these ethical trading initiatives and social auditing practices because of the labour-intensive nature of production (and the overwhelming dependence on female labour, a key focus of the high-profile anti-sweatshop campaign) and the environmental sensitivity of the production process (energy usage and waste water generation). 'Social audits' at the factory level have therefore become an important factor taken into account by apparel buyers (in particular speciality stores) in placing orders.[12] Buyers are now demanding not only better prices and timely delivery, but also better conditions for workers and environmental friendly production – 'greening of the industry' (Hale and Wills, 2007; McIntyre, 2008).

Sri Lanka's labour market regime, notwithstanding stringent regulations and procedures relating to the hiring and firing of workers, has been instrumental in preparing the apparel industry to effectively face the ethical workplace norms imposed by international buyers. Work conditions in Sri Lankan factories were already at a relatively high standard well before international buyers began to incorporate 'ethical trade' as an important element of their procurement policy. Sri Lanka had already become a signatory to (and remains the only country in Asia to do so) the 39 ILO Core Convention covering workplace practices prohibiting forced labour and child labour well before the export-oriented apparel industry took off.

The use of child labour has been curbed in Sri Lanka, and the minimum statutory age for employment is eighteen, with some conditional exemptions for those over sixteen. Compliance with these rules was rigorously enforced and monitored by the labour department and other bodies, including the BOI. Trade unions played an important role in ensuring adherence to these requirements (Perry, 2012). These initial labour market conditions reduced the likelihood of 'CSR transgression' by buyers in the form of adding an extra level of accountability for the apparel manufacturers (Perry, 2012).

Against this background, the upward movement in the value ladder of the Sri Lankan apparel industry has been accompanied by greater emphasis on ethical employment practices than in many of its Asian competitors (Fernando and

---

12 'When the buyers from Victoria's Secret and the other big brands come, working conditions is one of the first things they ask about. They have to, because they have customers asking them about it' – Mahesh Amalean, Managing Director of MAS Holdings, Sri Lanka's biggest clothing exporting firm (Friedman, 2000, 178).

Almeida, 2012; Ruwanpura and Wrigley, 2011). In this, MAS Holdings took the lead in the mid-1980s as part of its emerging role as a major supplier to Victoria's Secret (Athukorala and Ekanayake, 2014, Appendix 2). Following MAS's lead, the other major apparel firms have established their own CSR programmes such as women's empowerment programmes and professional, vocational and technical training programmes for employees. Most firms provide workers with transport facilities, free breakfasts, subsidized meals and medical care. They also actively engage in community services in those rural areas where the factories are located. The 'Garments Without Guilt' campaign launched by the Joint Apparel Association Forum (JAAF) has played a pivotal role in strengthening CSR commitments among apparel exporting firms and promoting Sri Lanka's name as an ethical clothing manufacturer (see Athukorala and Ekanayake, 2014, Appendix 1).

Some apparel factories in Sri Lanka have started to produce 'fair trade' clothing – clothing made out of organic and fairtrade cotton grown in India and Africa.[13] These factories import the cotton and then convert them into fabric in Sri Lanka. The three largest firms already supply organic cotton clothing for brand names such as Marks and Spencer and Tesco.[14] A number of local fabric companies like Ocean Lanka and Brandix Textiles have obtained fairtrade and organic accreditation from international certification bodies such as FLO-Cert GmbH in Germany and the Institute of Marketecology (IMO) in Switzerland. With increasing global concern regarding climate change, a number of apparel firms have started investing in environmentally friendly products and production processes. A number of large firms have embarked on building 'green factories', which meet international environmental standards.

Human capital base

The expansion of the apparel industry in Sri Lanka was aided by an ample supply of cheap, trainable labour. At the time of the reforms initiated in 1977, nearly a fifth of the total labour force of around five million was out of work, with the bulk of the unemployed concentrated in the 18–25 age bracket. The average monthly wage of a factory worker was about US$33, which amounted

---

13 'Fair trade' is a social movement whose stated goal is to help producers in developing countries achieve better trading conditions. Members of the movement advocate the payment of higher prices to exporters, as well as improved social and environmental standards.

14 Tesco sells clothing designed by Katherine Hammett, a designer known for her political T-shirts and her ethical business philosophy.

to about 12 per cent of that in Hong Kong and was also significantly lower compared to the other favoured locations of clothing production in the region, such as Malaysia, Indonesia, the Philippines and Mauritius (Athukorala and Rajapatirana, 2000, Chapter 4). Given the country's long-standing commitment to providing universal free education, the labour force had a much higher level of formal education (on average 10.3 years of schooling) compared to that in most other apparel exporting countries (Savachenko and Acevedo, 2010).

Another unique feature of labour supply to the apparel industry is that most of the female workers in apparel firms came with years of experience in using the standard household sewing machines, the basic technology of which was not very different from that of the industrial sewing machine.[15] Consequently, a female apparel worker who joined the labour force as a helper took only two to three months to pick up the skills required to become a machine operator, compared to the three to six months taken by her Bangladeshi counterpart.[16]

Owing to the country's long-standing commitment to universal free education up to the university level, Sri Lanka had a human capital base capable of acquiring the technical and managerial skills required for the apparel industry within a short time after the economy was exposed to foreign trade and investment through liberalization reforms. There has been a notable improvement in managerial and technical capability in the apparel industry over the past four decades, with public–private partnerships playing a pivotal role.

In 1984, the University of Moratuwa (the main public technical university in the country) started offering diploma-level design courses in textile technology in collaboration with the London School of Fashion Design. In 2004, it introduced a four-year degree course in fashion development offered in collaboration with the North Carolina State University College of Textiles. JAAF played an important role in initiating this programme. It has also taken the initiative to offer a post-graduate diploma in marketing in collaboration with the Chartered Institute of

---

15 In the late nineteenth century, the Sri Lankan subsidiary of the Singer Sewing Machine Company launched a hire-purchase scheme with affordable monthly instalment payments through an island-wide network. This scheme soon became so popular that the sewing machine became a ubiquitous household asset and part of bridal dowries. The combination of a higher level of formal education and basic training in using a household sewing machine has made Sri Lankan factory workers easily trainable compared to their counterparts in other countries in the region.

16 Based on an interview with a Sri Lankan firm with operations in Bangladesh, as well as a study by Savachenko and Acevedo (2010).

Marketing, UK, and established four training centres with financial and technical support from USAID to train sewing machine operators.

Brandix, the second largest apparel producer, has been running its own training institution, Brandix Clothing Training Institution (BCTI), since 1998. In 2004, BCTI started offering a master's programme in textile technology in collaboration with the RMIT University, Melbourne. In 2007, MAS Holdings, the largest apparel producer, inaugurated its own training school, the MAS Institute of Management and Technology (MIMT), to serve as a 'one destination solution' for all training requirements of its Sri Lankan and overseas operations. Recently Nike Corporation joined hands with MAS to set up a global training facility, the Nike Apparel Innovation and Training Centre (Nike-AITC), within MIMT. Nike-AITC trains over 100 employees annually from Nike vendors in over fifteen other countries.

In the beginning, the Sri Lankan apparel industry was heavily dependent on textile technicians imported from Hong Kong. This dependence on foreign textile technicians had virtually disappeared by the dawn of the new millennium. Sri Lanka has also become a supplier of textile technicians and managers to other apparel producing countries in the region and beyond (Jacob, 2013; Staritz, 2011).

Export performance

Between 1977 and 2004, the final year of the MFA regime, apparel exports increased from a mere US$15 million (2.1 per cent of total exports) to over US$2.8 billion (50.6 per cent) (Table 9.1). From 1992, apparel has become the single largest foreign exchange earner of the country. Over the years, the composition of manufactured exports has diversified into other labour and resource-based products, but in 2004, apparel still accounted for over 42 per cent of total merchandise exports and over 62 per cent of manufacturing exports. Sri Lanka's share in world apparel exports increased from 0.12 per cent in the mid-1980s to 1.1 per cent in 2004.

According to various predictions made in the lead-up to the MFA-quota abolition, Sri Lanka was among the countries expected to experience significant contraction in exports in the quota-free era (Adhikari and Weeratunge, 2007; Nordas, 2009; *The Economist*, 2008). The projected number of job losses ranged from 31,200 to 66,000, with a mean prediction of 49,000 (Wijesiri and Dissanayake, 2009, 163). These gloomy predictions have not materialized,

Table 9.1 Apparel exports[1] from Sri Lanka, 1970–2012

	US$ million (nominal)	Share of apparel in		Share in world apparel exports[3]
		Merchandise exports (per cent)	Manufacturing exports[2] (per cent)	
1970	1.4	0.4	0.9	–
1975	3.4	0.6	13.9	–
1977	15.1	2.1	13.8	–
1985	278.6	20.9	39.5	0.13
1990	637.0	33.3	53.2	0.76
1995	1,465.7	38.5	75.4	1.10
2000	2,775.8	52.0	76.6	1.23
2005	2,870.6	46.6	73.1	1.26
2006	3,048.8	45.1	72.1	1.28
2007	3,271.2	42.7	68.7	1.24
2008	3,434.3	42.1	67.5	1.25
2009	3,120.3	45.9	65.4	1.32
2010	3,178.3	42.0	56.9	1.23
2011	3,986.4	39.9	56.2	1.20
2012	3,783.8	43.1	57.1	1.18
2013	4,264.8	43.4	60.2	1.20
2014	4,682.3	44.2	61.8	1.28
2015	4,556.0	43.3	60.2	1.41

Source: Compiled from UN Comtrade database and Central Bank of Sri Lanka Annual Report (various years) and UN Comtrade database.

Notes: 1. Products belonging to the commodity code 841 to 845 of the Standard International Trade Classification (SITC). Based on importing-country customs records ('mirror export data').
2. Manufacturing is defined as SITC 5 to 8 – 68.
3. Figures for 1970, 1975 and 1977 are negligible (less than 0.1 per cent).

however. On the contrary, average annual Sri Lankan exports of apparel during 2005–15 amounted to US$3.564 billion, up from US$2.82 billion during the preceding five years (2000–04), a 26 per cent increase. Sri Lanka's share in world apparel exports did decline from about 1.10 per cent during 2000–04 to 1.01 during 2005–07, but has increased since then, reaching 1.42 per cent in 2015 (Table 9.1).

The MFA abolition triggered a massive set of restrictions in the Sri Lankan apparel industry. A number of firms, whose operations remained profitable under quota protection, went out of business, and the size distribution of the remaining firms shifted towards larger firms. According to customs export records, there were 817 exporting firms in 2004. This number declined to 671 in 2008 and to 450 in 2011. The size distribution of the surviving firms has become increasingly skewed to the right, with larger farms accounting for the bulk of exports. The three largest firms accounted for over 35 per cent of total exports in 2011, up from 13.4 per cent in 2004. In 2011, over two-thirds of exports originated from the top twenty firms, compared to 39 per cent in 2004.[17] Notwithstanding this shake-up, total employment in the apparel industry increased from 353,742 in 2013 to 395,979 in 2013.[18] According to information collected from interviews with managers of apparel firms, most of the small- and medium-sized firms now undertake subcontracting for the large firms, which have expanded production following the lifting of the quota constraints.

The performance record of the Sri Lankan apparel industry during the post-MFA era is particularly impressive when we take into account two important negative factors operating during this period. First, Sri Lanka is no longer a low-wage production base compared to many other apparel-producing countries in the region. The erosion of relative price competitiveness resulting from the trade preferences enjoyed by competitors has been compounded by a domestic labour shortage and increase in wages in recent years. Various news reports appearing during the first half of 2015 placed the number of unfilled vacancies between 50,000 and 100,000. The average hourly wage is now much higher than in Bangladesh, Vietnam, Cambodia (also possibly India and Indonesia), and is approaching the levels in China and other East Asian clothing-producing countries (Table 9.2). Wages in almost all apparel firms are now well above the minimum wage set by the government – Sri Lankan rupees 9,500 (about US$70).

---

17 Data compiled from firm-level apparel export data from unpublished customs records. Annual exports of US$10,000 used as the minimum cut-off point for enumerating exporting firms.

18 The data is from the Census of Industry (2003–04) and the Economic Census (2013–14) conducted by the Sri Lankan Department of Census and Statistics (http://www.statistics. gov.lk/?trk=profile_certification_title).

Table 9.2 Apparel manufacturing labour cost in selected Asian countries, circa 2008 (US$/hour)

Thailand	1.29–1.36
Malaysia	1.18
Philippines	1.07
China	0.51–1.08
Prime coastal provinces	1.08
Other coastal provinces	0.86–0.94
Remote provinces	0.55–0.94
India	0.51
Indonesia	0.44
Sri Lanka[1]	0.43
Vietnam	0.38
Pakistan	0.37
Cambodia	0.33
Bangladesh	0.22

Source: Jassin-O'Rourke Group (2008).

Note: 1. At the time of field work undertaken for this this study (the second quarter of 2015), the average hourly wage was about 0.58, with the large firms paying an average wage of over 0.70.

Second, unlike many of its competitors, Sri Lanka does not enjoy preferential access to the major markets in Europe and North America. On 15 February 2010, the EU suspended GSP+ concessions to Sri Lanka (with effect from 15 August 2010) due to concerns about the violation of human rights.[19] In addition to loosing preferential access to EU markets, Sri Lankan apparel exporters had to compete in the US market with exporting countries that enjoy handsome tariff preferences under the African Growth Opportunity Act (AGOA) and regional trading agreements with countries in Latin America.

What explains Sri Lankan apparel industry's success in maintaining dynamism in growth, notwithstanding these competitive disadvantages?

---

19 Under the EU-GSP scheme Sri Lanka is eligible for an average non-reciprocal preference margin of about 2.2 per cent on clothing exports (the average GSP rate of 9.0 per cent compared to an average MFA tariff rate of 11.2 per cent). In July 2005, Sri Lanka became eligible for additional tariff concessions under the newly introduced GSP+ scheme, which offered duty free access to 7,200 products (including almost all clothing items).

As discussed in the previous section, the Sri Lankan apparel industry had built a strong image of CSR, a particular feature being its compliance with internationally agreed employment practices, CSR and environmental standards. The human capital base and design capabilities of the industry had improved significantly, enabling it to swiftly respond to buyers' quest for variety. The growth of the domestic fabric base (mostly knitted textiles used in inner wear) and ancillary input supply industries hand in hand with the expansion of apparel production helped flexible manufacturing in order to respond appropriately to changing demand. The attractiveness of Sri Lanka as a source of procurement for leading brand marketers and speciality stores has also been strengthened by the industry's impressive record of CSR, in particular relating to compliance with ethical employment practices and internationally agreed environmental standards. These non-price factors seem to have played a pivotal role in enabling the Sri Lankan garment industry to make a notable structural shift from 'basic' apparel products to 'fashion-basic' products. [20]

Basic apparel products are the ones that remain in a retailer's or a manufacturer's collection for many seasons, such as men's white shirts or underwear. Fashion-basic products are variants on basic products that contain some (sometimes temporary) fashionable element (such as stone-washed jeans, trousers with pleats or trim, fashion lingerie and inner wear). Basic products account for over half of all internationally traded apparel products, with fashion-basic products accounting for about a quarter. However, over the past two decades, fashion-basic products have been the most dynamic, mainly because of the rapid increase in lean retailing. In basic apparel manufacture, low-wage nations, especially those with access to inexpensive textiles, have the potential for major market gains following the abolition of MFA quotas. The relative cost of basic products is fundamentally linked to the relative labour cost, which is the major determinant of international competitiveness in this sector; low-wage nations, especially those with access to inexpensive textiles, have the potential for major market share gains in the post-MFA era. In contrast, in fashion-basic products, exporting is more than a simple price–cost game; speed and flexibility are crucial capabilities for firms wrestling with product proliferation.

---

20 Here we draw on the three-way classification proposed by Abernathy *et al.* (1999): fashion products, basic products and fashion-basic products. Fashion products are high-end products, such as dresses from Paris and Italian-made suits, the demand for which is largely driven by social status and deep-rooted cultural values. These products are not typically imported from developing countries.

The available trade data does not permit (even at the highest degree of disaggregation that are available in customs records) precise disaggregation of total exports into these two categories. However, the data does point to a clear pattern of concentration of Sri Lankan apparel exports in the fashion-basic category in the post-MFA era. This pattern is also consistent with the analytical narrative of structural changes in the apparel industry in the previous section and the information collected from the firm-level interviews.

Data on the commodity composition of apparel exports from Sri Lanka between 2003–04 and 2014–15 are summarized in Table 9.3.[21] In the table, the top twenty apparel products identified as related to the export commotion in 2014–15 is used as the base for comparing changes in the product mix over time. The data shows a clear pattern of compositional shift in Sri Lankan apparel exports in favour of fashion-basic products. The degree of concentration of exports in these twenty products has increased from 65.4 per cent in 1990–91 to 90.6 in 2014–15. The two most rapidly expanding categories within this product group are brassières (SITC 84551) and panties (84482), which accounted for over 20 per cent of total apparel exports, compared to a mere 1.5 per cent in 1990–91. Among the top twenty products, the share of apparel for women, which generally possesses a higher fashion content, increased from 44 per cent to nearly 65 per cent. Between these two points in time, the combined share of these products in total exports increased from 7.5 per cent to nearly 20.5 per cent. The share of women's/girls' wear, which generally contains a higher fashion content compared to men's wear, increased from 60.1 per cent in 1990–91 to 66.7 per cent in 2014–15. Products such as men's business shirts and normal trousers (for both men and women), which generally have no fashion content, have virtually disappeared from the export product mix.

Table 9.3 Composition of Sri Lankan apparel exports,[1] 2003–04 and 2011–12

Product (SITC[2] code in brackets)	Composition (%)			World market share (%)		
	1990–91	2003–04	2014–15	1990–91	2003–04	2014–15
Top 20 products	65.40	76.54	90.57	0.89	1.30	2.54
Brassières (84551)	0.89	5.58	10.49	0.49	2.59	5.44
Women's panties knitted (8442)	0.64	3.65	9.29	0.42	2.14	7.55
Men's trousers woven (84140)	10.18	8.29	8.98	0.89	1.12	1.36

(*Contd.*)

21 Inter-temporal comparison is done using two-year averages relating to the end points of the period so as to reduce the impact of year-to-year fluctuations of trade flows.

(*Contd.*)

Product (SITC[2] code in brackets)	Composition (%)			World market share (%)		
	1990–91	2003–04	2014–15	1990–91	2003–04	2014–15
T-shirts/singlets knitted (84540)	2.24	6.05	8.60	0.36	0.85	1.16
Women's trousers woven (84260)	7.45	11.74	7.73	0.89	1.39	1.34
Jerseys and pullovers (84530)	8.70	10.28	7.05	0.44	0.76	0.64
Women's trouser knitted (84426)	0.75	1.45	6.77	0.35	0.99	2.76
Men's trousers cotton woven (85151)	7.04	4.35	4.31	1.32	1.61	1.67
Women's blouse woven (84270)	13.19	7.14	3.90	1.71	2.26	1.29
Babies' clothes knitted (84512)	0.66	1.62	3.88	0.39	1.04	2.54
Men's underwear knitted (84381)	0.01	0.94	3.77	0.02	1.00	4.00
Women's dresses knitted (84424)	0.82	0.43	2.70	0.70	1.21	1.45
Women's dresses woven (84240)	2.98	2.92	2.65	1.02	2.09	1.00
Women's/girls' swimwear knit (84564)	0.02	0.50	2.49	0.02	0.74	3.93
Men's trouser cotton(84371)	2.75	2.77	2.03	1.63	2.38	1.74
Other apparel knitted (84599)	0.33	0.72	1.79	0.26	0.76	1.51
Women's skirts woven (84250)	3.54	4.24	1.27	0.91	2.05	1.61
Women's blouses knitted (84470)	2.66	1.46	1.15	1.35	0.82	0.99
Babies' clothes woven (84511)	0.49	1.53	0.93	0.48	2.23	1.63
Women's underwear knitted (84489)	0.03	0.88	0.79	0.07	2.63	2.49
Other products	34.60	23.46	9.43	0.76	0.82	0.73

(*Contd.*)

(Contd.)

Product (SITC[2] code in brackets)	Composition (%)			World market share (%)		
	1990–91	2003–04	2014–15	1990–91	2003–04	2014–15
Total	100	100	100	0.81	1.25	1.34
US$ million	755	2485	4702			
Memo items: products classified by user type						
Women's apparel[3]	60.13	64.56	66.66	0.84	1.34	1.56
Men's apparel[3]	38.72	32.29	28.54	0.79	1.09	1.02
Babies' apparel	1.16	3.15	4.80	0.42	1.40	2.30

Source: Compiled from UN Comtrade database.

Notes: 1. Top 20 products identified based on the export composition in 2014–15. Figures are two-year averages. Women's apparel includes both women's and girl's wear. Men's apparel includes both men's and boy's wear. Products are listed in the designing order of the figure for 2014–15.

2. SITC: Standard International Trade Classification.

3. Values of unclassified items (for example, T-shirts, jerseys) classified on a pro-rata basis using shares collated from the classified (women/men) items.

The growing importance of Sri Lanka as a global supplier of inner wear (brassières and panties) within the broader category of fashion-basic products is clearly shown in Figure 9.1. In 2014–15, Sri Lanka accounted for 7.6 per cent

Figure 9.1 Sri Lanka's share in world apparel exports, 1988–2015

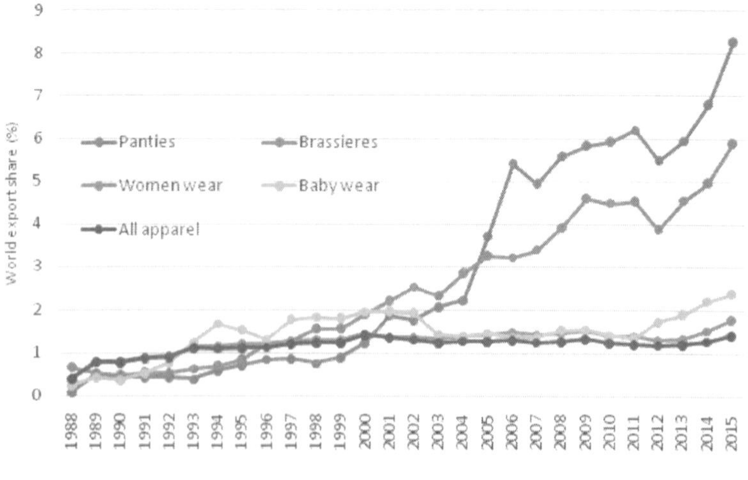

Source: Based on data compiled from UN Comtrade database.

Note: The top five apparel products were identified based on export values for 2011–12.

of total world exports of females pantyhose, up from 0.4 per cent in 1990–91. Sri Lanka's world market share in brassière manufacture increased from 0.49 per cent to 5.4 per cent between these time points. In the case of both products, the increase in world market share was faster during the post-MFA years. The market share of apparel for women in 2014–15 was 1.56 per cent, compared to a 1.34 per cent share for total apparel exports. The patterns of exports to the USA and EU of these products (data not reported here due to space constraints) are remarkably similar to this aggregate picture.

In Table 9.4, the composition of Sri Lanka's apparel exports in 2014–15 is compared with that of the seven other major apparel exporting countries in Asia. The first column of the table lists the top twenty apparel products exported by Sri Lanka, ranked by the export share value in 2014–15 which are stated in column 2. In other columns, the export share of each of the other countries is given for these twenty products. The data clearly shows Sri Lanka's unique role in exporting fashion-basic products among these countries, in particular when compared to Bangladesh, Cambodia, Indonesia, Pakistan and Vietnam. In the inner wear category (brassières and panties), which has perhaps the highest fashion content, all countries listed in the table other than Thailand have a much lower share compared to Sri Lanka. The market share for knitted apparel and women's wear are also greater for Sri Lanka compared to the other countries.

Table 9.4 Composition of apparel exports from Sri Lanka and the major apparel exporting Asian countries, 2014–15 (percentage)[1]

	Sri Lanka	Bangla-desh	Cambodia	China	India	Indonesia	Pakistan	Thailand	Vietnam
Top 20 products	90.6	87.1	79.4	68.4	82.8	73.8	80.5	75.1	64.6
Brassières (84551)	10.5	1.0	0.9	3.6	1.1	3.9	0.0	8.8	1.2
Women's panties knitted (8442)	9.3	1.3	1.2	1.9	1.7	0.7	0.4	7.9	1.0
Men's trousers woven (84140)	9.0	18.1	8.4	5.6	4.8	6.3	28.1	4.2	8.3

(*Contd.*)

218

(Contd.)

	Sri Lanka	Bangla-desh	Cambodia	China	India	Indonesia	Pakistan	Thailand	Vietnam
T-shirts/ singlets knitted (84540)	8.6	17.8	9.8	5.4	13.0	4.9	6.6	13.1	5.9
Women's trousers woven (84260)	7.7	10.5	9.4	7.1	4.1	6.7	18.9	2.3	7.6
Jerseys and pullovers (84530)	7.1	14.1	20.8	17.7	6.7	15.1	12.9	11.6	13.6
Women's trouser knitted (84426)	6.8	3.3	8.9	2.7	2.6	6.8	3.0	3.8	4.9
Men's trousers cotton (85151)	4.3	6.9	1.8	2.5	6.7	5.3	0.5	2.8	3.3
Women's blouse woven (84270)	3.9	2.2	1.3	3.8	13.6	7.6	0.4	2.7	2.7
Babies' clothes knitted (84512)	3.9	2.2	4.3	2.5	4.7	1.5	1.0	5.7	1.0
Men's under-wear knitted (84381)	3.8	1.1	1.4	1.2	2.1	0.4	1.3	3.4	2.1
Women's dresses knitted (84424)	2.7	1.0	3.3	2.7	2.5	2.7	0.2	0.6	2.8

(Contd.)

(Contd.)

	Sri Lanka	Bangla-desh	Cambodia	China	India	Indonesia	Pakistan	Thailand	Vietnam
Women's dresses woven (84240)	2.6	0.5	0.4	3.9	9.1	2.5	0.2	1.2	2.1
Women's swimwear knit (84564)	2.5	0.2	1.4	1.2	0.0	1.6	0.0	0.5	0.6
Men's trouser cotton (84371)	2.0	2.8	1.3	0.9	3.5	1.8	5.0	1.6	2.1
Other apparel knitted (84599)	1.8	0.7	1.7	1.4	1.3	2.0	0.8	1.5	1.5
Women's skirts woven (84250)	1.3	0.5	0.6	1.1	1.7	0.7	0.4	0.3	0.8
Women's blouses knitted (84470)	1.2	1.1	1.5	1.5	1.8	1.9	0.4	1.3	1.9
Babies' clothes woven (84511)	0.9	1.5	0.3	0.8	1.5	0.9	0.5	1.2	0.6
Women's under-wear knitted (84489)	0.8	0.2	0.7	0.7	0.3	0.3	0.1	0.4	0.5
Other products	9.4	12.9	20.6	31.6	17.2	26.2	19.5	24.9	35.4
Total	100	100	100	100	100	100	100	100	100
Value, US$ billion	4.7	29.30	8.8	130.0	14.4	9.6	4.7	3.1	21.1

(Contd.)

(*Contd.*)

	Sri Lanka	Bangla-desh	Cambodia	China	India	Indonesia	Pakistan	Thailand	Vietnam
Memo items: products classified by user type									
Women's	66.7	41.2	60.9	65.9	63.5	61.8	38.9	54.0	56.1
Men's	28.5	55.1	34.4	30.7	30.3	35.8	59.7	39.1	42.3
Babies'	4.8	3.7	4.6	3.3	6.2	2.4	1.4	6.9	1.6
Export similarity index[4]	100	61.5	66.7	64.4	63.0	67.6	48.0	70.7	64.4

Source: Compiled from UN Comtrade database.

Notes: 1. Figures are two-year averages. Women's apparel includes both women's and girl's wear. Men's apparel includes both men's and boys' wear. Products are listed in the designing order of the figure for 2014–15.

2. Top 20 products identified on the basis of Sri Lanka's export composition in 2014–15.

3. Values of unclassified items (for example, T-shirts, jerseys) classified on a pro-rata basis using shares collated from the classified (women/men) items.

4. Krenin-Finger (1979) index of export similarity. The figure in each column measures the degree of similarity of Sri Lanka's export composition to that of each of the other countries.

In order to compare Sri Lanka's exports composition across all product categories over this period, we estimated the export similarity index (ESI) as defined by Finger and Kreinin (1979) using export data at the five-digit level over the period 1950–2015. An ESI is a useful summary measure of the similarity of the commodity structure of a given country with another country or total world trade. The index is defined by the formula

$$S(ab, c) = \left\{ \sum_i Minimum \ [Xi(ac), Xi(bc)] \right\} 100,$$

where 'a' and 'b' denote two countries (or country groups) exporting to market 'c', Xi (ac) is the *share* of the commodity i in a's exports to c, and Xi (bc) is the *share* of the commodity i in b's exports to c. If the commodity distribution of a's and b's exports are identical [that is, Xi (ac) = Xi (bc)], the index will take on a value of 100. If a's and b's export patterns are totally different the index will take on the value zero. The index intends to compare only patterns of exports across product categories; it is not influenced by the relative size or scale of total exports.

ESIs calculated for comparing Sri Lanka's export composition with each of the other eight Asian countries are plotted in Figure 9.2. The index shows a high degree of variability among countries during the MFA era, reflecting the impact of periodic change in quota allocations during this period. However, the ESIs for more recent years shows a notable difference in Sri Lanka's export composition compared to each of the these countries. In 2014–15, the index varied in the range of 48.0 (Pakistan) and 70.7 (Thailand).

Figure 9.2 Export similarity index: Sri Lanka versus Asian apparel exporting countries, 1995–2015

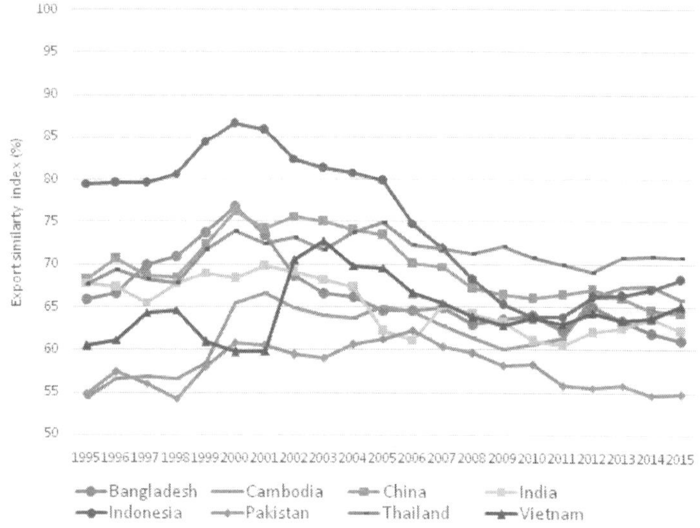

Source: Based on data compiled from UN Comtrade database.

The time patterns of value, price (unit value) and volume indices of apparel export from Sri Lanka are also consistent with the structural shift in the commodity composition exports towards high-value products (Figure 9.3). The theory of trade protection predicts a general decline in export prices following the abolition of quantitative export restrictions on a given product (Harrigan and Barros, 2009; Krishna and Tan, 2001).[22] In consistency with this postulate, a

---

22 There are two possible reasons for this. First, binding quotas push up the price of a product above the 'natural' market prices. Second, when the number of items that can be exported is limited, there can be a tendency on the part of the exporters to improve the quality of the product to maximize export value within the quota limit.

**Figure 9.3 Volume, unit value and volume indices of apparel exports from
Sri Lanka, 1985–2015 (1990 = 100)**

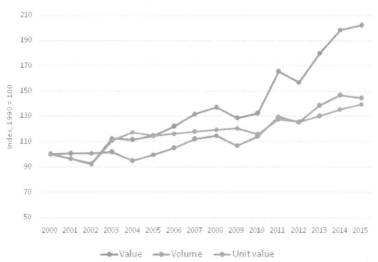

Source: Based on data compiled from Central Bank of Sri Lanka, Annual Report (various issues).

Note: Value and unit value series are in in US dollars. The original series in Sri Lankan rupees has been adjusted for changes in the average annual US$/Sri Lankan rupee exchange rate.

number of recent studies have found a significant decline in the prices of apparel imports in the USA and other major markets, and an additional decline in export prices at the individual exporting country level (Harrigan and Barrow, 2009; Startitz, 2010; USITC, 2011). However, in the case of Sri Lanka, both volume and price changes seem to have contributed to an increase in export values.[23] This pattern seems to mirror the structural shift in the commodity composition from basic products to fashion-basic (high-value) products. It seems that in the Sri Lankan case, the price-lowering effect of quota removal seems to have been counterbalanced by the structural shift in the commodity composition.

The success of the Sri Lankan apparel industry in carving out a niche in some high-value product lines under competitive market condition in the post-MFA era seems to have been helped by the ongoing process of increasing concentration of production in larger firms (as discussed in the previous section). Most of the Sri

---

23 In a comparative study of the export performances of South Asian countries, Tewari (2008b) has also found that unit values of exports from Sri Lanka (and India) to the EU remained high during the post-MFA era compared to those of other Asian competitors, including Bangladesh, Cambodia, China, Pakistan and Vietnam.

Lankan large firms are now full-package suppliers with the capacity to interpret designs, make samples, source inputs, monitor production quality and guarantee on-time delivery. In a quota-free world, buyers have a natural tendency to forge long-term procurement relations with large firms.

Conclusion

Following the economic liberalization reforms initiated in the late 1970s, which eliminated many of the crippling barriers on foreign trade and investment, Sri Lanka has emerged as a successful participant in the global apparel value chain. In contrast to the various gloomy predictions made in the lead-up to the MFA phase-out, Sri Lankan apparel industry has managed to sustain growth dynamism in the competitive market conditions of the post-MFA era. This performance record is particularly impressive given that Sri Lanka is no longer a low-wage production base compared to many other apparel producing countries in the region, and Sri Lanka, unlike many of its competitors, does not enjoy preferential access to the major markets in Europe and North America.

The Sri Lankan experience demonstrates that apparel is a bundle of differentiated products, not a homogenous commodity as commonly assumed by the trade flow modellers who came up with gloomy predictions in the lead-up to the MFA abolition. Sri Lankan apparel producers have carved out a niche in high-end markets for inner wear (female lingerie) and fashion-basic apparel products, with a strong customer base of leading brand marketers and speciality stores. Improvements in the human capital base and design capabilities have enabled the industry to swiftly respond to buyers' quests for variety and timely delivery in these highly competitive segments of the world apparel trade.

The managerial and technical capability of Sri Lanka's apparel industry has improved notably during the past four decades, with public–private partnerships playing a pivotal role. The industry's dependence on foreign textile technicians virtually disappeared and, from about the late 1990s, Sri Lanka has become a supplier of textile technicians and managers to other apparel producing countries in the region and beyond. As the industry expanded, the major apparel pricing firms began placing greater emphasis on ethical employment practices. The impressive record of compliance with ethical employment practices and internationally agreed environmental standards has enhanced Sri Lanka's attractiveness as a source of procurement for leading brand marketers and speciality stores.

Following the MFA abolition, the Sri Lankan apparel industry has also settled into the structure of a small core of larger firms, with small firms undertaking subcontracting for the large firms. Most of the large firms are full-package suppliers with the capacity to interpret designs, make samples, source inputs, monitor production quality and guarantee on-time delivery. In a quota-free world, buyers have started to forge long-term procurement relations with large firms, undermining the position of intermediary firms. The growth of the domestic fabric base (mostly knitted textiles used in intimate apparel) and ancillary input supply industries has helped apparel manufacturers respond swiftly to changing demand.

Foreign buyers and quota-hopping apparel producers from East Asia who came to Sri Lanka following the liberalization reforms played a pivotal role (as postulated by the GVC framework) in linking Sri Lankan firms to the global apparel value chain. In particular, the role of brand marketers was instrumental in setting the stage for a change in the composition of apparel products from mass-market products to niche products, lingerie, pantyhose and some fashion-basic casual wear. The process of export expansion and industrial upgrading through links forged with foreign buyers was immensely helped by an enabling domestic environment, which included a domestic work force capable of swiftly acquiring the required skills and an entrepreneurial class with colonial trade and business ties. The concurrent liberalization of foreign trade and investment regimes provided a viable setting for the collaboration of foreign partners and domestic suppliers. Labour market regulations inherited from the colonial era were instrumental in preparing the industry to uphold ethical trade norms, which international buyers in the upper end of the GVC have begun to emphasize as an important criterion in global sourcing. Collaborative actions by the industry and the government that facilitated an improvement in managerial and technical capability greatly eased the burden of adjustment to the abolition of MFA quotas, and helped take advantage of the opportunities that opened up in the post-MFA environment.

The GVC framework is a valuable analytical tool for analysing the export performance of a country within a demand-responsive industry such as apparel in the context of changing governance patterns of the global value chain. However, the Sri Lankan experience clearly demonstrates that, in order to capture the full picture of a country's engagement and industrial upgrading in the apparel value chain, it is necessary to incorporate the GVC approach in a more general economic analysis of export-oriented industrialization, paying attention to relevant country-specific characteristics and the policy context. The Sri Lankan experience also illustrates that, for understanding the role of foreign buyers (lead firms) as conduits for industrial upgrading, it is important to distinguish between mass retailers, speciality stores and brand marketers, instead of treating them all as a homogenous group. In the Sri Lankan case, it was speciality retailers and brand marketers who played a pivotal role in putting the Sri Lankan firms on a dynamic learning curve.

References

Abayasekara, A. 2013. 'GSP+ Removal and the Apparel Industry in Sri Lanka: Implications and Way Forward.' *South Asia Economic Journal* 14 (2): 293–316.

Abernathy, F. H., J. T. Dunlop, J. H. Hammond, and D. Weil. 1999. *A Stitch in Time: Lean Retailing and the Transformation of Manufacturing: Lessons from the Apparel and Textile Industries.* New York: Oxford University Press.

———. 2000. 'Retailing and Supply Chains in the Information Age.' *Technology and Society* 22 (1): 5–31.

Adhikari, R. and C. Weeratunge. 2007. 'Textiles and Clothing in South Asia Current Status and Future Potential.' *South Asia Economic Journal* 8 (2): 171–203.

Amaeshi, K. M., O. K. Osuji and P. Nnodim. 2008. 'Corporate Social Responsibility in Supply Chains of Global Brands: A Boundaryless Responsibility? Clarifications, Exceptions and Implications.' *Journal of Business Ethics* 81 (1): 223–34.

Amalean, M. 2001. 'The Apparel Industry of Sri Lanka: An Analysis of the Past Present and Future in a Global Context.' *Apparel Update* (Colombo), May–July: 5–8.

Appelbaum, R. P. 2008. 'Giant Transnational Contractors in East Asia: Emergent Trends in Global Supply Chains.' *Competition and Change* 12 (1): 69–87.

Athukorala, P. 2012. 'Sri Lanka's Trade Policy: Reverting to Dirigisme?' *The World Economy* 35 (12): 1662–86.

Athukorala, P. and R. Ekanayake. 2014. 'Repositioning in the Global Apparel Value Chain in the Post-MFA Era: Strategic Issues and Evidence from Sri Lanka.' Trade and Development Working Paper No. 2014-12. Canberra: Arndt-Corden Department of Economics, Australian National University.

Athukorala, P. and S. Rajapatirana. 2000. *Liberalization and Industrial Transformation: Sri Lanka in International Perspective.* New Delhi: Oxford University Press.

Bair, J. and E. D. Peters. 2006. 'Global Commodity Chains and Endogenous Growth: Export Dynamism and Development in Mexico and Honduras.' *World Development* 34 (2): 203–21.

Brandix Lanka Limited. 2015. *Built on Trust: The Sri Lankan Apparel Industry Pays Tribute to Martin Trust*. Accessed 12 May 2013. Available at http://www.brandix.com/built-on-trust.pdf.

CBSL (Central Bank of Sri Lanka). 2012. *Annual Report 2012*. Colombo.

———. 2015. *Annual Report 2015*. Colombo.

The Economist. 2008. 'Sri Lanka: Not Many Pleases.' 14 August. Accessed 17 May 2013. Available at http:/www.economist.com/node/11921197.

Evans, C. L. and J. Harrigan. 2005. 'Distance, Time, and Specialization: Lean Retailing in General Equilibrium.' *American Economic Review* 95 (1): 292–313.

Feenstra, R. C. and G. Hamilton. 2006. *Emerging Economics, Divergent Paths: Economic Organization and International Trade in South Korea and Taiwan*. Cambridge: Cambridge University Press.

Fernando, M. and S. Almeida. 2012. 'The Organizational Virtuousness of Strategic Corporate Social Responsibility: A Case Study of the Sri Lankan Family-Owned Enterprise MAS Holdings.' *European Management Journal* 30 (6): 564–76.

Friedman, T. L.2000. *Lexus and the Olive Tree*. New York: Anchor Books.

Fung, V., W. K. Fung and Y. Wind. 2007. *Competition in a Flat World: Building Enterprises for a Borderless World*. Upper Saddle River, NJ: Wharton School Publishing.

Finger, J. M. and M. E. Kreinin. 1979. 'A Measure of "Export Similarity" and Its Possible Uses.' *Economic Journal* 89 (356): 905–12.

Gereffi, G. 1994. 'The Organization of Buyer-Driven Global Commodity Chains: How US Retailers Shape Overseas Production Networks.' In *Commodity Chains and Global Capitalism*,edited by G. Gereffi and Korzeniewicz, 95–122. Westport, CT: Preager.

———. 1999. 'International Trade and Industrial Upgrading in the Apparel Commodity Chain.' *Journal of International Economics* 48 (1): 37–70.

Gereffi, G. and K. Fernandez-Stark. 2016. *Global Value Chain Analysis: A Primer*. Durham, NC: Duke Center for Globalization, Governance and Competitiveness. Accessed 13 March 2017. Available at http://dukespace.lib.duke.edu/dspace/handle/10161/12488.

Gereffi, G. and S. Frederick. 2010. 'The Global Apparel Value Chain, Trade and Crisis: Challenges and Opportunities for Developing Countries.' In *Global Value Chain in a Post-Crisis World: A Development Perspective*, edited by O. Cattaneo, G. Gereffi, and C. Staritz, 157–208. Washington DC: World Bank.

Hale, Angela and Jane Wills. 2008. *Threads of Labour: Garment Industry Supply Chains from the Workers' Perspective*. New York: Wiley.

Harrigan, J. and G. Barrows.2009. 'Testing the Theory of Trade Policy: Evidence from the Abrupt End of the Multifiber Arrangement.' *The Review of Economics and Statistics* 91 (2) 2009: 282–94.

Humphrey, J. and G. Schmitz. 2002. 'How Does Insertion in Global Value Chains Affect Upgrading in Industrial Clusters?' *Regional Studies* 36 (9): 1017–27.

Jacob, R. 2013. 'The Right Genes for Making Jeans.' *Financial Times*, 22 January. Accessed 17 May 2013. Available at http://www.ft.com/cms/s/0/d4191430-647b-11e2-934b-00144feab49a.html.

Jassin-O'Rourke Group, LLC. 2008. *Global Apparel Manufacturing Labour Cost Analysis*. Accessed 17 May 2013. Available at www.textileconnet.com/documents/resources/globalapparellabourcostsummary2008.pdf.

JAAF (Join Apparel Association Forum). 2012. *Chairman's Report to the Annual General Meeting*. Colombo: JAAF, November. Mimeo.

Jones, R. 2006. *The Apparel Industry*. Oxford: Basil Blackwell.

Keesing, D. B. and M. Wolf, M.1981. 'Questions on International Trade in Textiles and Clothing.' *The World Economy* 4 (1): 79–102.

Kelegama, S. and F. Foley. 1999.'Impediments to Promoting Backward Linkages from the Garment Industry in Sri Lanka.' *World Development* 27 (8): 1445–60.

Krishna, Kala M. and Ling Hui Tan. 2001. *Rags and Riches: Implementing Apparel Quotas under the Multi-Fibre Arrangement*. Ann Arbour: University of Michigan Press.

Lal, D. and S. Rajapatirana. 1989. *Impediments to Trade Liberalization in Sri Lanka*. London: Gower.

McIntyre, Richard P. 2008. *Are Worker Rights Human Rights?* Ann Arbour: University of Michigan Press.

Martin, W. and L. A. Winters. 1995. *The Uruguay Round: Widening and Deepening the World Trading System*. Washington DC: World Bank.

Neidik, Binnur and Gary Gereffi. 2006. 'Explaining Turkey's Emergence and Sustaied Competitiveness as a Full-packaged Supplier of Apparel.' *Environment and Planning A* 36: 2285–303.

Nordås, H. K.2003.'The Impact of Trade Liberalization on Women's Job Opportunities and Earnings in Developing Countries.' *World Trade Review* 2 (2): 221–31.

———. 2009. *The Global Textile and Clothing Industry Post the Agreement on Textiles and Clothing*, Geneva: World Trade Organization (WTO).

Perry, P. 2012. 'Exploring the Influence of National Cultural Context on CSR Implementation.'*Journal of Fashion Marketing and Management* 16 (2): 141–60.

Ruwanpura, K. N. and N. Wrigley. 2011. 'The Costs of Compliance? Views of Sri Lankan Apparel Manufacturers in Times of Global Economic Crisis.' *Journal of Economic Geography* 11 (6): 1031–49.

Savchenko, Y. and G. Lopez-Acevedo. 2012. 'Female Wages in the Apparel Industry Post-MFA: The Case of Cambodia and Sri Lanka.' Policy Research Working Paper 6061. Washington DC: World Bank.

Srinivasan, T. N. 1998. *Developing Countries and the Multilateral Trading System: From the GATT to the Uruguay Round and the Future.* New Delhi: Oxford University Press.

Staritz, C. 2011. *Making the Cut? Low-Income Countries and the Global Clothing Value Chain in a Post-Quota and Post-Crisis World.* Washington DC: World Bank.

Subramanian, Arvind and Devesh Ray. 2003. 'Who Can Explain the Mauritian Miracle?' In *In Search of Prosperity: Analytical Narratives of Economic Growth*, edited by Dani Rodrik, 205–43. Princeton, NJ: Princeton University Press.

Tewari, M. 2008a. 'Varieties of Global Integration: Navigating Institutional Legacies and Global Networks in India's Garment Industry.' *Competition and Change* 12 (1): 49–67.

———. 2008b. 'Deepening Interregional Trade and Investment in South Asia: The Case of the Textile and Clothing Industry.' Working Paper 213. New Delhi: Indian Council for Research on International Economic Relations.

Tokatli, N. and O. Kızılgün. 2010. 'Coping with the Changing Rules of the Game in the Global Textiles and Apparel Industries: Evidence from Turkey and Morocco.' *Journal of Economic Geography* 10 (2): 209–29.

USITC (United State International Trade Commission). 2011. *The Economic Effects of Significant U.S. Import Restraints (Seventh Update).* Washington D.C.: USITC.

Watson, N. 2010. 'MAS and the Women Go Beyond Programme. In United Nations Global Impact Project.' *Embedding Human Rights in Business Practice II*, 85–88. Geneva: United Nations.

Wijesiri, J. and J. Dissanayake. 2008. 'The Ending of the Multi-Fibre Agreement and Innovation in the Sri Lankan Textile and Clothing Industry.' *OECD Journal: General Papers* 8 (4): 157–88.

World Bank. 2004. *Sri Lanka Development Policy Review* (Report No. 29396-LK). Washington DC: World Bank.

10

Strategic Change in Indian IT Majors
A Challenge

Neetu Ahmed

Introduction

This chapter examines the need for a change in the growth strategy of Indian information technology (IT) service majors such as Infosys, TCS and Wipro. The chapter starts with the innovative global delivery model (GDM) that the Indian IT majors have implemented and the problems they may face if they continue on the same growth path. After this, it looks at the problem of path dependence and its manifestation in terms of low investment in research and development (R&D) and large cash build-ups. The chapter then looks at the challenges in bringing about a strategy change, the capabilities required and the role of both organic and inorganic growth.

The Indian IT services innovation model

The Indian IT software services industry was built on the basis of providing middle- to low-end programming services as part of an overall software service. The conception, design and architecture of the software were done by consultancy services such as IBM and Accenture, by the clients themselves, or by other IT consultancy companies. The Indian IT companies entered the picture to carry out programming, testing and maintenance of the software solution. In order to do this, the Indian industry innovated in coming up with what came to be known as the global delivery model (GDM), in which a software development service was broken up into a number of components. Some of the higher-end tasks requiring continuous or frequent interaction with the client were carried out on-site by the Indian firms' IT engineers, who were sent to work on the client's site. Other components of the work were carried out offshore by engineers in Indian offices. The completed and tested software service was finally put together for delivery to the client.

This GDM, with its division of onshore and offshore work, was able to utilize the difference between salaries paid to IT engineers in the high-income client countries (HICs) and the low- or middle-income provider countries, such as India. In addition, it was also able to 'follow the sun', with work continuing in India while offices in the USA or Europe closed for the day and vice-versa. The GDM reduced both the costs of IT service production and the time required for delivery. This innovation enabled the Indian IT service industry to capture a majority – more than 50 per cent – of the global market for IT services (Dossani, 2010). If China developed itself as the epitome of outsourcing in manufacture, India became the epitome of outsourcing in IT and related business services, often referred to as IT enabled services (ITES).

Current challenges

However, unlike a product, a process innovation such as a GDM for providing IT services is not something that can be patented. Nor can it be kept secret. Once the onshore/offshore model became known, firms in other countries could also copy the model. In particular, IBM and Accenture, the international IT services giants, set up middle- to low-end programming units in India to be able to provide end-to-end services, while using the advantage of lower salaries in India. In addition, many small- and medium-sized units sprang up in India, and some such service centres also developed in other developing countries like the Philippines.

Furthermore, disruptive technologies in the business environment are getting added every day like social, mobile, analytics and cloud (SMAC), augmented and virtual reality, drones and autonomous vehicles, blockchains, the Internet of Things (IoT) and artificial intelligence (AI), among others, forcing businesses to come out of comfort zones and change/transform their business models.

The list is growing every day with the advent of new technology or new ways to put it to use. Of immediate importance for the Indian IT companies, however, is that a lot of programming work can be automated. Programming is based on explicit knowledge, that is, on routines, such as 'if x then y'. The routines of programming can be automated. This reduces the cost of programming. It also reduces the employment intensity of IT service provision. However, Indian IT majors do not really have a choice between carrying out programming with an army of low-paid programmers and having it automated. Programming is and will be automated. If the Indian IT firms do not carry out this automation themselves, someone else will.

Another worry for the Indian firms is that the traditional outsourcers like banks and industrial firms have created subsidiaries for digital-only work, which have become part of their core functioning. For instance, Citibank has a unit called Citi FinTech in New York which, among other things, develops and manages Citi's mobile app, wealth management, money transfer services, and so on. The water-to-aviation conglomerate GE has a digital subsidiary as well. Both GE and Citibank were major outsourcers and have been among the top clients of Indian IT firms. As digital processes are now central to the functioning of such companies, it is difficult to convince them that it can be done overseas. For example, another large outsourcer, Bank of America, had a $3-billion digital innovation budget in 2016 to spend on financial technology (Fintech), which it ran almost entirely in-house (Singh, 2017).

IT is no longer just a tool to be used in some parts of firm activity, whether in manufacturing or services. It is a core technology that enables a firm to organize all its activities. As a result of this digitalization, large firms are less willing to outsource IT work, since they need in-house IT services for them to function. In supporting digitalization by clients, the role of specialized IT services is not to just provide services, but to work with clients in developing their digitalization systems.

The result is that the requirements of clients (from IT service providers) are also changing. As a vice-president of Gartner mentioned, now clients are looking at IT firms as partners, who will advise them, help them and work with them for co-discovery, co-sourcing and co-innovation (Chandran, 2016).

The consequence of all these above changes, as NASSCOM chairman Ganesh Natrajan said at the platform for 'Skills, Startups and Social Venture' in 2016, is that 'the Indian IT industry is facing a perfect storm', which is created by three forces. The first is digital transformation as clients are looking for new technologies like SMAC. The second is the automation of knowledge and processes, which is becoming a threat for the existing workforce. The third is the protectionist approach, which is reducing revenue opportunities and shrinking profitability by 10 per cent (Wharton, 2017).

The result is that Indian IT firms have been stuck as low-cost providers of middle- to low-end components of services, while they have not upgraded themselves to become high-end and/or full-service providers. Due to the threat posed by automation and political changes like Brexit and the USA's protectionist approach, the demand for offshore low-end services is falling and the scope for labour arbitrage is reduced. It is not that labour arbitrage has ceased to exist, as, for almost any given task, an Indian engineer would cost less than a North American or European engineer. However, the tasks required of IT service providers are changing.

According to the International Data Corporation (IDC), in 2017, '50 per cent of spends of organizations will be for third platform technologies, which refers to cloud computing, big data analytics, mobile computing and IoT and by 2018, at least half of the IT spending will be on cloud applications alone'. In the next two years, these new technologies will not remain new; they will become the core of what industry leaders do and how they operate. Consequently, Indian IT firms will have to change in order to be relevant for providing these new types of services. However, such a shift is stalled by the Indian IT majors' continued high reliance on their traditional GDM-based model.

Path dependence

The Indian firms have successfully faced many issues in the past like Y2K, the internet, e-commerce, social media and mobile platforms because the core skills required did not change dramatically and good programming skills with the capacity to train a large number of software professionals helped them to grow. However, new technologies like cloud computing, AI and digital technologies require a different set of skills which can only be developed through investment in R&D as well as general capability development. For example, IBM invested a very large amount of money in their WATSON project to develop AI, which created a new dynamic capability to keep the organization ahead of other competitor firms. By keeping in mind the changes in customer demand, global IT service providers are developing end-to-end service delivery capabilities, resulting in greater efficiency and productivity.

Changing the business model on which a firm has been built is, however, not an easy task. There is a strong tendency for an organization to continue with the model that was successful in the past – in this case, the one which enabled Indian IT majors to become companies worth US$10 billion. Their thinking and organization have been based on the successful GDM, and a substantial change has become difficult, though it is necessary. This path dependence is manifested in a few ways in the Indian IT industry, such as thinking of a dichotomy between service and product companies, a neglect of R&D and the piling up of cash reserves.

At a basic level, there is a tendency to think of the company as an 'IT services' firm and not an 'IT products' firm. However, products are goods that allow a service to be performed numerous times, with only minor tweaking of the programmes required. At the same time, even products are becoming services, for example, the cloud-based Microsoft Office Suite and other software, which allows hiring firms to pay by use and not for the product as a whole. The shift to products being sold as services was, in fact, initiated by Xerox, when it began charging its clients by the number of copies provided, rather than by selling the machines themselves.

Indian IT companies do have some of their own products, such as the banking software product Finacle of Infosys and BaNCS of TCS. However, the creation of such products for repeated services has not become the defining feature of their operations, which still remains that of services without products. What is necessary is to see these firms not as IT services or IT products providers but as technology firms in the IT space.

Low R&D spending

For continuing on an established growth path, there is not much need for R&D, though some R&D is always needed even to bring about incremental changes. When changing a firm's strategy, however, R&D for developing new capabilities and processes becomes absolutely crucial.

In the last few years, Indian IT firms have increased their spending on R&D for developing new technologies like AI, data science, IoT, automation, digital, and so on. Infosys, for instance, is investing in quite an aggressive way (1.3 per cent of sales) since 2007 in comparison to their Indian competitors (Table 10.1). However, the percentage should increase and they need to focus on digital technologies and product development.

How much any firm should invest in R&D will depend on the nature of the firm. In the case of technology firms with high growth, for example, they should spend about 10 per cent of their revenues on R&D, which is the average spending on R&D at the global level (CTIER, 2016). For example, global firms like Google and Microsoft spend almost 15 per cent of their revenues on R&D, whereas IBM spends about 7 per cent. Indian firms, which are very small in comparison to these giant IT firms, have also started spending more on R&D because of changes in the IT industry. The percentage spending of total revenue on R&D is still less than 1 per cent for Indian IT majors (Jalote, 2005). If we compare the R&D spending of global firms and Indian firms, we can see that Indian firms are way behind their foreign counterparts (Table

10.1) This behaviour can be easily explained as these firms were mainly service providers in the past few decades, which was supported by the profitability of the IT industry and the GDM.

There are about 275 global software and computer services firms in the top 2,500 global R&D spenders, of which 161 are from the USA, 32 from China, and only 5 from India, clearly highlighting the fact that India's IT industry has a long way to go (CTIER, 2016).

Table 10.1 R&D investment by global and Indian IT firms (2015)

Global/Indian IT firms	Company	R&D expenditure (US$ million)	Sales (US$ million)	R&D as % of sales
Global	Microsoft	9,922	77,078	12.9
	IBM	4,336	76,429	5.7
	Google	8,098	54,362	14.9
	SAP	2,307	17,560	13.1
	Capgemini	20	10,573	0.2
Indian	TCS	145	15,106	1.0
	Infosys	96	7,422	1.3
	Wipro	40	7,547	0.5
	HCL	29	2,735	1.1
	Rolta	33	583	5.6
	Mindtree	3	581	0.6

Source: CTIER (2016).

Companies like IBM and Accenture, who have R&D intensities of 5.7 per cent and 2 per cent respectively and are international rivals to the Indian IT companies, have invested significantly in new high-end services and are focusing increasingly on products to reinvent themselves. If the Indian IT industry is to truly become more competitive and move up the value chain, firms would need to increase their R&D expenditure on an average by 8 to 10 times more than what they currently spend and concentrate on developing new products (CTIER, 2016).

Idle cash

It is ironic that big Indian IT firms are sitting on a huge pile of cash and still losing business to multinationals at the global level. The next phase of development of IT firms depends on their ability to use this money, innovate and provide solutions to meet their clients' changed requirements. Today, technologies like SMAC are the disruptive force that plays a significant role in creating new enterprise business models.

What is the outcome of a cash build-up? It means that sustaining current revenues does not require much additional investment. This is fine when the old business model continues to serve as the engine of growth. However, when this model is challenged, it becomes necessary to invest some of that cash in developing or acquiring new capabilities.

Instead, Indian firms are using their cash for the buyback of shares as they are not sure about their acquisition strategies and wary of the cultural differences and risk associated with the same. They are improving their return on equity (RoE) by paying more to their shareholders and achieving higher valuations as companies that earn better returns on shareholder funds. Recently big IT firms like Tata Consultancy Services (TCS) and Infosys have distributed cash to their shareholders. TCS, which is India's highest-valued company on the stock market, recently announced a buyback of shares worth ₹ 16,000 crore (US$2.4 billion), the biggest ever in the Indian capital market. At that time, its cash hoard had gone up to ₹ 43,100 crore (US$6.4 billion), a staggering 9 per cent of its market cap (*TOI*, 2017). Apparently, this action was precipitated by the announcement of Cognizant's US$3.4 billion buyback over the next two years as a payout to shareholders after being pressured to do so by activist investor Elliott Management Corp (Sadam and Mukherjee, 2017).

Predictably, Infosys has followed suit with its own buyback announcement of ₹ 13,000 crore, or US$2 billion, from its cash reserves. This is hardly the fault of shareholders who are no doubt tired of seeing a growing pile of inert cash that is doing nothing for either the firm's fortunes or shareholders'. Also, the management in these firms, feeling the rising concern of slowing revenue growth, thinks it needs to placate its shareholders in some fashion before the axe falls on them.

Uncertain transitions

The challenges of changing the business model were exhibited recently in the turbulence in big firms like TCS, Infosys and HCL. Automation, data science and artificial intelligence are changing the contours of the industry very rapidly and grabbing everyone's attention.

These dire warnings centre around a shift from an old way of doing business, that is, focused on outsourced services, to evolving to provide software platforms and updating capabilities to cater to shifting customer demands and act as a business partner and less of an IT provider. As IT companies start working on newer technologies such as cloud computing, they are fast moving away from a people-led model, which means they need fewer employees.

Two ways in which firms can change their business capabilities are the development of new capabilities in the firm itself or the acquisition of new capabilities by buying up other firms with the required capabilities. The former can be called the organic and the latter the inorganic route to growth. Indian IT majors have adopted both these methods. Their implementation is discussed in the following sections.

Development of new capabilities

The Indian IT industry needs to harness emerging opportunities by developing new capabilities to move up in the global value chain (GVC). They need to move from providing low-value products to high-value customer-engaging products. The big international IT firms are continuously working to meet new challenges with the development of dynamic capabilities. These dynamic capabilities are considered to be crucial to a firm's attempts to constantly integrate, reconfigure, renew and recreate its resources and capabilities and, most importantly, upgrade and reconstruct its core capabilities in response to the changing environment to attain and sustain competitive advantage (Teece, Pisano and Schuen, 1997).

According to Soni (2013) Indian IT firms have at present adapted their strategies for the development of new capabilities, developing and maintaining current capabilities to keep pace with the advent of new technologies in the market (Table 10.2).

Table 10.2 Three prongs of dynamic capability building and response of Indian IT firms

Building dynamic capabilities	Response of Indian IT firms
Sense and shape opportunities and threats	Systematic innovation management programme
Seize opportunities and dynamic capabilities	Exploring new business models
	Sustainability and green

(Contd.)

(Contd.)

Building dynamic capabilities	Response of Indian IT firms
Maintain competitiveness through enhancing, combining, protecting and when necessary reconfiguring the business enterprise's intangible and tangible assets	Investment in intellectual property generation Embracing open innovation Talent supply chain management

Sources: Soni (2013) and Teece (2007).

It is difficult for competitors to copy the unique capabilities and these become the building blocks of the firm's strategy. According to Teece 'the strength of a firm's dynamic capabilities is fundamentally its ability to maintain profitability over the long term, including the ability to design and adjust business models' (Teece, 2018, 1).

The initial strategy of Indian IT firms was to grow organically and develop capabilities in-house. While Indian firms have been investing in new technologies in the last five years, they need to speed up the process to remain competitive and relevant in the industry. They need to increase investment by acquiring knowledge through internal processes as well as by hiring from top clients and from start-ups specialized in those particular skills. According to D. D. Mishra, Research Director at Gartner, 'thinking out of the box will differentiate the winners in the market'. As Sudin Apte, the CEO & Research Director at Offshore Insights, mentioned: 'Since Indian firms are mainly involved in growing by client pushed business growth, they are not good in corporate business like market research, consulting, planning, strategy' (Wharton, 2017).

However, things are changing. For example, Infosys has followed Accenture and set up an independent consulting unit, and Wipro started developing consulting capabilities around three years ago, leveraging its capabilities in the IT business. TCS has followed a somewhat similar approach, whereas Cognizant followed the strategy of hiring MBAs and business studies graduates and placed them in consulting roles.

In the past, TCS moved into new markets such as France and Japan by acquiring Citigroup's captive business process outsourcing (BPO) arm and France-based consulting services company Alti SA. This broadened TCS's portfolio to consulting, banking and financial services.

Initially Indian IT majors focused on building up and strengthening their in-house offerings. TCS has worked on developing its neural automation platform,

Igneo; Infosys has an AI platform called Mana; and Wipro has its AI platform Holmes, all of which will be crucial in helping them negotiate the difficult task of acquiring new business and retaining their old projects. Infosys has set up a US$100 million fund for a new product arm, building seven software products in sectors like data analytics and digital marketing (Dhanjal, 2016).

Tech Mahindra and MindTree are trying to promote innovation within their organizations by setting up start-up segments within them to encourage employees to work on disruptive technologies. Wipro is also encouraging its existing employees to look at new technology avenues through hackathons and fun training modules. The attempt is to internalize the start-up mentality.

Among the Indian majors, TCS seems more conservative in evaluating investment opportunities. According to Rajesh Gopinathan (CFO, TCS):

> Investments need to be evaluated for multiple things. One of the things they can deliver to you is strategic capability - new service line, new products, or new market access. It can be used as a mechanism for growth as well. We have always participated in the first two, but stayed away from the last one. (Nadhe, 2015, 1)

The key technological capability that the Indian IT majors have to acquire is artificial intelligence (AI) systems. As companies around the world become more digital in nature, there will be increased demand for AI systems that are central to this transition. As mentioned earlier, Indian IT majors have been working on AI systems and are carrying out substantial retraining of their professionals to carry out end-to-end provision of digital services. However, they do not have a place in MIT's list of 50 'smartest companies' in the world, in which there are five Chinese companies – Baidu, Huawei, Tencent, Didi Chuxing and Alibaba (MIT, 2017). That means that they still have a long way to go to translate their strategy and innovate to develop AI capabilities.

For these Indian companies to become truly competitive with the likes of IBM and Accenture, or even a consulting firm like Deloitte (which is becoming a serious player in the digital and design realm through acquisitions), Indian IT majors will have to buy their way out of trouble and they will have to do it very quickly. The acquisitions may be small in size and might not add substantially to the revenue or profit of these multi-billion dollar IT companies, but they do help send out the right signals to clients. Of course, internal capability building is necessary even to utilize acquisitions. Organic and inorganic growth are not necessarily opposed to each other.

Strategy of Indian IT firms with start-ups

Start-ups have an advantage over larger companies in that they can be bold in trying out new technologies and approaches without much risk. The majors have to keep worrying about factors like share prices, which make them less prone to taking risks. Will an increase in the percentage of shares held by the initial or main investors make the majors less worried about short-term turbulence in share prices? This step could have a positive effect on risk-taking, but one has to wait and see whether these majors develop a higher risk-taking appetite.

Indian IT firms are investing in start-ups to improve their capabilities or to acquire new capabilities. To develop a new technology like AI or cloud computing from scratch is a mammoth task in comparison to the process of acquiring or forming a partnership with a start-up having that particular skill set. Big firms are looking out for such engagements as these innovative start-ups are providing them a competitive advantage and differentiated technology, and helping them by compressing time-to-market and building solutions for new vertical segments.

While some firms like Infosys and Wipro have set up their own dedicated start-up funds, others are tracking small firms developing disruptive technologies in their own sectors. Unlike its rivals Infosys and Wipro, TCS has not created a venture fund to invest in start-ups. It uses its Co-Innovation Network (COIN) to work with start-ups as partners. The network is part of TCS's innovation labs and involves tie-ups with venture capital firms and university research labs. In the USA, the TCS COIN programme has alliances with venture firms such as Andreessen Horowitz, New Enterprise Associates and Norwest Venture Partners.

Infosys is soon expected to start inviting some of the start-up companies in the USA to present their technology at forums organized by the company, and will then shortlist some in 'incubation programmes' to help accelerate innovation in areas identified by the strategic team.

Innovation through investing in start-ups is easier than innovation through internal investment. People are afraid to take risks and challenge authorities; so it is easy if it is done as an individual entity separate from the main firm. It is similar to running a start-up inside the company with small teams. Most Indian IT companies, both large and small, have undertaken similar initiatives. (Table 10.3)

Table 10.3 Acquisition/partnership of Indian IT firms with start-ups

Companies	Start-ups	Year	Mode	Money spent (USD)	Start-up corpus fund
TCS	–	–	–	–	COIN (Co-Innovation Network) – US$500 million innovation fund – internal company programme started in 2004 to partner with start-ups
Infosys	Cloudyn	2016	Minority investments (5–10%)	4 million	US$100 million innovation fund
	DWA Nova LLC	2015		15 million	
	Airwiz	2016		2 million	
	Whoop	2016		3 million	
HCL	–	–	–	–	Internal Venture fund
Wipro	Opera Solutions Corp.	2013	Acquisition	30 million	US$100 million
	Axeda Corp.	2013	Acquisition	5 million	
Tech Mahindra ltd	FixStream Networks	2014	Acquisition	10 million	US$50 million internal interpreneurship programme
	i5 Startnet	2013			
Cognizant	Itaas		Acquisition		Cognizant Capital internal fund

Source: Collected by author from annual reports and newspaper articles.

In the last year, Infosys has made a few more acquisitions like Trifacta, Waterline Data, CloudEndure, ANSR Consulting, Whoop, Airwiz and Cloudyn. It spent at least US$43 million from its US$500-million venture fund in making these investments. However, because of internal challenges (primarily from investors), the acquisition strategy is in question and most of its executives in the mergers and acquisitions (M&A) department have left (Nirmal, 2017).

Acquisitions to increase capabilities

Any organization, large or small, cannot cater to everything on its own, which is where the role of acquisitions becomes important. The bigger firms are forced to look at product innovation through acquisitions to come out of the traditional IT services model; they have to look for ideas outside their existing frameworks/ think-tanks. Over time, engagements that begin as partnerships and strategic investments can lead to mergers and acquisitions. The newer services can also be integrated with the ones that the larger firms already provide to customers.

However, if we take the case of Indian IT firms very few acquisitions have occurred in previous years. Firms possess large amounts of spare cash, but they are not utilizing it for developing capabilities by acquiring firms. The acquisitions undertaken by these firms in the past are also not very high-value in nature. TCS, for instance, has made only three major acquisitions in the last ten years – E-Serve International (Citibank's BPO arm) in 2008, the Pune-based Computational Research Laboratories in 2012 and Alti (an enterprise solutions provider from France) in 2013.

In the same period, Infosys made seven acquisitions, three of which happened after Vishal Sikka took over as CEO in 2014 – Panaya (automation provider), Skava (a digital solutions provider) and Noah Consulting (an information service management provider). HCL Technologies is looking at acquisition opportunities in areas like engineering and R&D services as well as digital technologies to drive growth. In the past few months, it has announced the acquisition of companies like Geometric (for US$200 million) and Butler America Aerospace for US$85 million (*Deccan Chronicle*, 2016). Tech Mahindra is planning to acquire the US-based healthcare IT consulting company CJS Solutions group for US$110 million to expand its presence in the healthcare sector (Kurup, 2017).

However, if we count only those deals that involved digital technology firms, the number is fewer. Digital acquisitions in the last five years have included just these few firms: Wipro's acquisition of Appirio – a SaaS (Software as a Service) provider – for US$500 million in 2016 and Designit (a design company) for US$95 million in 2015; HCL Technologies acquiring Power Objects (a provider of the Microsoft Dynamics CRM) for US$46 million in 2015; and Skava by Infosys for US$120 million (Nirmal, 2017).

On the other hand, Accenture shelled out US$2.5 billion for thirty-eight acquisitions in the last three years. Sixty per cent of it was in 2016 alone, and all the acquisitions were in the area of digital technologies. This resulted in their business growing by 35 per cent in the digital sector alone (John and Phadnis, 2016).

Table 10.4 Some of the biggest acquisitions by Indian IT services companies

Company	Target	Deal size (US$)	Business
TCS	E-Serve International, Citi Bank's BPO (USA)	512 million	Banking and financial services
	Computational Research Laboratories (India)	34 million	High-performance computing and cloud services Enterprise solution provider
Infosys	Alti (France)	97.5 million	
	Panaya (Israel) Kallidus (USA) Noah Consulting LLC (USA)	200 million 120 million 70 million	Automation technology E-commerce services Consultancy for energy sector
	Lodestone Mgt Consultants (Europe) Skava (USA)	345 million 120 million	Management consultancy Digital solutions
Wipro	Designit (USA) Viteos (USA)	94 million 130 million	Design firm BPO technology for capital firms
	Appirio (USA)	500 million	SaaS provider
HCL	Power Objects (USA) Geometric LTD (India) Butler America aerospace (USA)	46 million n/a n/a	CRM consulting PLM and engineering services Engineering and design
Tech Mahindra	SOFGEN Holdings (Switzerland) Pininfarina (Italy) – controlling stake Target Group (UK) Bio Agency (UK)	30 million 53 million (EUR) 164 million 66 million	Consulting and services Automotive and industrial design

Source: Collected by author from annual reports and newspaper articles.

These days, IT clients are looking for complete solutions instead of obtaining them piecemeal, and Indian IT firms will quickly find themselves at a disadvantage if they do not develop the correct end-to-end capabilities. To its credit, Cognizant did buy Toronto-based Idea Couture (a digital innovation and design firm) last year, but this has proven an exception rather than the rule in the IT sector in India (*The Hindu*, 2016).

'When their clients hear about an acquisition in a particular space, they understand that the company is serious about the area, and will start discussions on how they can work together not just on the traditional business side but even on new technologies,' Shashi Bhusan, senior vice president at investment banking services firm IDFC Securities, told *Quartz* (Punit, 2016).

However, there are links between internal capabilities and acquisitions. Firms have to develop their own capabilities in order to utilize and integrate acquisitions with the rest of their operations. This itself is a challenge requiring a strategic vision of the capabilities that need to be built, both internally and through acquisitions.

Conclusion

The IT majors are involved in various attempts at upgrading – through the development of internal capabilities, promoting start-ups (and even a start-up culture among their own employees) and by acquisitions. However, they are doing all this without the visible sense of urgency that other global companies seem to be demonstrating. Instead of acquisitions, all of them are announcing buybacks of shares to keep investors happy in the short term. For strategic change, however, they need to utilize the cash for R&D investment and for acquisitions. The legacy of low R&D investment and large cash holdings, combined with the pressures of sustaining share prices, remain obstacles to be overcome in meeting the challenges of technological change.

At the global level, organizations are looking for new-age solutions based on digital technologies, cloud computing, customer engagement, business analytics, social collaboration tools or wearable computing devices, which are transforming their business models. New technology firms such as Uber, Airbnb, Facebook and Google are working with Accenture, but not with any legacy Indian service provider. In this situation, Indian IT firms need to see and then reposition themselves not as limited IT service providers, but as technology firms per se, involved in the creation and application of digital technologies.

Indian IT firms need to restructure their internal organizational set-up to become more open to the acquisition of firms dealing in new technologies, which may add new capability skills to these firms. Indian firms still do not seem to be aggressive on acquisitions and continue to believe in organic growth to avoid risky investments and cultural differences between firms of different sizes, at different locations. Innovation is a difficult proposition in large firms, whereas it is easy to do with start-ups, where these big firms are not directly associated and need not risk their investment decisions.

As growth based on revenues from exports of services is reducing because of changes in clients' business models, automation, protectionism and restrictions on visa availability, Indian firms need to also focus on domestic business. Indian businesses are by and large lagging behind in the adoption of digital technologies. However, global competition will force the domestic demand for IT services to grow in a significant way, with the support of the 'Digital India' initiative of the Government of India.

Due to uncertainties in the market with respect to new technologies whose demand is growing, Indian firms need to develop those technologies in-house and also adopt the inorganic path of acquiring these capabilities. Learning from the fate of formerly strong brands like Nokia and Kodak, who could not adjust to the technological changes in their industries, Indian IT firms need to act with a sense of urgency in restructuring their business models to ensure their importance in the fast changing IT-ITES industry. IT is a general-purpose technology and it will affect every aspect of economic functioning. Supporting businesses, both global and domestic, in becoming digital is the capability that Indian IT firms need to develop.

References

Chandran, Pradeesh. 2016. 'Age of the Digital Dawns on Indian IT Industry.' *The Hindu*, 23 May. Accessed 4 August 2017. Available at http://www.thehindu.com/business/Industry/Age-of-the-digital-dawns-on-Indian-IT-industry/article14335171.ece.

CTIER. 2016. 'Indian IT Industry: Future Competitiveness Demands Increased R&D Spending.' *CTIER Brief*, 2 October. Accessed 28 July 2017. Available at http://www.ctier.org/pdf-event/2016-10-CTIER-Brief-IT%20Industry.pdf.

Deccan Chronicle. 2016. 'HCL Tech Bets on Acquisitions to Drive Growth.' 23 October.

Accessed 10 August 2017. Available at http://www.deccanchronicle.com/business/companies/231016/hcl-tech-bets-on-acquisitions-to-drive-growth.html.

Dhanjal, Swaraj Singh. 2016. 'Infosys Looking at Three Pronged Strategy to Work with Start-Ups: Pravin Rao.' *Livemint*, 12 February. Accessed 15 July 2017. Available at http://www.livemint.com/Industry/F3kgvw7Np2c67qBqrLu2FJ/Infosys-looking-at-three-pronged-strategy-to-work-with-start.html.

Dossani, Rafiq. 2010. 'Software Production: Globalization and Its Implications.' In *The Service Revolution in South Asia*, Part II, edited by E. Ghani, 5–44. New York: OUP and the World Bank.

The Hindu. 2016. 'Cognizant Acquires Idea Couture.' 18 October. Accessed 15 July 2017. Available at http://www.thehindu.com/business/Industry/Cognizant-acquires-Idea-Couture/article14513248.ece.

IDC. 2017. 'IDC Forecasts $1.2 Trillion in Worldwide Spending on Digital Transformation Technologies in 2017.' *IDC Media Center*, 23 February. Accessed 4 July 2017. Available at http://www.idc.com/getdoc.jsp?containerId=prUS42327517.

Jalote, Pankaj. 2005. 'Research Investments in Large Indian Software Companies.' India IT Forum, Singapore, September 2005. Accessed 17 August 2017. Available at https://www.iiitd.edu.in/~jalote/GenArticles/ResearchInITcosLarge.pdf.

John, Sujit and Shilpa Phadnis. 2016. 'India is the Powerhouse of Accenture: India CMD Rekha Menon.' *Economic Times*, 9 August. Accessed 19 July 2017. Available at http://tech.economictimes.indiatimes.com/news/corporate/accenture-india-is-the-powerhouse-of-accenture-india-cmd-rekha-menon/53610889.

Kurup, R. 2017. 'Tech Mahindra to Buy CJS Solutions for $110m.' *The Hindu BusinessLine*, 6 March. Accessed 11 July 2017. Available at http://www.thehindubusinessline.com/info-tech/tech-mahindra-to-acquire-usbased-healthcare-it-consulting-firm/article9572329.ece.

MIT. 2017. '50 Smartest Companies 2016.' *MIT Technology Review*. Accessed 4 September 2017. Available at https://www.technologyreview.com/lists/companies/2016.

Nadhe, Shivani Shinde. 2015. 'TCS Eyes Organic Growth.' *Business Standard*, 19 May. Accessed 18 July 2017. Available at http://www.business-standard.com/article/technology/tcs-sees-massive-organic-growth-opportunity-115051800383_1.html.

Nirmal, Rajalakshmi. 2017. 'IT's Time for ctrl+alt+delete.' *The Hindu*, 26 February. Accessed 28 July 2017. Available at http://www.thehindu.com/todays-paper/tp-business/its-time-for-ctrlaltdelete/article17370307.ece.

Punit, Itika Sharma. 2016. 'India's $146-billion IT Industry Has No Idea What Will Happen to Its European Business Now.' *Quartz India*, 24 June. Accessed 4 August

2017. Available at https://qz.com/716157/indias-146-billion-it-industry-has-no-idea-what-will-happen-to-its-european-business-now.

Sadam, Rishika and Supantha Mukherjee. 2017. 'Cognizant to Return $3.4 Billion to Shareholders, in Deal with Elliott.' *Livemint*, 9 February. Accessed 5 August 2017. Available at http://www.livemint.com/Companies/9oeLbN9GB602jhycFY hopK/Cognizant-to-appoint-3-directors-buy-back-34-billion-wor.html.

Singh, Shelly. 2017. 'Indian IT: Action Shifting from Traditional Services to Digital Technology.' *The Economic Times*, 14 February. Accessed 20 July 2017. Available at http://economictimes.indiatimes.com/tech/ites/indian-it-action-shifting-from-traditional-services-to-digital-technology/articleshow/57135869.cms.

Soni, Pavan. 2013. 'Innovation in the Indian IT Industry: A Dynamic Capabilities View.' In *Servitization, IT-ization and Innovation Models: Two-Stage Industrial Cluster Theory*, edited by H. Hirakawa, K. Lal, S. Naoko and N. Tokumara, 106–15. London: Routledge.

Teece, D. J. 2007. 'Explicating Dynamic Capabilities: The Nature and Micro-Foundations of (Sustainable) Enterprise Performance.' *Strategic Management Journal* 28 (13): 1319–50. DOI: http://doi:10.1002/smj.640.

———. 2018. 'Business Models and Dynamic Capabilities.' *Long Range Planning* 51 (1): 40–49. Available online 23 July 2017. DOI: https://doi.org/10.1016/j.lrp.2017.06.007.

Teece, D. J., G. Pisano and A. Shuen. 1997. 'Dynamic Capabilities and Strategic Management.' *Strategic Management Journal* 18 (7): 509–33. Available at http://links.jstor.org/sici?sici=0143-2095%28199708%2918%3A7%7C509%3ADCAS M%3E2.0.CO%3B2-%23.

TOI (*The Times of India*). 2017. 'TCS Board Approves Rs 16,000 Crore Share Buyback, Biggest in India.' 20 February. Accessed 19 July 2017. Available at http://timesofindia.indiatimes.com/business/india-business/tcs-board-approves-rs-16000-crore-share-buyback/articleshow/57251790.cms.

Wharton. 2017. 'Has the "Dream Run" for Indian IT Ended?' *Knowledge@Wharton*, 14 April. Accessed 16 July 2017. Available at http://knowledge.wharton.upenn.edu/article/dream-run-indian-ended.

11

Moving from OEM to OBM?
Upgrading of the Chinese Mobile Phone Industry[1]

Huasheng Zhu, Fan Xu and Qingcan He

Introduction

More and more developing countries have been directly or indirectly integrated into global production networks. Despite being at the low end of global value chains (GVCs) and exposed to the risk of being replaced by other countries with lower production costs, it is believed that these developing countries are capable of industrial upgradation (Gereffi, 1999, 49–55). For developing countries, the model of upgrading from being an original equipment manufacturer (OEM) to becoming an original brand manufacturer (OBM) is considered to be a practical one (Gereffi, 1999, 55–57; Leonard-Barton, 1995; Hobday, 1995). As far as the four types of economic upgrading (Gereffi, 1999, 2005, 171; Barrientos, Gereffi and Rossi, 2011, 323–24) are concerned, developing countries generally encounter far less difficulty in process and product upgrading than in functional and chain upgrading (Humphrey and Schmitz, 2002, 1023).

However, in other literature on this issue, it is argued that integration into the GVC contributes little to industrial upgrading for developing countries, not only because over-dependence on trade with a couple of multinational companies (MNCs) would hinder the process of upgrading and transformation for a firm in less developed economies, but also because MNCs tend to prevent their suppliers in developing countries from catching up with them (Humphrey and Schmitz, 2002, 1024). Besides the reluctance to undertake the risk of upgrading (Barrientos *et al.*, 2011, 333–34), there are still other difficulties for OEM firms in developing countries seeking to fill the gap between the requirements for being an OEM and an OBM,

1   The research is supported by the National Science Foundation of China (Project Codes: 40701039, 41171098) and the Fundamental Research Funds for the Central Universities (Project Code: 2014KJJCB03).

such as the lack of sales channels, and very limited knowledge spillover from MNCs which occupied the high end of the value chains (Schmitz and Knorringa, 2000). Conversely, companies with successful experiences of upgrading in developing countries are domestic-market oriented or export their products to other less developed economies (Bazan and Navas-Aleman, 2001), by manufacturing cheaper products with inclusive innovation to occupy the subsistence marketplaces and build up their brand value (Weidner, Rosa and Viswanathan, 2009). These companies have managed to accumulate technological capability and obtain global research and development (R&D) resources (Fan, 2006a), especially exploiting many opportunities in growing and emerging technologies for industrial upgrading in collaboration and competition with MNCs (Jin and Zedtwitz, 2008, 332). Such cases in East Asian countries also highlight the indispensable role of governments (Fan, 2010) whose policies and whose fostering of innovative milieus are conducive to the upgrading process (Humphrey and Schmitz, 2002).

In recent years, the issue of how to transform from 'Manufacturing China' to 'Innovative China' has been put forward as an important one concerning national strategy in China. It is not only related to China's low-profit and low-end status in the GVC, but also to the sustainable growth and international competitiveness of the national economy. The risk of the OEM model has been exposed in some areas of southeastern China and industrial upgradation is an urgent issue.

The Chinese mobile phone industry has experienced the same problem. Started as an assembly shop of MNCs in the 1990s (Zhou, 2005, 20), China saw rapid development in mobile phone manufacturing. Within a very short period of time, a large number of domestic mobile phone manufacturers (MPMs) emerged, which led to the establishment of a complete industrial chain (Kong, 2010, 41–42), ranging from equipment and material components production to industrial design, assembling and sale services (Wen, 2008, 149–50). It seems that the standard pattern of industrial upgradation from OEM through ODM (original design manufacture) to OBM has been proved to be effective in China. However, most independent design houses (IDHs) closed down subsequently. Chinese manufacturers also encountered a sharp decline in the domestic market share since 2005 (Tian, 2008). This seemed to demonstrate the technological weakness of China.

At present, two facts about Chinese mobile phone manufacturing are frequently mentioned. One is related to the value chain of Apple's iPhone. As an OEM of Apple Corporation, Foxconn's factories in the mainland of China earned a small profit, accounting for less than 5 per cent of Apple's production cost (Li, 2012). This fact indicates that China is still at the low end of value chain of global mobile phone industry. The other fact, which is inspiring, is that a group of vendors represented by ZTE and Huawei have changed the market competition (Lei, 2007) and their products became popular in the domestic market, and went on to corner a considerable share of the world market. ZTE and Huawei have already ranked among the world's top ten in terms of mobile phone sales (Fang, 2012) though they still lag far behind globally renowned MNCs such as Samsung and Nokia in production.

Does what has happened in Chinese mobile phone manufacturing mean that there has been industrial upgrading from OEM to OBM? Can the success of some domestic companies be explained through this upgrading model? Can this upgrading model be considered as the so-called inclusive innovation in other developing countries (Fressoli *et al.*, 2014, 278; Papaioannou, 2014)? This chapter aims to answer these questions. The data for this analysis is collected from various sources, such as official websites, professional journals and academic literature in China. It also makes use of interviews with representatives of four major domestic companies and one inwards MNC, which took place in December 2012 and November 2015. The remainder of this chapter is organized as follows. The first part describes the current status of the Chinese mobile phone industry. The second part analyses three successful experiences of domestic companies in developing and marketing mobile phones. The third and fourth parts explore the possibilities for OEMs, joint ventures and IDHs to upgrade to OBMs. The fifth part provides the conclusion to this analysis.

Development of the Chinese mobile phone industry

Started as an outsourcing manufacturing destination in the early 1990s by a couple of MNCs, China has not only expanded its scale of production, but has also accumulated mobile communication technologies and built up its own brands with increasing popularity at home and abroad. In combination with Gereffi's definition of upgrading (Gereffi, 2005, 171), Tokatli's complementary viewpoint (Tokatli, 2012), and Chu's (2009) description of OEMs, ODMs and OBMs, five indicators, namely market share, brands, extension of value chain, patent application and profit rate, are used to examine the development of the Chinese mobile phone industry.

Growing market share of Chinese mobile phone companies at home and abroad

In the early 1990s, China was involved in the global production networks of foreign MNCs manufacturing mobile phones. Some domestic companies began to assemble mobile phones as electronic manufacturing services (EMS). Factory No. 522 of the former Ministry of Posts and Telecommunications, the predecessor of Eastern Communications, was the first company in China to produce mobile phones for Motorola in 1991. Since the late 1990s, mobile phone license regulations laid down by the former Ministry of Information Industry greatly encouraged Chinese companies to build up their own brands and further stimulated the development of China's mobile phone manufacturing industry. Thereafter, the share of domestic brands in terms of mobile phone sales in the Chinese market increased quickly. Figure 11.1 shows how domestic companies rapidly expanded in China, increasing their market share from 5.46 per cent in 1999 to 58 per cent in 2003. Since 2004, however, Chinese companies encountered great difficulties and their market share in China declined to 23 per cent in 2008. Some evidence indicates that the situation has been getting better recently. The market share of domestic companies accounted for 37.5 per cent at the end of 2011 (Nie, 2012), and increased to 80 per cent at the end of 2014 (Huang, 2015). Therefore, at the moment domestic mobile phone manufacturers once again dominate the Chinese market.

Figure 11.1 Changes of the market share of domestic mobile phone manufacturers in China from 1999 to 2015

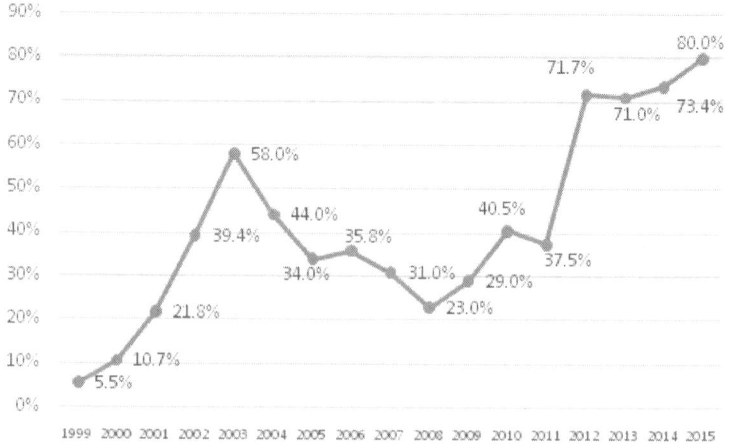

Sources: http://www.ccidconsulting.com/, http://www.tech.163.com/, http://www.ccidnet.com/, http://wegou.wehefei.com/ and http://znzd.cena.com.cn/.

Meanwhile, as far as the export of mobile phones is concerned, China has become an important manufacturing country in the world. Figure 11.2 shows that the total export volume of domestic mobile phone enterprises expanded from 510,000 units in 2002 to nearly 130 million in 2009, and the share of domestic MPMs (including 'copycat' phone-makers) on the international market increased from 0.17 per cent to 15.13 per cent over the same period. Furthermore, according to TrendForce's data, the market share of domestic mobile phones had increased to 42 per cent, which was close to the combined market share of Samsung and Apple (Beijie, 2016).

Figure 11.2 Export volume and the share of Chinese domestic MPCs in the international market from 2002 to 2009

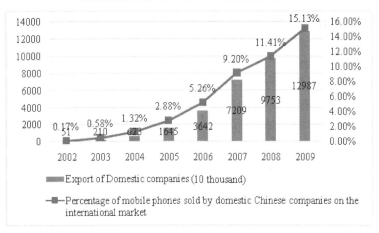

Source: http://www.ccidnet.com/.

A couple of emerging brand manufacturers

As mentioned earlier, due to the Chinese national policy which provided mobile phone making licenses to domestic companies in the late 1990s, a group of domestic manufacturers with economic and technological power (such as KEJ, ZTE, Bird, TCL, KEJ, Konka and Amoi) quickly sprung up (Zhu, 2004) and made an impact on the market, which used to be dominated by foreign giants such as Motorola, Nokia and Ericsson. In spite of some obvious disadvantages in scale economy and technology, these domestic companies took a differentiation strategy and had advantages as far as their sales channels were concerned. As a result of that, their products were very popular in the low-end market of China and captured a considerable market share. The top three domestic mobile phone manufacturers (Lenovo, Bird and Amoi) had a 14.3 per cent national market share in 2006 (see Figure 11.3), nearly 8.8 per cent higher than the combined market share of all domestic manufacturers in 1999.

Over the past ten years, a couple of other domestic manufacturers have built a good reputation and become competitive in the domestic market in China. In the 3G mobile phone market, the combined market share of the top three domestic companies (Coolpad, Huawei, and ZTE) reached 16.2 per cent in 2010 (Figure 11.4). Chinese brand manufacturers occupied 37.5 per cent of the domestic market share in 2011, while the four MNCs – Nokia, Samsung, LG and Motorola – accounted for 41.5 per cent. Six Chinese companies were part of the list of the top ten mobile phone brands on the domestic market in the same year. ZTE, Huawei, Coolpad and Lenovo are considered to be the four most competitive Chinese companies, according to a manager from Nokia (China) Investment Co. Ltd.

China's mobile phone market has changed a lot in recent years. Among the top ten mobile phone companies in the Chinese market in 2015, only two are foreign companies (Apple and Samsung). The other eight are indigenous Chinese companies. MI, the emerging company founded in 2010, is the one with the highest market share. Nokia, which used to be the most popular mobile phone brand, saw a massive decrease in the number of users and could not get into the top ten.

Figure 11.3 Market share of Chinese mobile phone brands in 2006

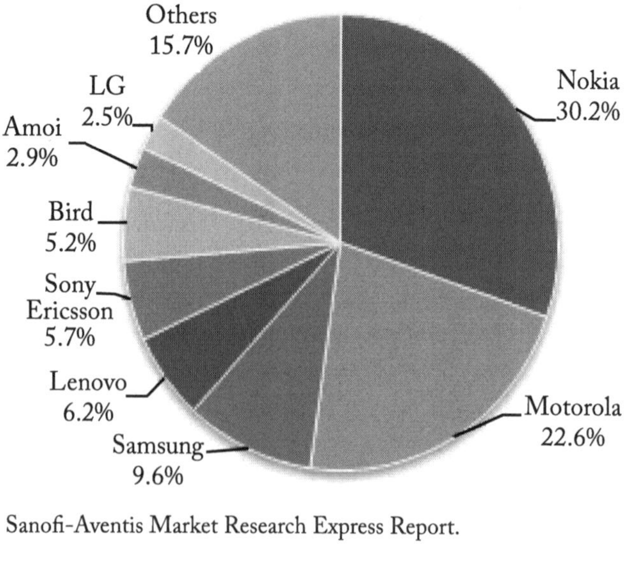

Source: Sanofi-Aventis Market Research Express Report.

Figure 11.4 Market share of Chinese 3G mobile phone brands in 2010

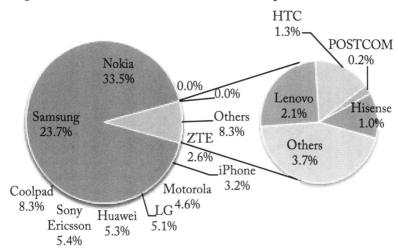

Source: 2010–11 research report of China's mobile phone market.

Figure 11.5 Market share of Chinese mobile phone brands in 2015

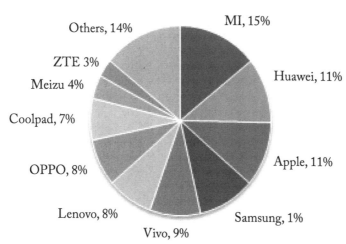

Source: IHS Technology.

Extended value chain of mobile phone manufacturing in China

Mobile phone manufacturing covers many sophisticated value-added activities (Figure 11.6) and components. Chinese companies have extended their business from mere hardware assembly to industrial design, integrated circuit (IC) design and even to the operating system (OS) for smartphones. Consequently, the value chain of mobile phone manufacturing has been gradually built up in China. Domestic and foreign companies not only have their own OBM factories, but also have a close cooperative relation with domestic electronic manufacturing services and ODMs (Figures 11.7 and 11.8).

Figure 11.6 Evolution of mobile phone manufacturing value chain in China

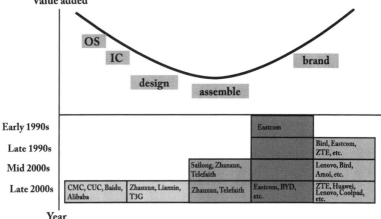

Source: The authors' interviews with company officials in 2012 and 2015.

Figure 11.7 Business linkages of domestic brand companies with EMSs and ODMs

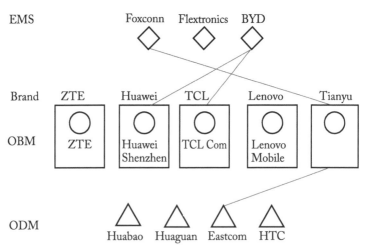

Source: The authors' interviews with company officials in 2012 and 2015.

Figure 11.8 Business linkages of foreign companies with EMSs and ODMs

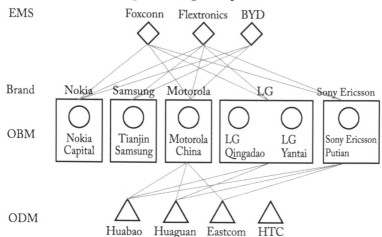

Source: The authors' interviews with company officials in 2012 and 2015.

Increasing patent applications in China

Although many domestic MPMs have encountered a major barrier while attempting to export mobile phones involving technology patents, a group of large companies in China have started paying attention to technology innovation. As a consequence, the number of patent applications increased recently. Figure 11.9 shows the increase in the total number of patent application in the field of smartphone technology.

Figure 11.9 The number of application patents related to smartphone technology in China between 2000 and 2010

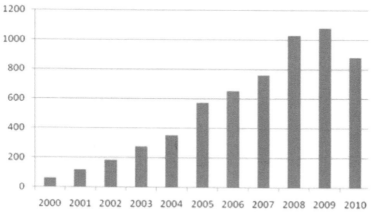

Source: Patent Examination Cooperation Centre of Beijing (http://www.sipo.gov.cn).

Human–computer interaction technology (HCIT) represents a high level of technology in the field of smartphones. Between 2000 and 2011, among the global top ten companies in terms of patents concerning human–computer interaction technology, there were only two Chinese companies, HTC and ZTE (Figure 11.10). However, in the Chinese market, five leading companies with Chinese backgrounds – ZTE, Huawei, Coolpad, Lenovo and HTC – have made significant achievements in this field, narrowing the gap with the top three foreign companies in the Chinese market (Apple, Samsung and LG) (Figure 11.11).

Figure 11.10 The number of HCIT patent applications of companies in the world between 2000 and 2011

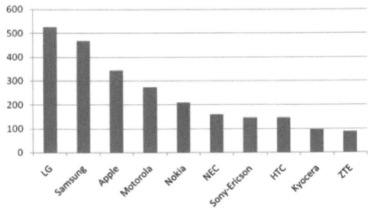

Source: Patent Examination Cooperation Center of Beijing (http://www.sipo.gov.cn).

Figure 11.11 The number of HCIT patent applications of companies in China between 2000 and 2011

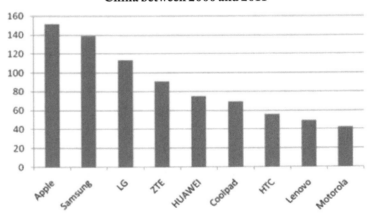

Source: Patent Examination Cooperation Center of Beijing (http://www.sipo.gov.cn).

Continuing low profit rate

Despite the fact that China has achieved much in the mobile phone manufacturing sector, there is still a large gap between Chinese companies and foreign MNCs in terms of international competitiveness. Statistical data shows that domestic mobile phone production had reached 1.13 billion units in 2011; the same year's export volume reached 880 million, accounting for nearly 80 per cent of global exports (Wang, 2012). However, between January 2012 and August 2012, the average general export trade price of a Chinese mobile phone sold under a Chinese brand name was only $33.30. Apple and Samsung combined earned 99 per cent of the global mobile phone profits in 2012. Both these facts demonstrate that most domestic companies have still not properly entered into the high-end market at present (Wang, 2012).

Beyond OEM: Emerging brand companies with a technologically relevant background

In the late 1990s, many domestic companies entered the mobile phone manufacturing industry due to the perceived high profits. Lacking crucial technology, many companies depended on independent design houses and foreign manufacturers which did not have a mobile phone license. Many manufacturers preferred not to invest in R&D and technology innovation. Therefore, when the license policy was cancelled in the mid-2000s, these companies faced great difficulty and their domestic market share declined sharply. However, a couple of innovative companies with mobile phone manufacturing licenses made use of business opportunities in the initial period and accumulated crucial technology. Generally, there are three kinds of innovative manufacturers with different development paths.

ZTE: The successful horizontal expansion of a telecom equipment manufacturer

ZTE, a leading global provider of telecommunications equipment and network solutions, set up its own mobile phone manufacturing plants in 1998. ZTE began to be an important equipment provider for many telecommunication network operators in many countries since 1996 and has set up a stable business relationship with these local network operators. These relationships actually acted as marketing channels through which ZTE could quickly occupy a considerable market share in the host country. For example, ZTE co-operated with the Indian company Reliance to set up the largest ALL-IP network on the planet, and Reliance set a record by selling 1 million ZTE mobile phones in a single week in October 2007 (Sun, 2008). As a provider of telecommunications equipment and network solutions, ZTE pays much attention to technology innovations concerning telecommunications equipment and mobile phones. Due to this, ZTE became one of the few companies in the world that could manufacture 2G, 3G and 4G mobile phones.

As the percentage of revenue from mobile phones to its total revenue increased from 20 per cent in 2006 to 28.3 per cent in 2014, mobile phones have been treated as one of ZTE's strategic products. In the fourth quarter of 2011, ZTE ranked fifth in the world in terms of mobile handset production, manufacturing 17.1 million handsets and comprising 4 per cent of the international market (C. Liu, 2012). In 2015, ZTE produced 56 million smartphones and its growth rate was 16 per cent, being higher than the industry average of 11 per cent (Dong, 2016). According to Gartner's report, ZTE has become the second-fastest growing smartphone manufacturer behind Apple (Wang, 2012) and the fourth largest mobile phone manufacturer in the world (ZTE website). The company is striving to become one of the top three companies in the world in this sector (Yang, 2012). ZTE's success in the mobile phone business can be largely attributed to its manufacture of customized cell phones for telecommunication network operators. For instance, the sales volume of the ZTE BladeV880, a customized phone for China Unicom – one of the major operators in China – was more than 4 million units in 2010, which made up a major share of the low-end market.

Existing business relationships and marketing channels in developed countries contributed to the success of the company's expansion to the mobile phone industry in those regions. ZTE collaborated with operators in the USA such as Verizon and AT&T. With the help of these network operators, the market share of ZTE in America increased to 8.2 per cent in 2015 (Li, 2014). However, in an advanced economy, high-quality but low-price handsets are more important. For example, ZTE smartphones have high sales volumes in Manhattan, New York City, where most of the buyers are attracted by its cheaper price and high quality. Other than that, ZTE focuses on the prepaid market, which is full of low-income customers, where there is the possibility of faster growth. With the high-quality, low-price handsets, ZTE became the second largest mobile phone manufacturer in the prepaid market (Li, 2014).

Another example from a different market confirms this trend. In 2005, 300,000 WCDMA mobile phones (the F866 model), which were customized by ZTE for Hutchison Whampoa, successfully entered the UK market. A couple of telecom network operators in the global top twenty were very suspicious about their quality because ZTE was a new entrant in the 3G mobile phone sector. However, the F866 eventually won the acceptance of Hutchison Whampoa after more than 3,000 strict tests, but in a three-month period instead of the usual six months. These tests also showed that the repair rate was less than 2 per cent (Mi, 2008).

ZTE has paid great attention to technology innovation and international co-operation, building eighteen state-of-the-art R&D centres in China, France and India, and has employed over 30,000 research staff. The company spent 9 billion Yuan on R&D in 2014, which was 11.06 per cent of its annual revenue (ZTE website). The company transferred its experience in undertaking incremental innovation in telecommunication equipment manufacturing to build an innovation-oriented strategy for mobile phone making. The company set up an industrial design centre in Shanghai in 1998 on the basis of 'design-driven research and development'. The ID centre has expanded to accommodate more than 300 professional designers and engineers. The company has also established six design groups in Nanjing, Xi'an and Shenzhen in China, as also centres in Dallas in the USA and Gurgaon in India (Chen, 2011). In 2002, ZTE signed a memorandum of cooperation with Intel for the development of 3G technology.

Over a ten-year period, the company has managed to obtain a large number of patents related to mobile phone technology. ZTE has more than 12,000 patent applications related to mobile phones. Its volume of patent applications ranked third in the world in 2014. In China, though, ZTE has the largest number of patent applications related to mobile phones (around 6,000). Among its 2,000 international patents concerning mobile phones under the Patent Cooperation Treaty (PCT), more than 70 per cent are related to 3G mobile phones, far ahead of other Chinese companies (Wang, 2012). The company has also won fifteen international design prizes, including the Red Dot Design Award in the field of mobile phone design in 2011. Through innovation in mobile phone design, ZTE has turned to the high-end segment of the mobile phone market, trying to build a more high-end brand image. The Blade, the brand name of its newly designed star product, was very popular in the UK, France, Japan and other countries. Its sales volume reached 2 million by the end of the first half of 2011. The Blade V7, the latest version of the series, was widely acclaimed at the Mobile World Congress in 2016. It was listed among the 'The Top Ten Smart Phones' by the *International Business Times* and also won other prizes (Wang, 2016). Now, ZTE has a greater market share in many countries. For instance, ZTE ranked fourth in the USA (in terms of sales numbers) with the sale of 15 million smartphones in 2015, and it was among the top five sellers in Australia, Russia, Turkey and other countries (Dong, 2016).

Lenovo: The amazing turnaround of an electronic computing 'giant'

Lenovo Corporation, one of the world's largest IT vendors, was founded in 1984 with a technological and academic background. The company set up Lenovo Mobile to enter the mobile phone manufacturing sector in 2002. Lacking crucial technology at that point, the company utilized schemes from mobile phone design companies in Japan and South Korea. However, Lenovo did not achieve great success in this functional mobile phone era and eventually decided to sell this business. After the arrival of the smartphones era, Lenovo realized the huge possibilities if it transferred its expertise in electronic computing into mobile phone manufacturing. The other important reason for Lenovo's decision to return to the mobile phone world is because the profit margins in the personal computer sector decreased quickly and telecommunication networks, cable television and the Internet tended to start becoming integrated.

New Lenovo Mobile was set up in 2008, and functioned on the principle of 'customers, innovation, and efficiency' (Hou, 2012). Lenovo adopted the differential strategy to meet different demands in segmental markets, and built up four major product lines (S, A, P and K) of music phones which provide various online services including music broadcasting, downloading and uploading. Consequently, Lenovo underwent speedy growth and was ranked second in the domestic mobile phone market in the first half of 2012, with a market share of 14 per cent (Pang, 2012), nearly 10 per cent higher than that in 2005. Initially, the rapid expansion of Lenovo in China's smartphone market relied heavily on collaboration with telecommunication networks operators in China, and nearly 70 per cent of its mobile phones were sold in the business halls of networks operators. Customers could get a smart mobile phone at a lower price through the prepayment of a small amount of the mobile network service fee (Ding, 2015). With the collaboration with the mobile network operators and the advantage of low production costs based on Xoceco (an electronic manufacturer in China) technology (Wang, 2006), in 2012, Lenovo obtained a market share of 14 per cent in China. Since 2011, the network operators have subsidized low-priced smartphones in order to popularize the use of 3G (Zhang and Ma, 2015, 48–49).

Lenovo's success in the smartphone industry not only depends on its information technology capabilities, brand awareness and widespread marketing channels in the personal computer world, but is also due to its regular programmes of learning and innovation. The Apple corporate model set a good example for Lenovo for extending its business from personal computers to mobile phones. However, Lenovo realized that there was a big risk if a Chinese company completely adopted Apple's business model. Therefore, Lenovo finally made an important change by moving from a closed operating platform to an open Android platform. Unlike other mobile phone manufacturers, Lenovo had, very early on, started regarding mobile handsets as mobile computing tools. According to a manager of MIDH (Mobile Internet and Digital Home Business Group) in Lenovo, the company has laid emphasis on application functions in mobile phones and has set up R&D centres for research on mobile phone technology in Beijing, Shanghai and Xiamen. After Motorola's withdrawal from Nanjing, Lenovo established a new R&D centre there and hired about thirty former Motorola Nanjing employees. The personnel working on the end-to-end design of mobile phone software currently exceeds 300. Around 20 per cent of technology involving its mobile phones is attributed to Lenovo's independent R&D and 80 per cent of its products are manufactured in-house. In terms of the number of patent applications, Lenovo had the third highest among Chinese mobile phone companies. In total, it owned forty-nine patents related to human–computer interaction during the period between 2000 and 2010 – a number exceeded only by ZTE and Huawei. Moreover, Lenovo acquired Motorola in 2014, which could cut down 20 per cent of the production cost of some of its smartphones, because Lenovo would no longer need to pay Motorola for certain patents since Lenovo now owns them directly (Shi, 2016).

Lenovo did not begin to expand into overseas markets until recently. In November 2012, Lenovo smartphones emerged in the Indian market. Based on the mature sales and service network of its personal computers and other electronic products, Lenovo has managed to enter the Indian mobile phone market and has been successful there. In the fourth quarter of 2015, its market share of smartphone sales was 11.6 per cent, on the heels of Samsung and Micromax (a local brand). After acquiring Motorola in 2014, Lenovo sped up its pace to enter more developed markets using the Motorola brand, extant market channels and the key patents (Hou, 2014), to which it added its own standards of high quality and innovation. Meanwhile, it expanded in emerging markets through the cheaper Lenovo smartphones (He, 2015). Consequently, the ratio of its overseas market smartphone sales to domestic market sales reached 65 per cent in 2015, nearly 50 per cent higher than that in 2014 (Zhou, 2015).

MI: A rising star with the background of a mobile internet service provider

MI Corporation was founded in April 2010 as a smartphone software developer and mobile internet service provider. Its founders were all former senior employees of famous domestic and foreign IT companies, such as Jinshan, Microsoft, Google and Motorola. With their professional experience and entrepreneurship skills, the company grew very quickly. From August 2011 to July 2014, MI launched eleven different new models of smartphones, averaging one product launch every 3.2 months.

With the strong belief that mobile phones will become the most convenient calculating tool for daily life (instead of personal computers), MI worked out a long-term strategy for the business of mobile phones called the 'circuitous path', which involved using its advantage as a mobile internet providing service, and then extending it to mobile phone manufacturing (Wang, 2011). As an experienced software developer, MI concentrates on secondary development based on the Android system, and also has its own mobile operating system – MIUI. MIUI became widely used across twenty-three countries, with 30 million mobile phone enthusiasts around the world in one year. This was due to MI's model of continuously implementing improvements after taking serious consideration of user feedback. MI has built an internet forum (MIUI.com) to publish its operating system and gather users' opinions about the system. The company publishes an updated version once a week, which would be tested voluntarily by multiple users and be further improved based on the users' feedback (Dong and Cheng, 2014, 81). The forum is an open platform where anyone can download and use the MIUI system and then let MI know about their experiences and expectations. So every user who contributes is actually involved in the creation of each version of the MIUI system. The company often reveals ideas to its users through forums before new product development, and invites them to make an evaluation before a new product launch (S. Liu, 2012). From this perspective, the company follows the way of inclusive innovation (Kuang, 2012).

Miliao, a kind of online communication software with a requirement for real-name registration, was launched at the end of 2010. 300 million users registered within the first six months. The large number of MI fans and its good reputation among users are valuable assets and have made a great contribution to its expansion into mobile phone manufacturing. The company launched its first smartphones under its own brand name in August 2011. MI's mobile phones were very popular – the leading online handset retailer in Hong Kong, RingHK.com, announced that MI's phones ranked third in terms of CTR (click-through rate), after Samsung and Sony-Ericsson.

MI outsources its production to Inventec and Foxconn and applies the world's most advanced mobile terminal technology and components in every new mobile phone. Moreover, MI adopts the order-oriented e-commerce model, which means that the company has set up production plans based on the volume of online orders and purchases components accordingly from its suppliers. This business model is conducive for implementing zero inventory management. The company uses diverse channels for sales (such as network direct sales, collaboration with operators, and social networks), and constantly maintains this core competency through resources integration (Ding, 2012). Consequently, the company is effectively able to improve the product quality, cut down the production costs and lower business risks. Its products are much cheaper than that of many manufacturers. According to a survey, MI phone users are mainly the generation born in the 1980s and 1990s. Most of them desire smartphones with lower prices. MI has gained great success for its cost management performance in the domestic market (Wei, 2014).

MI has received financial support from venture capital institutions for its innovation capabilities and business potential. MI obtained an investment from the Morningside Group, Qiming Venture Partners and IDG in October 2010. With a combined investment of $41 million from Morningside, Qiming and IDG, MI's market value reached $250 million in 2011. In December 2011, the company got $90 million from QiMing, IDG, the Shun Fund, Temasek, Qualcomm and Morningside Financing (DoNews, 2012). MI got an investment of $216 million in June 2012 and $1.1 billion in December 2014, and its market value increased to $45 billion (Zhang, 2016). MI has not required external investment since 2015, because it made enough profit to support its development.

However, MI is facing patent risks; the number of its patent applications related to smartphones is far lower than many domestic and foreign manufacturers, which is a potential barrier to its future development. MI has not engaged in manufacturing but relies on more than 400 suppliers; therefore, MI is exposed to some serious risks in its complicated supply chain (Li, 2014). For instance, MI used Qualcomm's central processing unit (CPU) in its smartphones to keep its price advantage; however, Qualcomm was penalised by the Chinese government because of its monopoly in 2014. After that, the cost of MI phones increased because of the higher patent fee of Qualcomm's CPU (Wang and Li, 2015). Therefore, in order to have a stable supply of CPUs, MI began to develop its own CPU with Leadcore Technology since late 2014. CPU was used for the first time in its new smartphones MI 5C in 2017 (Wang, 2017).

It is clear that MI's development mostly relies on its users and factories. From product design to development and testing, users can involve themselves in the whole process where they can express their demands and point out the defects of the mobile phone, which actually leads to inclusive innovation. Through these actions, MI has created and cultivated the loyalty of customers. Without its own factory and the loss of its own patents, MI has to use existing components to manufacture mobile phones, which has led to more influence from suppliers.

Difficulties of OEMs and joint ventures in upgrading to OBMs

Compared to the three companies mentioned above, the majority of joint ventures, which were considered to be the leading firms in the development of the Chinese mobile phone industry, have not strengthened their competitiveness. Only a handful of small- and medium-sized manufactures have succeeded in setting up their own brands, but have encountered great difficulty in improving the status of their products from their position in the low-end segment in the world market.

The difficult transformation of the offshore manufacturing base in China

Shenzhen, a city in the southeastern Guangdong province, has already become the largest manufacturing base of mobile phones in China. Initially, the city focused on export-oriented manufacturing with a large number of OEM factories, but now has transformed into hub of the global production network with a complete industrial chain of mobile phone manufacturing facilities, ranging from R&D and industrial design, components making, final product assembly to sales and marketing. The percentage of handset shipments from

Shenzhen to the total number of global shipments reached 25 per cent in 2010 (S. Liu, 2012), and the global top ten OEM firms manufacturing mobile phones are based in this city. Due to the increasing number of domestic OEMs, the average price of mobile phones decreased dramatically and the profit per product exported to other developing countries decreased to 2–5 per cent for OEM firms.

Shenzhen has been working hard for upgrading these firms from OEMs to OBMs. Moving to OBM status is a transformation strategy for some OEMs in Shenzhen, with the encouragement of the local government. A handful of firms such as Coolpad, G'Five, Tianlong and Yidalong (besides ZTE and Huawei), have sold mobile phones abroad under their own brand. The mobile phone companies have been concerned about their product quality and thus have made a lot of investment in technology innovation (Yi, 2012). In spite of the improvements in brand image and technology, mobile phone manufacturers in the city still have some difficulty in upgrading from OEM to OBM status. Jinli, usually treated as a successfully transforming company, has not yet obtained a good enough reputation on the domestic market. G'Five, one of the leading mobile phone manufacturing companies in Shenzhen, has encountered great challenges from its major former clients after building up its own brand. Due to a large amount of investment in its own brand, G'Five was burdened with high costs and lower profits (Lu, 2011). Furthermore, according to Shenzhen customs, the average export price of each product was $54.30 in January 2013, a decrease of 25 per cent compared to the value in the same period in 2012. Moreover, almost half the mobile phone exports in Shenzhen are still OEM-related (Shenzhen customs, 2013).

Failure of joint ventures to upgrade to OBMs

There were a couple of domestic manufacturers who started mobile phone businesses in the early 1990s. Compared to other peer companies in China, these manufacturers had some specific assets (such as being formerly government-owned), the possession of up-to-date communication technology, and established co-operation with international mobile phone manufacturing giants such as Motorola and Nokia. Such collaboration was believed to contribute to industrial upgradation of domestic companies from OEMs to OBMs. However, that is not the case as most of these companies did not improve their brand image, and some of them even exited the mobile phone market (see Table 11.1). The reasons behind this are very complicated (for example, in some cases, an enterprise management system was a key point), but an over-dependency on foreign resources caused an unbalanced power structure in the business collaboration, which meant that there was little opportunity for Chinese companies to obtain cutting-edge technology and build up their own brands. For example, Hangzhou East Communications Equipment Factory (Eastcom), a state-owned company, introduced manufacturing technology from Motorola in 1990 to build China's first advanced mobile phone production lines, and became Motorola's first partner in the Chinese mainland. Compared to other private firms, Eastcom easily got access to financial support, especially from the government. In 1997, the company launched mobile phone development projects and even established an R&D department in Silicon Valley in the United States. In 1999, Eastcom produced a mobile phone under its own brand, the EG580. The company did not achieve great success in its branded products and eventually has become a production base for Potevio, Eastcom's parent company (Wang, 2006). Two other state-owned companies, Capital and Kejian, had similar experiences.

Unlike the three companies mentioned earlier, Bird was a private-owned pager manufacturer. In 1999, Bird signed a cooperation agreement on the development and production of mobile phone technology with Sagem. They set up a joint venture plant at the end of August 2002 and jointly established R&D institutions in 2005 (Shen, 2005). However, in spite of established market channels, Bird failed to seize smartphone development opportunities due to the lack of crucial technology. Moreover, expansion to the automobile industry and real estate led to Bird's neglect of investment in technological innovation in order to secure competitive advantage. At present its main business is still related to mobile phones, such as motherboard production and sales, and the design and production of mobile phone accessories, but its brand is less influential than before.

Limited knowledge spillover of foreign MNCs

Chinese mobile phone manufacturing originated in foreign investments in OEMs, though cooperation with foreign manufacturing giants did not bring about the development of companies selling products under their own brands. With the increasing importance of the Chinese market and because of Chinese high-quality-but-low-cost professional talent, MNCs set up R&D institutions in China (see Table 11.2). These foreign R&D institutions act as professional training centres and contribute to the prosperity of the local talent market through talent flow. In fact, many founders of the previously burgeoning IDHs have a professional background in these institutions. Additionally, according to a respondent, Lenovo made a decision to set up a new mobile phone research centre in Nanjing in 2012 merely based on the fact that Motorola closed down its R&D centre in that city. The research personnel who shifted to Lenovo were expected to be a bridge for knowledge and technology flow. Such issues need to be carefully explored in the future.

In sum, in the early stages, cooperation with MNCs helped Chinese companies accumulate related technology and gain resources for management and training (Fan, 2010). It was conducive for domestic companies for building their own brands. However, with the increase of their market share, Chinese companies faced serious challenges from non-Chinese MNCs. Conflicts concerning technological patents between domestic companies and MNCs happens frequently (Cui, 2010, 79), which to some extent hinders the upgrading process of domestic companies. Increasing market competition or cost-cutting pressure has led some innovative companies to develop their own technology and market expansion.

Table 11.1 Cooperation between multinational companies and Chinese manufacturers

Multinational companies	Chinese partner(s)		Primary cooperative projects	Current situation
	Company name	Background		
Motorola	Hangzhou Communications Equipment Factory (HZCEF)	A state-owned communication company	In 1990, Eastcom introduced manufacturing technology from Motorola and built China's first advanced mobile phone production lines	Eastcom has transformed into a production base of Potevio (its parent company) and shelved its own brand
Nokia	Beijing Post & Telecom Equipment Factory (predecessor of Capitel)	A state-owned telecommunications equipment factory	NCT – a joint venture with Nokia was established in 1995. In 2000, Capitel and Nokia jointly invested 10 billion Yuan to build Beijing Xingwang Industrial Park for integration of industrial chains	Capitel has focused on digital communication

(Contd.)

(Contd.)

Multinational companies	Chinese partner(s)		Primary cooperative projects	Current situation
	Company name	Background		
Samsung	China Kejian Co. Ltd	A state-owned research institute of digital technology	In1999, Kejian invested $612,000 in a joint venture – SKSMT – with Samsung and Hong Kong Keyao to develop the GSM mobile communication technology. Kejian and Samsung also invested in another joint venture, SSKMT, in 2001.	Kejian exited the mobile phone market in 2005
French SAGEM	Fenghua Bird Co. Ltd	A private pager manufacturer in Ningbo, Zhejiang	Bird and Sagem set up a joint venture plant at the end of August 2002. They also jointly established R&D institutions in 2005	The company still focuses on the mobile phone business, but its brand value is less influential than before

Sources: http://www.motorola.com.cn/; http://www.nokia.com/zh_int/guanyunuojiya-0; http://www.samsung.com/cn/; http://www.sagemcom.com.

Notes: 1. NCT refers to Beijing Nokia Communication Technology Co. Ltd.
2. SSKMT refers to Shenzhen Samsung Kejian Mobile Telecommunication Technology Co. Ltd.

Table 11.2 R&D centres of foreign multinational companies in China

Foreign MNCs	R&D centre	Year	Main function
Motorola	Nanjing Software Centre	1997	Software development
	Motorola China Research and Development Institute	1999	Personal communications product development, the latest mobile communication solutions
	Beijing R&D Centre of Personal Communications	1999	Mobile phone design and R&D
	Beijing R&D Center	2004	Wireless communications technology, particularly the development of 3G technology
	Hangzhou R&D Centre	2006	Software and hardware development related to 3G CDMA and UMTS technology, system testing, and development of new products

(Contd.)

(*Contd.*)

Foreign MNCs	R&D centre	Year	Main function
Nokia	Beijing R&D Centre	1998	The first R&D centre, which began the research and development related to high-end mobile phones
	Xingwang Industrial Park (Beijing)	2001	China's first high-tech industrial base
	Hangzhou R&D Centre	2002	3G software and platform technology development
LG	LG Electronics China R&D Centre (Beijing)	2002	R&D centre for mobile phones and digital TV
	LG Yantai R&D Centre	2011	R&D and production centre
Samsung	BST (Beijing)	2000	Standardization and commercialization for Chinese mobile communication market
	SCRC (Nanjing)	2004	Core application platform and technology
	SGMC(Guangzhou)	2008	Large mobile phone R&D institution

Sources: http://www.motorola.com.cn/; http://www.nokia.com/zh_int; http://www.lg.com/cn/about-lg; http://www.samsung.com/cn/.

Boom and bust cycles of IDHs in China

Mobile phone licenses granted by the Chinese central government in the late 1990s led to the growth of domestic mobile phone vendors in China. Most of them had disadvantages in terms of not possessing core technology and good enough industrial design centres, and had to outsource design-intensive components to foreign design consultancies. With the expansion of the mobile phone market, more and more research staff employed by MNCs such as ZTE, Motorola, Nokia, Ericsson and Samsung started to set up IDHs of their own, bringing about rapid growth in the design service sector.

Three development stages of IDHs

Until today, Chinese IDHs have experienced three stages. They are:

1. The initial period (1999–2003)

China's first mobile phone design company, CLP Cellon, was established in

1999, and by 2004, there were about fifty IDHs in China. These IDHs provided design services for over 400 design plans in total, and their net profit reached 70 per cent of total sales during 2001–03 with a 120 per cent growth rate (Tian, 2008). At this stage, most IDHs were small-sized and invested little on R&D. They mainly focused on the provision of some application software, handset appearance and industrial design.

2. The rapid growth period (2004–06)

IDHs developed quickly to cater to the increasing domestic demand for mobile phones with various requirements. When the mobile phone license regime was abolished, the lower entry threshold further stimulated the expansion of domestic mobile phone manufacturing. Experienced IDHs, such as Techfaith, even began to work on overseas projects. IDHs still made high profits.

3. The recession period (since 2006)

As international vendors lowered their prices almost to the same level as domestic products, domestic market competition increased. Under such circumstances, the weaknesses of small manufacturers in term of product quality were exposed, and many of them had to exit the market. A couple of companies established their interior design departments. Moreover, MTK, a chip manufacturer from Taiwan, China, launched turnkey solutions integrating various applicant services into the chip and greatly simplifying the manufacturing process. The demands for design services declined heavily and many IDHs had to close down due to the lack of business. Even some large IDHs did not survive. CLP Cellon is a case in point. Techfaith and Ginwave had to dismiss a large number of employees. The rate of profit in the mobile phone design industry decreased heavily from 300 per cent in 2002 to 5.1 per cent in 2007 (Li, 2007).

In general, the failure of Chinese IDHs can be attributed to various reasons. Among them, an important one was that many IDHs were opportunistic and paid little attention to investment in technology innovation. As a result, they did not build up their core competencies properly. The few IDHs surviving the decline have transformed from being design consultancies to ODMs, and aspire to become OBMs in future.

Surviving IDHs' transformation: The case of Techfaith

In 2002, more than a dozen designers and engineers left Motorola and established Techfaith. In the early stages, Techfaith introduced design programmes from South Korea for secondary development. Owing to its high-quality

R&D team, Techfaith soon gained a reputation among domestic mobile phone manufacturers for its good design service. Subsequently, with financing from NEC, Qualcomm, Intel and other strategic investors with a technical background, the company made great progress in design capability. Some famous foreign MPMs such as Nokia, NEC, Alcatel, Mitsubishi and Siemens commissioned handset designs from Techfaith. Eight of the top ten domestic companies (such as Lenovo and Haier) became Techfaith's long-term customers. In 2005, although many domestic IDHs began to decline, Techfaith was listed on the NASDAQ, raising more than $100 million. The company pays a great deal of attention to R&D investment. In the field of smartphone design, Techfaith has begun to develop software based on open operating systems including Linux and Windows Mobile, and the company has the ability to implement and even customize high-end smartphones for special customers. The company has approximately 2,400 professionals, of whom 90 per cent are engineers. Half of the 2,000-strong research staff of the company were involved in software development. In 2006, a European network operator spent $7 million buying a new type of mobile phone designed by Techfaith that could be used to watch television programmes.

Due to the decline of the domestic market share of Chinese mobile phone vendors since the mid-2000s, and especially after the financial crisis in 2008, the demand for original design services dropped significantly. In August 2009, Techfaith spent a total of $12.5 million in order to acquire a smartphone maker, QIGI Future Technology (Beijing) Co. Ltd. (hereinafter referred to as 'QIGI') (Yi, 2010), with the objective of transforming from a design consultancy to a manufacturer with its own design ability and brand. However, due to the lack of popularity of the QIGI brand, the sales volume of their mobile phones is relatively low. It was reported that Techfaith's annual shipments of its own brand was around 300 million, while sale of the QIGI phone was only 100 million units (Cheng, 2010). Therefore, Techfaith is still an ODM rather than an OBM. Table 11.3 shows that the share of design service revenue in the company's total income has decreased since 2006, while the sales revenue of specific products has grown.

It is Techfaith's entrepreneurial team from Motorola that made the company display good economic performance and also achieve a successful transformation, while the vast majority of IDHs went bankrupt or closed down.

Table 11.3 Income of Techfaith's main business sections from 2006 to 2011
(unit: '000 US$)

Years	2006	2007	2008	2009	2010	2011
Mobile phone design service	42,860	41,721	19,123	4,482	3,512	3,914
Product sales revenue	37,944	101,723	189,727	206,106	268,365	319,886
R&D expenses	21,970	30,876	18,195	12,040	11,613	13,541
The total net income	80,804	143,444	208,850	211,076	271,877	323,800
The share of design service to the total net income	53%	29%	9%	2%	1%	1%
Proportion of product sales revenue to total net income	47%	71%	91%	98%	99%	99%

Source: Techfaith annual report, http://www.techfaithwireless.com/.

Conclusion

Through nearly twenty years' development, China has been moving from an offshore outsourcing destination of multinational mobile-phone manufacturers towards a technology- and design-oriented manufacturing base, cultivating a number of its own brands. Gereffi's four types of economic upgrading can be found in the Chinese mobile phone industry; however, domestic leading companies have still encountered embarrassing situations involving their low-end products with low profits in the global market. Upgrading to OBM status is an ongoing process for the majority of Chinese mobile phone companies.

The model of industrial upgrading from OEM to OBM is considered as a development path for companies in developing economies involved in the global production system. However, the evidence shows that almost half of the total mobile phone export volume in Shenzhen is still OEM-related, and the majority of IDHs ended up being shut down or merged. It is not very easy to successfully make a transformation from being an OEM to an OBM. Industrial upgrading also depends on innovative companies, which have focused on the domestic market and are not integrated into the global production network as OEM firms. Moreover, these companies have paid much attention to long-term benefits rather than short-term returns, and permanent innovation instead of opportunistic investments. In addition, participation in international business deals and collaborations have exposed these companies to global competition and have contributed to strengthening their core competencies and brand popularity.

Foreign investment did bring about the rise of the Chinese mobile phone industry. Joint ventures depended heavily on technology introduction knowledge from their foreign partners, but made few efforts to develop cutting-edge technology or build up its own brand. However, as real role models and competitors, the existence of foreign companies (especially these global giants) highlighted the importance of technology innovation, which forced domestic companies to improve their creativity. Additionally, the establishment of foreign R&D centres in China could be conducive to the accumulation of human capital in the long run.

The experiences of ZTE, Lenovo and MI prove that upgrading can be achieved by making use of the knowledge acquired from one sector in another. That also means that investments for knowledge accumulation are very important in the long term for industrial upgradation in a country. In this process, these domestic companies have continuously engaged in obtaining new technology and institutional development, have paid attention to building and strengthening their own advantages in niche markets, and have taken care to effectively communicate with customers and gauge their changing tastes. This upgrading can be considered as incremental improvement, and not a breakthrough or radical innovation. Investment, R&D (for every part of the manufacturing process) and technology-oriented acquisition facilitated access to cutting-edge or crucial technology, further increasing upgradation opportunities for domestic companies. An upgrade is never a final stage, but an ongoing process, which has a knock-on effect. Companies or personnel involved in the mobile phone industry may make great contributions to the upgrading processes of other industries in future.

References

The titles of all articles in Chinese have been translated by Huasheng Zhu.

Barrientos, S., G. Gereffi and A. Rossi. 2011. 'Economic and Social Upgrading in Global Production Networks: A New Paradigm for a Changing World.' *International Labour Review* 150 (3–4): 319–40.

Beijie. 2016. 'The Share of Chinese Domestic Mobile Phones on the International

Market was 42% in 2015, and There Were Seven Chinese Companies in the Top Ten of the Volume of Production [in Chinese].' Accessed 1 January 2016. Available at http://www.expreview.com/45175.html.

Chen, S. 2011. 'ZTE Handsets Win 15 International Design Awards in 5 Years [in Chinese].' *Shenzhen Economic Daily.* Accessed 9 March 2013. Available at http://szsb.sznews.com/html/2011-07/25/content_1674062.htm.

Cheng, J. 2010. 'TechFaith "Take-All" [in Chinese].' Ifeng website. Accessed 1 March 2013. Available at http://finance.ifeng.com/roll/20101028/2785189.shtml.

Chu, W. 2009. 'Can Taiwan's Second Movers Upgrade via Branding? [in Chinese].' *Research Policy* 38 (6): 1054–65.

Cui, X. 2010. 'Foreign Investment and the Development of China's Mobile Phone Industry [in Chinese].' *Practice in Foreign Economic Relations and Trade* 4: 77–79.

Ding, C. 2015. 'The Strategy of Late Comers in the Chinese Smart Phone Market: The Cases of MI, Huawei and Lenovo [in Chinese].' *Brand* 8: 6–7.

Ding, R. 2012. 'MI's Business Model and Innovation [in Chinese].' *Business* (5): 83–84.

DoNews. 2012. 'The MI Has Completed the C Round of Financing, the Russian DST Group Is the Lead Investor [in Chinese].' Finance Sina website. Accessed 1 March 2013. Available at http://finance.sina.com.cn/chuangye/investment/20120606/100512236397.shtml.

Dong, Q. 2016. 'ZTE Announced the Volume of Smart Phone in 2015: Only 15 Million Sold in China [in Chinese].' Pcpop website. Accessed 1 January 2016. Available at http://www.pcpop.com/doc/1/1818/1818698.shtml.

Dong, L. and J. Chen. 2014. 'Seamless Open Innovation: The Product Innovation Model of Xiaomi in the Internet Ecosystem [in Chinese].' *Science Research Management* 35 (12): 76–84.

Fan, P. 2010. 'Developing Innovation-Oriented Strategies: Lessons from Chinese Mobile Phone Firms.' *International Journal of Technology Management* 51 (2/3/4): 168–93.

Fang, N. and Rui Xie. 2012. 'Huawei, ZTE and HTC are in the Top Ten of Global Mobile Phone Sales [in Chinese].' Sohu IT Website. Accessed 1 February 2013. Available at http://it.sohu.com/20130216/n366183900.shtml?utm_source=tuicool.

Fressoli, M., E. Arond, D. Abrol, A. Smith, A. Ely and R. Dias. 2014. 'When Grassroots Innovation Movements Encounter Mainstream Institutions: Implications for Models of Inclusive Innovation.' *Innovation and Development* 4 (2): 277–92.

Gereffi, G. 1999. 'International Trade and Industrial Upgrading in the Apparel Commodity Chain.' *Journal of International Economics* 48 (1): 37–70.

———. 2005. 'The Global Economy: Organization, Governance and Development.' In the *Handbook of Economic Sociology*, Second edition, edited by Neil J. Smelser and Richard Swedberg, 160–82. Princeton, NJ: Princeton University Press/Russell Sage Foundation.

Gereffi, G., J. Humphrey and T. Sturgeon. 2005. 'The Governance of Global Value Chains.' *Review of International Political Economy* 12 (1): 78–104.

He, T. 2015. 'Lenovo Implement Two-Brand Strategy, Focusing on Overseas Market [in Chinese].' Tencent Technology Website. Accessed 3 March 2015. Available at http://www.nbd.com.cn/articles/2015-03-03/900441.html.

Hobday, M. 1995. *Innovation in East Asia: The Challenge to Japan*. Cheltenham, Glos.: Edward Elgar Publishing.

Hou, X. 2012. 'Lenovo PC + Strategy Produce Results, and Mobile Phones Reach Beyond Nokia [in Chinese].' *Chinese Business News*. Accessed 3 March 2015. Available at http://tech.qq.com/a/20120805/000020.htm.

Hou, Y. 2014. 'From PC to Mobile Phone, Lenovo has an Innovation in the Business Model [in Chinese].' 21CN Website. Accessed 11 November 2014. Available at http://it.sohu.com/20141111/n405930643.shtml.

Huang, Y. 2015. 2014. *Annual Report of Good Mobile Phones in China* [in Chinese]. CNETNEWS Website. Accessed 4 February 2015. Available at http://www.cnetnews.com.cn/2015/0204/3045848.shtml.

Humphrey, J. and H. Schmitz. 2002. 'How Does Insertion in Global Value Chains Affect Upgrading in Industrial Clusters?' *Regional Studies* 36 (9): 1017–27.

Jin, J. and M. von Zedtwitz. 2008. 'Technological Capability Development in China's Mobile Phone Industry.' *Technovation* 28: 327–34.

Kuang, D. 2012. 'Reveal the R&D and Marketing Process of MI: The Same Team of Production and Sales [in Chinese].' Tencent Technology Website. Accessed 1 April 2012. Available at http://tech.qq.com/a/20120401/000166.htm.

Lei, B. 2007. 'Large Shocks of Domestic Mobile Phone Pattern Due to the Rise of the ZTE and Huawei [in Chinese].' *Communications Information Report*. Accessed 25 September 2007. Available at http://tech.hexun.com/2007-09-25/100800003.html.

Leonard-Barton, D. 1995. *Wellspring of Knowledge: Building and Sustaining the Sources of Innovation*. Cambridge, MA: Harvard Business School Press.

Li, J. 2014. 'ZTE Plans to Transformation: Get Rid of the Dependence of Network Operators [in Chinese].' Eeo Website. Accessed 8 November 2014. Available at http://tech.ifeng.com/a/20141108/40861879_0.shtml.

Li, L. 2007. 'Series of Mobile Phone Design Companies Closed Down Due to the Innovation Absence and Plagiarism [in Chinese].' *IT Time Weekly* (15): 40–41.

———. 2012. 'To See the Status of Our Country in International Trade and Measures to Improve its Position from Apple iPhone [in Chinese].' *Times Finance* 5: 212.

Li, Y. 2014. 'The Mystery of MI's Manufacturing [in Chinese].' *China Economy and Informatization* (8): 28–37.

Liu, C. 2012. 'ZTE Handsets Ranks Fifth in the Global Market Share [in Chinese].' Communication Industry Website. Accessed 1 February 2013. Available at http://www.ccidcom.com/zhongduan/20120203/MRYPqF5R3QtqmQOo.html.

Liu, S. 2012. 'Do Not Take the OEM Road and Adhere to Its Own Brand [in Chinese].' *Shenzhen Economic Daily*, 20 February. Accessed 9 March 2013. Available at http://szsb.sznews.com/html/2012-02/20/content_1932805.htm.

Lu, J. 2011. 'G'Five Leading Mobile Phone Manufacturers Transformation Tide in Shenzhen [in Chinese].' *Shenzhen News*, 26 September. Accessed 24 March 2013. Available at http://www.sznews.com/zhuanti/content/2011-09/26/content_6086935.htm.

Mi, Y. 2008. 'Business with 100 Customers, ZTE's Global Custom Layout [in Chinese].' Tencent Website. Accessed 1 February 2013. Available at http://digi.tech.qq.com/a/20080925/000102.htm.

Kong, L. and Q. Yang. 2010. 'Analysis of Status and Reason of Chinese Manufacturing Firms in the Global Value Chain Division of Labor [in Chinese].' *Theory Horizon* 3: 41–42.

Nie, X. 2012. 'Domestic Mobile Phone Share Ascends to 37.5% [in Chinese].' C114 Website. Accessed 1 February 2013. Available at http://market.c114.net/186/a670109.html.

Pang, R. 2012. 'Interview with Lenovo Feng Xing: Improve Profit Margins to Maintain Market Share [in Chinese].' Yesky Website. Accessed 1 March 2013. Available at http://mobile.yesky.com/286/33859786.shtm.

Papaioannou, T. 2014. 'How Inclusive Can Innovation and Development Be in the Twenty-First Century?' *Innovation and Development* 4 (2): 187–202.

Qin, S. 2011. 'Lei Jun Engages in Angle Investment [in Chinese].' ICEO Website. Accessed 1 March 2013. Available at http://www.iceo.com.cn/chuangye/60/2011/0808/226370.shtml.

Shen, L. 2005. 'Bird Company Is Exploring a New Mode of Transnational Integration [in Chinese].' Accessed 30 June 2016. Available at http://www.p5w.net/stock/news/gsxw/200512/t133485.htm.

Shenzhen Customs. 2013. 'The Number of Mobile Phone Eports at Shenzhen Port Increased under the Price Fall in January 2013 [in Chinese].' Accessed 8 March 2013. Available at http://shenzhen.customs.gov.cn/publish/portal109/tab61275/info418921.htm.

Shi, N. 2016. 'Lost 4 Billion in Three Months, Yang Yuanqing Responded to the Losses of Lenovo for the First Time [in Chinese].' Tech Ifeng Website. Accessed 12 March 2016. Available at http://tech.ifeng.com/a/20160312/41562087_0.shtml.htm.

Sun, Y. 2008. 'ZTE Handsets Development Strategy Surfaced, Aiming at the World's

Top Five [in Chinese].' Yicai Website. Accessed 8 March 2013. Available at http://tech.163.com/08/0311/03/46NOFJSN000915BE.html.

Tian, C. 2008. 'Study on the Development of Chinese Mobile Phone Design Houses [in Chinese].' Doctoral dissertation: Beijing University of Posts and Telecommunications.

Tokatli, N. 2012. 'Toward a Better Understanding of the Apparel industry: A Critique of the Upgrading Literature.' *Journal of Economic Geography* 13 (6): 1–19.

Wang, J. 2006. 'Eastern Communications Went Back to OEM Helplessly.' Sina Website. Accessed 1 March 2013. Available at http://tech.sina.com.cn/t/2006-08-01/10501064638.shtml.

Wang, L. 2016. 'With the Great Innovation and R&D, ZTE Got International Awards Continuously in MWC [in Chinese].' Mobile China. Accessed 8 March 2016. Available at http://www.cnmo.com/news/540004.html.

Wang, P. 2012. 'The ZTE Smartphone Patent Ranks Fourth in the World, the First in China [in Chinese].' Accessed 1 March 2013. Available at http://www.cctime.com/html/2012-3-16/2012316106413905.htm.

Wang, P. and C. Fan. 2012. 'Profits Are No More Than 1% of Global Mobile Phone Sales even though China Has Exported 1 Billion Mobile Phones [in Chinese].' The Xinhua News Agency. Accessed 26 February 2013. Available at http://news.xinhuanet.com/fortune/2012-10/23/c_113467802.htm.

Wang, S. and M. Li. 2015. 'Decode Supply Chain of MI: Lei Jun Has the Initiative, Hundreds of Companies Supply Dispersedly [in Chinese].' *Money Weekly*. Accessed 30 March 2015. Available at http://tech.ifeng.com/a/20150330/41028505_0.shtml.

Wang, X. 2011. 'Lei Jun: Reveal the Secret of MI [in Chinese].' Donews Website. Available at http://www.donews.com/people/201108/567057.shtm.

Wang, Y. 2017. 'MI Released Its Own-developed Chip Surging S1 to Compete with Xiaolong 625/P20 [in Chinese].' Tengxun Website. Accessed 31 July 2018. Available at http://digi.tech.qq.com/a/20170228/042588.htm.

Wang, Z. 2006. 'Why Lenovo Mobile Can Buck the Trend?' *China Daily*, 13 February.

Wei, Y. 2014. 'Why Is "MI" So Good? [in Chinese].' *Import and Export Manager* (6): 46–48.

Weidner, K. L., J. A. Rosa and M. Viswanathan. 2010. 'Marketing to Subsistence Consumers: Lessons from Practice.' *Journal of Business Research* 63 (6): 559–69.

Wen, H. and X. Jin. 2008. 'Study of Influencing Factors on Derivation and Reintegration of Value Chain—The Case of Chinese Mobile Telephone Value Chain.' *China Industrial Economics* (6): 148–57.

Wu, D. 2016. 'Would MI Begin to Use Its Own CPU in the Latter Half of 2016? [in Chinese].' Leifeng Website. Accessed 24 February 2016. Available at http://tech.ifeng.com/a/20160224/41554571_0.shtml.

Wu, Y. 2007. 'ZTE: Find the Phone Gold Mine [in Chinese].' *IT Ceocio China* (22): 67–68.

Yang, H. 2012. 'ZTE Phone: Seek Positive and Robust Development Strategy, Interview with Vice President He Shiyou [in Chinese].' C114 Website. Accessed 1 March 2013. Available at http://www.c114.net/news/127/a668727.html.

Yi, D. and J. Chen. 2012. 'Transformation and Upgrading of Shenzhen Mobile Phone Industry in the Renovation [in Chinese].' *Shenzhen Special Zone Daily*, 24 December.

Yi, F. 2010. 'The TechFaith Completed the Acquisition of QIGI Future Transactions [in Chinese].' 21CN Economic Report. Accessed 1 March 2013. Available at http://tech.sina.com.cn/t/2010-01-05/20383740329.shtml.

Zhang, L. 2016. 'Lei Jun: The Account of MI Is Over Ten Billion, Doesn't Start New Financing [in Chinese].' Donews. Accessed 7 March 2016. Available at http://www.donews.com/net/201603/2919449.shtm.

Zhang, Y. and Y. Ma. 2015. 'Make an Operation to Lenovo Mobile Phone [in Chinese].' *New Economy* (27): 48–49.

Zhou, L. 2015. 'Lenovo Smart Phone: The Share in the Overseas Market Is 65% [in Chinese].' Sina Website. Accessed 13 August 2015. Available at http://tech.xinmin.cn/2015/08/13/28370258.html.

Zhou, S. and J. Li. 2005. 'Evolution and Development of the Chinese Mobile Phone Manufacturing Industry [in Chinese].' *Mobile Communications* (6): 19–22.

Zhu, S. 2004. 'Research of Current Domestic Handset Industry Strategy [in Chinese]. Master's thesis, Beijing Capital Economic and Trade University.

ZTE Website. 'Introduction of ZTE Company [in Chinese].' Accessed 7 March 2016. Available at http://www.zte.com.cn/china/about/corporate_information.

12

Indian Pharmaceutical Industry

Policy and Institutional Challenges of Moving from Manufacturing Generics to Drug Discovery

Dinesh Abrol and Nidhi Singh

Introduction

Catching-up requires the Indian pharmaceutical industry to catch up in the creation of knowledge for drug discovery and process innovations (Jiasu, Lin and Sha, 2016). During the post-TRIPS (Trade Related Intellectual Property Rights) era, in January 2000, India's policymakers laid down explicitly for the first time a policy for the promotion of drug discovery and development efforts.[1] It was with the announcement of this policy that India's policymakers declared

---

1 In January 2000, the Pharmaceutical Research and Development Committee (PDRC), headed by Dr R. A. Mashelkar, suggested a series of measures to bring about an improvement in the level of pharmaceutical research and development (R&D) in the country. The PDRC, in this report, enunciated a vision for the Indian pharmaceutical industry aimed at providing an increased amount of intellectual capital to make available safe, cost effective, contemporary therapeutics to the people of India to help reduce the mortality and morbidity rates in the country and make India a significant player in the global market place. The report established five 'Gold Standards' for pharmaceutical companies for availing themselves of exemption from the Drug Price Control Order (DPCO). These measures included a minimum investment of 5 per cent of the total turnover in R&D, employment of at least 1,000 scientists, a turnover of at least ₹ 10 crore, registration of at least ten patents, and current good manufacturing practices (CGMP) approval for manufacturing facilities. The report had set out priority areas for the Indian pharmaceutical industry to deal with the R&D challenges of drug discovery and development for the priority diseases, while at the same time requiring Indian companies to become globally competitive with products based on new molecules and new drug delivery system. The fiscal and non-fiscal support measures included suggestions such as the establishment of the Drug Development Promotion Foundation to promote R&D as an autonomous organization, venture capital financing, mandatory collection of 1 per cent of the maximum retail price (MRP) of all formulations sold in the country and a pharmaceutical R&D support fund.

their ambition of not only developing contemporary therapeutics to help reduce the rates of morbidity and mortality for the country, but also of becoming a significant global player on the strength of domestic firms' investments in drug discovery research and development (R&D).

In India, the process of creation and accumulation of firm-specific advantages by domestic firms began under the new patent regime with the passing of FERA regulations and the New Drug Policy 1978 to reduce activities of multinational corporations (MNCs) in the sector. Although the pioneering domestic pharmaceutical firms took some time to export to the highly regulated markets of the US and Europe, but what is really important is that the route taken was one of developing in-house capabilities for generic manufacturing and R&D with the help of the capabilities of the public-sector industry and R&D institutions in place in India. The entry of domestic firms into the US market started when Ranbaxy developed an alternative process for manufacturing Eli Lilly's patented drug Cefaclor. The American company sensed that it would lose its markets to Ranbaxy's low-cost substitute in countries that did not recognize product patents. To make the best of a bad situation, Eli Lilly offered a manufacturing contract to Ranbaxy for producing 7 ACCA, intermediate for Cefaclor. In 1993, Ranbaxy laboratories signed a contract manufacturing agreement with Eli Lilly (Pradhan, 2006).

This chapter examines the contribution of domestic pharmaceutical firms to the drug discovery efforts undertaken after the implementation of the TRIPS Agreement in India. It assesses their contribution towards system-building activities. The policy impact is tracked in terms of the progress made in the strengthening of in-house capabilities and the development of system-wide links and relations for the creation of knowledge for drug discovery. The authors analyse how the tasks of steering and coordinating policies for upgrading of in-house R&D, publicly funded R&D, intellectual property, the domestic industry and the healthcare system were tackled by the policymakers in theory and practice.

The analysis focuses on the contribution of the in-house R&D activities of domestic pharmaceutical firms, foreign technology transfer through alliance making, collaboration, and overseas R&D (ORD) undertaken in India. It suggests that the challenge of path construction for innovation system building remains largely unaddressed even after a period of more than fifteen years and that a fundamental change in the policy path is required to obtain success in drug discovery. Policymakers need to redefine their ambitions and the expectations from domestic firms as far as drug discovery is concerned. Changes in the priorities of the government, the creation of public-sector research institutes, and collaboration with universities and hospitals will help realize the targets better.

The analysis indicates that the weak connection between domestic firms and public-sector research organizations is the weakest link in the pharmaceutical innovation system in India. In the post-TRIPS era, domestic pharmaceutical firms in India were put on the pathway of a global integration of learning processes and competence building due to the adoption of a specific policy path. Domestic firms continue to pursue innovation-making strategies in line with their thinking that their limited in-house R&D efforts, when combined with contributions from strategic alliances and collaborations with foreign firms, will ultimately enable the national pharmaceutical innovation system to catch up with the pharmaceutical R&D systems and innovation originating from the USA and Europe.

This study suggests that the contribution of all the main actors to the landscape of pharmaceutical product, process and manufacturing innovation is embedded in the concept of learning, competence building and innovation-making, which is 'heroic' in terms of knowledge creation for new drug development. This is also the reason why India is becoming alarmingly 'dependent' on foreign firms for competence building in terms of capacity creation for drug discovery, development, manufacturing and regulation. At home, the current R&D and innovation strategies of the Department of Pharmaceuticals (DOP), the Department of Science and Technology (DST), the Department of Scientific and Industrial Research (DSIR) and the Department of Biotechnology (DBT) place insufficient emphasis on building industry–academia and academia–industry–hospital relationships, and also on cooperation for learning and competence building within India.

The analysis also indicates that the efforts of domestic firms have not been successful in the development of in-house capacity for drug discovery R&D. Domestic firms have also failed in the establishment of closer relationships with public-sector research institutes, universities and hospitals – a pathway that could help with capability building. Domestic firms have not even been able to generate adequate demand for research manpower capable of undertaking drug discovery and development research at home. They have not been able to help much with the strengthening of the fundamental and strategic research capacity of public-sector research institutes and universities – a pathway that India should have followed for the development of partnerships for meeting domestic demand to help with the reduction of the morbidity and mortality burden.

Another conclusion reached is that India's policy-dependent failures have arisen primarily due to the inability of domestic firms to accelerate their pace of contribution towards system-building activities for the upgradation of national innovation system (NSI) structures in order to catch up in one step in both export-oriented generic manufacturing as well as drug discovery efforts for global markets. Domestic firms have failed to sustain their investment in the building of in-house capacity for drug discovery research. Their own in-house structures of knowledge creation for drug discovery and development are close to becoming entirely dependent on the offers of supply of contract research services emerging from the side of foreign firms. India will have to deal with the challenge of how to prevent the domestic firms from becoming dependent on the imports of key starting materials (KSMs), intermediates and active pharmaceutical ingredients (APIs) on most urgent basis. Dependence on critical imports from China is today an import security concern of the government as well as of the domestic pharmaceutical industry.

The analysis focuses on the challenge of the diagnosis of the root cause of the problem of why system-building activities could not be nurtured by domestic firms in India. While it is a step forward that India's policymakers are now aware that domestic firms cannot blindly continue on the path of paying attention only to alliance-making and collaborations with foreign firms, the crucial thing is to understand why, in the period of less than two decades, the view adopted by these firms has caused these path-dependent failures to emerge so acutely and rapidly. The authors suggest that India needs to get its domestic firms to follow a path of development which would allow them to simultaneously upgrade pharmaceutical manufacturing to stay competitive in the generic medicine business at home and abroad. The policy options that are still open for the realignment of the existing path are briefly examined.

The authors indicate that various types of system-building failures in India are being experienced because most of the stakeholders have not been subject to a matching policy and institution-building framework that could guide and enable domestic firms to contribute with adequate investment in system-building for pharmaceutical innovation. It is recommended that these firms should be encouraged to contribute to the development of science-based clusters which can be prioritized for nurturing by the government, industry, hospitals and the public research systems with an eye on both domestic disease priorities as well as export priorities.

The authors recommend that India's policymakers need to implement a mission-based approach. The infusion of public investment, product development partnerships, procurement and prizes should get due importance.

The government will have to give priority to the development of pharma clusters by bringing together public-sector R&D institutions and domestic firms for the diffusion of knowledge of technology of continuous manufacturing to remain competitive in respect of exports to the highly regulated pharmaceutical markets of the United States and Europe. Domestic firms will have to jointly take up the tasks of developing the structures of national innovation system to simultaneously enable accelerated drug discovery and competitive generic manufacturing. They argue that the reliance of the government on stronger intellectual property rights (IPRs) is not going to yield much success with drug discovery and generic manufacturing upgradation.

TRIPS, policymaking and pharmaceutical innovation

The vision and direction of industrial upgradation changed significantly in the case of domestic pharmaceutical industry from the year 2000 onwards, for all types of complementary policy measures under implementation in India. The Indian government devised a policy in support of separate R&D companies and gave liberal tax concessions to domestic pharmaceutical firms for the promotion of exports to regulated markets.[2] It was also a time when several important academic contributions explicitly favouring the argument of stronger IPR regime in their writings were advocating India to embrace the path of external liberalization and abandon that of internal liberalization which had allowed domestic pharmaceutical firms to promote their footprint in domestic as well as export markets in a competitive way (Lall and Albaladejo, 2002; Keely, 2000; Granville and Leonard, 2003). This policy path had the assumption that the route of strategic alliances, R&D collaborations and out-licensing agreements would allow the domestic firms to acquire capabilities for drug discovery and marketing of generics. India would be able to achieve the possible synergy by combining the emerging characteristics of automatic diffusion of pharmaceutical production with the existence of the conditions of a strong base in science education and the practice of public health spending.

Contrary voices were raised from within Indian academia, the civil society and the local pharmaceutical industry. First, these voices argued in

---

2   Most of these R&D companies do not exist anymore as separate entities and have been integrated into and are controlled by the parent firms. Achievements in the sphere of export of formulations are limited by the weakening of innovation in manufacturing of pharmaceuticals and the growing dependence of domestic pharmaceutical firms on the imports of KSMs, intermediates and APIs from the Chinese state-owned enterprises (SOEs).

favour of the position that India needed to fully exploit the transition period, making use of exemptions obtained through international negotiations on trade and investment in the World Trade Organization (WTO). Abrol (2015) analyses the kind of benefits domestic firms have been able to derive from the delayed implementation of the TRIPS Agreement in the case of pharmaceuticals in India. Second, these contrary voices also argued for the adoption of the policy of 'selective delinking', the strengthening of the public sector, positive discrimination in favour of private sector companies practising indigenous innovation, and new product development for the benefit of Indian priority diseases with the help of innovative public procurement should be followed.[3] It was pointed out that the path of delayed external liberalization – holding back the freedom to establish subsidiaries to foreign pharmaceutical firms, postponing the implementation of product patents until 2005, and adopting stricter criteria for patentability reflected in Section 3(d) of the India Patent Law (amended in 2005) – has paid the domestic pharmaceutical firms handsomely. However, the influence of the other school on the policymaking process was obviously stronger.

Patents, domestic firms and innovation

In this section, we undertake an assessment of the effects of the pharmaceutical innovation system resulting from the adoption of this path of catching-up on the pharmaceutical industry in India. Our assessment of the resulting efforts for the catching-up process in the post-2000 phase of pharmaceutical innovation making indicates that while the full legal effects of the TRIPS Agreement were suspended during the transition period, its effects on India were nonetheless substantial (Abrol *et al.*, 2015). The worst effects could also be avoided because of the dominant academic response and the contrary impact of the TRIPS Agreement on R&D innovation within the industry and on the policymakers working within the Indian government. With a looming deadline for TRIPS implementation and the fear of losing ground in the local market, Indian firms began to look for the opportunity of exporting generics to regulated markets in the USA and Europe. This led domestic firms to look in two directions – towards the export of products going off-patent and towards R&D for the development of incremental process and product innovations to stay in the business of pharmaceutical exports. All the measures were targeted

---

3   See Abrol (2004), Chaudhuri (2005) and Dhar and Gopakumar (2006).

at leveraging the developed country markets. India was able to achieve a positive trade balance in pharmaceuticals in the late 1980s. Domestic firms were increasing their focus on exports to unregulated markets in developing countries. Although the developed world has the most lucrative markets for generic drugs, extensive regulation restricts entry.

Domestic firms began to develop the necessary organizational and technological capabilities through the acquisition of foreign firms as well as strategic alliances and collaborations for learning, competence building and innovation making, using the opportunities being made available at that time in the global pharmaceutical industry. Although the domestic firms took some time to develop in-house competence for the export of off-patent generics to regulated markets, they have continued to steadily invest in the inventive activity required to be carried out for the success of this path. It is because, till then, domestic firms had chosen to rely on the capabilities of the public sector industry and R&D institutions – a discontinuity which some characterized as a sign of a rising star was nothing more than a sign of the locking-in of domestic firms into a dependent path of industrial development.

An analysis of the industry-wide patenting activity indicates that innovation-making activities continue to focus on the development of capabilities, innovations and technological know-how for off-patent generics that the industry is interested in exporting to regulated markets in Europe and the USA. The number of patents filed for new chemical entities (NCEs) is still small. An analysis of the different types (in terms of numbers) of patents in Table 12.1 suggests that the economic opportunity created by the Hatch-Waxman Act of 1984 remained an important stimulus for domestic pharmaceutical firms to invest in the processes of learning, competence building and innovation making during the post-2000 period. See Table 12.1 for the historical timeline of capability development profiles mapped by the authors on the basis of patents filed by the Indian pharmaceutical industry with the United States Patent and Trade Mark Office (USPTO).

Table 12.1 Pharmaceutical patenting in the United States from the Indian pharmaceutical industry, 1992–2013

Sl. no.	Nature of patent	1992–95	1996–99	2000–03	2004–07	2008–13	Total
1.	Process patent		11	51	133	176	371
2.	NDDS patent			18	23	10	51

(*Contd.*)

(*Contd.*)

Sl. no.	Nature of patent	1992–95	1996–99	2000–03	2004–07	2008–13	Total
3.	NCE patent		3	6	10	–	19
4.	Method of treatment, dosage, formulation composition, combination and product patent	14	26	102	261	202	403
5.	New forms of substances		6	63	156	250	475
Grand total		**14**	**46**	**240**	**583**	**638**	**1,521**

Source: Patents granted to top twenty domestic pharmaceutical companies by USPTO.

Chemistry-driven research processes leading to non-infringing processes for APIs; the identification and characterization of impurity profiling pertaining to APIs; the reduction of impurity levels; acceptable dosage forms and formulations have come to be pursued by the domestic firms as their main priority in the sphere of pharmaceutical innovation during the post-TRIPS period. Bedi and Bedi (2015), using databases like Ekaswa (TIFAC) and the official websites of the European Patent Office and the Indian Patent Office (IPO), also confirm that the majority of the applications for the top eleven large pharmaceutical companies up to 2010 were related to inventions in the field of new or improved processes for products than for the products themselves. Their analysis also confirms that product-related applications are concerned with intermediates and formulations, with maximum concentration on modified dosage forms.

While Bedi and Bedi (2015) indicate that there has been a small increase in the number of product patent applications filed by the top eleven large pharmaceutical companies, especially after 2005, our own analysis, which covers a longer period, shows that this type of inventive activity has neither been sustained, nor has it led to a significant increase in NCE patenting. In fact, Table 12.1 shows that NCE activity does not even figure in the trends list after 2010. Furthermore, we would like to highlight that foreign firms dominate the process patent scene as well; there are very few patents granted to domestic firms for NCEs.

Figures 12.1 and 12.2 contain information on the nature of patents granted to both domestic and foreign firms by the IPO. The number of product patents granted to foreign firms by the IPO is much higher than that of domestic firms. Further, dosage and formulation and process patents account for close to 99 per cent of patents filed at the IPO.

Figure 12.1 Nature of patents granted to domestic and foreign firms in IPO (2005 to March 2013)

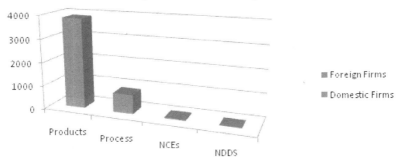

Source: Compiled and analysed by the authors from the database created by Indian Patent Office (IPO).

Figure 12.2 Nature of patents granted in IPO (2005 to March 2013)

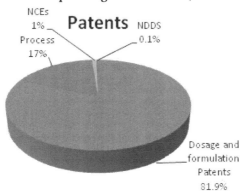

Source: Compiled and analysed by the authors from the database created by the Indian Patent Office (IPO).

New-product related inventive activity is still to emerge as a game changer in the creation of competitive advantages for domestic pharmaceutical firms in the domestic or export market. While some domestic companies are known to have also increased their investment in R&D and the filing of patents, abbreviated new drug applications (ANDAs) and drug master filings (DMFs) to become only valuable for acquisition rather than becoming competitive in the global or domestic pharmaceutical market landscape,[4] in the case of others like Ranbaxy, their investment behaviour relating to innovation making is to foray into regulated markets for quick profits, which has landed the Indian pharmaceutical industry in serious trouble.[5]

Domestic firms, drug discovery and new product development

While it is true that the face of the Indian pharmaceutical industry has gradually changed owing to an R&D-based domestic industrial sector which is competent enough to participate in the processes of learning, competence building and innovation making for the supply of off-patent generics to regulated markets, yet even here the bulk of its 'innovative outputs' still belong to the areas of dosage/formulation/composition of matter related R&D work. This point needs emphasis because scholars studying industrial dynamics tend to become overly optimistic in their conclusions regarding the progress made by the domestic segment of the Indian pharmaceutical industry. Our own analysis is that we need to take a long-term view because catching-up involves complex relationships between scientific research and industrial innovation, for which the industry will have to undertake lasting measures.

Evidence-building undertaken on new product development from the information made available by companies on their websites indicates that initially only ten or twelve Indian pharmaceutical companies had earnestly started working on the development of new drugs. However, there has been a decline in the growth of investment in new product development. The problem of weak in-house capabilities in the domestic pharmaceutical industry as far as the discovery and development of new drugs is concerned continues to be a major handicap for the 'national innovation system' in India. The examples mentioned here based on the analysis of the collaborative R&D activities of domestic firms indicates that the current level of activity of compound development and testing by domestic companies is still quite small compared to global standards. Domestic firms underestimated the challenges that come with drug discovery and innovative drug development. Many Indian companies are now pursuing a strategy that will lower their costs and risk factors. The usual strategy is to find a new drug within an existing family that has been discovered, that is, to find a compound, that is, analogous to a discovered compound.

---

4   Fresinus Kabi and Matrix are two such examples which come to mind in respect of such
    behaviour in competence building and innovation making.

5   The promoters of Ranbaxy did not realize the seriousness of their folly when they tried
    selling their assets to a Japanese MNC (Daichi Sankhyo).

Take, for example, the case of Giltazones – one of the compounds of Dr. Reddy's Laboratories (DRL) on which Sankhyo was doing work. This strategy of DRL choosing a known family of compounds for development undoubtedly cut down on the risk. Several domestic firms investing in drug discovery took this easy route. The other strategy is out-licensing where an Indian company takes some lead compounds to the pre-clinical stage. In this case, DRL's strategy was to collaborate with a foreign company to jointly pursue clinical development.[6] If all the tests are cleared by the lead compound, the company can strike a deal with an MNC that has the right to market the compound in a particular foreign market. The Indian company gets milestone payments for each stage of clinical trials cleared by the compound. DRL is still one of the most determined domestic companies in the area of drug discovery and development. All big companies, namely Ranbaxy, DRL and Glenmark, follow the out-licensing route to develop new drugs. DRL has entered into a deal with Novartis for further work on an anti-diabetic compound (DRF, 4158). Ranbaxy entered into a deal with Bayer for Cipro NDDS (Novel Drug Delivery System) and RBx 2258 (benign prostatic hyperplasia or BPH). Glenmark has entered into a deal with Forest of the USA and Tejin of Japan to experiment with compounds that could provide treatment for asthma.

The success rates and timelines indicate that with the exception of Phase 1 trials, for which the success rate of 54 per cent lies within the range for global industry, the chances for transition to higher phases are considerably lower. The drug discovery process at Indian companies is considerably far less efficient than the global industry average. With slightly over eighty active compounds in the pipeline, India is nowhere close to becoming a competitor. The R&D expenditure of the top fifteen Indian pharmaceutical firms is still far behind the costs being incurred by generic drug companies in Israel and Europe. Dabur, Nicholas Piramal, Wockhardt and Shanta Biotech have had to divest important parts of their pharmaceutical business to foreign companies. In many cases, these divestures have also involved R&D-based segments. However, it is true that DRL, Cipla, Glenmark, Lupin, Cadila, Wockhardt, Sun Pharma and Torrent are still around as integrated Indian pharmaceutical companies which have built substantial foreign sales.

An analysis of the current status of new drug development efforts of the domestic firms clearly indicates that most molecules have not progressed very far and many of them have been completely abandoned by the firms (Differding, 2014). A few positive outcomes certainly exist in terms of drug discovery; the

---

6   A company can reduce some of the uncertainties of new drug research through this process, though this may not produce a blockbuster drug.

number of success stories, however, is small and not yet significant in terms of contribution. In June 2013, Zydus Cadila launched Saroglitazar, the first drug discovered and developed by an Indian pharmaceutical company and the first glitazar in the world to be approved for the treatment of diabetic dyslipidemia or hypertriglyceridemia in patients with Type 2 diabetes. In April 2012, Ranbaxy launched India's first domestically developed drug, Synriam, a combination of arterolane maleate and piperaquine phosphate, for the treatment of plasmodium falciparum malaria. Although arterolane was discovered not in India, but by a collaborative drug discovery project funded by the Medicines for Malaria Venture (MMV), Ranbaxy partnered in 2003 to carry out development work for which it was granted a worldwide license.

Glenmark and US partner Salix Pharmaceuticals gained approval from the US Food and Drug Administration (FDA) in December 2012 for crofelemer, licensed from Napo Pharmaceuticals, for treatment of non-infectious diarrhoea in patients undergoing antiretroviral therapy for HIV/AIDS. Crofelemer, a purified oligomericproanthocyanidin isolated from the latex of the South American Sangre de Grado tree (Croton lechleri), has a new mechanism of action: it blocks two structurally unrelated chloride channels in the gut, thereby decreasing the excretion of water and reducing the duration of diarrhoea.

Discussions about where hope lies for new drug development have led some to suggest that India's first innovative drug could come from a new generation of pharmaceutical companies. In recent years, ambitious new start-up discovery firms backed by private equity investors such as Pune-based Nova Lead and Indus Biotech have come up. They gained success where Indian pharma goliaths wandered into and faltered (BW Online Bureau, 2014). Not surprisingly, the *Business World* article 'Death of a Dream' questioned if this was the end or the beginning of the story? Whether this dream can be revived for the Indian domestic pharmaceutical firms is in need of rigorous analysis if the policy design is to be worked out appropriately.

Our analysis of the disease focus of NCEs confirms that the Indian companies undertaking drug discovery and development work consider the domestic market to be of too small a size and not attractive enough to take up development work on new products in the drugs and pharmaceutical sector, and they are not as enthusiastic about investing in new drug development as they were at the beginning of this decade. See Table 12.2 for company-wise figures of investigational new drugs (INDs) registered by domestic companies.

Table 12.2 Investigational new drugs (INDs), 2008–13

Company name	2008	2009	2010	2011	2012	2013
Dr. Reddy's Laboratories		2	2	2	4	3
Ranbaxy	1	7	5	6		
Aurobindo					1	1
Wockhardt		2		2		
Glenmark		8	14	16	9	8
Piramal Healthcare		1			3	3
Sun Pharma	1	9	18	8	10	5
Lupin		4				
Cipla		9	4	11	4	
Cadila	2	14	21	11	12	7
GlaxoSmithKline (foreign)		7	1			
Novartis (foreign)		1	3			
AstraZeneca (foreign)	2	9	12	8	10	1
Total	**6**	**73**	**80**	**64**	**53**	**25**

Source: Compiled by the authors.

Domestic firms and the contract research route

There is more investment from domestic pharmaceutical firms towards broadening of activities and services as well as for deepening of the skills required for the contract research route. From what were initially custom chemistry services based on the country's long tradition in chemical manufacturing, many of the major Indian contract research organizations (CROs) have evolved towards higher value added activities such as medicinal chemistry, biology, ADME (absorption, distribution, metabolism and excretion), animal pharmacology and safety studies, and integrated drug discovery capabilities. The terms of recent deals have evolved from fee-for-service (FFS) and full-time equivalent (FTE) agreements to collaborative research agreements and partly shared risk collaborations, with milestone payments and eventually royalty payments in addition to research fees.

To a large extent, this evolution has been driven by the need of Western pharmaceutical companies to address the declining productivity of drug discovery. Outsourcing and partnering with companies in emerging low-cost countries remains an option for them to address rising costs. Most of the major Western pharmaceutical and biotech companies have been investing in valuable resources in India for a number of years through strategic collaborative partnerships and alliances to fuel their in-house discovery and development pipeline. Pharmaceutical companies have been outsourcing non-IP (intellectual property) sensitive chemistry activities to India since the late 1990s, when only a limited number of CROs were offering such services.

Several contract research companies capable of pursuing drug discovery collaborations have emerged (Advinus, Aurigene, Jubilant and Syngene, for example) while many others are closely following (for example, GVK Bio, Orchid, TCG Lifesciences, Torrent and Zydus Cadila). These collaborations have produced seventy-one patent applications and publications. Close to twenty-five collaborations have been entered into, which illustrate the extent to which major pharmaceutical companies have initiated research activities in India. All the different approaches taken by them in their collaborations with Indian CROs and biotech companies reveal some interesting results with respect to the IP scenario. At least seven out of the top twenty pharmaceutical companies have filed patent applications on the basis of these collaborations. Far less IP is, in contrast, generated in India by pharma companies in the top twenty-one to hundred (Differding, 2014).

According to Edmond Differding (2014), out of the eighty companies studied, only five domestic companies had applied for patents. Western pharmaceutical companies are on a learning curve in their alliances with Indian companies. Many of them have already learned how to successfully generate IP with Indian inventors. It will not be unreasonable to speculate that other pharmaceutical and biotech companies will follow. According to a 2011 Boston Consulting Group (BCG) survey of forty global biopharma companies, more than 70 per cent of executives were satisfied with their Indian R&D alliances and three out of four expected to increase their R&D activities in India. This survey reveals how the R&D game is being played. It is clear that India will not be able to gain much IP from this game. India will not be able to close the skill gap capacity by depending on strategic alliances and collaborations.

So far, several of these alliances have been quite productive for Western companies. This is evidenced not only by the significant number of patent applications and publications, but also by the rising number of disclosed pre-clinical and clinical development of pharmaceutical drug candidates that have been injected into R&D pipeline projects of Western pharmaceutical companies. The vast majority of pharmaceutical companies are opting for multiple partners, with the advantages of sharing of the inherent risk of drug discovery by the partners, and of being potentially more competitive, as it allows them to select best-in-class partners for each project, such as Endo, Forest, Janssen, Merck Serono, Merck Sharp, Dohme and Novartis. Others prefer a strategic collaboration with one carefully selected key partner, thereby decreasing complexity, along with internal management and communication needs.

Technology acquisition by domestic firms

The claimed benefits of increased technology transfer to domestic firms through contract, alliances and joint ventures are also not evident in the case of India. Foreign technical collaborations have not been important for export; therefore, only small- and medium-scale firms have entered into such collaborations, mostly to cater to the domestic market. Expectations from the route of contract manufacturing are also not clear with regard to technology acquisition. Exploiting contract manufacturing will not improve the prospects of technology transfer by itself because there are no new technologies being transferred. Production capabilities can certainly get better on account of the enforcement of good manufacturing practices (GMP) in the case of some firms. Analysis indicates that though players like Matrix Laboratories, Divi, Shasun Chemicals and Cadila have made much use of this opportunity to grow, their technological capabilities have not been upgraded despite the provision of contract manufacturing services. Apart from Ranbaxy and Cipla, which were warned by the USFDA for not adhering to quality control regulation, Matrix was the third drug company working from India for the US market to get a warning from the regulatory authorities of the USA.[7] More than forty companies have been warned for not adhering strictly to the quality control practices recommended by the USFDA.

There is evidence that as far as the terms and conditions of contract manufacturing of bulk drugs are concerned, the deals being entered into by Indian firms in the post-TRIPS era are far from being equal. Ranbaxy

---

7   When it comes to manufacturing, India ranks only second to the US in the number of global DMFs every year. DMF is essentially permission to enter the US bulk actives market with the objective of either supplying to a large US generics player or captive consumption. DMFs by Indian companies rose to 19 per cent of the world filings in 2003 compared to 2.4 per cent in 1991. For the April–June quarter of 2003, India accounted for 34 per cent of the world's filings.

and Lupin Laboratories were among the first Indian companies to bag manufacturing contracts from multinational companies – Ranbaxy from Eli Lilly and Lupin from Cynamid. In the pre-TRIPS period, manufacturing contracts came through when Ranbaxy developed an alternative process for manufacturing Eli Lilly's patented drug, Cefaclor, because the US firm sensed that it would lose its markets to Ranbaxy's low-cost substitute in countries that did not recognize product patents. Eli Lilly offered a manufacturing contract to Ranbaxy for producing 7 ACCA, an intermediate for Cefaclor, to make the best of a bad situation.

Today, the situation has changed due to the implementation of the TRIPS Agreement. Take, for example, the case of Nicholas Piramal. It entered into a joint venture (49:51) with Allergan Incorporated, USA, to earn business for the manufacture of bulk drugs. The same is true for its negotiations with the UK-based firm Baker Norton to earn business in the form of contract manufacturing. It seems that the growth in contract manufacturing will come about due to the efforts of companies such as Divi, Sashun and Nicholas Piramal India (now taken over by Abbot Laboratories, USA), which have been willing to accept 'subordinate relationships' in their collaborations. See Table 12.3 for a glimpse into the pattern of contract research and manufacturing services (CRAM) activities being undertaken by large domestic pharmaceutical firms since the adoption of the TRIPS Agreement in India.

Table 12.3 Pharmaceutical companies in CRAM activities in India

Companies in contract research (excluding clinical trials)	Clinical trials
Nicholas Piramal	Clingene (Biocon)
Aurigene (Dr. Reddy's)	Jubilant Clinsys (Jubilant Organosys)
Syngene (Biocon)	WellQuest (Nicholas Piramal)
GVK Biosciences	Synchron
Jubilant Organosys	Vimta Labs
Divi's Laboratories	Lambada
Suven Life Sciences	Siro Clinpharm
Dr. Reddy's Laboratories	Reliance Life Sciences
Vimta Labs	Asian Clinical Trials (Suven Life Sciences)

Sources: *Annual Report* and IDMA News, 2007 (International Disease Management Alliance).

It needs to be stressed that not all modes of collaboration lead to enhanced competencies. In-licensing and out-licensing of compounds for further development are primarily market penetration strategies targeted towards increasing time and cost efficiency.

Nature of capability building and exports to regulated markets

The export of generic drugs to regulated markets in the USA and Europe should not be considered as a reliable, long-term option for domestic firms to undertake industrial upgrading for the development of capabilities for manufacturing and product innovation. Domestic companies are currently investing a lot of money into the generic market with the intention of making maximum profits where market competition is less and margins high. As such, things are possible only in the beginning when drugs become off-patent. They file four to five ANDAs every year to be the first in the market and exploit the period of exclusivity available under the US drug regulation laws. Experience, however, indicates that the road ahead for the export of generics to the regulated market is likely to be tedious and full of hurdles.

To be specific, in the USA, under the Hatch-Waxman Act, the government has a system of patent term 'restoration' which can extend the monopoly of the original patentee for a maximum of five years, in addition to the initial patent term. In the EU, too, there exists a scheme for a supplementary protection certificate (SPC). In the USA, no ANDA can be submitted until five years after the referenced brand name product gets its first FDA approval if the originator product was the first drug product to gain approval which contained a particular active ingredient. Similarly, an ANDA cannot be submitted for three years if an originator's new drug application or supplementary application is supported by new clinical investigations conducted by the applicant and is essential for approval (normally, for a new indication). As of 1997, the USA now allows for an additional six months of exclusivity as a reward for studying drugs to be utilized in the case of children. In the USA, the first version of an orphan drug is entitled to seven years of exclusivity, preventing approval of an ANDA. The US also allows, as a reward, 180 days' exclusivity to the first generic manufacturer to file a successful Paragraph IV certification alleging that a listed patent is invalid or not infringed. Thus, as far as the question of export of generics is concerned, it faces important IPR-related hurdles today in overseas markets.

It is clear that Indian pharmaceutical firms cannot expect that the opportunity for developing traditional pharmaceutical generics will automatically fall into their lap. As evidence shows, even in the area of bio-generics, a tough fight is in waiting for the Indian pharmaceutical industry. The recombinant products market has been led so far by imports of established global brands and marketing of the products either by local subsidiaries (SmithKline Beecham, Novo) or through marketing arrangements as in the case of Nicholas Piramal and Roche. Similar changes were seen in the case of firms such as Shanta, Bharat, Panacea and Wockhardt in the Indian market for products like the Hepatitis B vaccine, Interferon-Alpha, insulin and EPO. Indian policymakers are expecting litigation to grow in the case of bio-generics. The Indian pharmaceutical industry is getting a taste of this at an early stage. Of late, almost all export-oriented Indian firms have faced this challenge in the USA.

Studies differ in their degree of optimism about the positive effects of stronger patents on product development by local firms based on disclosed foreign patents and on additional R&D efforts. In the domestic sector today, only a handful of firms have been able to increase their R&D investments. Some of these have earlier demonstrated that they can, with the help of public sector research, hone their expertise in the creation of new processes for patented products. Dr Reddy's Group was the first domestic company to file the first two product patent applications for anti-cancer and anti-diabetes substances in the USA. However, it is clear that Dr Reddy's Group does not want to engage autonomously in new drug development. It has been selling its rights to foreign partners because it does not have the capacity to invest further. In fact, it has stopped working after the drug discovery phase. Examples of Wockhardt joining hands with Rhein Biotech GmbH, Germany; Ranbaxy shaking hands with Eli Lilly for development work; and Cipla undertaking custom synthesis and collaborations with Japanese and Swiss firms indicate the limitations of and opportunities available to Indian firms.

Based on her investigative interviews with executives of domestic firms, Sophia Ackerhans (2016) suggests that the twenty-two firms and industry experts considered the political framework and government incentives aimed at facilitating R&D collaboration to be of lowest importance. The access to public funding of the host/home government was evaluated with the lowest divergence, followed by the desire to support the regulatory framework and adapt to the market or regulatory environment.

India does not seem to figure much in the increased strategic R&D alliance activity of global biopharmaceutical and biotechnology firms. Federica (2014) reveals that a gap exists between R&D deals and manufacturing/marketing deals, despite some progress. This study also shows that sixty companies out of the isolated 123 did not report any alliances during the period of observation. There is a simple explanation for this: in biopharmaceutical research the distribution of capabilities is the major determinant of the partner and the mode of alliance. The dynamic of biotechnology in India is also dependent on the overall movement of internationalization of R&D. Outsourcing markets in clinical trials, R&D and production are becoming accessible to the locally bred firms of countries like India. Due to many short-term benefits, it is obviously tempting to direct the industry totally or mainly for these markets.

The examples of DRL and Biocon are especially useful for discussion on the conditions for gains to accrue from the contract work being undertaken by these two companies. Both these companies have created several entities, each of them corresponding to a different strategy. DRL is involved in the development of recombinant DNA-based products and has an internal programme of BT-based (biotechnology-based) drug targets discovery. It has also set up a company named Molecular Connections Pvt. Ltd. and a contract research company named Aurigene, involved in chemical and biological research for drug discovery. Similarly, Biocon, whose core activity is manufacture of industrial enzymes, has set up a contract research subsidiary named Syngene and a clinical research organization named Clinigene.

However, as far as the contribution of these domestic firms to meet the product development challenge for neglected diseases is concerned, our analysis makes it clear that the current level of opportunities which limit Aurigene, GVK Bio and Syngene to cloning and getting the genes to express will not allow these companies to build an industry capable of doing cutting-edge biotechnology research. At the moment, the mother companies have no intention of interfering with their subsidiaries because of confidentiality agreements signed by them with partners who have outsourced the part of drug discovery or clinical research to them. This means that no technological information can circulate between the company in charge of contract research work and the parent company involved in its own research.

From the standpoint of priorities of public health protection, the moot question is: how will it benefit the country in terms of promotion of indigenous drug discovery and development efforts? As mentioned earlier, it is clear that under the existing policy environment and the emerging conditions of competition in the global pharmaceutical industry, locally bred firms of developing countries are likely to be lured by the multinational corporations to work for the Western markets. At the same time, the situation as it stands is that pharmaceutical research is largely directed towards the needs of Western markets. The message is clear: the industry is least concerned with undertaking R&D for neglected diseases of the poor.

Nature of emerging industrial and science links

An assessment of relationships forged through acquisitions, alliances, collaborations and agreements while undertaking outward foreign direct investment (OFDI) indicates that for the establishment of appropriate industrial networks, these firms have failed to give priority to the objective of capability building for development of new drugs. See Table 12.4 for details on the pattern of functions being served through acquisitions of foreign firms and divisions made by these fourteen firms. Analysis suggests that R&D-related acquisitions are far fewer in number than acquisitions for marketing and production activities. In case of all fourteen firms, the number of alliances, collaborations and acquisitions remained skewed in favour of purposes relating to marketing, manufacturing and the supply of R&D services.

Acquisitions were mainly for strengthening their foreign markets. The assessment also indicates that a very small number of firms are involved in asset augmentation for the purpose of manufacturing. R&D alliances and collaborations involve still fewer firms. Compared to the acquisition of manufacturing and distribution arms abroad by each and every firm in the sample, only a small number of companies have acquired firms abroad with the motive of upgrading R&D capabilities. As far as the number of acquisitions made for the purpose of boosting drug-discovery R&D is concerned, it is a small number reflecting the bias of ties and connections under establishment. See Tables 12.4 and 12.5 for details on the types of R&D being served through acquisitions made by these firms during the period under observation.

Table 12.4 Pattern of R&D and marketing acquisitions for fourteen leading Indian firms, 1999–2011

R&D acquisitions		Sub total	Marketing/Production acquisitions		Sub total	Total number of acquisitions
Domestic acquisitions	Foreign acquisitions		Domestic acquisitions	Foreign acquisitions		
2	20	22	3	72	75	97

Sources: Individual company websites, press releases, news, archives and other data accessed as on November 2011.

Notes: The top fourteen leading Indian pharmaceutical companies are: Ranbaxy Laboratories, Cipla Ltd., Dr Reddy's Laboratories, Cadila Healthcare, Biocon Ltd., Sun Pharmaceuticals, Lupin Ltd., Piramal Healthcare, Glenmark Pharmaceuticals, Torrent Pharmaceuticals, Strides Arcolab, Wockhardt Ltd., IPCA Laboratories, Orchid Pharmaceuticals.

Table 12.5 Types of R&D acquisitions with industries, 1999–2011

Companies	Discovery R&D DA	Discovery R&D FA	Sub total	Clinical development DA	Clinical development FA	Sub total	Research services DA	Research services FA	Sub total	Grand total
Top fourteen Indian pharmaceutical companies							2	20	20	22

Source: Compiled by the authors from news and website press releases.

Notes: DA: Domestic acquisitions; FA: Foreign acquisitions

Table 12.6 Types of R&D alliances, collaborations and licensing agreements, 1999–2011

Top fourteen Pharmaceutical Companies in India		R&D alliances			R&D collaborations			In-licensing			Out-licensing		
		Discovery R&D	Clinical development	Research services	Discovery R&D	Clinical trial	Research services	Discovery R&D	Clinical trial	Research services	Discovery R&D	Clinical trial	Research services
RI/AI	Domestic	2		1	5	3	1		1				
	Foreign				2	4	3						
Industry	Domestic		1		1	1			1				
	Foreign	2	2	8	12	17	19	5	6			4	5
Grand total		4	3	9	20	25	23	5	8			4	5

Source: Compiled by the authors.

Notes: RI-research institution, AI-academic institution; alliances and collaborations have been distinguished on the basis of the time horizon involved, alliances involving longer term ties.

See Table 12.6 for details on the types of alliances, collaborations and agreements signed by these firms with research institutions and other firms, both foreign and domestic. An analysis shows that R&D acquisitions have been made mostly for the purpose of establishing research service facilities for the benefit of facilitating the entry of generics into the markets of USA and Europe. The research services function seems to dominate acquisitions made with the objective of establishing facilities in the host country for preparing dossiers and undertaking laboratory work. Foreign firms account for the maximum number of alliances, collaborations and licensing agreements entered into by these firms during the period under observation.

In the case of R&D-related ties, research services function dominated the relationships forged with foreign companies. It is also clear that these firms did very little to use the alliances, collaborations and agreements to strengthen their drug discovery infrastructure. Discovery R&D was the objective of forging a relationship with foreign firms in far fewer cases compared to research services and clinical trials.

Not only are domestic pharmaceutical firms ready to out-license clinical development of their NCEs to firms that have considerable market operations in the drugs and pharmaceuticals sector in India, but they are also entering into in-licensing deals for undertaking bio-equivalence studies in the area of formulations and dosages. In-licensing arrangements are being used to build a portfolio for the purpose of growing in the domestic market. For example, Nicholas Piramal has had arrangements with Roche for launching products relating to cancer, epilepsy and AIDS. Glenmark has in-licensed Crofelemer, Napo's proprietary anti-diarrheal compound. Wockhardt has had arrangements for the in-licensing of Syrio Pharma SpA for dermatological products. Ranbaxy has had arrangements with KS Biomedix Ltd for EMRs to market Trans MID in India with an option to expand into China and other southeastern Asian countries.

Foreign firms are apparently gaining financially. They control far more R&D and marketing relationships than they would normally forge through OFDI. Consider the examples of out-licensing and in-licensing agreements being signed by these companies. In case of in-licensing agreements, payments to foreign firms are on a recurrent basis with guaranteed returns. An imbalance is also evident at the level of number of agreements entered into by these companies for marketing and research. Marketing as a purpose dominates the agreements. In-licensing agreements in the R&D area are for bioequivalence studies. With respect to product development, the area of bioequivalence is not a gap that can be filled through in-licensing agreements. However, this is not the case when one analyses the out-licensing deals because the agreement pertains to clinical development in earlier phases and pre-clinical toxicology studies.

Domestic ties with research institutions and academia have received the least attention from emerging Indian pharmaceutical multinationals. Although domestic firms are the major beneficiaries of R&D services sourced from public-sector research laboratories, there are very few alliances for undertaking collaborative drug discovery and development-related R&D work between domestic firms and public-sector research institutions. Just two firms used domestic R&D institutions for the purpose of R&D alliances. See Table 12.7 for the pattern of ties built with domestic R&D institutions for clinical and discovery R&D by these firms during the period 1999–2011.

Table 12.7 Types of R&D alliances with RI/academia

Companies	Clinical and discovery R&D		Sub total	Research services		Sub total	Grand total
	DA	FA		DA	FA		
IPCA Laboratories	1		1				1
Piramal Healthcare	1		1	1		1	2
Total	2		2	1		1	3

Source: Compiled by the authors from an analysis of governmental and industry websites.
Note: Among the fourteen leading pharmaceutical companies, only IPCA and Piramal have conducted alliance-style cooperation with RI/academia. DA-Domestic acquisitions; FA-Foreign acquisitions.

Table 12.8 also has details on the strengthening of market function through new ties with foreign firms. It is evident that marketing-related relationships dominate alliances and collaborations. Some Indian pharmaceutical firms prefer to rely only on marketing alliances abroad instead of setting up subsidiaries or production facilities.

Table 12.8 Pattern of marketing alliances, collaborations and licensing agreements, 1999–2011

Top fourteen pharmaceutical companies in India	Marketing alliances		Marketing collaborations		In-licensing (Marketing)		Out-licensing (Marketing)	
	Domestic	Foreign	Domestic	Foreign	Domestic	Foreign	Domestic	Foreign
	10	111	5	101		21	2	6

Source: Compiled by the authors from an analysis of governmental and industry websites.

Further, we also note with some concern that most of these domestic firms have chosen to enter into alliances, collaborations, and agreements with foreign firms that already have a presence in the Indian market. By forging a close relationship for the supply of contract research and manufacturing services with these foreign actors, such firms have made it clear that they have no plans to compete with big pharmaceutical companies, either in the domestic market or the foreign market. Lupin has a marketing alliance with Cornerstone to market Suprax. DRL has an alliance with Pilva for the development and marketing of oncology products in Europe; DRL and GlaxoSmithKline have a multi-product agreement; DRL is collaborating with Pharmascience Group for the development and marketing of generic products in Canada; and Glenmark has a supply and marketing agreement with Lehigh Valley. Certainly, some of these marketing alliances reflect an element of strategic choice. At the moment DRL, Glenmark and Lupin are seemingly examples of strategic elements guiding their relationships. Shorter term considerations are becoming far more pervasive in the case of most firms whose relationships we have analysed.

Evidence of dominance of the marketing function is clearly indicated in different types of relationships forged by each of these fourteen firms. Cases of domestic R&D institutions being targeted for in-licensing agreements are very few. In some cases, global pharmaceutical companies are out-licensing their products to Indian firms. This relationship brings regular royalty payments with minimum investment and wider geographical coverage for their products. Strides Acrolab Ltd. has entered into a number of such deals with companies in the USA, UK, Japan and Europe. Clinical outsourcing is also being treated as a lucrative strategy by some Indian firms. Cadila Healthcare has entered into alliances with Atlanta Pharma, Schering AG and Boehringer Ingelheim. Lupin has a licensing agreement with Cornerstone Bio Pharma Inc. for clinical development of novel drug delivery systems (NDDS) for an anti-infective product.

Ranbaxy has entered into a few collaborative research programmes involving global pharmaceutical firms, for example, with Medicines for Malaria Venture (MMV), Geneva, for an anti-malarial molecule, Rbx 11160; with GlaxoSmithKline for drug discovery and clinical development for a wide range of therapeutic areas; and with the University of Strathclyde, UK, for an NDDS. Ranbaxy also has a collaborative relationship with Eli Lily, Pfizer and Novartis in drug discovery and with Vectura (a drug delivery company) for development of platform technologies in the area of oral controlled release systems. Ranbaxy, DRL, Lupin, Glenmark, Torrent, Sun Pharmaceuticals, Cadila and Biocon figure prominently in the agreements, collaborations and alliances entered into for the purpose of R&D. However, there are only a few examples of collaborative R&D programmes which involve some kind of risk-sharing through joint ventures or collaboration with other pharmaceutical companies in order to develop and commercialize products. They have largely entered into one-way relationships, which may not be advantageous in the long run.

Torrent has entered into a collaborative research programme for drug discovery in the area of the treatment of hypertension with Astra Zeneca. Cipla has entered into a collaborative programme of the risk-sharing type with a domestic company set up by a non-resident Indian, namely Avesthagen Laboratories, to produce a biogeneric drug for arthritis, N-Bril. Although Avesthagen has an ongoing collaborative programme with Nestle, Bio Mereleux of France and other companies, Cipla's relationship with Avesthagen is unlikely to prove compromising and can be handled independently. Dependent or potentially compromising relationships will not benefit the firms as much and can the affect the national system of innovation adversely when pressure is being mounted on the industry to accept TRIPS plus provisions of data exclusivity. Of course, there are some exceptions.

Table 12.9 Domestic pharmaceutical activities of commercialized/ launched generic compounds

Domestic companies	1999–2001			2002–04			2005–07			2008–11			Total
	Disease type												
	I	II	III	I	II	III	I	II	III	I	II	III	
Top fourteen Indian pharmaceutical companies	5			27	4	2	52	6	4	79	20	3	202

Source: Data collected from individual websites and latest annual reports of individual pharmaceutical companies and Cygnus Research, accessed in November 2011.

Notes: Disease type (Type-I, Type-II, Type-III): *Type-I - diabetes, cancer, metabolic diseases, hepatitis, influenza, cardiovascular, infectious diseases, inflammatory diseases, allergy, respiratory diseases; *Type-II – HIV/AIDS, tuberculosis, malaria; *Type-III - leishmaniasis, trypanosomiasis, lymphatic filariasis, leprosy, diarrhoea.

Domestic companies consider the domestic market to be too small and not sufficiently attractive for taking up development of new products in the pharmaceutical sector. See Table 12.10 for the pattern of disease orientation of compounds launched. Most of the compounds in demand belong to the category of Type I diseases. In the absence of a stimulus for augmentation of home country demand, the conditions continue to favour the target of low value-added products required by global markets. It is this imbalance in policy design that is reinforcing skewed research priorities in the public-sector research system. From the point of view of the current public health situation, this certainly does not suit the country on whose shoulders the domestic industry still depends.

There is evidence of a shift in R&D priorities. An analysis of the evidence processed by us shows that all the important developments that we see in respect of the creation of R&D capabilities for new drug discovery and development within Indian firms have a global market favouring R&D orientation. As things stand now, it is clear that pharmaceutical research is largely directed towards the needs of the regulated markets of the USA and Europe. Even high-burden disease areas in India have not been able to attract locally bred firms. Analysis indicates a preponderance of medium-burden disease areas – cancer (3.4 per cent), tuberculosis (2.8 per cent), HIV/AIDS (2.1 per cent), malaria (1.6 per cent), respiratory diseases (1.5 per cent), blindness (1.4 per cent), diabetes (0.7 per cent) – being covered by the firms in their relationships with academic institutions and industry networks. See Table 12.10 for the pattern of coverage of different types of diseases in academic alliances and collaborations.

Table 12.10 Pattern of coverage of different types of burden of diseases in academic collaborations and alliances, 1999–2011

Companies	Collaborations and alliances for discovery and clinical R&D with RI/academia					
	Domestic institutions			Foreign institutions		
	High-burden disease areas	Medium-burden disease areas	Low-burden disease areas	High-burden disease areas	Medium-burden disease areas	Low-burden disease areas
Top thirteen Indian pharmaceutical companies	4	15	3		1	

Source: Individual company websites and companies annual reports.

Table 12.11 Pattern of coverage of different types of disease burden for new chemical entities (NCEs) under development by Indian pharmaceutical companies, 1999–2011

Companies	NCE pipeline		
	High-burden disease areas	Medium-burden disease areas	Low-burden disease areas
Top thirteen Indian pharmaceutical companies	17	34	32

Source: Individual company website press releases, news, archives, and so on.

See Tables 12.10 and 12.11 for the pattern of coverage of diseases as focus of development of NCEs under development by these firms. An analysis of the development of NCEs through the alliances formed with foreign firms for drug discovery and clinical trials indicates that the focus is on medium-burden diseases like cancer, tuberculosis, HIV/AIDS, malaria, asthma, bronchitis, blindness and diabetes. Diseases for which capability development is being undertaken with the help of foreign firms are those in which the developed world has more interest. Of late, high-burden disease areas in India have garnered the least interest.

Impact of government R&D schemes

While the industry is complaining about the rather small amount of government funding for the direct benefits of R&D for the industry, it is interesting to note that they are not utilizing the existing schemes in any major way. Medium-burden diseases are a major focus of the projects undertaken by the industry. This is because of the worldwide emphasis on many of those diseases at the level of R&D funding. The impact of OFDI connections on the lack of balance in R&D priorities is starkly visible in case of the use of government schemes by emerging Indian pharmaceutical multinationals. Table 12.12 indicates that most of the emerging Indian pharmaceutical multinational companies have not been leveraging government funding for undertaking industrial R&D.

Table 12.12 Pattern of coverage of different types of burden of diseases in industrial collaborations and alliances of fourteen leading Indian companies, 1999–2011

Collaboration and alliances for discovery and clinical R&D with industry					
Domestic firms			Foreign firms		
High burden disease areas	Medium-burden disease areas	Low-burden disease areas	High-burden disease areas	Medium-burden disease areas	Low-burden disease areas
1			15	31	19

Source: Compiled by the author from the analysis of information provided on websites and press releases.

More than half of these fourteen large domestic firms chose to ignore – almost completely – the schemes formulated by the government for industrial research financing. Only six firms out of the fourteen undertook government-funded projects for the creation of facilities and activities required for development of new drugs. But large, domestic firms accounted for just 15 projects in the portfolio out of the 104 sanctioned by the government. See Tables 12.13 and 12.14 for the groups of diseases covered by domestic firms while using government-funded programmes and schemes initiated for the benefit of pharmaceutical innovation.

Table 12.13 Pattern of government funding agencies' programmes/schemes-funded burden of diseases by industry, 2005–11

Funding agencies	High burden	Medium burden	Low burden	Total
DPRP	23	30	13	66
BIPP	6	5	1	12
SBIRI	2	14	10	26
Grand total	**31**	**49**	**24**	**104**

Source: Compiled by the authors from the information available on these schemes.

Table 12.14 Firm-wise pattern of government funding agencies' programmes/schemes-funded burden of diseases by industry, 2005–11

Companies	DPRP			BIPP			SBIRI		
	High burden	Medium burden	Low burden	High burden	Medium burden	Low burden	High burden	Medium burden	Low burden
Total number of projects in different classes of disease burden	23	30	13	6	5	1	2	14	10
Torrent Pharma	-	1	4	-	-	-	-	-	-
Ranbaxy Laboratories	-	5	-	-	-	-	-	-	-
Strides Arcolab	1	-	-	-		-	-	-	-
Lupin Pharma	1	-	1	-		-	-	-	-
Cadila Healthcare	-	3	-	-	-	-	-	-	1
Biocon Ltd	-	-	-	-	1	-	-	-	-
Total	**2**	**6**	**5**	**-**	**2**	**-**	**-**	**-**	**1**

Source: Compiled by the authors from the websites of the ministries administering these schemes.

Since domestic firms have not come forward in a big way to use government schemes for R&D and innovation of therapeutics for tackling priority diseases, it is obvious that the national links of these firms with the public research institutes are only getting weaker instead of becoming stronger. Despite the central government agreeing to cede the ownership of IPRs to collaborating firms, there is a lack of interest among emerging Indian pharmaceutical multinationals in these schemes. Some of these firms have now been sold by their promoters to foreign firms. Therefore, the OFDI connections of the emerging Indian pharmaceutical multinationals are adversely affecting the plans of Indian policymakers for the development of a national system of innovation for the benefit of the Indian pharmaceutical industry.

Medical research is lacking in both learning and reflection; the government is yet to give attention to the creation of this capacity. Mechanisms are required to be created for a systematic medical research system analysis to be undertaken on a periodical basis by the Department of Health Research. Other concerns are also required to be taken care of for the promotion of R&D and S&T (science and technology) departments' extra-mural research priorities, funding stability, network development and access-related IP management issues. Evidence collated as a part of the preliminary health research system analysis (HRSA) undertaken has confirmed important gaps and mismatches in many specialities, a narrow research base in many areas, a fragmentation of research efforts, lack of coherence, a development gap, inadequate competence in biology for drug discovery, and so on.

Some examples of imbalances in respect of manpower and expertise development for the benefit of R&D are given here. For example, there is underdevelopment of toxicology research and drug development for the treatment of arsenic and lead poisoning. Similarly, there are imbalances in the generation of manpower for such research (Sharma, 2013). There is obviously a large gap between the demand for and the availability of qualified personnel. While there is considerable activity going on currently in public-sector research organizations in the fields of genomics and proteomics in India, the investment from domestic firms is unable to take advantage of this activity. While it is possible to conceive of public–private partnerships to give momentum to the field of discovery and development research in the area of pharmaceuticals that will take care of the priorities of national public health and neglected diseases of the poor of the developing world as a whole, this path can be better created with the public mission approach. Although, at this moment, the future of pharmaceutical production innovation appears to be – in a critical way – in the hands of these companies' potential partners abroad, the outcomes of public-sector R&D can be leveraged to align their priorities with public health goals if the paths and models of innovation can be redirected suitably by increasing public investment and involving the private sector in the implementation of the mission around public health priorities.

Conclusion

Contrary to the expectations of policymakers, growing global integration is failing to generate the 'best case conditions' predicted to be prevailing for the prospects of industrial upgrading of the pharmaceutical sector and knowledge creation for the acceleration of the catching-up process and for the benefit of the public health system in India. Large-sized domestic firms are making far more investments in marketing activities than in competence building, interactive learning, and innovation making activities. Domestic firms have failed to utilize the strategic advantage of industrial capabilities developed with the help of public investment. The primary incentive to invest in R&D, whether for NCEs, modifications, or development of generics, has not arisen in a big way from the new TRIPS-compliant product patent regime in India. In the post-TRIPS era, while the government has been able to accelerate the contribution of in-house R&D to the emerging pharmaceutical innovation-making landscape because of the anticipated shrinkage of off-patent opportunities for domestic firms, it is also true that even in the absence of TRIPS, such R&D activities would still have been undertaken by quite a few domestic firms because of their decision to enter regulated markets to take advantage of the opportunities opened for generics.

While R&D activities have diversified, no NCE has yet been developed. Domestic pharmaceutical firms are yet to prove their competence in respect of the development of new products. There have been several setbacks and the partnership model has not always worked properly. Little has changed to dispute the traditional wisdom that developing countries should not grant product patent protection (Chaudhuri, 2007).[8] It is necessary to accelerate the processes of learning, competence building and innovation making by establishing a clear national strategy with the aim of strengthening the place of domestic pharmaceutical firms and of enhancing the systemic autonomy and coherence of a national system of innovation. Policy intervention by way of increasing the size of the domestic market and rapidly expanding the knowledge base in the public sector with the aim to encourage domestic firms to undertake more technological activities directed at meeting the needs of Indian people has been suggested as a remedial step.

Coming to the beginning of the change in the composition of drivers of funding for research for health in favour of Type III diseases and traditional medicine, in India, the enabling environment to steer, co-ordinate, manage, appraise, articulate demand and appropriate IPRs is still missing. Markets for

---

8   Recently, Chaudhuri, Park and Gopakumar (2010) explored the issue of policy options in light of the experience of the Indian private sector and the public–private partnerships initiated in India for the development of new drugs and suggested the expansion of public–private partnerships to include organizations from other innovative developing countries such as Brazil and China.

knowledge and technology are by no means a neutral space; policy interventions for industrial upgrading have to take into account that there is an international division of labour being constituted through the route of outsourcing. Innovation systems must stay clear of the traps that this division of labour is laying down for domestic firms. As things stand today, it would not be possible for domestic firms to grow beyond a point through the selected routes of export of generics and contract work in research and manufacturing. These routes can be used to only supplement the strategy of expanding the domestic market. However, to depend mainly on these routes for further growth would take the domestic firms away from the real needs-based innovation. It is likely that most domestic firms will ultimately settle down to accept the role of junior partners in the new game of proteomics and genomics-based innovation, wherein the R&D platform/tools are already monopolized via the route of strong IPRs.

Prospects for domestic R&D for neglected diseases and conditions will improve only when the constraint of the market size is suitably eased for the benefit of local pharmaceutical firms. To alleviate the constraint of small market size, the Indian government must also step in to improve the demand conditions. Recently, health expenditure has been declining across the board in India. This is a direct consequence of the implementation of neoliberal fiscal strategies. It is too much to expect from domestic pharmaceutical firms – whose revenues are insecure – to contribute to R&D investment for neglected diseases if there is declining public health expenditure. Policymakers will also have to seek significant changes on the side of the supply of innovation capacities if their new strategies for industrial upgrading are to obtain significant success. They need to get the private sector to coordinate with the public sector in the creation of a programme for upgrading innovation capacities in order to play a positive role in drug development for diseases of the poor in India. Policymakers will also have to provide direct support for R&D facilities for clinical trials. Domestic firms should not get incentivized for inappropriate product targets. Dependent relationships being forged through excessive reliance on low-quality contract work in both manufacturing and research will have to be discouraged.

Decoupling of research costs from product prices can be an important step in the appropriate direction. Rewards for R&D financing need to be redesigned to discourage inefficient and unfair innovation work. For example, the encouragement to invest in India in the case of open source drug discovery (OSDD) movement does not rely on monetary incentives. It also offers the model for emulation to achieve the goal of decoupling of R&D from the price of the product. Licensing mechanisms need to be used to maximize access. Pressure on the Indian government to desist from issuing compulsory licenses (CLs) and moving away from the implementation and strengthening of Section 3(d) of the Indian Patent Act (amended 2005) need to be opposed. The focus of the public sector with regard to the implementation of the IPR regime should be looked into from the standpoint of where the innovation policy needs to redirect the efforts in the public interest.

As far as the impact of the pro-TRIPS domestic innovation policy on the contribution of domestic firms to pharmaceutical innovation is concerned, evidence is building up to contradict the claim that the adverse effect on the prices of patented medicines would be adequately compensated by the diffusion of new technological capabilities and advanced pharmaceutical knowledge.[9] Apparently, the activity of mergers and acquisitions prompted the Department of Industrial Promotion and Policy (DIPP) to express concern with regard to access to medicines in a White Paper issued on 30 November 2011. Control of the home market was perceived to be gradually moving away from the hands of domestic firms. Foreign firms are better placed to use the Indian production base, charging higher prices for medicines because of their growing market power (Chaudhuri, 2010).

After a gap of almost fifteen years, the policy space is seemingly opening up in favour of policy measures which would be able to provide public policy support to the promotion of manufacturing innovation. The domestic pharmaceutical industry is waking up to the challenge of rejuvenating the local production of key starting materials, intermediates and APIs, and is seeking technology from the CSIR system once again. Concerns of national security, import dependence and export protection have emerged as key triggers within both industry and policymaking circles with regard to the operationalization of schemes for the collaboration of research institutes and the industry. It is apparent that India wishes to retain a position in the regulated markets. The domestic industry can continue exporting generic medicines only through the development of clusters for fermentation products, critical starting materials, intermediates and APIs, fluorination, biopharmaceuticals, and so on (Iphex Pharmaexcil,

---

9   Recently, this apprehension was confirmed by an official White Paper of the Department of Industrial Promotion and Policy (DIPP) of Government of India (DIPP, 2011). The paper has attempted to bring issues concerning the regulation of foreign direct investment (FDI) and the use of provisions of compulsory licensing to deal with the policy challenge once again on the agenda of the Indian government.

2017). R&D and innovation for drug discovery and new drug development will have to wait for the pharmaceutical innovation system to gain maturity and progress further.

As far as drug discovery and new drug development is concerned, while smaller research-intensive biotechnology companies specializing in niche areas of expertise with their focus on specific disease areas or target classes are doing better compared to established pharmaceutical companies, their capacity to commercialize the technological knowledge is very weak. Overall R&D investment in both chemistry- and biology-based drug discovery is lagging much behind the global industry average. More biotech companies need to be created. Although the Indian government aims to stimulate the launch of 2,000 start-ups in life sciences over the coming five years, it is unlikely that most of these start-ups will venture into new drug development and drug discovery based on their own proprietary NCEs.

Policymakers will have to try getting established domestic firms to concentrate their efforts on the real needs-based innovations and strategies that will free the Indian firms from getting into dependent relationships with foreign firms. The worldwide practice of negative innovation emanating from the pharmaceutical sector under the strategy of 'innovation for profit' has never been supportive of the Type III diseases of developing countries. Indian policymakers have a social responsibility to ensure that the institutions of health sciences remain geared to producing more of public goods rather than market goods. In particular, they have a duty to use the instruments of public-sector R&D and government support for innovation in the private sector in a targeted way.

In order to accelerate the processes of knowledge creation for the benefit of acceleration of the catching-up process, the Indian pharmaceutical industry is shown to be in urgent need of creating complementarities and linkages to establish the new pathways of growth. Steps that are considered necessary to bring about a radical change in the impact of active policies under implementation are identified as challenges facing policymakers with respect to the tasks of domestic market-building, dealing with information externalities arising out of a weak institutional research base, and remedying the coordination failure and various other such problems involving the promotion and regulation of technology development.

References

Abrol, D. 2004. 'Post-TRIPs Technological Behaviour of the Pharmaceutical Industry in India.' *Science Technology and Society* 9 (2): 243–71.

———. 2005. 'Post-TRIPs Development Strategies of Indian Pharmaceutical Industry.' *Proceedings of the National Seminar on Drug Policy*, JSA, Kolkata, 16–17 April.

———. 2006. 'Conditions for the Achievement of Pharmaceutical Innovation for Sustainable Development: Lessons from India.' *World Review of Science, Technology and Sustainable Development* 3 (6): 344–61.

———. 2010. 'Public Engagement on Intellectual Property Rights: Lessons from the Campaign on TRIPs in India.' In *Science and the Public*, Vol. 15, Part 2, edited by Ashok Jain, 183–224. New Delhi: Centre for Studies in Civilizations-PHISPC.

Ackerhans, S. 2016. 'Challenges and Opportunities for the Innovation of Novel Drugs: An Analysis of R&D Collaborations within the Sectoral Innovation System of the Indian Pharmaceutical Industry.' Master's thesis, Copenhagen Business School. Accessed 6 August 2017. Available at http://www.grin.com/en/e-book/324120/ challenges-and-opportunities-for-the-innovation-of-novel-drugs.

Athreye, S., D. Kale and S. V. Ramani. 2009. 'Experimentation with Strategy and the Evolution of Dynamic Capability in the Indian Pharmaceutical Sector.' *Industrial and Corporate Change* 18 (4): 729–59.

Bedi, N. and P. M. S. Bedi. 2015. 'Patenting and R&D Trends in Indian Pharmaceutical Industry: Post-Trips Scenario.' *Journal of Intellectual Property Rights* 18 (2): 105–10.

Bhaumik, S. K. *et al.* 2003. 'Survey of FDI in India.' DRC Working Paper No. 6. London: Centre for New and Emerging Markets, London Business School, April.

Branstetter, L., R. Fisman, and F. C. Foley. 2005. 'Do Stronger Intellectual Property Rights Increase International Technology Transfer? Empirical Evidence from U.S. Firm-Level Panel Data.' NBER Working Paper No. 11516. Cambridge: National Bureau of Economic Research July. Accessed 6 August 2017. Available at http:// www.nber.org/papers/w11516.

BW Online Bureau. 2014. 'Death of a Dream.' *Business World*, 8 November. Accessed 6 August 2017. Available at http://businessworld.in/article/Death-Of-A-Dream/08-11-2014-65256/.

Chaudhuri, S. 2005. *The WTO and India's Pharmaceuticals Industry: Patent Protection, TRIPS and Developing Countries*. New Delhi: Oxford University Press.

———. 2007. 'Is Product Patent Protection Necessary in Developing Countries for Innovation? R&D by Indian Pharmaceutical Companies after TRIPS.' WPS No. 614, September. Kolkata: Indian Institute of Management, Calcutta.

———. 2010. 'R&D for Development of New Drugs for Neglected Diseases in India.' *International Journal of Technology and Globalisation* 5 (1/2): 61–75.

Chaudhuri, S., C. Park and K. M. Gopakumar. 2010. *Five Years into the Product Patent Regime: India's Response*. New York: United Nations Development Programme. Accessed 6 August 2017. Available at http://content.undp.org/go/cms-service/download/publication/?version=live&id=3089934.

Dhar, B. and K. M. Gopakumar. 2006. 'Post-2005 TRIPS Scenario in Patent Protection in the Pharmaceutical Sector: The Case of the Generic Pharmaceutical Industry in India.' Geneva: UNCTAD and IDRC.

Dhar, B. and N. Rao. 2002. 'Transfer of Technology for Successful Integration into the Global Economy: A Case Study of the Pharmaceutical Industry in India.' UNCTAD/ITE/IPC/Misc.22. This paper is part of the series of case studies carried out by Investment Policy and Capacity Building Branch, DITE. Accessed 6 August 2017. Available at unctad.org/en/docs/iteipcmisc22_en.pdf.

Differding, E. 2014. 'Drug Discovery Alliances in India – Indications, Targets, and New Chemical Entities.' *ChemMedChem* 9 (1): 43–60. DOI: 10.1002/cmdc.201300341.

Federica, A. 2014. 'With the Help of a Foreign Ally: Biopharmaceutical Innovation in India after TRIPS.' *Health Policy Plan* 29 (3): 280–91. DOI: 10.1093/heapol/czt015.

Glasgow, L. J. 2001. 'Stretching the Limits of Intellectual Property Rights: Has the Pharmaceutical Industry Gone Too Far?' *The Journal of Law and Technology* 41 (2): 227–58.

Government of India. 2007. *The Working Group Report of Eleventh Five Year Plan on Biomedical R&D and Health Systems Research*. New Delhi: Planning Commission.

Granville, B. and C. S. Leonard. 2003. 'Markets for Pharmaceuticals and Absorptive Capacity in Developing Nations: The Case of Transition Economies.' London: The Royal Institute of International Affairs. Accessed 6 August 2017. Available at http://www.univ-tlse1.fr/idei/Commun/Conferences/pharmacy/Papers/Granville-Leonard.pdf.

Hudson, J. 2000. 'Generic Take-up in the Pharmaceutical Market Following Patent Expiry: A Multicountry Study.' *International Review of Law and Economics* 20 (2): 205–21.

Iphex Pharmaexcil. 2017. Discussion at the Technical Session of the 'International Expo for Pharma and Healthcare', 27–29 April. Hyderabad: Pharmaceuticals Export Council of India.

Jiasu, L., B. Lin, and S. Sha. 2016. 'Catching-Up Pattern among Countries in Science-Based Industries: A Case Study in Pharmaceutical Industry.' *Journal of Industrial Integration and Management* 1 (1): 18 pages. DOI: 10.1142/S2424862216500044.

Keely, L. C. 2000. 'Pathway from Poverty? Intellectual Property in Developing Countries.' Special Report 14. London: Centre for Economic Performance, London School of Economics. Accessed 6 August 2017. Available at http://cep.lse.ac.uk/pubs/abstract.asp?index=623.

Kumar, N. 1995. 'Intellectual Property Protection, Market Orientation and Location of Overseas R&D.' Working Paper 9501. United Nations University (UNU).

Lall, S. and M. Albaladejo. 2002. 'Indicators of Relative Importance of IPRs in Developing Countries.' Oxford: Queen Elizabeth House Working Paper QEHWPS85.

Maria, A., J. Ruet, and M. H. Zerah. n.d. 'Biotechnology in India.' *Final Report*. French Embassy. Accessed 6 August 2017. Available at http://www.cerna.ensmp.fr/Documents/AM-JR-MHZ-Biotech-Summary.pdf.

Maskus, K. E. 2000. 'Intellectual Property Rights in the Global Economy.' Accessed 6 August 2017. Available at www.colorado.edu/economics/courses/maskus/4999/ch6finalrev.doc.

Pradhan, J. P. 2003. 'Liberalisation, Firm Size and R&D Performance: A Firm Level Study of Indian Pharmaceutical Industry.' New Delhi: RIS. Accessed 6 August 2017. Abvailble at http://www.ris.org.in/dp40_pap.pdf.

———. 2006. 'Global Competitiveness of Indian Pharmaceutical Industry: Trends and Strategies.' ISID Working Paper 2006/05, June. Accessed 6 August 2017. Available at http://isidev.nic.in/pdf/wp0605.pdf.

13

Revisiting the Miracle

South Korea's Industrial Upgrading from a Global Value Chain Perspective

Joonkoo Lee, Sang-Hoon Lee and Gwanho Park

Introduction

South Korea has been known for its successful economic development in the post-World War II world economy. In 1960, the country's gross domestic production (GDP) per capita was just US$156, lower than Ghana's. However, it has rapidly grown since then, reaching $25,977 in 2013. In 1996, South Korea joined the Organisation for Economic Cooperation and Development (OECD) and become only the second Asian member of this rich countries' club, after Japan. South Korea's economic development was mainly driven by exporting manufacturing goods. The country's exports rose from $122 million in 1960 to $703 billion in 2013, with manufacturing accounting for more than 80 per cent of the exports. It has become one of the ten largest trading economies in the world.[1] The rapid expansion of exports was largely attributable to the constant upgrading of export product composition to higher value-added, more technologically sophisticated products, which coincided with upgrading the country's industry structure to focus on high-tech sectors, such as electronics and information technology (IT). In this regard, South Korea is an example of successful 'economic upgrading', defined as moving up to higher value-added activities with improved technology, knowledge and skills (Gereffi, 2005).

In explaining South Korea's economic growth, two opposite explanations have been presented. A market-based perspective highlights export-push strategies, openness to foreign investment and technology transfer as the key factors of the growth (World Bank, 1993). In contrast, state-centred views

---

1   Compiled from the World Development Indicators (WDI, http://data.worldbank.org/data-catalog/world-development-indicators).

emphasize the key role of the state's active industrial policy in prodding local firms to upgrade and compete in global markets (Amsden, 1989; Chang, 1993; Evans, 1995). The debate following the economic crisis of the late 1990s centred on the development state was eclipsed by a 'neoliberal turn', or its strength was maintained with newly mandated roles (Chu, 2009; Kalinowski, 2008; Pirie, 2008). Missing in these explanations, however, is the role of global–local linkages in economic development (Hamilton and Gereffi, 2009). Economic development and industrial upgrading take place in a global economic context and through the interaction of global and local actors. Furthermore, just focusing on macro-economic settings or the role of the state fails to explain commonalities and differences in the patterns and trajectories of upgrading across different sectors and time periods.

To address these lacunae, this chapter revisits South Korea's experience of industrial upgrading from a global value chain (GVC) perspective. Specifically, it examines the upgrading paths of three sectors – apparel, automobile and animation, focusing on sectoral and temporal differences in upgrading paths and the role of changing global–local linkages in shaping the trajectories. A GVC refers to the full range of activities that firms and workers do to bring a product or service from its conception to its end use and beyond, including research and development (R&D), product design, production, as well as sales and marketing (Gereffi and Fernandez-Stark, 2011). The GVC perspective highlights fragmented and dispersed value chain activities across countries and the role of global buyers as the integrator of decentralized production networks. It focuses on the linkage between global buyers and local suppliers and its impact on the economic upgrading of countries, firms and workers engaged in the value chain. Therefore, from the GVC perspective, this chapter examines how South Korean firms changed their position in the GVCs of the three sectors and how they addressed upgrading challenges. It also investigates how the role of the state changed across and within the sectors over the period, particularly after the economic crisis of the 1990s.

The chapter is organized as follows:The next section reviews the literature of industrial development and upgrading in GVCs in the context of South Korea. A case study of upgrading trajectories in the three sectors is presented next. The final section discusses the findings from the study, highlighting sectoral characteristics in upgrading paths, the role of the state and changes in post-crisis upgrading dynamics.

Industrial development and upgrading in GVCs: The South Korean context

Two dominant perspectives have been presented regarding East Asian industrial development. One is market-based, notably presented in the World Bank's *The East Asian Miracle* (1993). According to the neoclassical economic perspective, rapid economic growth in post-war Asian countries was mainly attributed to their market-friendly approach, or 'getting the price right'. Industrial development was driven by export-push strategy, openness to foreign investment and technology transfer, combined with market-minded, 'careful policy interventions' by governments (World Bank, 1993, 24). In contrast, an alternative view emphasizes the role of non-market institutions, particularly the state, in economic growth. According to a state-centred version of this view, strong and bureaucratic East Asian states effectively intervened in the economy with various industrial policies, often highly sector-specific ones, to correct and prevent market failure ('getting the price wrong') and to prod local firms to upgrade and compete in more challenging export markets than domestic ones (Chang, 2006; Evans, 1995; Woo-Cumings, 1999).

The GVC approach provides a distinctive perspective from these market and state-oriented approaches with regard to the major sources of learning and capability-building for industrial development. It highlights the role played by *organizational* processes, specifically the coordinated forms of inter-firm linkages between global buyers and local suppliers in the upgrading of the latter. It illuminates the varied roles of global–local linkages in economic development, which were downplayed by the two mainstream explanations (Hamilton and Gereffi, 2009). Global buyers provide technology, information and market access that can be used by local suppliers as resources for upgrading (Pietrobelli and Saliola, 2008; Schmitz, 2006), although the relative importance of global resources in local supplier upgrading is varied by sector, the buyer–supplier relationship and the type of upgrading (Navas-Alemán, 2011; Schmitz, 2004; Schmitz and Knorringa, 2000). For instance, re-examining East Asian industrial development from a GVC perspective, Feenstra and Hamilton (2006) highlight the significant role played by the rise of large retail buyers – mostly American – in South Korea's and Taiwan's export growth. The global buyers developed new forms of offshore manufacturing, organizationally supporting the emergence of 'demand-responsive' suppliers in East Asia. These suppliers organized their production systems and developed their capabilities to effectively respond to the demand from global buyers in GVCs.

In addition, the GVC approach redefines economic development as upgrading into higher value-added activities in a fragmented production system (Gereffi, 2009; Giuliani, Pietrobelli and Rabellotti, 2005; Lee, 2010). Industrial upgrading is defined as the process by which a country or a firm moves to higher value-added activities in GVCs (Gereffi, 1999; Humphrey and Schmitz, 2002). Innovation is critical for upgrading. In a 'smile curve', higher value-added activities – for example, R&D and product development– tend to be innovation-intensive, while lower value-added ones like assembly are increasingly labour-intensive, relying on semi- or un-skilled workers, often with a temporary contract (Mudambi, 2008). The GVC literature distinguishes different forms of upgrading: (*a*) process upgrading: making production processes more efficient by reorganizing the production system and using advanced technology, (*b*) product upgrading: moving into more sophisticated or high-value product lines, (*c*) functional upgrading: occupying more profitable nodes within a chain and (*d*) inter-sectoral upgrading: moving into a more profitable value chain (Humphrey and Schmitz, 2002). Process and product upgrading can occur in any node of the chains, although product upgrading is more related to pre-production such as R&D and product design rather than the production process, in which process upgrading is critical. Functional upgrading indicates moving up along the smile curve into higher value-added functions, such as from assembly to branding and marketing. Inter-chain upgrading refers to moving up to higher value-added industries; for example, Taiwanese firms upgraded into the computer manufacturing sector by building upon their competence in producing television (TV) sets and, later, monitors (Humphrey and Schmitz, 2002). While process and product upgrading is important for increased exports and jobs, functional and inter-chain upgrading is more critical for sustained economic development in the long run by protecting local firms from price competition and deteriorated value capture.

The literature on industrial development in South Korea, and broadly East Asia, presents a plethora of evidence on upgrading in various forms. The 'Asian Tigers' have been known for their ability to upgrade industrial capabilities, learn from various sources and move from imitation to innovation (Amsden and Chu, 2003; Evans, 1995; Gereffi and Wyman, 1990; Kim, 1997). Consequently, East Asia became a centre of post-war economic growth and industrial upgrading (Chang, 2006; World Bank, 1993). Furthermore, East Asian economies have shifted to more innovative products with focus on R&D and product design, and moved up to more technology- and capital-intensive sectors such as IT and biotechnology (Chu, 2009; Kim, 1997; Wang, 2007; Wong, 2004). However, every East Asian country did not follow the same path – for example, there were notable differences between South Korea and Taiwan (Feenstra and Hamilton, 2006). Functional upgrading to original brand manufacturing (OBM) was highly favoured by Korean firms, particularly large diversified conglomerates called *chaebol*. Meanwhile, in Taiwan, specialized suppliers that focused on process and product upgrading became the cornerstone of the small- and medium-sized enterprise (SME)-oriented economy (Hsieh, 2011; Lee, Kim and Lin, 2016).

Less attention has been paid to the diversity of upgrading by sector and upgrading type in one country as well as whether the upgrading dynamics have changed since the economic crisis of the late 1990s. First, upgrading paths and the roles of global and local actors therein may vary by sector. Although many South Korean industries experienced a rapid expansion in exports and upgrading, the nature of such industrial development could be different by sector. Different sectors – for example, producer-driven (such as the automobile sector) and buyer-driven (such as the garment sector) (Gereffi, 1994) – have distinctive dynamics in upgrading, and the relative importance of global buyers as opposed to local actors – *chaebol*, SMEs and the state – in shaping upgrading outcomes may be not equal in different sectors. Furthermore, the role of the state in prodding local producers for upgrading may also be varied, depending on the sector and the form of upgrading. The important role played by the state in South Korea's industrial development is acknowledged by both state-centred and market-oriented approaches but to different degrees. From a GVC approach, a more intriguing question, however, is whether the form of government intervention was varied by sector or by the different types of upgrading required in different periods. For instance, government policy might have a more direct impact on functional or inter-sectoral upgrading than product or process upgrading, or in more technologically sophisticated sectors, which requires greater financial and technological resources.

The final question to be examined is whether upgrading dynamics have changed since the economic crisis of the late 1990s. The literature presents contrasting views regarding the characteristics of South Korea's post-crisis development dynamics; some characterize them as a neoliberal turn of the Korean political economy, which entailed market-friendly reforms and the demise of the development state (Pirie, 2008), whereas others emphasize the persisting relevance of state intervention in the recovery from the crisis (Kalinowski, 2008; Woo, 2007) as well as the state's newly found role as a facilitator of post-industrial transition (Chu, 2009; Lee, 2015; Wang, 2007). Meanwhile, firms began to diverge in the wake of the economic crisis. Some *chaebol*s have become better established in global markets than before the crisis while others fell behind. A new generation of SMEs has emerged since the crisis, particularly in sectors like IT, media and entertainment. The question is whether and how upgrading dynamics have changed since the crisis, paying close attention to the change in the relative role of global and local actors in post-crisis upgrading.

Tales of three value chains: Apparel, automobile and animation

This section examines South Korea's upgrading and innovation experiences in three sectors: textile and apparel, automobile and animation. By examining multiple sectors that are different in the type of technology they use, the level of technological sophistication and GVC governance, we aim to identify the key characteristics of South Korea's experience in upgrading, as well as the commonalities and differences across the sectors.

The textile and apparel sector, as in many other developing countries, was one of the key export sectors in Korea's early industrialization. It is known for its buyer-driven nature, where global buyers play a critical role in engaging developing countries and firms into GVCs. Automobiles are much more complicated products, requiring a higher level of technological capabilities, and automobile value chains are typically characterized as producer-driven, with large capital-intensive automakers playing a key role in organizing production networks, although the power of mega-suppliers is recently expanding (Foy, 2014). After a series of difficulties in foreign markets, South Korean automakers have experienced global success over the last decade or so. Finally, animation is different from the other two in that it is a cultural product and creativity-intensive. Animation GVCs are changing in governance; they were traditionally driven by buyers like large TV networks. While their power is still strong, there is an increasing role of international co-production between various firms. South Korean animation producers, long known for their strong performance in outsourcing-based exports, have made a successful transition to a more creativity-intensive form of animation-making in recent years. In the analysis that follows, we examine the trajectories of upgrading and innovation in each of the three sectors.

Textile and apparel

The textile and apparel industry was one of the key export-driven sectors in the early period of South Korea's post-war economic development. As Figure 13.1 shows, South Korea's exports in the textile and apparel sector rose dramatically over the few decades from the 1960s, as did its share in the country's total exports. Between 1961 and 1972, the sector's share in the country's total exports increased from 10 per cent to 54 per cent, with $572 million worth of textile and apparel exports in 1972. Since then, exports continued to grow rapidly, reaching a peak in 2000 with $18.8 billion. Through this impressive drive of industrial development, South Korea emerged as an original equipment manufacturing (OEM) supplier base for global clothing brands and one of the major garment exporters by the end of the 1980s. With domestic petrochemical complexes established and chemical and synthetic fibre domestically supplied, a fabric-production segment was vertically integrated.

Figure 13.1 South Korea's textile and apparel exports

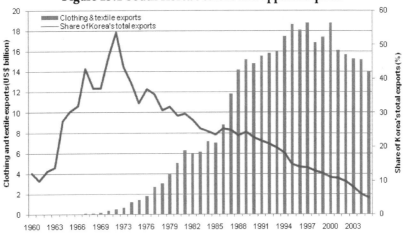

Source: Global Trade Statistics System, Korea International Trade Association (KITA).

However, due to weakened price competitiveness in global markets in the 1990s, South Korean apparel firms chose to relocate labour-intensive value chain activities to lower-cost countries, with other local firms striving to move onto high value-added activities like branding and high-tech products. Since the early 2000s, the export value has been declining, mainly attributed to the growing offshoring of apparel production in the face of China's accession to the World Trade Organization (WTO) and the phase-out of the Multi-Fibre

Arrangement (MFA). Also, the sector's contribution to total exports declined as the country diversified its export portfolio to a broader range of manufacturing goods, such as automobiles, ships and electronics. In 2000, textile and apparel represented only 11 per cent of South Korea's total exports.

Rising from ashes: Multi-front upgrading and export growth (1960s–80s)
During the era of colonial rule by Japan (1910–45), Korea served as one of Japan's major cotton suppliers and Japanese capital built factories to capitalize on raw materials and abundant labour in the colonial periphery. This laid the early foundation of South Korea's modern clothing industry. As of 1940, textile production represented 12 per cent of the entire industrial production in Korea (Lee, 2012, 28). The Korean War (1950–53), however, destroyed most of the existing textile factories in the area now known as South Korea. This made industrial rebuilding an urgent post-war task.

After the War, foreign aid played a key role in reconstructing the sector. Almost every machine and type of material was imported in various forms of foreign aid. A great deal of raw cotton was imported at very low prices from the United States, which eased a farm surplus there. Modernized textile-production facilities began to be founded with aided equipment. In the 1950s, textile and apparel production largely focused on meeting domestic demand, substituting imports in the basic consumer goods sector. The Korean government supported import-substituting production with various policy measures, outlined in the Emergency Cotton-Spinning Reconstruction Plan (1953–57), including import restrictions, high tariffs, import quotas and low interest rates (Lee, 2012, 34).

In the 1960s, as foreign aid began to dry out, the clothing industry shifted gear to export-driven development, spurred by the transition of the overall economy to export-led industrialization. The transition was accelerated by fast-growing consumer demand in advanced economies. At the same time, it was facilitated by the rising outsourcing of labour-intensive tasks by US and western European producers to developing countries in the face of rising wages at home, heralding the era of a new international division of labour (Fröbel, Heinrichs and Kreye, 1980). The geographic shift of production was particularly evident in light manufacturing: for example, the garment sector. From the mid-1960s, as Japan moved up to higher value-added nodes like textile production, more labour-intensive garment production shifted to other East Asian countries like South Korea, Hong Kong and Taiwan (Gereffi, 1999).

South Korean firms and the government responded to this opportunity by strengthening export-oriented manufacturing sectors. The groundwork was laid in five-year economic development plans, which started in 1962. As part of the plans, the Guro Industrial Complex (GIC) was founded in Seoul in 1964 to attract foreign investment in the apparel sector, initially from Korean residents in Japan, and outsourcing orders from Japanese general trading companies (*sogo shosha*). The ensuing rise of trade and investment flowing between South Korea and Japan reconnected their historical ties. The garment sector became the largest export sector for decades in the nation's first industrial complex. For much of the earlier years, garment firms in GIC mostly engaged in outward processing production (for example, cut-make-trim) with raw materials mostly supplied by foreign buyers and the final products were exported to Japan, the USA and Europe. The garment sector achieved gradual process upgrading largely in the labour-intensive segments, and rapidly expanded its exports. Between 1971 and 1981, South Korea's clothing exports grew more than sixteen times, from $388 million to $6.3 billion.

A bigger step forward related to upgrading was made in the 1980s as South Korea succeeded in localizing the production of chemical and synthetic fibres (Korea Federation of Textile Industries, 2014). On the one hand, the localization of key input materials was attributed to technology flows from Japan. Japan expanded chemical-fibre production facilities thanks to special procurement demands during the Korean War, starting the production of synthetic fibres like nylon. The technology flowed into South Korean firms like Kolon, one of the local textile giants that later became a *chaebol*, and so did second-hand machinery from Japan. In the midst of restructuring, Japanese clothing firms expanded equipment exports and technology transfer to South Korea (and Taiwan) through joint investment instruments (Korea Institute for Industrial Economics and Trade, 1997, 579). On the other hand, the upgrading to chemical-fibre production was also facilitated by the establishment of local petrochemical complexes in the 1970s. As part of the state-led Heavy and Chemical Industry Promotion Initiative, large-scale petrochemical complexes were built in two southern cities, Ulsan (1972) and Yeocheon (1979). This enabled South Korean firms to localize the supply of key input materials and build vertically integrated linkages leading from fibre production to textile and garment production. As exports continued to grow, the country emerged as one of the largest Asian garment exporters by the end of the 1980s.

Global shifts, factory relocation and new upgrading challenges (1990s–present)

The decade starting in 1985 represented the golden era of South Korea's clothing sector as its exports recovered from the slowdown caused by the second oil crisis. This successful adjustment was facilitated, on the one hand, by the government and the industry's quick response to the crisis, including the enactment of the Textile Industry Modernization Promotion Act (1979). On the other hand, the international trade environment following the Plaza Accord (1985) provided favourable conditions for South Korea's exports as a strong yen undermined Japanese firms' competitiveness in global markets. South Korea's clothing exports more than doubled in the period 1985–95, from $7 billion to $19 billion.

By the mid-1990s, however, South Korea's textile and garment exports began to slow down, as shown in Figure 13.1. At the same time, South Korean firms began to relocate production facilities abroad. In 1978–2001, evidence shows 1,911 instances of foreign direct investment (FDI) (stock-based) had occurred in fifty-nine different countries with a total worth of $1.8 billion. The FDI count represented 22 per cent of South Korea's total FDI count in manufacturing, while in value those amounted to just 12 per cent of the country's total, indicating that apparel FDI was small-scale and driven by SMEs. The overwhelming majority of the investment (84 per cent) was in the garment sector and only 16 per cent in more upstream nodes such as fibres, textiles and dyeing. Geographically, 83 per cent of the investments were in Asia – mostly in China (Moon, 2003).

This increased offshoring in South Korea's clothing sector was attributed to a few factors. First, South Korean firms had to address competitiveness challenges from Japan, China and other Asian countries in global markets. Japanese firms, in the face of a strong yen, expanded their overseas production in China and South-East Asia, posing a challenge to South Korean firms. At the same time, more exports from China and other developing Asian countries pushed South Korean firms into a corner as they confronted various domestic challenges from the 1980s, including rising wages, frequent industrial disputes and labour shortages. Finally, the MFA incentivized South Korean producers to move production to non-signatory nations or countries whose quota was not exhausted by domestic producers.[2]

---

2   The MFA governed the world trade in textiles and garments from 1974 to 2004, imposing quotas on the amount developing countries could export to developed countries. It expired in 2005.

The relocation of production abroad created a vacuum in the domestic clothing sector, as well as the need to upgrade to higher value-added activities, such as branding, design and R&D. In response, the South Korean government launched the Seven-Year Plan for Clothing and Textile Structural Improvement in 1989, aiming to produce high-quality products for the domestic fashion market and exporting high-end woven products. The new emphasis lay in small-batch production, using new material fibre, deploying creative designs, and moving from OEM to original design or brand manufacturing (ODM or OBM). South Korea put more focus on fabric production, including processing and producing raw material, yarn, and textiles which required a great deal of know-how and capital investment (Lee, 2012, 60). South Korean garment factories relocated abroad were supplied materials imported from South Korea and which in turn exported the final products to the USA, Japan, the European Union, as well as back to South Korea. This generated a triangular pattern of trade between South Korea, the rest of Asia and final markets in advanced economies (Gereffi, 1999). The new focus on product and functional upgrading deepened after the industrial restructuring that followed the Asian financial crisis of the late 1990s, China's accession to the WTO and the final phase-out of the MFA in 2005 (Lee, 2005), which further accelerated the relocation of Korean manufacturing to China and declining garment exports.

Meanwhile, as the income level of many South Koreans generally increased, changing patterns of consumption facilitated the growth of the domestic market for high-end fashion products and clothing with high functionality (for example, for sports and leisure activities). However, at the same time, the market became more competitive as it attracted more foreign brands. One of the notable developments is a growing influence of foreign SPA (specialty retailer of private label apparel) brands, such as Uniqlo, Gap, Zara and H&M.[3] Foreign SPA brands have become increasingly influential in the domestic market, competing with numerous domestic brands. They significantly cornered the market by constantly offering a variety of products in different

---

3   Also known as 'fast fashion', SPA refers to apparel producers with strategies to design and manufacture up-to-date styles of clothing quickly and cheaply so that the mainstream consumer can buy such products at a lower price. Such strategies are facilitated by the apparel firm exclusively managing and streamlining the entire supply chains from planning to design, production, distribution and sales, with sophisticated information technology systems. Fast fashion has become a key trend in global apparel business (Tokatli, 2008).

styles with low prices. In 2013, three global SPA brands – Uniqlo, Zara and H&M – recorded more than 1 trillion won of combined revenue in the Korean market (Byun, 2014).

This has prompted local apparel brands to expand from design-oriented or middle-market strategies to SPA business strategy. Since the 2000s, several new local SPA brands were launched, such as Codes Combine (2002), SPAO (2009), MIXXO (2011), 8seconds (2012) and TOP10 (2012). These local brands, however, are facing difficulties in building highly coordinated global or regional supply chains – which is what foreign SPA brands did – that offer the latter critical competitive advantages, such as low prices, small-batch production and mass merchandising stores. Forerunners like ZARA and H&M keep pioneering new sourcing locations ahead of competitors and supporting their business and price decision systems with cutting-edge mathematical models to optimize stock (Caro and Gallien, 2009). Such business models and supply chain management techniques require a great deal of tangible and intangible investment in innovation and other activities. Thus, new-born South Korean SPA brands are now faced with a catching-up challenge to address the structural shifts in the apparel GVC towards more flexible just-in-time sourcing and production.

Automobiles

The automobile industry in South Korea has a relatively short history, but has impacted the society widely and profoundly. No other industry matches its influence as it spurs other industries such as machinery, shipbuilding, oil, petrochemicals, steel, industrial design as well as electronics. In just three decades starting from 1984, South Korea's automobile production skyrocketed from 0.2 million to 4.5 billion vehicle units (Figure 13.2). In 2012, 70 per cent of the vehicles produced were exported. Automobiles accounted for 13 per cent of South Korea's total exports in value that year, making it a top export item (KAMA, 2013, 6). The country is the home of Hyundai Motors and Kia Motors, which together constitute the world's fourth largest automotive group (OICA, 2013). Understanding the spillover effect of automobile production, many developing countries have attempted to build a robust automotive industry, but only a handful of them have been successful (Dicken, 2011). In this regard, South Korea is exceptional, although the ride to success was not entirely smooth.

Figure 13.2 South Korea's automobile production and exports, 1971–2013

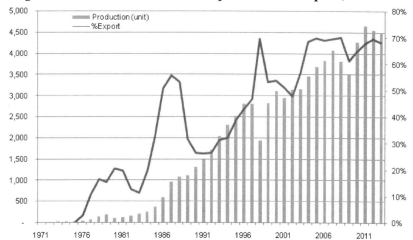

Sources: KAMA Korean Automobile Industry: *50th Anniversary History Book* (2005); *KAMA Korean Automobile Industry Annual Report* (2013); OICA Production Statistics (2013).

A bumpy ride towards an export-oriented sector (1970s–90s)

Until the 1980s, the focus of South Korean carmakers lay on acquiring the technologies required to manufacture a car. They had numerous technical tie-ups with Japanese and US firms: Shinjin and Toyota; Hyundai and Ford; Asia and Fiat; Kia and Mazda; and Hyundai and Mitsubishi. Development plans for the automotive industry required firms to achieve technological independence, which was the requirement for starting their business. Progress, however, was slow to come till the late 1960s, due to the lack of incentives and penalties in place despite various government-led supportive policies and sectoral development plans. Local carmakers' technological levels in manufacturing, design, basic (fundamental) technology and R&D remained low throughout the 1960s and 1970s. Semi-knock-down (SKD) and complete build-up (CBU) manufacturing was the common practice.[4] The technological independence ratio, which indicates how many parts were supplied domestically, was 5 per cent in 1962, 21 per cent in 1967, and 38 per cent in 1969 for compact cars and sedans (KAMA, 2005, 127, 149, 151).

---

4   Under the CBU scheme, cars are assembled in the country of origin and exported whole to the destination market. In contrast, a knocked-down (KD) scheme refers to importing a kit containing the parts needed to assemble a product in the destination country. A complete or incomplete set of parts is imported, and the latter is referred to as SKD.

A breakthrough came in the mid-1970s with the Heavy and Chemical Industries Promotion Initiative, followed by the Long-Term Automobile Industry Development Plan (1974) to achieve technological independence for engines, components and assembly. These plans included restricting imports of auto components as well. South Korean firms decided to develop unique and distinct models and build all-around plants. The representative models were Kia's Brisa (introduced upon Mazda's Familia model) and Hyundai's unique Pony model (in collaboration with British Leyland Motors Corporation and Mitsubishi for engine and transmission and for design with Italdesign Giugiaro). Hyundai's decision was justified by plans to develop and export a unique model, despite rival firms focused on increasing the technological independence of models already in the market. As a result of these efforts, the technological independence ratio rose to 90 per cent in 1977 and South Korean automotive firms had accomplished almost 100 per cent localization by the mid-1980s, although many key parts were still made based on imported technology (KAMA, 2005, 272). Overall, the joint upgrading efforts by the government and local firms to localize parts and components and build a unique model were the stepping stone for the entire industry to upgrade further.

Thanks to increased demand in the local market and the commencement of exports starting from 1975, South Korean automotive firms experienced unprecedented growth. Hyundai used Canada as a test bed for the North American market, marking an initial success in the early 1980s. Encouraged by this success, it advanced into the US market in 1986, once again attaining high sales. The growth, however, did not sustain, due to quality and consumer satisfaction issues (KAMA, 2005, 337–38). Hyundai eventually experienced a huge loss in sales. In response, local carmakers diversified market and product portfolios to reduce risk. The fast-growing demand of automobiles in the domestic market helped them overcome hardships in their initial foreign expansion (KAMA, 2005, 590).

Despite the considerable progress, there was still a significant gap in productivity and quality between South Korean carmakers and their foreign competitors. South Korean automakers' productivity (for example, the average assembly time) lagged behind that of Japanese or North American makers. In 1993, the recorded number of defects in Hyundai's new cars were more than two times higher than that of cars made by General Motors (GM), Toyota or Honda (Lansbury, Kwon and Suh, 2007). The economic crisis in 1997–98 prompted an industry-wide restructuring driven by the government, focusing on enhancing managerial transparency and improving the financial structures of automotive firms (KAMA, 2005, 604). As part of the restructuring, crisis-stricken local carmakers were acquired by their domestic or foreign rivals; Hyundai acquired Kia to form the Hyundai Motor Group (HMG), and Daewoo Motors and Samsung Motors were acquired by foreign automakers – GM and Renault, respectively. This led to a significant consolidation in the South Korean auto industry, now dominated by Hyundai.

Post-crisis upgrading and the globalization of value chains (2000s–present)

Ever since the disappointment in the US market in the late 1980s, Hyundai has focused on increasing customer satisfaction through tighter quality control, improved product design and better brand management. A significant improvement in quality came in the early 2000s, as the company put quality management as its key priority across its production lines, R&D and after-service. Also, Hyundai established Hyundai Mobis that specializes in developing and supplying core components of its vehicles. As a result, in 2004, Hyundai was ranked second after Toyota in J. D. Power's Initial Quality Study (IQS) (Brown, 2012). It also launched a long-term product warranty programme to gain consumer confidence (Holstein, 2013). In design, Hyundai consolidated research centres across Hyundai and Kia, including their design centres, to Namyang Technology Center in South Korea (Kim, 2014a). Simultaneously, it expanded design centres and studios overseas; they are located in Germany, the USA, China, India and Japan (Hyundai Motor Co., 2014). Kia's design has significantly improved after recruiting Peter Schreyer from Volkswagen and putting design as the key strategy of the company (Park, 2014a). Improved design management has won Hyundai and Kia various car design awards worldwide (Collett, 2014). With the growing emphasis on quality and design, the brand value of Hyundai has climbed the ladder to match those of global carmaker brands. Aggressive marketing strategies and brand campaigns have also played an important part in building a global brand. Hyundai first entered Interbrand's *Best 100 Brands* list in 2005 and rose to forty-third in 2013 (Interbrand, 2014). All these accomplishments indicate the concurrence of significant process and product upgrading.

Simultaneously, the supply chains of South Korean automobile firms have considerably changed with the rising importance of first-tier suppliers and the increasing globalization of production and other value chain activities. The role of mega-suppliers has been growing during decades of outsourcing in R&D and production, leaving auto assemblers increasingly dependent on such suppliers. With suppliers investing more capital into R&D for new technology and innovation of core components, it is likely that suppliers will gain even more power over customers in the market (Foy, 2014). Another prevailing trend is collaboration between industries, that is, carmakers cooperating with suppliers in the electronics/IT industry and the chemical industry. This is attributed to the high proportion of electronics within vehicles and efforts to develop next-generation vehicles, which require automakers to not only nurture their own capabilities but also build a strategic alliance with other firms in various technology domains, such as software, semiconductors, new materials and car batteries (Mo and Park, 2013).

In response to this changing demand, Hyundai and Kia Motors have completed vertical integration along their supply chain, starting from materials, components and assembly (*Forbes Korea*, 2014). Not only have they established Hyundai Mobis (the world's sixth largest supplier by revenue), but also other specialized suppliers such as Hyundai Wia, Hyundai Powertech and Hyundai Dymos, all ranked among the top 100 global suppliers (Yonhap News, 2014). R&D activities are handled flexibly through collaboration between these subsidiaries and the assemblers. This is facilitated by emphasizing modular production, leading to improved quality, lower costs and higher productivity in the assembly process. This gives the companies relatively more power than other assemblers in handling global mega-suppliers (Jeong, 2014).

Hyundai Motor Group's car production has also expanded globally. Their production plants are located in ten different countries, strategically dispersed throughout continents. These include the USA, China, India, Brazil, Turkey, the Czech Republic, Slovakia and Russia. The establishment of overseas factories started in 1997 and gained momentum in the early 2000s, when exports and global sales skyrocketed. In 2013, Hyundai and Kia produced 7.6 million cars, with 54 per cent being produced outside South Korea (KARI, 2014). This rising offshore production is expected to continue in the near future, as indicated by planned factory expansions in China, Brazil and Mexico (Park, 2014b). At the same time, the co-location of components suppliers has become a common trend for Hyundai and Kia. First-tier and second-tier suppliers move with car manufacturers, establishing production facilities and thus forming huge production belts within an area. One notable example is the production belt in the USA, spurred by HMG across three neighbouring states – Georgia, Tennessee and Alabama – where forty-five first-tier and second-tier South Korean suppliers are currently co-located, with this number set to increase (Chae and Kim, 2014).

Looking ahead, 'eco-friendly' has been the keyword and main trend in the automobile business. Since the 1990s, the shift in R&D activities has been mainly targeted towards alternative fuel vehicles (AFVs), instead of the dominant internal combustion engine (ICE) (Sierzchula *et al.*, 2012). The development of fuel-efficient, light-weight material, eco-friendly engines and batteries has become the main criteria for 'eco-friendly' vehicles. Global brands have been experimenting with different technologies that best reflect consumers' needs (Shin, 2014). Autonomous vehicles are another trend in next-generation automobiles. Global carmakers including Hyundai Motors and IT firms such as Google have moved beyond the development and test operation stages of self-driving vehicles (Chae, 2013). Suppliers including traditional firms and IT firms are collaborating to develop new systems, software and operating systems for the cars (Park, Kang, and Mo, 2014). It is perceived, however, that Hyundai, Kia and their suppliers currently lag behind global leaders in the field of technology for next-generation vehicles and have failed to gain the attention of experts and consumers (Kim, 2014b). This suggests that, despite the recent phenomenal global success of South Korean automakers, they have once again become followers and will have to confront a rapidly changing technological and market landscape in the global auto industry, as they have done earlier in the last few decades.

Animation[5]

The animation industry in South Korea has a much longer history as an export sector than other cultural and creative sectors that the country has recently become known for, such as K-pop music and drama (Shim, 2006). From the beginning, the industry developed through close linkages with the global animation industry (Lent, 1998; Lent and Yu, 2001). South Korean animators were first engaged in animation GVCs as offshore suppliers in the late 1960s. Incremental upgrading within the labour-intensive segments of the GVCs enabled a rapid growth of animation exports to the USA, Japan and Europe (Figure 13.3). However, the geographical shift of animation GVCs and the resulting decline of Korea's outsourcing exports in the early 2000s prompted local studios to upgrade to new products like 3D computer animation as well as their own original animation by engaging more in creativity-intensive segments of the value chain. This has generated a new linkage to GVCs such as international co-production and renewed export momentum.

---

5   This section draws from the first author's research on Korea's animation industry (Lee, 2011, 2015).

Figure 13.3 South Korean animation exports, 1982–2013

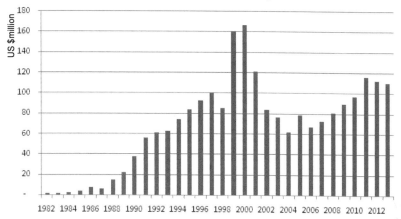

Sources: 1982–1993, Yi (1994); 1994–1996, Korea Broadcasting Development Institute (1997); 1997–2002, *White Paper on Cultural Industries*, annual volumes; 2003–10, *White Paper on the Animation Industry*, annual volumes; 2011–13, content industry statistics.

Outsourcing-based export growth without government support (1970s–90s)

From the late 1960s, South Korean animation producers began to engage as offshore outsourcing suppliers in labour-intensive, low-valued segments in GVCs driven by foreign buyers. They initially served Japanese studios. Later, they served US and European firms as they expanded outsourcing abroad. As in the clothing industry, rising wages and increased labour disputes in Hollywood throughout the 1970s prompted more American studios to contract out labour-intensive work to offshore studios in East Asia – initially Japan, followed by Taiwan, South Korea and the Philippines (Sito, 2006). In response, newly established suppliers mushroomed in these countries to take advantage of the outsourcing opportunities and lower labour costs (Lent, 2001; Yu, 1999).

Generally, animation production consists of pre-, main- and post-production. Pre-production includes creativity-intensive tasks, such as script writing and model creation. Main-production involves translating the stories and model characters onto the screen, including layout, animation, colouring, inking and composition. Lastly, post-production adds sounds and special effects onto the animation to get it ready for release (Raugust, 2004). Main-production is considered more labour-intensive than pre- or post-production. South Korean firms first assumed the most labour-intensive parts of main-production, such as colouring and inking, and gradually moved up to higher value-added activities within main-production, such as drawing key animation.

In the early years of exporting, much of the learning and skill development for such upgrading was facilitated by the presence of overseas supervisors at the supplier studios. Dispatched by foreign (mostly US) buyers to monitor the overall production process, they trained South Korean animators, who had had virtually no opportunity to get trained elsewhere as animators. These supervisors also served as 'translators' between the creators and South Korean animators, as well as the two cultures. Over time, the role of foreign supervisors in skill development gradually declined as South Korean producers and workers improved their capabilities and upgraded to more skill-intensive main-production tasks like layout and key animation.[6] In addition, skill upgrading was also facilitated by strong competition among Korean offshore suppliers. To secure lucrative orders from established foreign buyers, they were keen to attract more skilled animators, often poaching workers from competitors (Vallas, 1997).

It is notable that US and Japanese buyers had distinctive impacts on the upgrading of South Korean firms (Lee, 2011). South Korean suppliers historically specialized in any one of the two major buyer groups, and they experienced differing paces and modes of upgradation. Generally, US buyers outsourced more higher-budget projects to South Korea than Japanese counterparts. US firms also outsourced a broader range of main-production tasks, for example, the entire main-production from layout to composition. It required the supplier to have a high level of managerial capability, but also gave it more freedom in planning and managing production. In contrast, Japanese buyers exerted more direct control of the supplier's production schedule and process, utilizing the geographic proximity between the buyer and the supplier. Furthermore, Japanese studios maintained their control across main-production until more recently, limiting the scope for the offshore supplier to functionally upgrade. These differences in the type of upgrading affected the growth patterns of local suppliers: South Korean firms generally grew bigger and faster in US-led chains than in Japanese-led chains.

Overall, the animation sector in this period was driven by SMEs working for foreign buyers as OEM suppliers. Exports grew faster, by over sixteen times from $6.2 million to $100 million between 1987 and 1997, during the so-called golden age of South Korean animation exports (Vallas, 1997). However, the amount of animation exports was virtually negligible compared to other

---

6   While their presence in offshoring studios continued until the late 1990s, their presence
     was more for assuring the speed and quality of supplier production than skill training
     (Lee 2011).

manufacturing sectors, given the fact that clothing exports amounted to $19 billion in 1997 (see Figure 13.1). Due to the small size of exports, combined with the country's inclination towards manufacturing, the animation sector failed to draw attention from the government, as well as from *chaebol*s. Until the mid-1990s, the government showed little interest in animation exports, let alone in providing any support for export promotion. This was also attributed to the authoritative government's antipathy to the genres of cartoons and animation, exemplified by its characterization of them as 'social evils' that did harm to children (Hŏ, 2002). Local animation firms did not have an industry association until the mid-1990s to represent their interest. In this situation, foreign buyers played a critical role in the growth and upgrading of local suppliers.

Export crisis and upgrading to original animation (2000s–present)

The conditions surrounding the South Korean animation industry dramatically changed in the early 2000s. The most important was the rapid decline of outsourcing-based exports. As shown in Figure 13.3, South Korea's animation exports were cut by more than half in between 2000 and 2004, from $166 million to $61 million. After a brief export boom in 1999–2000, thanks to the weak post-crisis Korean won, many South Korean studios experienced a sharp decline of exports – something that was somewhat unexpected and unprepared for, even by major outsourcing suppliers (Lee, 2011).

The rapid decline of animation exports was attributed to multiple changes in the global animation industry. First, the worldwide boom in animation in the 1990s ended, which shrank the overall global demand for animation. Furthermore, a growing popularity of new entertainment media, such as video gaming and the internet, began to undermine animation markets. More importantly, in the face of rising labour costs in existing supplier bases in South Korea and Taiwan, foreign buyers increasingly shifted their offshoring destinations to lower-cost countries, such as China, India and Vietnam. Finally, the transition of many US major studios to digital 3D animation diminished the role of South Korean suppliers (who had long been famous for traditional hand-drawn 2D animation) in favour of the rising powerhouses of computer animation, such as India.

In response, South Korean animation studios pursued upgrading into higher value-added products and chain activities. Not only did they begin to work on 3D computer animation, but more producing firms reduced their work-for-hire projects for foreign buyers, shifting their focus to creating original animation. They newly assumed pre- and post-production activities, which tended to be more creativity-intensive and higher value-added, but also riskier and requiring more capital and a high-quality workforce, compared to main-production. The number of original animation titles produced by South Korean studios increased. In 2002, the overwhelming majority of exports consisted of outsourcing-based production. In 2007, nearly 50 per cent of animation production was original production, while the share of contract-based production, both for domestic and foreign markets, declined to less than 50 per cent (Table 13.1).

Table 13.1 Original and contract animation production in South Korea, selected years

Export-based (US$ '000)	1999	2002	Industry revenue-based (KRW million)	2006	2007
Original production	4,626 (2.9%)	8,173 (9.7%)	Original production	107,292 (47.2%)	137,322 (47.5%)
Outsourcing	156,185 (97.1%)	74,852 (89.2%)	Contract-based production	107,784 (47.4%)	135,025 (46.7%)
Other	-	276 (0.3%)	Other	12,197 (5.4%)	17,021 (5.8%)
Total export	160,811 (100.0%)	83,870 (100.0%)	Total industry revenue	227,173 (100.0%)	289,368 (100.0%)

Sources: 1999 – *Statistics of Cultural Industries 2000*, cited in Kang and Ch'oe (2001, 7); 2002–2004 – KOCCA (2004, 18–19); 2006 and 2007 – KOCCA (2009a, 27).

This upgrading to original production was largely driven by SMEs. They continued to play a key role as in the earlier phase, unlike in many other sectors in South Korea, which were increasingly driven by large conglomerates. However, the SMEs that drove upgrading in this period were not the same as offshore outsourcing suppliers in the earlier phase; most of them were young and established in the late 1990s and afterwards with virtually no experience in offshore outsourcing. The post-crisis start-up boom in the early 2000s attracted talented creative and business people to form or join young studios that focused on original production. For example, Iconix, now one of the leading South Korean animation studios, was spun off in 2001 from a *chaebol* to successfully produce several popular TV animation shows, including *Pororo, the Little Penguin* (2003), that churned out a number of serials and commercially successful mechanizing products. The studio does cover almost the entire value chain leading up to sales and marketing, and targets both domestic and foreign markets from the beginning of a project (Lee, 2011).

The upgrading efforts have been assisted by foreign firms, but the type of the firms was different from those of the earlier outsourcing phase. Foreign buyers, whose interest lay primarily in the quality and on-time delivery of outsourcing suppliers' work, were reluctant to assist their suppliers to upgrade functionally and create their own products – findings similar to studies about other GVCs (Bazan and Navas-Alemán, 2004). Furthermore, the new generation of South Korean studios with no outsourcing experience had little connection with foreign buyers. Instead, they began to build links with different types of foreign firms through different channels. International co-production emerged as the major outlet for their animation. It refers to a form of commercial partnership by which firms from different countries collaborate to develop, produce and distribute audio-visual products (Hubka, 2002; Strover, 1995). The partners jointly contribute money and professional services (for example, script writing and animation drawing) to a project in exchange for profits and rights (for example, distribution and merchandizing) (Raugust, 2004). By engaging in co-production with foreign studios and distributors, whose main interest lies in tapping creative and market capabilities as well as the skilled animators their international partners employ, South Korean studios can distribute their own or joint projects through prominent foreign distributors. Also, foreign partners can provide the Korean producers with creative and marketing inputs which help increase the marketability of the project in foreign markets. Finally, the Korean firms can learn from their foreign partners in the fields of creative development, marketing, distribution and other areas in which they are less capable. Therefore, international co-production has become a new springboard for South Korean studios to upgrade with their own projects (Lee, 2015).

Finally, this functional upgrading was heavily supported by the state, in stark contrast to its earlier ignorance of the animation sector. The government has significantly expanded its policy measures to support the animation industry since the late 1990s, as part of a broader government initiative to nurture globally competitive cultural and creative industries (Yim, 2002). The support focused exclusively on creating and bringing original animation to global markets. The government has helped South Korean animation studios and products increase their exposure to global markets and build relationships such as international co-production with foreign firms. It invested in public–private joint funds dedicated to fund a promising start-up project in animation. Also, a TV animation quota system was installed in 2005, which mandated TV networks to broadcast newly produced local animation for a certain amount of their airtime to expand a distribution channel for local studios (MCT, 2007).

In addition, the government signed international co-production treaties with Canada (1995), France (2006) and New Zealand (2008) (KOCCA, 2009b). Finally, the Korea Creative Content Agency (KOCCA) was established in 2001 as a government agency dedicated to cultural industries and tasked to support local firms' efforts in creative development, sales and marketing at home and abroad (MCST/KOCCA, 2008, 30–31).

Discussion

This chapter has examined the upgrading trajectories of three industries in South Korea: apparel, automobiles and animation. All these sectors exhibited dynamic growth and multiple forms of upgrading over several decades. The textile and clothing sector led the growth of South Korea's manufacturing exports in the 1970s and 1980s, generating a large number of entry-level manufacturing jobs. In the automobile sector, South Korea has become exceptional among developing countries as it established a robust domestic auto sector, which remains competitive in the global market. The animation industry illustrates the country's successful adaptation to a post-industrial economy. In all three sectors, various forms of upgrading – process, product and functional – occurred throughout the period.[7] The geographic shift of global and regional value chains, especially in apparel and animation, posed an industrial crisis, providing momentum for further upgrading. In this analysis, our findings are reflected upon, focusing on our three themes: (*a*) sectoral characteristics in upgrading paths and the relative importance of key actors, (*b*) the role of the state and (*c*) changes in post-crisis upgrading dynamics.

First, we have found the difference between process/product upgrading and functional upgrading in terms of the relative role of key actors. In all three sectors, process and product upgrading, which involves acquiring, learning and implementing key technologies regarding basic production processes and products, was a key challenge in the initial phase of development, and linkages to foreign buyers and partners appeared to be critical in this mode of upgrading. A key role of learning from buyers or 'learning-by-supplying' in the apparel sector is well known (Schmitz and Knorringa, 2000). In animation, the presence of overseas supervisors played an important role in early skill development. In

---

7   The sector cases in study here do not provide any evidence of meaningful inter-sectoral connection, at least in South Korea. Little was found regarding any significant cross-sectoral investment, ownership and upgrading between and among these three sectors.

automobiles, emphasis was placed on more formal arrangements for technology transfer, such as technical tie-ups with foreign automakers, although informal flows of information played a part as well. Regarding the role of foreign buyers, it is interesting that, in the animation industry, there was a difference between Japanese and American buyers in terms of the way they outsourced and the way they affected supplier upgrading. Functional upgrading was more facilitated in the US chains than the Japanese chains, although upgrading remained largely limited within main-production in both chains.

Functional upgrading, particularly, posed a bigger challenge to South Korean firms and the government, thus requiring greater joint efforts by the two. In apparel, localizing chemical and synthetic fibre manufacture, a big step forward for entering new product markets, was facilitated by a 'big push' by the state and big businesses, notably the Heavy and Chemical Industry Promotion Initiative, which also facilitated upgrading in the steel, petrochemical, shipbuilding and other manufacturing sectors. Also, the localization of the manufacture of key auto components and building an original domestic model required joint efforts by the government and local firms, and the rewards were considerable. South Korea's localization ratio in auto component manufacture jumped significantly since the 1970s, and the country became an exporter of assembled cars to advanced economy markets by the 1980s. Furthermore, functional upgrading requires a different form of firm capabilities from what is needed for process or product upgrading. For example, upgrading to being able to do pre- and post-production in animation required South Korean studios to hire and nurture workers with different skills (for example, computer animation), build new business contacts (for example, foreign distributors) and implement a distinctive managerial approach (for example, greater risk-taking). That is also the case for government support. Network-building has become the new centrepiece of government policies to support the upgrading of local firms to original animation producers by facilitating international co-production and overseas marketing.

Second, the South Korean state has become known for its active role in post-war industrial development with sector-specific interventions. Our cross-sectoral assessment illustrates that its role was more prominent in a larger manufacturing sector like the automotive industry, where the state was strategically involved multiple times in technological acquisition and transfer. The state also involved itself more critically in functional upgrading, which requires a greater amount of financial and technological resources and industry-wide coordinated efforts. For example, the state's push for creating heavy and chemical industries was a turning point in upgrading in textile and apparel to upstream segments like input production. However, state involvement for upgrading was virtually non-existent for most of the animation sector's high-growth era with foreign buyers and local suppliers playing a greater role.

At the same time, the role of the state has been changing over time in all three sectors. The turn to original animation shows the importance of state support. The government strategically selected the sector as one of the post-industrial sectors for its policy push in the 1990s, focusing on removing key bottlenecks for functional upgrading, such as creative development, financing, distribution and marketing. Furthermore, the government has found a new role in network-building for upgrading, as exemplified in its push for supporting globalization efforts of local producers. This growing role of the state contrasts with its diminishing role in other sectors. The government's role has become less prominent in the textile and apparel sector, partly due to the increasing delocalization of apparel production. The same applies to the auto sector but for a different reason; *chaebol*s like HMG have become capable of addressing upgrading challenges with their own resources available at home and abroad, decreasing their dependence on the state.[8]

Therefore, this chapter illustrates the Korean state's adaptability to the changing landscape of GVCs as well as the shift of the Korean economy to higher value-added activities and more technologically advanced or creativity-intensive sectors. Government policies have continued to shift their emphasis to the next big thing within and across sectors, with their role changing accordingly. However, as firms constantly confront a moving target of upgrading, so does the state. As upgrading to new products and technologies such as eco-friendly and self-driving vehicles or new functions like retail-oriented fast fashion in apparel (which are often both disruptive and innovative) becomes important for future growth in these sectors, it is posing a new challenge for policymakers to find the right role for state action.

Finally, our findings map the change in upgrading dynamics over this period. In both clothing and automotive sectors, the 1990s represent a major industrial crisis; for the former, it was caused by the rise of offshoring and factory migration to lower-cost countries, while quality problems in foreign markets posed the challenge in the latter. The situation was only intensified by the economic crisis

---

8   While not examined here, this also applies to electronics, where Samsung and LG have emerged as giant global electronics makers, with increasingly less dependence on government support in R&D and other activities.

of the late 1990s, making restructuring and upgrading in all aspects more urgent. In animation, while the crisis came a little later, it was driven by the geographical and technological shift in animation GVCs, prompting major upgrading efforts. In all three sectors, functional upgrading became a key challenge as well as a major goal. Moving into design, marketing and branding was pursued commonly in all the sectors. In addition, new technologies such as high-performing textile manufacture and 3D computer animation have to be mastered and higher quality standards have to be met to compete in global markets. South Korean firms are trying to catch up again, but in a different league.

One notable development is a shift in emphasis towards combining global and local capabilities for upgrading. For example, Hyundai and Kia have integrated their capabilities in production at home with newly acquired talent in R&D abroad to improve the quality of their products and to make their designs more attractive in global markets. At the same time, they tapped into lower-cost workforces by establishing factories in China, India and other emerging markets. The same holds true for animation. The skilled production that South Korean studios are proud of has to be combined with advanced capabilities in creative development and resources in finance and distribution to make their animation compete in global markets. International co-production has emerged as a channel to access such assets. This form of 'glocal' upgrading strategy is different from the unidirectional process of learning and absorbing foreign knowledge and technology that characterized the earlier phases of upgrading. This does not mean that local learning and innovation are no longer important; rather, finding the right mix of local and global capabilities and managing global–local linkages effectively and dynamically has become more important. This also explains why network-building has become an important task for the state in promoting upgrading in changing GVCs.

References

Amsden, Alice H. 1989. *Asia's Next Giant: South Korea and Late Industrialization.* New York: Oxford University Press.

Amsden, Alice H. and Wan-wen Chu. 2003. *Beyond Late Development: Upgrading Policies in Taiwan.* MIT Press.

Bazan, Luiza and Lizbeth Navas-Alemán. 2004. 'The Underground Revolution in the Sinos Valley: A Comparison of Upgrading in Global and National Value Chains.' In *Local Enterprises in the Global Economy: Issues of Governance and Upgrading,* edited by H. Schmitz, 110–39. Cheltenham: Elgar.

Brown, Jacob. 2012. 'The Hyundai and Kia Manifesto.' *Motor Trend*, 6 January. Accessed 6 July 2017. Available at http://www.motortrend.com/news/the-hyundai-and-kia-manifesto.

Byun, Jin-kyung. 2014. 'Fast Fashion in Full Swing [in Korean].' *SisaIN*, 3 November. Accessed 11 November 2014. Available at http://www.sisainlive.com/news/articleView.html?idxno=21648.

Caro, Felipe and Jérémie Gallien. 2009. 'Inventory Management of a Fast-Fashion Retail Network.' *Operations Research* 58 (2): 257–73.

Chae, Soohwan and Dongeun Kim. 2014. 'The Increase of 5,000 Jobs at the Largest Automobile Production Base in Southeast U.S. [in Korean].' *Maeil Business Newspaper*, 16 July. Accessed 12 August 2014. Available at http://news.mk.co.kr/newsRead.php?year=2014&no=998931.

Chae, Youngseok. 2013. 'Autonomous Automobiles: Shaking the Fundamentals of the Automobile Industry [in Korean].' *Global Auto News*, 22 February. Accessed 14 August 2014. Available at http://auto.naver.com/magazine/magazineThemeRead.nhn?seq=158.

Chang, Ha-Joon. 1993. 'The Political Economy of Industrial Policy in Korea.' *Cambridge Journal of Economics* 17 (2): 131–57.

———. 2006. *The East Asian Development Experience: The Miracle, the Crisis and the Future*. Penang and London: Zed Books and Third World Network.

Chu, Yin-wah. 2009. 'Eclipse or Reconfigured? South Korea's Developmental State and Challenges of the Global Knowledge Economy.' *Economy and Society* 38 (2): 278–303.

Collett, T. 2014. '2014 Red Dot Design Awards: Kia Soul, Hyundai Genesis, i10 and Mazda 3.' *The Motor Report*, 26 March. Accessed 16 July 2017. Available at http://www.themotorreport.com.au/58500/2014-red-dot-awards-kia-soul-hyundai-genesis-i10-and-mazda3.

Dicken, Peter. 2011. *Global Shift: Mapping the Changing Contours of the World Economy*. New York: Guilford Press.

Evans, Peter B. 1995. *Embedded Autonomy: States and Industrial Transformation*. Princeton, NJ: Princeton University Press.

Feenstra, Robert C. and Gary G. Hamilton. 2006. *Emergent Economies, Divergent Paths: Economic Organization and International Trade in South Korea and Taiwan*. New York: Cambridge University Press.

Forbes Korea. 2014. 'Global 2000: Vertical Integration as the Growth Engine [in Korean].' 23 June. Accessed 12 August 2014. Available at http://jmagazine.joins.com/forbes/view/302228?aid=302228.

Foy, Henry. 2014. 'Age of Mega Supplier Heralds Danger for Carmakers.' *Financial Times*, 18 May. Accessed 5 July 2017. Available at https://www.ft.com/content/50c272c4-dce9-11e3-ba13-00144feabdc0?mhq5j=e3.

Fröbel, Folker, Jurgen Heinrichs and Otto Kreye. 1980. *The New International Division of Labor: Structural Unemployment in Industrialised Countries and Industrialization in Developing Countries.* Cambridge: Cambridge University Press.

Gereffi, Gary. 1994. 'The Organization of Buyer-Driven Global Commodity Chains: How U.S. Retailers Shape Overseas Production Networks.' In *Commodity Chains and Global Capitalism*, edited by Gary Gereffi and M. Korzeniewicz, 95–122. Westport, CT: Greenwood Press.

———. 1999. 'International Trade and Industrial Upgrading in the Apparel Commodity Chains.' *Journal of International Economics* 48 (1): 37–70.

———. 2005. 'The Global Economy: Organization, Governance, and Development.' In *The Handbook of Economic Sociology*, 2nd Edition, edited by N. J. Smelser and R. Swedberg, 160–82. Princeton: Princeton University Press.

———. 2009. 'Development Models and Industrial Upgrading in China and Mexico.' *European Sociological Review* 25 (1): 37–51.

Gereffi, Gary and Donald L. Wyman. 1990. *Manufacturing Miracles: Paths of Industrialization in Latin America and East Asia.* Princeton, NJ: Princeton University Press.

Gereffi, Gary and Karina Fernandez-Stark. 2011. *Global Value Chain Analysis: A Primer.* Durham, NC: Center on Globalization, Governance and Competitiveness. Accessed 14 January 2015. Available at http://www.cggc.duke.edu/pdfs/2011-05-31_GVC_analysis_a_primer.pdf.

Giuliani, Elisa, Carlo Pietrobelli and Roberta Rabellotti. 2005. 'Upgrading in Global Value Chains: Lessons from Latin American Clusters.' *World Development* 33 (4): 549–73.

Hamilton, Gary G. and Gary Gereffi. 2009. 'Global Commodity Chains, Market Makers, and the Rise of Demand-Responsive Economies.' In *Frontiers of Commodity Chain Research*, edited by J. Bair, 136–61. Stanford: Stanford University Press.

Hŏ, In-uk. 2002. *Han'guk Aenimeisyŏn Yŏnghwasa [A History of Korean Animation].* Seoul: Sinhan Media.

Holstein, William J. 2013. 'Hyundai's Capabilities Play.' *Strategy and Business*, 28 February. Accessed 13 August 2014. Available at http://www.strategy-business.com/article/00162?pg=all.

Hsieh, Michelle F. 2011. 'Similar Opportunities, Different Responses: Explaining the Divergent Patterns of Development between Taiwan and South Korea.' *International Sociology* 26 (3): 364–91.

Hubka, David. 2002. 'Globalization of Cultural Production: The Transformation of Children's Animated Television, 1980 to 1995.' In *Global Culture: Media, Arts, Policy, and Globalization*, edited by D. Crane, N. Kawashima and K. Kawasaki, 233–55. New York: Routledge.

Humphrey, John and Hubert Schmitz. 2002. 'How Does Insertion in Global Value Chains Affect Upgrading in Industrial Clusters?' *Regional Studies* 36 (9): 1017–27.

Hyundai Motor Co. 2014. 'Global Networks.' Accessed 5 August 2014. Available at http://worldwide.hyundai.com/WW/Corporate/Network/GlobalNetworks/index.html.

Interbrand. 2014. 'The Best Global Brands Previous Years 2013.' Accessed 5 July 2017. Available at http://interbrand.com/best-brands/best-global-brands/previous-years/2013/.

Jeong, Gi-su. 2014. 'High Tech Modules, the Global Competitiveness of Hyundai Mobis [in Korean].' *Inews24*, 30 June. Accessed 15 August 2014. Available at http://news.inews24.com/php/news_view.php?g_serial=832028&g_menu=022100&rrf=nv.

Kalinowski, Thomas. 2008. 'Korea's Recovery since the 1997/98 Financial Crisis: The Last Stage of the Developmental State.' *New Political Economy* 13 (4): 447–62.

KAMA. 2005. *Korean Automobile Industry: 50th Anniversary History Book* [in Korean]. Seoul: Korea Automobile Manufacturers Association.

———. 2013. *Annual Report 2013: Korean Automobile Industry*. Seoul: Korea Automobile Manufacturers Association. Accessed 5 July 2017. Available at http://www.dgfez.go.kr/eng/img/download/Automotive_Industry-2.pdf .

Kang, Man-sŏk and Chong-il Ch'oe. 2001. *Kungnae Aenimeisyon Sanŏp Palchŏn Pangan Yŏn'gu [A Study of the Development Plan for Domestic Animation]*. Seoul: Han'guk Pangsong Chinhŭngwŏn.

KARI. 2014. *2014 Korean Automotive Industry*. Seoul: Korea Automotive Research Institute. Accessed 7 August 2014. Available at http://kari.hyundai.com/publish/publishDetail.do?masterId=9&no=18.

KBDI. 1997. *Aenimeisyon Sanŏp Yuksŏng Chŏngch'aek [A Policy for the Promotion of the Animation Industry]*. Seoul: Korea Broadcasting Development Institute.

Kim, Dal. 2014a. 'Ipnomics: The Number of Hyundai and Kia Motors Intellectual Property [in Korean].' *Electronic Times*, 1 October. Accessed 29 October 2014. Available at http://www.etnews.com/20141001000050.

Kim, Linsu. 1997. *Imitation to Innovation: The Dynamics of Korea's Technological Learning*. Boston: Harvard Business School Press.

Kim, Seungyong. 2014b. 'Domestic Carmakers Not Seen in the Fierce Race for Autonomous Vehicles [in Korean].' *Digital Times*, 1 January. Accessed 28 August 2014. Available at http://www.dt.co.kr/contents.html?article_no=2014010302010132614002.

KOCCA. 2004. *Taehanmin'guk Aenimeisyon Sanup Paeksŏ 2004 [White Paper on the Korean Animation Industry 2004]*. Seoul: Korea Cultural Content Agency.

———. 2009a. *2008 Aenimeisyon Sanup Paeksŏ [White Paper on the Animation Industry 2008]*. Seoul: Korea Cultural Content Agency.

————. 2009b. *Aenimeisyon Kukche Kongdong Chejak Hwalsŏnghwa Pangan Yŏn'gu* [*A Study of Promotion Policies for International Animation Coproduction*]. Seoul: Korea Creative Content Agency.

Korea Federation of Textile Industries. 2014. 'History of Textile Industries [in Korean].' Accessed 15 August 2014. Available at http://www.kofoti.or.kr/textile/history.asp.

Korea Institute for Industrial Economics and Trade. 1997. *Han'gugŭi Sanŏp: Palchŏnnyŏksawa Mirae Pijŏn* [*Industries in Korea: History of Development and Future Visions*]. Seoul: Korea Institute for Industrial Economics and Trade (KIET).

Lansbury, Russell D., Seung-Ho Kwon and Chung-Sok Suh. 2007. *The Global Korean Motor Industry: The Hyundai Motor Company's Global Strategy*. London: Routledge.

Lee, Im-ja. 2005. 'Sŏmyuk'wŏt'ŏ P'yechi Ihu Ŭilyusanŏpŭi Muyŏksŏngkwa Pyŏnhwa [Changes in the Trade Performance of the Garment Industry in the Post-MFA Era]. *KIET Sanŏpkyŏngje* [*KIET Industrial Economy*], November, 54–68. Accessed 29 July 2014. Available at http://www.kiet.re.kr/kiet_web/?sub_num=12&state=view&idx=30625.

Lee, Jae-Duk. 2012. *Economic Development Model of the Development in Skill-Intensive Textile Industry*. Seoul: Ministry of Strategy and Finance, Republic of Korea. Accessed 28 July 2014. Available at http://www.ksp.go.kr/publication/modul.jsp?syear=&sage=&skey=&stem=&stype=&pg=9&idx=37.

Lee, Joonkoo. 2010. 'Global Commodity Chains and Global Value Chains.' In *The International Studies Encyclopedia*, edited by R. A. Denemark, 2987–3006. Oxford: Wiley-Blackwell.

————. 2011. 'Animating Globalization and Development: The South Korean Animation Industry in Historical – Comparative Perspective.' PhD dissertation, Duke University. Available at http://hdl.handle.net/10161/5655.

————. 2015. 'Globalization, Upgrading and Regional Engagement: International Coproduction and the Korean Animation Industry in Asia.' In *After-Development Dynamics: South Korea's Contemporary Engagement with Asia*, edited by A. P. D'Costa, 65–84. Oxford: Oxford University Press. Available at http://hdl.handle.net/10161/5655.

Lee, Joonkoo, Jong-Cheol Kim and Jinho Lim. 2016. 'Globalization and Divergent Paths of Industrial Development: Mobile Phone Manufacturing in China, Japan, South Korea and Taiwan.' *Journal of Contemporary Asia* 46 (2): 222–46.

Lent, John A. 1998. 'The Animation Industry and Its Offshore Factories.' In *Global Productions: Labor in the Making of the Information Society*, edited by G. Sussman and J. A. Lent, 239–54. Creskill, N.J.: Hampton Press.

————. 2001. *Animation in Asia and the Pacific*. Bloomington, IN: Indiana University Press.

Lent, John A. and Kie-Un Yu. 2001. 'Korean Animation: A Short but Robust Life.' In

Animation in Asia and the Pacific, edited by J. A. Lent, 89–100. Bloomington, IN: Indiana University Press.

MCST/KOCCA. 2008. *Aenimeisyon Sanŏp Chungjanggi Palchŏn Chŏllyak Ch'ujin Hyŏnhwang Mit Bowan Kyehoek (2006–2010)* [*The Progress and Complementary Plan of the Mid- and Long-Range Development Strategy for the Animation Industry, 2006–2010*]. Seoul: Ministry of Culture, Sports, and Tourism; Korean Cultural Content Agency.

MCT. 2007. *Aenimeisyon Ch'ongryangje Punsŏk Mit Sanŏp Yuksŏng Chŏngch'aek Yŏn'gu* [*An Analysis of the Animation Quota System and a Study of Industry Promotion Policy*]. Seoul: Ministry of Culture and Tourism.

Mo, Sejun and Jaewoo Park. 2013. '2013 Global Components Competition. Seoul: Automotive Research Institute [in Korean].' Accessed 3 September 2014. Available at http://kari.hyundai.com/publish/publishDetail.do?masterId=32&no=3.

Moon, Nam-Cheol. 2003. 'Movement of Foreign Locations of Korean Textile-Clothing Industry [in Korean].' *The Geographical Journal of Korea [chirihagyŏn'gu]* 37 (4): 409–26.

Mudambi, Ram. 2008. 'Location, Control and Innovation in Knowledge-Intensive Industries.' *Journal of Economic Geography* 8 (5): 699–725.

Navas-Alemán, Lizbeth. 2011. 'The Impact of Operating in Multiple Value Chains for Upgrading: The Case of the Brazilian Furniture and Footwear Industries.' *World Development* 39 (8): 1386–97.

OICA. 2013. '2013 OICA Production Statistics. Paris: International Organization of Motor Vehicle Manufacturers (OICA).' Accessed 16 November 2014. Available at http://www.oica.net/wp-content/uploads//all-vehicles-2013.pdf.

Park, Byung-il. 2014a. 'Why Hyundai and Kia Motors Is Strong: Shaking the World with Its Core Fluid Sculpture and K-Family Look Design Concept [in Korean].' *Asia Today*, 18 July. Accessed 27 August 2014. Available at http://www.asiatoday.co.kr/view.php?key=20140717010010313.

Park, Jaewoo, Sandul Kang and Sejun Mo. 2014. *Strategy for the Development of Core Components of Adas: Software* [in Korean]. Seoul: Korea Automotive Research Institute. Accessed 10 October 2014. Available at http://kari.hyundai.com/publish/publishDetail.do?masterId=32&no=36.

Park, Soojin. 2014b. 'Hyundai's Winning Move to Build Additional Overseas Plants and Develop Eco-Friendly Vehicles [in Korean].' *The Korea Economic Daily*, 10 October. Accessed 14 November 2014. Available at http://www.hankyung.com/news/app/newsview.php?aid=2014100909951.

Pietrobelli, Carlo and Federica Saliola 2008. 'Power Relationships Along the Value Chain: Multinational Firms, Global Buyers and Performance of Local Suppliers.' *Cambridge Journal of Economics* 32 (6): 947–62.

Pirie, Iain. 2008. *The Korean Developmental State: From Dirigisme to Neo-Liberalism.* London: Routledge.

Raugust, Karen. 2004. *The Animation Business Handbook.* New York: St. Martin's Press.

Schmitz, Hubert. 2004. *Local Enterprises in the Global Economy: Issues of Governance and Upgrading.* Cheltenham: Edward Elgar.

———. 2006. 'Learning and Earning in Global Garment and Footwear Chains.' *European Journal of Development Research* 18 (4): 546–71.

Schmitz, Hubert and Peter Knorringa. 2000. 'Learning from Global Buyers.' *Journal of Development Studies* 37 (2): 177–205.

Shim, Doobo. 2006. 'Hybridity and the Rise of Korean Popular Culture in Asia.' *Media, Culture and Society* 28 (1): 25–44.

Shin, Dong-yun. 2014. 'The Keywords for Automobile Trend in the Paris Motor Show: G (Gorgeous), D (Deutschland), P (Plug in Hybrid Vehicle) [in Korean].' *Herald Economy*, 10 October 10. Accessed 12 November 2014. Available at http://news.heraldcorp.com/view.php?ud=20141006000864&md=20141009005445_BK.

Sierzchula, William, Sjoerd Bakker, Kees Maat and Bert van Wee. 2012. 'Technological Diversity of Emerging Eco-Innovations: A Case Study of the Automobile Industry.' *Journal of Cleaner Production* 37: 211–20.

Sito, Tom. 2006. *Drawing the Line: The Untold Story of the Animation Unions from Bosko to Bart Simpson.* Lexington: University Press of Kentucky.

Strover, Sharon. 1995. 'Recent Trends in Coproductions: The Demise of the National.' In *Democracy and Communication in the New Europe: Change and Continuity in East and West,* edited by F. J. Corcoran and P. Preston, 97–123. Creskill, N.J.: Hampton Press.

Tokatli, Nebahat. 2008. 'Global Sourcing: Insights from the Global Clothing Industry–the Case of Zara, a Fast Fashion Retailer.' *Journal of Economic Geography* 8 (1): 21–38.

Vallas, Milt. 1997. 'The Korean Animation Explosion.' *Animation World Magazine* 2 (6): 33–38.

Wang, Jenn-Hwan. 2007. 'From Technological Catch-up to Innovation-Based Economic Growth: South Korea and Taiwan Compared.' *Journal of Development Studies* 43 (6): 1084–104.

Wong, Joseph. 2004. 'From Learning to Creating: Biotechnology and the Postindustrial Developmental State in Korea.' *Journal of East Asian Studies* 4 (3): 491–517.

Woo-Cumings, Meredith. 1999. *The Developmental State.* Ithaca, N.Y.: Cornell University Press.

Woo, Meredith Jung-En. 2007. 'After the Miracle: Neoliberalism and Institutional Reform in East Asia.' In *Neoliberalism and Institutional Reform in East Asia,* edited by Meredith Jung-En Woo, 1–31. New York: Palgrave Macmillan.

World Bank. 1993. *The East Asian Miracle: Economic Growth and Public Policy*, New York: Oxford University Press.

Yi, Byŏng-uk. 1994. 'Manhwa Ch'aenŏl Sinsŏlŭl Wihan Ŏpkye Hyŏnhwangkwa Panghyang Mosaek [The Current State of Business and the Future Direction for New Cartoon Channels].' *Monthly Cable TV* 9 (June): 41–44.

Yim, Haksoon. 2002. 'Cultural Identity and Cultural Policy in South Korea.' *International Journal of Cultural Policy* 8 (1): 37–48.

Yonhap News. 2014. 'Hyundai Mobis, Car Parts Supplier, Ranks 6th in World.' *Yonhap News Agency*, 18 June. Accessed 10 October 2014. Available at http://english.yonhapnews.co.kr/business/2014/06/18/81/0503000000AEN2014061800370003 20F.html.

Yu, Kie-Un. 1999. 'Global Division of Cultural Labor and Korean Animation Industry.' In *Themes and Issues in Asian Cartooning: Cute, Cheap, Mad, and Sexy*, edited by J. A. Lent, 37–60. Bowling Green, OH: Bowling Green State University Popular Press.

14

Evolutionary Demand, Innovation and Development[1]

Smita Srinivas

Unconnected economic sub-systems

A characteristic of developing economies is the complex production layers that coexist, often disaggregated and disconnected from each other. Hirschman (1958) and Arthur Lewis (1954) were among the influential development economists who recognized the challenge of dispersed, isolated sectors. Their approaches were consistent with the later rise of the neo-Schumpeterian evolutionary tradition that also focuses on non-equilibrium, dynamic characteristics of production systems. These approaches include the non-traded aspects of the domestic economy which constitute heterogeneous production. While there is much written on why these coexisting and evolving systems are not easy to describe in neoclassical economics, there is still a limited body of work addressing what this dynamism means for development and the roles of states. Indeed, the open-ended and evolutionary aspects of this technological change may have been understated. What draws these different economics traditions together, however, is the importance they all placed, admittedly in very different ways, on the institutional permutations through which the sectors connect. This chapter emphasizes that the unconnected sub-systems raise at least two challenges: one, that there are many productive sub-systems within which innovation occurs and coordination is no easy task. This has been well recognized in scholarship; the second aspect, however, has not received the attention it deserves: that demand evolves in these different, inter-linked sub-systems. Determining how demand emerges is no straightforward task.

---

1   I thank Meenu Tewari, Sandip Sarkar and Dev Nathan for the invitation to submit this chapter which advances the arguments of prior writing.

While global value chains (GVCs) reflect influential changes in the production structure of industrializing economies in trade, these linkages offer some complexities and important omissions. Structurally and cognitively, the 'ends of the chain' constitute extensive networks of small firm suppliers. Even when GVCs exist or dominate, the economy may have a large un-traded component, comprising a large mix of 'informal' micro and small firms involved in both domestic and international trade, and economic activity that is characterized by piece-rate, own-account, self-employed and subsistence activities (Chen, 2005). Size is not the only qualification; the institutional contexts in which people can productively work and innovate are. How people innovate with an institutional mix that lies largely outside that favouring GVCs deserves attention (Srinivas and Sutz, 2008), and how we consider time t=0 matters in any evolution of a sub-system, even that of the now dominant GVC (see Srinivas, 2009).

Structural transformation could be characterized in several ways: a move towards greater fractions devoted to global trade; concentration of greater market share within certain sectors; and if not a reduction of the informal economy, at least greater 'formalization' emblematic in the growing size and revenues of firms; sometimes a wider tax base; and, always, some degree of movement from agriculture towards manufacturing and services. Furthermore, this is accompanied by a difference in the quality, certification and standards of exported products and services. It is a characteristic of many developing economies that a vibrant domestic trade flourishes in export products that are 'rejects', that is, which do not make the export certification or quality bar. These may include items as vastly different as garments, surgical instruments, building materials and consumer electronics. These rejected products continue to constitute a sizable fraction of domestic goods; the price differentiation in these goods and other products never intended for exports make up important affordability criteria in the domestic markets. The fact that domestic demand is high for many of these products shows us that a spectrum of possible price and quality differentiators exist, but also, in some cases, that the use of these products is quite varied. For instance, washing machines might be used in some countries to wash vegetables, and in others, automotive tires are diverted from landfills and redesigned completely into a range of further products.

To situate innovation within the industrial context requires some attention to these processes because price, quality and use differentiation tells us more about the evolution of demand. Thus, while innovation creates demand, demand creates innovation as well (see discussion in Srinivas, 2014).

Demand in economic development

The idea that economic development is a learning process is not new (Lall, 1982, 1984, 1992; Amsden, 1989; Nelson, 1993; Malerba and Nelson, 2012). Neither is the notion that a core part of this learning is the development of technological capabilities in firms. However, the emphasis on technological learning in contemporary scholarship has primarily been focused on the supply side: building these capabilities in competitive (especially international) frameworks and in deepening organizational change. Supply-side analyses have overwhelmingly driven 'catch-up' studies and comparative development scholarship. What we seem to know far less solidly is how economic development relates to the demand side.

The demand side is dynamic and uncertain; thus it is especially interesting for theory and development outcomes. Demand is not an area focused on correct pricing alone. Rather, it is an essential element of the characteristics of innovation that Schumpeter (1938) well recognized: new products, processes, markets, input sources and organizations. On the demand side, the meso and macro enquiry can be targeted towards understanding how otherwise unconnected and dispersed sectors might provide crucial signals to each other in the process of structural change. This tradition is represented most notably by Hirschman (1958) who sees the core question of economic development as a challenge of structural change where multiple sectors exist unconnected to each other. Demand between sectors in his scheme creates the knock-on effect where increasing returns become crucial, and firms and regions becomes reorganized to deal with these dynamic, non-equilibrium interlinkages.

Of course, not all sub-sectors come into the world fully formed, and it is the *dynamic* of demand formation *and* sector build-out and connections that constitutes the terrain of what we classify as economic development. GVCs are notably one such crucial inter-linkage within and across sub-sectors, but they do not constitute the full dynamic of development. From an evolutionary and systemic standpoint, we can view economic development as the coordination and legitimacy of multiple market and non-market institutions, specifically focused on advancing technological change and innovation (Nelson, 2005; Srinivas, 2009, 2012). Technological change is equally central to the way in which the state evolves and learns alongside firms. These multiple coexisting channels of production and innovation leave some stark choices for development plans and policies. If the primary task is coordination between these different production and innovation supply sub-systems, what types of responses to demand shape the learning and consequently the productivity of sectors, allowing the possibility of knock-on effects between sectors?

The emphasis on the non-equilibrium, dynamic attributes of demand in dispersed sectors has an important micro-tradition visible in the work of Hirschman, Lewis and several other industry sector specialists. Many *dirigiste* economists such as Amsden (1989) emphasized targeting as a way to move past the multiple coexisting sectors, converting the developmental question into one primarily of an industrial policy focused on manufacturing. But beyond this earlier agenda of development economics and political economy, the Schumpeterian, evolutionary approaches have demonstrated the difficult open-ended policy questions centred on innovation and technical change, with special attention to unexpected ways in which institutional change occurs and the economy evolves over time (examples include Pasinetti, 1981; Nelson, 1993; Lundvall, 1992; Metcalfe, 1998, 2007). Although many neo-Schumpeterian and evolutionary economics approaches have been less concerned with developing economies, there are important strands of scholarship linking the traditions. Srinivas (2012) analyses technological capabilities in the health industry using multiple countries as examples, underscoring the fundamental industrial and health policy dilemmas of the state to legitimize, create and balance multiple and successive markets towards some semblance of coordination between production, demand and delivery capabilities (see also Chataway and Smith, 2006; Chataway *et al.*, 2014; Mackintosh *et al.*, 2016). Moreover, the neo-Schumpeterians pay closer attention to technological learning within firms, and the non-equilibrium, dynamic feedback loops within firms to other organizations. A sub-set focus on the challenges of coordinating policy shifts that connect innovation and industrial policies with social policies, driven by interests in addressing inequality through the deliberate inclusion agenda of welfare states (Arocena and Sutz, 2010; Albuquerque, 2007; Srinivas, 2009, 2012). These various approaches to analysing co-evolving sub-systems recognizes to varying degrees that production constitutes only one element of a wider evolutionary scholarship on the endogeneity of technical change and the origin and evolution of preferences (Metcalfe, 1998). The states 'co-ordination' economy, therefore, is hardly a 'command and control' one – rather, it is a complex regulatory process where political legitimacy and information problems exist, and through which an institutional menagerie has to be juggled over time (Srinivas, 2012). Sub-systems of demand and delivery must evolve alongside production capabilities (Srinivas, 2012, 8) This coordination is a fundamentally non-equilibrium process, packaged with value-propositions of plans and power that usually remain hidden from public scrutiny. These values regarding the means and ends of innovation and dynamic productive systems are expressed unevenly in scholarly sub-traditions of neo-Schumpeterian, evolutionary analysis (Papaioannou and Srinivas, 2016).

It is worth emphasizing that, even within the 'developmental' end of evolutionary analysis, scholars emphasize quite different aspects that connect production and innovation to demand: in some (Albuquerque, 2007; Srinivas, 2009, 2012; Arocena and Sutz, 2010), the challenge lies in reconciling industrial priorities of knowledge with social policies or welfare states. Alternately, Pasinetti's (1981) demand can be dealt with at the micro level of preferences but as with Hirschman, focused at the meso level where the knock-on effects of price differences and differential demand between sectors becomes important. Demand can also be framed as the consumption question of different income elasticities of demand so that sectors evolve differently (Metcalfe, 2007, 113). This approach is closer to the ways in which Hirschman connects structural change to disparate industrial sectors and whose 'forward–backward' linkages provide the growth dynamism required to propel the economy. Both studies focused on specific industry sectors and those on more generalized, meso-level evolutionary dynamics are consistent with those on structural change through the 'long wave' (Perez, 1983, 1985).

Of course, industry sector studies provide special vantage points into this debate because the way the state governs technological change and the evolution of demand in individual industry sectors is not straightforward. For instance, in the health industry, Srinivas (2012) demonstrates the state's challenges in reconciling or managing the dimensions of consumption and delivery in the health industry, even when its supply is highly successful. It is tempting, of course, to narrowly approach demand in such industry studies and divide up the world of GVCs into the health, automotive, garments, renewable energy, coal and computer sectors, but this would be a mistake. Individual sector studies have often split the economic world into exports versus domestic demand and narrated national successes through a story of import-substitution versus export-driven industrial development. However, various industry studies in the neo-Schumpeterian and evolutionary traditions offer other useful viewpoints on development and structural change. Dutrenit and Katz (2005) highlight the enduring challenges for several Latin American economies in domestic institutional design even where substantial export sector gains have occurred; Mackintosh et al. (2016) show how technological capabilities in several African health industries have generated substantial gaps in dealing with domestic demand. Srinivas (2012, 8) forces us to an even longer timeline of intervention where case studies involving different countries can be contrasted. In the institutional triad of production, consumption and delivery of one industry, the separate institutional 'axes' of the triad can be seen as industrial sectors in their own right. Rather than being subservient to 'production' (manufacturing in its narrowest sense) demand generates its own manufacturing and service sub-sectors, for example, insurance, information and communication technologies (ICTs), logistics, trucking, cold chain, advertising, and so on.

Thus the interdependency of productivity rates between sectors can be seen under the umbrella of single industry studies as well. The tradition of scholarship of the supply-side industrial production narrative is just one element of a complex, mutually reinforcing or disintegrating economic dynamic. The advantage of the single-industry, multiple subsector, analysis in the evolutionary tradition is that an autarkic model is unnecessary: foreign demand is easily incorporated. For example, over time, domestic health firms may increasingly rely on the procurement and delivery capacities of foreign welfare states (Srinivas, 2006, 2012; Albuquerque, 2007). Similarly, experimentation, failure, selection and other aspects of institutional design can be incorporated without resorting to a crude biological analogy of evolution.

Analytically speaking, however, one of the challenges is to understand if and how micro-level case studies of individual products, firms or even industry structures can be connected with macro-level analyses of the effects of demand (such as Keynes or Kaldor). Demand is necessarily evolutionary in scope because the fundamental emphasis is on how individual preferences, inter-sector dynamics and instituted economic coordination all reflect the different scales and governance institutions of the economy. Hirschman (1958), in the tradition of regional economics, resolved some of the conceptual questions of increasing returns and forward–backward linkages, but not necessarily the methodological challenges of the micro- and meso-scales of industry analysis. This gap makes using Hirschman's work more challenging when trying to understand technological change and learning in regional development. More productively perhaps, some evolutionary economists have developed analytical models to understand open-ended growth by making assumptions that the growth of capacity within the sector matches the growth of demand (for example, Metcalfe, 2007). This permits increasing returns, creating a situation where the productivity growth between sectors becomes mutually interdependent (see also Young, 1928).

Framing domestic demand

Naturally, the question of 'underdevelopment' is not neatly resolved through demand and market-facing instruments alone, but calls on political economy to explain the governing abilities and priorities of the state. We might argue that it is precisely this inability to govern the institutional mix that politically defines 'underdevelopment'. This reflects the Latin American structuralists' scepticism that market demand, even robust export demand, would resolve the considerable challenges of economic transformation and inequality. This scepticism had both structural and institutional roots: structural because industrial policies were presumed biased towards satisfying the domestic demand of elites who emulated the consumption patterns of industrialized economies. It also reflects a scepticism about institutional capacity that even if the state were to be the final arbiter of appropriate consumption patterns, it would require politicians and bureaucrats to alienate those with deep pockets and take the side of those without. This scepticism regarding the ability/willingness of the state (including the judiciary and bureaucracy) to side with the economically and politically disenfranchised extends from Latin American to South Asian development scholarship. While this type of structural and institutional bias towards demand is quite familiar in scholarship on structuralism, there has been far less attention to how demand emerges in the process of technological innovation itself. This is worrying because the domestic political question continues to loom large in industrially heterogeneous economies (Dutrenit and Katz, 2005), and because technical and organizational capabilities are crucial in firms as well as for capable bureaucrats at regional and municipal levels (Cassiolato *et al.*, 2002). Yet development-generating innovations require experimentation, demonstration pilots, scale-up and testing, all of which require governance norms and state strategies, which are absent.

The debate of innovations being 'inclusive' must therefore be positioned not merely in the context of the state's selective exercise of power, but whether innovation itself emerges in novel ways in specific structural and cognitive conditions. Problematically, 'inclusion' has come to mean a confusion of several normative developmental expectations – from products that are better suited to certain populations, more affordable innovations, innovations that include wider classes of people, innovations that can reach more individuals and groups even at the same price, and innovations that include populations within the developing economies (especially those that are industrializing) which are not the focus of industrialized nations. In other words, inclusion has been taken into the realms of price, new population groups, different geographies, better logistics and more adaptable design.

This attention to the equitable outcomes of innovation is understandable. In part this is perhaps a delayed response concern of equity in Schumpeterian terms (see Papaioannou and Srinivas, 2016). Furthermore, terminology can add to the confusion: some of the debates deploy the terms 'frugal', 'scarcity-induced', 'resource-constrained', 'appropriate', or 'inexpensive', or 'bottom of the pyramid' (BoP) as if they are synonymous. This would be unhelpful because these diverse innovation frameworks make strong and often conflicting assumptions about innovation and production's relationships to demand. For instance, the BoP approach may be seen as assuming willingness to pay 'at the bottom', that is, an unmet demand, while 'scarcity induced innovation' is agnostic about where the demand might come from, not focusing on cheap products or low-income customers, but rather, problem-framing for local contexts through which new customers might be found (low- or high-income), and where new markets (domestic or overseas) might emerge. Thus, while the BoP sees a large demand through low-income consumers, scarcity-induced innovation is agnostic on price, concerned with customization and neglected groups who may nevertheless constitute a large potential demand.

Furthermore, beyond the noticeably important differences in these 'inclusive' debates about innovation are strong development differences about the relationship of innovation to industrial transformation itself. The traditional science and technology policy, 'appropriate technology' and 'scarcity-induced innovation' approaches are all fundamentally concerned with structural transformation but have different emphases regarding the scale and pace of technological learning, and the role of state and lead (often large) firms in economic development. The cost of products per se is not the prime consideration for demand, except for approaches that emphasize the buying power of welfare states in basic needs, affordability concerns and the impact of welfare states on structural transformation. Consequently, 'inclusive' debates about innovation can be typified by their approaches to needs and demand, and to structural transformation. These differences are reflections on the challenges of framing innovation and their developmental benefits within the context of wider production systems. Furthermore, because innovation provides a vital dynamic of industrial production, we would need to enquire whether or not the technological capabilities and learning involved in such innovative processes are domestically circumscribed in any way or freely available across national boundaries through specific types of privileged firms.

If we are to enquire a little further, we would see several dynamics in play. Innovation creates new demand which increases productivity that in turn generates process innovations. These process innovations embody technical advances in new capital equipment, generating a wave of demand because the old capital is now obsolete. New entrepreneurs take up and utilize these innovations in further experimentation and deployment. Relative profits stimulate investment, and a Kaleckian 'adaptation mechanism' is the supply of innovations in the face of effective demand from entrepreneurs and firms. If Schumpeter can be seen to represent the supply side story, then Kalecki represents the conversion to the demand side (Kalecki, 1968; see also Rothbert, 1942; Courvisanos, 2009).

As individual consumers can express their preferences for specific products and processes, so can firms. Schmookler (1966) hypothesized that market size induces process innovations more than product innovations, while other scholars have emphasized that the engagement of specific users generates product innovations (Myers and Marquis, 1969; Von Hippel, 2005; Fontana and Guerzoni, 2008).

While innovation creates demand and, in turn, demand creates innovation, the mismatch between demand and innovation offers a clear institutional path for policy and planning. Several actors then attempt to realize economies of scale and establish competitive advantages through first mover strategies by investing in technological learning. Specific industrial policy instruments can consequently play a crucial role in establishing the importance of the market's size (especially domestic market size) for the benefit of firms. These instruments may include setting technical standards requirements for products and processes, and establishing market size and scope through preferred procurement for those firms satisfying such requirements. This process of establishing the contours of market size is hardly an inevitable 'natural' process, but one deeply politically embedded in the culture of state intervention, and the legitimacy and extent of market intervention. These are framed in every nation by the political context in which such intervention is deemed in the public interest and, of course, the capabilities of local firms (foreign-owned or indigenous) to respond. These types of political legitimacy as well as caution and influence by the state is inevitably rationalized in rhetoric on various grounds: affordability, skills-building, quality and access, supply-side efficiencies, international competitiveness, or even national pride. One might argue that the late industrializing state's vital economic and political function is precisely to convert effective demand and market size into competitive advantages while responding to essential domestic needs to different degrees (2014, 89). Technological advances per se are therefore not evidence of development in this wider sense.

The extent of public intervention depends both on the political rationale for involvement as well as the economic mechanisms through which such involvement can grow sustainably. States, markets and other institutions determine the improvement access and inclusion through a range of demand measures from lowering costs and raising incomes to widening the range of access channels (Srinivas, 2014, 90). This is where economic and social policy has become closely intertwined and areas such as health, water, food and energy become a means of both industrial and social policy interventions (see also Albuquerque, 2007; Arocena and Sutz, 2010). Furthermore, increased consumption can occur through higher productivity rates, which in the best of worlds reflect higher wages and therefore greater demand. More promisingly, sustained social policy can raise real income more directly. Rising wages and incomes are not the only ways in which access to innovations increases; fundamental rights may do the same, making it possible to increase access, if not the ability or willingness to pay. The process of urbanization can also increase the effective demand and the importance of state intervention in a range of ways, both through industrial as well as social policy interventions (Srinivas, 2014). State-legitimized investments can create urban and regional demand opportunities and also foster monopolies with high windfall profits. Entrepreneurs, innovators and financiers are attracted by this type of widespread public intervention and by the social legitimacy and marketing claims they can make in the name of public benefit. Examples from across the industrialized and industrializing world's history exist in sectors such as urban electricity, construction and real estate, as well as water and sanitation (Hughes, 1993a, 1993b; Reddy, 2004).

Demand and the cognitive frames of problem-framing

As mentioned earlier, the reason demand is so crucial is that innovation simultaneously involves both cognitive and structural frames through which the world is filtered. Srinivas and Sutz (2008) consider this mix of cognitive and structural elements as providing the conceptual basis for splitting the world of innovation into four quadrants that connect the industrializing (Developing Countries, DC) and industrialized economies (Advanced Industrial Countries, AIC) (see extensive discussion in Srinivas, 2009, 2014). The axes of Figure 14.1

denote the location (DCs, AICs) where the problems are framed and efforts expended (searched or found innovations). For instance, a problem may exist in a developing country, but the firms (or governments) of advance industrial economies may be impervious to this problem in both cognitive terms (the problem effectively is absent in their world) and structural terms (the demand for such products is irrelevant because no export market exists). Thus, some classes of problems in developing countries require firms that will expend suitable effort, and institutional conditions such that markets for such products can develop over time.

Figure 14.1 A taxonomy of innovation in developing countries

	Problems for which solutions have been found in AICs	Problems for which solutions have not been searched or found in AICs
Problems for which solutions suitable for DCs conditions exist	The vast majority of solutions acquired through technology transfer	Solutions to problems mainly posed in DCs and developed locally
Problems for which solutions suitable for DCs conditions do not exist	'Canonical' solutions exist, but for different scarcity reasons they are not suitable for DCs conditions	No solutions (yet) Typically health issues like vaccines against cholera of AIDS

Source: Srinivas and Sutz (2008, 136).

The four quadrants differentiate, as the structuralists hypothesized, the world of industrializing and industrialized economies, and their interactions. However, the four quadrants also differentiate interactions of the two types of economies not merely in terms of trade (with which the structuralists and *dependistas* were concerned) but in the cognitive mix of 'make or buy' options in which some technological innovations are solutions to problems framed and solved locally, while others are not. Thus, this heuristic offers a mechanism to explore why and how national environments reward certain types of domestic problem-framing and problem-solving through technological innovation. These four quadrants create a taxonomy of innovation in which some types of structure and cognition priorities are recognized and rewarded through policy and plans, and others quite dramatically sidelined.

Furthermore, the four quadrants together offer separate demand prospects for generating greater numbers of economic participants and signalling new consumers, products and processes. Beyond prices, a range of other institutional options – including champions, prizes or other incentives – become more visible to signal and reward innovations. For example, there is no *a priori* role for individual or institutional actors in innovation. The histories of antibiotics, vaccines, water filtration systems, prosthetics, electricity supply, and ecological and housing mechanisms across history has shown us all ways that different actors make the institutional system come alive (see discussion in Srinivas, 2014).

In some product categories, firms participate in complex traded encounters with lead firms which are located in other countries. When this dynamic is strong, the upper left-hand quadrant dominates economic priorities. In this case, the policy challenge is the degree to which the government's control and incentives are agile enough to respond to firms that drive specific technological innovation imperatives. Lead firms may mould incentives and pressures 'within the chain', and the incentives provided by government (unless a public sector firm is in the lead) may not have the intended effect. On the other hand, if the government's role is to ensure that firms steer their priorities towards domestic needs which are not reflected in effective demand, specific industrial instruments such as fiscal incentives, procurement, selected patent protections and privileged market access can signal demand to make lead firms or dominant suppliers adjust their strategies. The history of innovation tells us that such institutional nudging of policy incentives, from recognizing need to building effective demand, can be initiated by the state, non-state actors and firms themselves. Firms may use traditional research and development (R&D) departments or 'external' foundations, think-tanks or other mechanisms to identify future demand segments and the means to build this demand.

The evolution of need to demand

Because the four quadrants are closely tied together, even if some are policy pariahs, coordinating their relative effects is the main challenge of policy design and planning processes. Although the upper left-hand quadrant grows and thrives through global inter-linkages, it represents only a portion of demand and mostly ignores the cognitive challenge of steering education, training and industrial policies towards honing problem-framing and problem-solving skills. The quadrants in Figure 14.1 are institutionally and geographically connected in multiple ways, making it all the more critical for articulated policy priorities and timeline for intervention. An evolutionary approach to demand is far from a linear progression, and it allows for open-ended outcomes, with non-equilibrium behaviour of sectors where no 'stages' exist. In Figure 14.2 below, a simple heuristic can display unrecognized need, followed by recognized need, (effective) demand and unfulfilled demand. The parentheses between these categories remind us that evolution is open-ended, not stages of inevitable progression from left to right, and the mechanisms between these are still questionable.

Figure 14.2 The evolution of demand

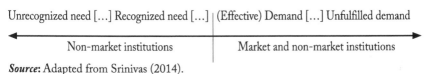

Unrecognized need [...] Recognized need [...] | (Effective) Demand [...] Unfulfilled demand

Non-market institutions   Market and non-market institutions

Source: Adapted from Srinivas (2014).

Arguably, needs which are subjective, socially circumscribed and politically defined are largely situated within the sphere of non-market institutions, while potential demand – when needs are 'converted' by institutional design – is situated within the realm of both markets and non-market institutions. For instance, the effects of advertising, social customs and election outcomes (and not prices alone) might change effective demand. The degree to which markets and firms respond to effective demand gives us the remainder, that is, unfulfilled demand at the right end of the spectrum.

If we think in terms of agents and politics, the spectrum between left and right offers the opportunity for different organizations and interventions to mediate the relationships between (mostly invisible) needs and those needs that they recognize. Policy, after all, is an important institutional market for transforming some needs into recognized categories to which the state responds. Similarly, crossing the threshold from need to demand is an institutional barrier that may be hugely assisted or stymied by the state, but often requires active organizations and institutional experimentation. Note that the spectrum on the left or right sides says nothing about actors, efficiency or time. Inclusion/exclusion challenges can be found all along it, even though the preponderance of low-income challenges lies in the left half in the ambit of non-market institutions. The figure raises some questions of what 'inclusive innovation' means. It should be clear that these four points along the spectrum reflect different institutional design opportunities for inclusion, and different degrees to which market instruments can be effective. We can see that along the spectrum also lies the social challenge (agents, politics) of recognized need and the difficulty of converting unrecognized needs to recognized needs. The recognition of needs by state or non-state agents hardly guarantees that those needs are met, but it may nevertheless help converting to and meeting the demand. The evolutionary dynamic is necessarily politically constituted and may never easily convert into market-facing demand or provide any reassurance that such demand will in fact be fulfilled. However, the heuristic displays how the willingness to pay and affordability considerations remain only one of several criteria by which technological innovations come into being, and one of several dynamic processes through which demand is expressed.

The agents matter. Not-for-profit organizations, business firms, religious, spiritual or civic associations, third-party monitoring and the state can all play important roles in ensuring different forms of recognition and legitimacy of needs and in building demand. Equally, responding to demand can occur in a multitude of ways, not only through market mechanisms. My past research found that in the case of vaccines, a special type of product and nuanced public good, there was only one instance where a non-profit organization decisively shaped and legitimized the R&D and manufacture of a vaccine over time. This was the case of the March of Dimes which drove the R&D and licensing of a polio vaccine. In every other instance, the public sector played a decisive role. The state, and, in many instances, either public firms or the army, proved instrumental in the creation of vaccines. Even where private firms played active roles, the public role remained pivotal (Wilson, Post and Srinivas, 2007, 20, 46–47.) Today there exist more consortia-style hybrid organizations (for example, IAVI, GAVI) which traverse the traditional public and private divide involved in vaccine development, recognizing that mixed models offer some advantages such as enhanced revenues, testing, infrastructure, the ability to include 'orphan' products and wider regulatory oversight. The state has usually been at the heart of converting recognized need to effective demand, not through individual consumption (because vaccines are heavily subsidized or often free) but through the state's strategic industrial policy instruments such as procurement, or through social policy and welfare state buying. In most product innovations, a range of organizations including non-governmental organizations (NGOs) and unions may create the momentum from unrecognized to recognized need, but a non-state actor can rarely amass the momentum and appropriate fiscal (or other demand) instruments to convert this into market demand.

The Jaipur Foot prosthetic offers another example of a non-state, charitable organization, the Bhagwan Mahaveer Viklang Sahayata Samiti (BMVSS), that intervened to first clarify the prosthetic needs that existed. It took the BMVSS enormous effort to differentiate the potential scale and diversity of need, the market-facing exercise to situate demand, the explorations into subsidizing their in-house learning to improve products, the identification of new needs, and eventually the creation and legitimization of a subsidized and rapidly growing global marketplace for prosthetic products. Neither state nor private firms played an important role until newer R&D collaborations. In contrast, such prosthetics-enhancing roles for the state have existed in other countries, notably in the USA, Canada and western and northern Europe. These involve measures such as making the urban built environment more disability-friendly, and insurance provisions making it easier to afford and use prosthetics. War-recovery zones which require prosthetics do show some variation in their state-led responses, but the BMVSS is arguably the organization that truly clarified needs, demand and set the relevant global market formation in motion. In the prosthetics case, there is vast unfulfilled demand that remains, requiring a much wider ecosystem of organizations and policy experimentation. We might term this a new type of industrial targeting and demonstration. Indeed, as part of the wider evolutionary attributes of policymaking, we can see the spectrum as a new type of what has been termed 'evolutionary targeting' (Avnimelech and Teubal, 2009).

In the context of urban electricity, the stories of Mysore state and the state of New York are extremely different. Even though the Indian state might have been arguably more progressive in attempting to extend electricity to the masses and to Kolar gold mines (Reddy, 2004), in New York, with similar technologies and protagonists, government and firms (led by Edison) focused not on 'inclusive' electrification for low-income housing, but rather on the commercial use of electrical lights for street lighting and entertainment. The rollout of electricity to New York low-income tenement housing came later (Hughes, 1993a, 1993b).

Therefore, although the state in many nations has successfully boosted many aspects of technological innovation (pharmaceuticals, seeds, building materials, post-harvest storage, solar panels), it has been unevenly able to sustain the innovation objectives and industrial policy clarity towards widespread problem-framing and adaptation of firms . While in sectors such as water, sanitation and transportation facilities, states have arguably been quite successful in leading with a 'light touch' to public benefit, the challenges in energy or agriculture also require 'crowding in' private firms and not-for-profit organizations. Problems of coordination across sectors, agents and organizations create political opportunities as well as dilemmas for the state. For instance, in urban sanitation and water purification, decentralized solutions are increasingly required along centralized infrastructure and capabilities. Similar mix-and-match combinations of actors are evident in education, health services and delivery, agriculture, pharmaceuticals, water and sanitation, and energy innovation (see various authors in Ramani, 2015).

Non-market institutions often emerge to respond to these complexities of market organization. Lobbying becomes an obvious form of perverse rent-seeking to ensure the shift of governmental priorities. The move from recognized need to effective demand can also institutionalize time delays or regressive relationships. For example, the later the state recognizes public health priorities, the faster firms can work to expand the effective demand for tobacco. Inversely, tobacco advertising identifies 'unrecognized need' among teen smokers, converting this population group to adult smokers (effective, growing demand). Export demand also acts to convert unrecognized need (in this case untapped foreign needs) into effective demand (domestic and foreign). GVCs in tobacco, automobiles, garments or leather products thus require different governance mechanisms regulating the product design and industrial goals. In Srinivas and Sutz's (2008) scheme, policy design represents the continued pressures and attractions to innovators of the upper left-hand quadrant (GVCs) relative to others.

The institutional characteristics of this GVC quadrant are distinct and powerful in economic terms, linking to other types of innovation through various dynamics: lead firms exert powerful influences from their home country markets; the science and technology policy design required for this quadrant seemingly limits the existing R&D structure and the priorities of large and mid-size business firms; the technology intensity of innovations in this GVC-led quadrant in developing economies may be similar to those in industrialized contexts; and specific product and process innovations in this quadrant reflect various social aspirations (the dependency scholars might have flagged this as well: better cars, better consumer electronics, more fashionable clothes and accessories, better housing, and so on). Perhaps, most importantly, this quadrant reflects the familiar form of global economic integration, that is, traded links to firms overseas and consumption patterns that are now firmly ingrained in our social psyche through global mimicry and organization efficiencies. In turn, these processes are identified with administrative and planning procedures across ministries such as industry and commerce, trade, external affairs, labour, or science and technology.

In sharp contrast, the off-diagonal quadrants (for example, the Hib vaccine from Cuba) reflect 'idiosyncratic', 'non-canonical' forms of problem-framing and solutions originating in non-industrial, often differentiated, local contexts (Srinivas and Sutz, 2008). Not only are these different from the characteristics of the upper left-hand quadrant, but sometimes these can also become global markets by solving an intractable problem whose solution now travels well into those other contexts that might not otherwise have invested the efforts in such a product or process. Ironically, these innovations, innovative precisely because they are able to work through complex institutional and resource constraints, offer a different cognitive and structural model of innovation ('scarcity-led'). Yet these tend to be crowded out or practically invisible in policy circles (the Cuban Hib vaccine is a happy science and policy exception because of the formidable extant costs of the incumbent vaccine).

The political economy challenge, therefore, is one of transition from different paradigms reflected in the four quadrants and towards integrating the quadrants more closely and deepening the institutional strengths of each. Coexistence of these innovation worlds, however, is no ideal solution. The bridging between quadrants does not occur easily because technological choices reflect the entrenched political challenges of redistribution within economic paths (Kaplinsky, 2011); substantial policy inertia remains in each within which innovators and financiers must take risks. Even GVCs are not exempt from this uncertainty. GVCs may well have 'innovation under the radar' (Kaplinsky, 2011), but there are undoubtedly challenges at the 'end of chain' stage to induce and support innovation in small firms. The greater the attention to GVCs as the primary form of development, the more challenging it is to find other ways (quadrants) in the innovation debate towards alternate markets, product differentiation, pricing and infrastructure strategies. Can GVCs integrated with a wide range of idiosyncratic and non-canonical innovations and take us to a different development paradigm?

The contrast is worth emphasizing in individual industry sectors where traded and non-traded products coexist. For example, certain tools in the construction industry may be geared towards micro- and small-firm segments as well as to domestic trade. A polisher may use an important piece of equipment which is available at a lower price, but may also have access to cheaper, more ubiquitous or customized polishing instruments in the domestic market. Similarly, export rejects have quite innovatively adapted to the local market, reigning supreme because they may have failed to meet export criteria for a range of reasons with fewer consequences domestically (technical standards and testing, just-in-time production, labelling, different safety standards, and so on). Off-diagonal elements in Srinivas and Sutz's (2008) dynamic of Figure 14.1 focus on a specific local challenge of coexistence and integration – the struggle to scale up. The problem is not technological innovation per se, which does emerge, but on their permeability within the industrial economy. The Cuban Hib vaccine bucked this trend. It offered a scientific and technological innovation that not only framed and solved a critical health challenge, but in doing so was able to restructure the global market beyond Cuba for such vaccines. It offered both a domestic and global solution to a problem with different pricing and availability criteria defined by public health goals. Similarly, private-sector-led public benefits are generated by water filtration products sold at different prices and geographies with the necessary design for the availability of clean water.

Development plans: Coordinating multiple production and innovation sub-systems

As stated here, the political economy challenge for technological innovation is not so much that many different systems exist alongside in a complex economy, but that planning processes and policy design often privilege some types of innovation over others, thus relegating specific forms of learning and institutional design to secondary policy priority. The point made by Srinivas and Sutz (2008) is that the dominant policy model is to recognize innovation and industrial processes that are characterized by GVCs in the upper left-hand quadrant (see Figure 14.1). Similarly, Figure 14.2 implies that more attention needs to be paid to the creation and active facilitation of demand by diverse agents that can undergird the quadrants of Figure 14.1. Industrial policies and innovation policies within wider development plans (not command and control, but a guidance and incentive structure) can have enormous benefits for pushing more learning in firms and other organizations. One can go further to state that experimenting with demand evolution and the coexisting of different types of innovation worlds should constitute a vital element of industrial policy and planning. These may include the specifics of design to encourage innovation, from the use of bulk procurement in agencies to the deployment of subsidies for boosting individual consumption of specific products, or by studying and incorporating lead user improvements for essential goods and services. Without this, neither the scaling up of innovations nor the benefits of full use of the domestic market are achieved.

This evolutionary approach can be seen in the long-term evolution of industry sectors, but might also be the basis of experimentation and divergent paths in industrial policies.

This experimentation is vital because, as the figures indicate, no one-size-fits-all planning process or policy design is possible. On a case-by-case basis from health to electricity, water to transport, one can analyse relationships from need (both unrecognized and recognized) to demand (met and unmet). The story of individual protagonists often goes hidden in providing institutional vision and leadership. These individuals may not be scientists or 'star' innovators. For instance, in the case of the Jaipur Foot, although the individuals may be important, the organizational leadership of BMVSS has to be noted in changing the way in which prosthetics were perceived. Even in New York's electrification and that of Mysore state the role of the public and private sector was vital but hardly predictable. In New York, Edison combined his technical skills with business acumen to highlight viable business models already existing in gasworks to illustrate how his own lighting system might revolutionize cities (Basalla, 1988, 47). At the time of his intervention, alternate lighting systems existed in Europe and the USA: one generated by central gasworks underground, another through electric arc lighting, which, in serial connections, meant that lighting in public places could only be turned on or off together, allowing for no individual lighting. Edison's genius was not narrowly technical; he highlighted the pollution and disadvantages generated by gas lighting *and* arc lighting while simultaneously advancing his own unit-based light system innovations as a remedy for both private and commercial use. Simultaneously, recognizing their continued and perhaps inevitable coexistence, he made his own system malleable enough to mimic and comply with gas industry statutes and regulation. Similarly, he included several measures: the strategic use of light meters, analogous to gas meters, using terminology for electricity systems mimicking that of the gas industry, underground workings, and compatibility with gas powered motoring created a selective and modified component system, while he '[...] constantly kept the technology and economics of gas lighting in mind' (Basalla, 1988, 49).

Therefore, from a philosophical standpoint, while discontinuity and individual genius often appear to be attractive explanations for technological change, in reality, a much more evolutionary hypothesis is strengthened by closer case analysis. As Srinivas (2012) indicates, in the health industry, the nemesis of states is the 'market menagerie' of managing multiple coexisting institutions representing innovation in the spheres of production, consumption or delivery. The evolutionary and co-evolutionary perspective reminds us that few countries succeed in this juggling act or for any length of time. At best, the state may be selectively able to act as the lead user, procurer or other legitimizing protagonist, but this role is rarely sustainable over time. Technological advances also mean that alternative problem-framing and problem-solving modes ('idiosyncratic, non-canonical', see Srinivas and Sutz, 2008) may pop up over time, yet be far less integrated with other policies and production systems in which global production networks may be the more easily recognizable and dominant economic reward system. The more GVCs dominate, the higher the odds will be against alternate approaches to innovation. Mergers and acquisitions can be a response to shifting policy and consumer demand over time, making it more likely that 'mainstream' products give way to idiosyncratic ones, and firms make and buy to adapt to demand (for example, consumer product firms invest in former 'NGO' products such as prosthetics and solar lighting; firms create new product features (washing machines having a 'grey water' mode or modifications so that they can wash vegetables), or meat and dairy conglomerates start producing or increasing their vegan products. What was earlier external competition is now internalized.

If indeed innovation is not invention but the adaptation of products and processes in new markets and organizational systems, then the divorce of in-country innovation sub-systems from each other through an insulated coexistence signals deep structural schisms. While some scholars (for example, Schumacher and Furtado) and nationalists (Gandhi) have cautioned against 'big' production for a range of different reasons (appropriate scale, skewed elitist demand, meaning and skills), the emphasis remains far more on the importance of integration of different developmental engines which the different productive capacities and scales represent.

In an earlier piece of writing (2014), I likened the spectrum of Figure 14.2 to an iceberg where effective demand is only a small visible part of the iceberg, and the evolutionary policy tasks for growth, targeting and developmental benefits are the lower portions, but these tasks are neither single-dimensional nor easily sequenced. Welfare and urbanization policies can offer enormous potential to shape demand and to signal priorities for the problem-framing capabilities within and between the four quadrants of Figure 14.1. While manufacturing has been the engine of structural change and learning of the twentieth century, its share of gross domestic product (GDP) has not grown as much as many would like (UNIDO, 2016).

The very large informal economy and tight interlinkages with GVCs in many sectors makes the co-ordination and legitimization of co-existing production and innovation sub-sectors even more stark. While earlier, national development plans directed industrial policy at considerable policy distance, larger nations and those with devolved responsibilities struggle with industrial policy design at urban and regional levels.

The evolutionary perspective when focused on demand, as in Figure 14.2, illustrates how need and demand are institutionally recognized through different human-made policy mechanisms, socially circumscribed preferences or consumption patterns. There may be other goals of innovation beyond inclusion: creativity, experimentation, competition, nationalistic/individual freedom and quality-of-life improvements. In principle the burden of proof is higher since public plans are involved: to demonstrate good use of public investment, the crowding in of private investment (or further public investment), the attracting of entrepreneurs, and boosting the growth and business cycle. Innovation as a developmental process rarely has the state entirely absent but this hardly exonerates it.

The case of electrification allows a type of natural experiment about diffusion rates within and across countries, compatibility between gas and electricity across countries, or utilities reform, or wind versus solar energy. Was large-scale industry's use of electricity sufficient in some Indian states but not in others to electrify the homes of the very poor? Mysore state's early expansion of electrification using the Kolar gold mines as a lead user was an example of a lead industry experiment with limited, wider impact (see Reddy, 2004).

The jury is still out about exactly how to design and diffuse innovations for low-income consumers, and equally about how lead users (institutional or individual) might make this happen. It is a sign of political correctness to argue that innovation that includes the lowest-income groups is somehow 'better' but there are difficult questions to answer in this stance. By what criteria and time-scale will it be 'right' or 'better' for such groups? With such goals, can products be better tested or customized? Will they necessarily be cheaper or best adapted? Should low-income communities be guinea pigs for innovative measures, or are they the real drivers of new problem-framing and solutions, lead users and innovators in their own right? If the four schematic gradations from needs to demand are considered, and four quadrants taken into account, we might gain some clarity on how forms of inclusion can come about by linkages between unconnected or under-connected sectors. There are no automatic steps from one to the other and no *a priori* protagonists to make the linkages. For-profit firms have the freedom to pursue their own competitive strategies, and NGOs their social aims, but public plans require a higher burden of proof in supporting the coordination and integration of different sub-systems in the economy. Converting this planning power into more transparent processes with value-premises made explicit remains the development challenge. The economics of innovation and demand can begin here: to analyse if and how innovation and upgrading under GVCs can coexist and co-evolve with other means for production and development.

References

Albuquerque, E. M. 2007. 'Inadequacy of Technology and Innovation Systems at the Periphery.' *Cambridge Journal of Economics* 31 (5): 669–90.

Amsden, A. H. 1989. *Asia's Next Giant: South Korea and Late Industrialization.* New York: Oxford University Press.

Arocena, R., and J. Sutz,. 2010. 'Weak Knowledge Demand in the South: Learning Divides and Innovation Policies.' *Science and Public Policy* 37 (8): 571–82.

Avnimelech, G. and M. Teubal. 2008. 'Evolutionary Targeting.' *Journal of Evolutionary Economics* 18 (2): 151–66.

Basalla, George. 1988. *The Evolution of Technology.* Cambridge, UK: Cambridge University Press.

Cassiolato, J. E., H. M. M. Lastres and M. M. L. Maciel, eds. 2003. *Systems of Innovation and Development.* Cheltenham: Edward Elgar.

Cassiolato, J. E., M. H. Szapiro and H. M. M. Lastres. 2002. 'Local System of Innovation under Strain: The Impacts of Structural Change in the Telecommunications Cluster of Campinas, Brazil.' *International Journal of Technology Management* 24 (7–8): 680–704.

Chataway, J. and J. Smith. 2006. 'The International Aids Vaccine Initiative (IAVI): Is It Getting New Science and Technology to the World's Neglected Majority?' *World Development* 34 (1): 16–30.

Chataway, J., R. Hanlin, and R. Kaplinsky. 2014. 'Inclusive Innovation: An Architecture for Policy Development.' *Innovation and Development* 4 (1): 33–54.

Chen, Martha Alter. 2005. 'Rethinking the Informal Economy: Linkages with the Formal Economy and the Formal Regulatory Environment.' Working Paper 10/2005. Helsinki: United Nations University, World Institute for Development Economics Research.

Courvisanos, J. 2009. 'Political Aspects of Innovation.' *Research Policy* 38 (7): 1117–24.

Dutrénit, G. and J. Katz. 2005. 'Introduction: Innovation, Growth and Development in Latin-America: Stylized Facts and a Policy Agenda.' *Innovation* 7 (2–3): 105–30.

Fontana, R. and M. Guerzoni. 2008. 'Incentives and Uncertainty: An Empirical Analysis of the Impact of Demand on Innovation.' *Cambridge Journal of Economics* 32 (5): 927.

Fujita, K. 2003. 'Neo-industrial Tokyo: Urban Development and Globalization in Japan's State-Centered Developmental Capitalism.' *Urban Studies* 40 (2): 249–81.

Hirschman, A. O. 1958. *The Strategy of Economic Development*. New Haven: Yale University Press.

Hughes, T. P. 1993a. *Networks of Power: Electrification in Western Society, 1880–1930*. Baltimore: Johns Hopkins Press.

———. 1993b. 'The City as Creator and Creation.' In *Berlin/New York: Like and Unlike: Essays on Architecture and Art From 1870 to the Present*, edited by Josef Paul Kleihues and Christina Rathgeber, 13–32. New York: Rizzoli.

Kalecki, M. 1968. 'Trend and Business Cycles Reconsidered.' *The Economic Journal* 78 (310): 263–76.

Kaplinsky, R. 2011. 'Schumacher Meets Schumpeter: Appropriate Technology below the Radar.' *Research Policy* 40 (2): 193–203.

Lall, S. 1982. 'Technological Learning in the Third World: Some Implications of Technology Exports.' In *The Economics of New Technology in Developing Countries*, edited by F. Stewart and J. James, 165–86. Londres: Frances Pinter.

———. 1984. 'Exports of Technology by Newly-Industrializing Countries: An Overview.' *World Development* 12 (5–6): 475.

———. 1992. 'Technological Capabilities and Industrialization.' *World Development* 20 (2): 165–86.

Lewis, W. A. 1954. 'Economic Development with Unlimited Supplies of Labour.' *The Manchester School* 22 (2): 139–91.

Lundvall, B. A. 1992. *National Innovation System: Towards a Theory of Innovation and Interactive Learning*. London: Pinter.

Mackintosh, M., G. Banda, W. Wamae and P. Tibandebage, eds. 2016. *Making Medicines in Africa: The Political Economy of Industrializing for Local Health*. Basingstoke: Palgrave Macmillan.

Malerba, F. and R. Nelson. 2012. *Economic Development as a Learning Process*. Cheltenham: Edward Elgar.

Metcalfe, J. S. 1998. *Evolutionary Economics and Creative Destruction*. London: Routledge.

———. 2007. 'Instituted Economic Processes, Increasing Returns and Endogenous Growth.' In *The Evolution of Economic Institutions: A Critical Reader*, edited by G. M. Hodgson, 98–119. Cheltenham: Edward Elgar, in association with the European Association for Evolutionary Political Economy.

372 Smita Srinivas

Myers, S. and D. G. Marquis. 1969. *Successful Industrial Innovation*. Washington: National Science Foundation.

Nelson, R. R., ed. 1993. *National Innovation Systems: A Comparative Analysis*. Oxford University Press.

Papaioannou, T. and S. Srinivas. 2016. 'Innovation as a Political Process of Development: Are Neo-Schumpeterians Value Neutral?' Paper first presented at SPRU's 50th Anniversary Conference on Transforming Innovation, 7–9 September 2016. Science Policy Research Unit (SPRU), University of Sussex.

Pasinetti, L. L. 1981. *Structural Change and Economic Growth: A Theoretical Essay on the Dynamics of the Wealth of Nations*. Cambridge: Cambridge University Press.

Perez, C. 1983. 'Structural Change and the Assimilation of New Technologies in the Economic and Social System.' *Futures* 15 (5): 357–75.

———. 1985. 'Microelectronics, Long Waves and the World Structural Change: New Perspectives for Developing Countries.' *World Development* 13 (3): 441–63.

Ramani, S., ed. 2014. *Innovation in India: Combining Economic Growth with Inclusive Development*. Cambridge University Press.

Reddy, A. K. N. 2004. 'Science and Technology for Rural India.' *Current Science* 87 (7): 889–98.

Rothberth, E. 1942. 'Review of Business Cycles, by J. A. Schumpeter.' *The Economic Journal* 52 (206/207): 223–29.

Schmookler, J. 1966. *Invention and Economic Growth*. Harvard University Press.

Srinivas, S. 2009. 'Industry Policy, Technological Change, and the State.' Background Paper No. 7 for *The State and Development Governance*, United Nations Conference of Trade and Development (UNCTAD), Least Developed Countries (LDC) Report, February.

———. 2012. *Market Menagerie: Health and Development in Late Industrial States*. Stanford: Stanford University Press.

———. 2014. 'Demand and Innovation: Paths to Inclusive Development.' In *Innovation in India: Combining Economic Growth with Inclusive Development*, edited by S. Ramani, 78–106. Cambridge University Press.

Srinivas, S. and J. Sutz. 2008. 'Developing Countries and Innovation: Searching for a New Analytical Approach.' *Technology in Society* 30 (2): 129–40.

UNIDO. 2016. *The Role of Technology and Innovation in Inclusive and Sustainable Industrial Development*. Industrial Development Report. Vienna: United Nations Industrial Development Organization.

Von Hippel, E. 2005. *Democratizing Innovation*. Boston: MIT Press.

Wilson, P., S. Post and S. Srinivas. 2007. 'R&D Models: Lessons from Vaccine History.' Policy Research Working Paper #14. New York: International AIDS Vaccine Research Initiative (IAVI), June.

15

GVCs and Development Policy

Vertically Specialized Industrialization[1]

Dev Nathan

Introduction

This chapter is an attempt to answer the 'so what?' question. After all the experience and analyses of global value chains (GVCs), what does it mean for development policy? The chapter starts by first looking at whether GVCs are just the flavour of the year (or the decade?) or they represent a form of firm restructuring that will not go away anytime soon. After summarizing what was pre-GVC development policy, the chapter looks at the benefits for developing countries of entering into GVCs, even at the very lowest level of low-value labour-intensive production.

Having established the rationale for and benefits from being in a GVC, the chapter then looks at the first steps of upgrading in GVCs – of functional upgrading leading to the earning of process rents. Policies to support such functional upgrading are outlined, rejecting the market fundamentalist (or Washington Consensus) approach of letting the market alone hold sway. In the attempt to earn such rents, the obstacles placed by the Prebisch-Singer thesis, applied to GVC upgrading by Raphael Kaplinsky (2005), are discussed; monopsonistic market structures allow lead firms from high income countries to capture the benefits of productivity increases in the supplier firms from developing countries. But it is pointed out that the growth of supplier economies and the growing market itself are factors that mitigate the dissipation of rents that would otherwise hold sway.

This is followed by discussion of GVC-specific industrial policy, based

1   An early version of this chapter was delivered as a lecture at the ICSSR-ISID refresher course for teachers of economics in May 2017. Thanks to Satyaki Roy and the participants for the opportunity to present my thoughts and for their questions and comments. Thanks also to some of the usual GVC-suspects for their very helpful comments – Stephanie Barrientos, Gary Gereffi, Will Milberg and John Pickles. The usual caveats apply.

on vertically specialized industrialization (Milberg and Winker 2013) or concentration on GVC segments rather than entire sectors or products, the development of capabilities in adjoining tasks, reverse engineering and the reorganization of labour as important in moving firms from just earning competitive profits to securing some rents, and for developing countries from low-income to middle-income status.

Having managed catch-up industrialization (Nayyar, 2015), many economies have experienced the well-known 'middle-income trap'. What policies are needed to overcome the middle-income trap? The importance of developing capabilities in carrying out non-routine tasks, the need for developing economies to establish their own lead firms, the importance of not just being in GVCs but also, sometimes, of leaving them in order to form one's own GVC, the importance of frugal engineering in developing economies, the limits to reverse innovation based on modifications of existing products, and the difficulties in moving from knowledge utilization (catch-up in production) to knowledge and technology creation, the move from middle-income non-specialization to high-income specialization – these are all discussed as policies for overcoming the middle-income trap. The concluding section looks at some similar ways in which the issues raised in the chapter can be framed.

Why are there GVCs?

With 80 per cent of world trade now estimated to be conducted through GVCs (UNCTAD, 2013) it is necessary to consider how the rise of GVCs affects development policy. Before we take that up, we deal with a preliminary question: is the organization of trade on the basis of GVCs a passing phenomenon – something that is not likely to last – particularly under the current attacks from Donald Trump in the USA or other nationalist politicians?

There are two factors underlying the organization of world trade through GVCs. As pointed out by Nathan, Tewari and Sarkar (2016), the first factor is the management doctrine of concentration on 'core competence' (Prahalad and Hamel, 1990) while outsourcing the rest of the tasks to other firms in whose core competence the tasks lie. This provides the benefits of specialization, with each task or set of tasks being carried out by firms who have a specialized competence in carrying out those tasks. The Indian telecom company Airtel contracted IBM to provide all of its IT service requirements. Its CEO argued that IBM, dealing with IT service supply and solving the problems of many clients, would have far greater competence in the supply of IT services than an IT department of Airtel could develop (Damodaran, 2016).

However, being able to outsource all but core functions requires the capability to compartmentalize a production process with detailed specifications that need to be conveyed to other firms. This has been made possible by the development of information and communication technologies (ICTs), through which detailed specifications can be both delineated and transmitted between firms. ICTs increased both the speed and the volume of information that could be transmitted.

The benefits of both specialization and scale in outsourcing to specialized service providers ensure that the splintering of production or vertically specialized industrialization (Milberg and Winkler, 2013; Davis, Kaplinsky and Morris, 2017) are not ephemeral. Of course, future technological developments may make possible some other configuration of tasks in production, but at present one can say that with the development of ICT the splintering of production is not something that depends on the whims of trade policy.

The technology of ICTs and the management doctrine of core competence can lead to the splintering of production. This splintering does not have to be global, however. It can well be within firms in a concentrated locality, as has been the case with Japanese 'just-in-time' production systems. For value chain organization to become global, two more conditions are required. One is low-cost international transport, made possible by cheap fuel and containerization. A more important factor is the availability of the required production capabilities at a lower cost than in the 'headquarter' economies – the term that Richard Baldwin (2016) uses to describe the economies that host the lead firms. The development of manufacturing and service production capabilities in firms and the management-cum-workers they employ is critical to outsourcing becoming offshoring. Moreover, these capabilities must be available at a lower cost than in the headquarter economies. With equipment costs not varying by much between countries, it is land (as in, land with developed infrastructure) and labour costs that can vary substantially from country to country. Arbitrage in costs, particularly labour costs, then becomes crucial to the global outsourcing or GVCs.

The two factors – the benefits of specialization and scale in outsourcing and the existence of multiple wage rates in a world of globally mobile capital – mean that the organization of world production and trade in GVCs is not something that is going to go away until a new technological revolution changes the balance between in-house and outsourced production, or the world becomes flat in the sense of wage rates being equalized around the world, in which case outsourcing would not necessarily be global.

Phases of development policy

The key question in this chapter is: what difference has the GVC mode of production made to development policy? This discussion needs to begin with a characterization of pre-GVC development policy. Some of these are:

1. The Lewis-Kuznets model of the transfer of surplus labour out of agriculture into modern industry, chiefly manufacturing. This is based on the Kaldor analysis of the importance of increasing returns, presumed to be possible in manufacturing, for increasing per capita income.

2. The need to develop manufacturing in entire sectors of production, such as consumer goods or producer goods. Economic thinking in the pre-GVC era was almost solely in terms of entire products or sectors. Thus, this became part of development policy too.

3. The importance of heavy industry or capital goods production in developing an industrial structure. This was based on the Soviet Union's Feldman model, modified in the Indian Mahalanobis model, both of which stressed the key role of the production of capital goods or the machinery-producing sector in sustaining industrialization.

4. The difficulty of developing countries in competing with developed countries in the market for manufacturing and thus the need to protect infant industries from foreign competition in import-substituting industrialization (ISI).

5. The inelastic global demand for developing countries' exports of primary goods and agricultural products, modified by the Prebisch-Singer thesis of monopsonistic market structures denying developing countries the benefits of increases in productivity in the production of primary goods. In short, export pessimism about the possibility of exports financing necessary imports of capital goods.

6. All of the above development criteria required a high level of investment – a big push to shift the economy from a low-growth to a high-growth trajectory. The rate of growth would depend on the level of investment, which needed to be higher than the low domestic savings of low-income developing countries.

7. Both export pessimism and the need to increase investment above the low domestic savings threshold led to the need for foreign aid or foreign capital inflow in the early phases of development.

Through the 1950s and 1960s much of decolonized Asia and Latin America went through substantial development through this development policy that was centrally characterized as import-substituting industrialization (ISI). However, in the 1970s it was difficult to sustain this model of industrialization as export earnings failed to keep pace with import requirements for production. The Prebisch-Singer phenomenon of the difficulty of primary producers to increase their export earnings came in with a vengeance to lead to large foreign exchange deficits, financed through debt. With the debt crisis, which was most severe in Latin America, development policy shifted in the direction of managing the external balance through a stress on export-oriented industrialization (EOI) versus the old ISI.

In this second phase of development policy dating from the 1970s the emphasis on planning was substituted by an emphasis on the market. This meant, in particular, the use of a developing country's comparative advantage based on abundant labour and scarce capital. This comparative advantage could be used to move beyond primary goods export with their Prebisch-Singer immiserizing possibilities to that of export of labour-intensive manufactured products, such as garments. The Washington Consensus led by the World Bank and the International Monetary Fund (IMF) stressed the need to reduce price distortions brought about by import duties in the infant industry manner, or export subsidies. In supporting exports of labour-intensive products, it supported policies of allowing wages to reach their market levels and not go higher, so that they would not erode the developing countries' comparative advantage in these labour-intensive export industries.

The 'Asian Tigers' – South Korea, Taiwan, Hong Kong and Singapore – were the exemplars of this export-oriented industrialization, though there were debates about the extent to which the polices followed the Washington Consensus prescriptions (see Amsden, 2001). The Washington Consensus development policies are usually characterized as being neoliberal in nature. A more effective characterization of them, however, would be that they are market-fundamentalist, in that they are based on the doctrine that policy should only facilitate market functioning and not replace market-based decisions of firms by market-substituting policies, whether in the case of import duties, export subsidies or even setting wages.

These policies were criticized by many economists, most picturesquely by Ha Joon Chang (2003) as being one of 'kicking away the ladder' of development by confining development countries to stagnate in low-level manufacturing. One country that famously utilized the export possibilities of labour-intensive manufacture but also pushed the development of more advanced manufacturing in heavy industries and the chemical sector was South Korea. Its policies, characterized as heterodox (Amsden, 2001), first provided protection for heavy industry and thus subsidized their exports, as discussed in Chapter 13 in this book. A feature that this export-oriented industrialization had in common with import-substituting industrialization was the focus on whole products or sectors, such as automobiles or the chemical sector.

Moreover, even while following such heterodox policies, one feature of the labour-intensive exports that was not realized in analysis and policy was that these exports were within value chains. Korea, Taiwan and Hong Kong all produced garments, shoes and toys based on designs supplied by global brands. They supplied the brands with the manufactured goods for retail sale. This was already a value chain type of development, a firm-level policy of manufacturing through insertion into a value chain. The value-chain method of developing exports was introduced into economic analysis by Gary Gereffi (1994) with the notion of 'buyer-driven' commodity supply chains.

Of course, not all products were produced or exported in this manner. South Korea's manufacture and export of automobiles was not based on this value chain approach; the attempt was to build the whole chain, rather than a part of it. While state policy built entire sectors, such as chemicals or heavy industries, firm-based export decisions very much followed the logic of GVCs, taking up the easier components to enter segments of labour-intensive manufacturing while functioning as contracted suppliers in GVCs.

Benefits of being in a GVC

For a developing country, or rather a firm from a developing country, the first point of a GVC-focused development policy is not to try working on every component of a product, but to concentrate on segments. Gereffi and Sturgeon point to the need to 'target special niches in GVCs' (Gereffi and Sturgeon, 2013, 354). One can start with a segment that requires easily acquired skills, such as the cut-make-trim (CMT) segment of garment manufacture, leaving aside design, branding and marketing. Not only is such CMT manufacture something that is easily done, but being part of a value chain means that the developing country firm does not have to struggle for a market. GVC sales are typically contracted sales for large markets, so the developing country gets the advantage of producing on a large scale without having to undertake the difficult task of marketing.

This advantage of sales within a GVC is not given sufficient attention as a means of being able to take advantage of economies of scale in export production. Can one imagine firms from Bangladesh, Cambodia or any other garment exporter being able to sell US$20 billion worth of garments on the world market all on their own? Instead, the garments are sold under the brands for which the developing country firms carried out contracted production.

As argued in Kaplinsky (2005), Nathan and Sarkar (2011) and Nathan *et al.* (2016), a GVC is based on a structure of the monopoly strength of the lead firms (buyers) and the weakness of suppliers in competitive markets that are easy to enter with relatively low or medium knowledge requirements. Rents as surpluses over competitive profits are concentrated in the lead firms, while competitive suppliers secure merely competitive profits. This would be the characteristic manner of GVC participation, particularly in the case of entering developing country firms.

Are there any benefits to such participation in trade when the developing country firms only make competitive profits? Is there any gain from trade for these developing countries?[2] The first gain is, of course, access to a global market on a much larger scale than the domestic market. All the domestic value accrued in the GVC cannot be taken as the gain from trade, since labour and capital would have been employed otherwise in the absence of this trade. It is only the excess over any such alternate use, or the excess over the opportunity cost, that can be considered to be the gain from trade. In the case of labour, this would be the excess of the GVC wage over alternate employment in, say, the rural unorganized sector from which these workers migrate.

In the case of Bangladesh, for example, one can compare garment workers' wages with earnings in the rural micro-enterprise sector, assuming that to be the likely alternative employment of the women workers. Again, since many of the workers in the labour-intensive segments in garments and leather products

---

2   This, in fact, was the question posed by Deepak Nayyar, when the author presented this structure of GVC production and the resulting distribution of income during a seminar on GVCs at the New School in New York. In a sense this section is an answer to that question.

are young women who are first-time entrants into the labour force and might have remained outside any employment otherwise, their entire wages would be considered to be a gain from such trade.

For capital, the alternate employment, even at a similar rate of profit, would have been on a much lower scale. Even competitive profits from GVC supply are likely to be higher than, say, agriculture, because of the economies of scale. Thus, the increase in the scale at which profit is earned is a gain from trade. The same would be true for any taxes the government collects on the GVC segment. Of course, governments tend to reduce the taxes they earn through various forms of concessions (duty drawback and so forth) so that these benefits are transferred to the manufacturing firms.

Thus, the excess earnings of labour and capital in GVCs compared to earnings when put to alternate use constitute the gain from GVC trade, even when the GVC structure leads to developing-country suppliers earning only competitive profits. This direct income gain from trade, however, is not all there is to the story. There are also some other gains from trade. As the Kaldor analysis emphasizes, increasing a country's per capita income is a matter of shifting into economic activities that provide economies of scale, leading to increasing returns. GVC-based manufacturing or service production is such an increasing-return activity. Let alone smaller countries like Bangladesh and Cambodia, one could argue that even China was able to move into increasing-return activities through large-scale entry into GVC segments in garments, leather products, toys, and so on, which provided increasing returns. The first phase of China's participation in GVCs was based on its cheap labour. This allowed the Lewisian shift of a large portion of rural surplus labour to urban industry.

Mention has already been made of the benefit to labour from wages above what would have been earned in the next-best alternative employment. In addition, there are two other positive factors in such development of labour-intensive GVC segments. There is the Lewisian shift of surplus labour from agriculture or other low-return rural activities. This shift is central to the development process. It benefits not only the migrating workers, but also those left behind, as labour surpluses are reduced and rural wages go up. A longitudinal study of the state of Bihar in India pointed to the important role of migration in tightening the labour market in Bihar and leading to a rise in wages (Rodgers et al., 2013). Overall, in India, there has been an increase in rural real wages of above 2 per cent per annum between 1999–2000 and 2011–12 (Ajit Ghose, 2016). Studies of China point out that with the absorption of labour in industry, there has been a tightening of the national labour market and an increase in wages (Fang and Wang, 2010; Zhu, Chapter 4).

Besides increased employment, there is also the dynamic effect of knowledge spillover. The assembly of manufactured good for global markets requires the ability to manufacture quality goods on time. This learning enhances production capabilities. Firms that produce for export tend to use the same methods when they produce for the domestic market, as was verified in discussions with Indian garment exporters (Nathan and Harsh, Chapter 3).

However, will competitive profits enable higher investments – something that is a *sine qua non* of development for a low-income country (LIC)? If, in the usual manner of economic analysis, whether classical or Keynesian, we take all wages to be consumed and investment to come only out of profits, then competitive profits will not lead to higher investment. The competitive profits will only be sufficient to allow reinvestment to maintain the firm and not for expansion. But the fact is that a lot of investable funds come out of household savings. In China, household savings are usually in excess of 50 per cent of the household income. This high level of savings has been a key part of overall savings, going up from 20 per cent of the gross domestic product (GDP) in 1981 to 30 per cent in 1988 and then remaining steady at around 40 per cent of GDP. High levels of investment are crucial for investment in an LIC. The growth of wages, even if not of the wage share, is a contributor to high investment through deposits in the banking system. One can argue that China's full-fledged adoption of GVC-based industrialization, when compared to India's half-hearted adoption of the same (Sarkar *et al.*, 2014), could account for the growth differences through the two decades after they both opened up. Where India did adopt a GVC approach, such as in the supply of IT services, it grew very rapidly, accounting for more than 50 per cent of global offshore services; while in manufacturing, where the adoption was half-hearted, India has lagged behind China and the rest of Asia.

Upgrading in GVCs

While entering into GVCs even in low-value earning labour-intensive segments is of some benefit in absorbing surplus labour from rural into increasing-returns activities in manufacturing, what is the GVC-specific policy that should be followed by developing country firms (supported by their respective states) for subsequent development? The GVC literature identifies some forms of increasing value capture that developing country firms have adopted, usually under the notion of forms of upgrading (Humphrey and Schmitz, 2000).

In functional upgrading, firms take on more functions than simple assembly. This functional upgrading can lead to what is called 'full package supply'. This involves taking on all production stages after the design stage – or even after the idea or conception of a product, from 'sketch to scale', as is quoted in Chapter 2. Increasing the number of functions, even if the rates of return do not increase for each additional function, will increase the total domestic value captured.

Besides functional upgrading there can also be process upgrading, where the supplier firms economize on process costs and increase productivity. While this can work for individual supplier firms who can cut costs below those incurred by competitors supplying at the same prices, it may not work when all firms in a segment undertake such process improvements because of the likely Prebisch-Singer effect in monopsonistic markets. Similarly, an individual country may be able to secure cost advantages for its firms by investing in infrastructure that reduces logistics costs, or in housing and other benefits for workers that increase their productivity. However, when all competing supplier countries or even a large number of them undertake such logistic and productivity-enhancing measures, there could be the same fallacy of composition that comes into play when all or many firms undertake process improvements. We will return to this important topic a little later.

However, at this point, it should be noted that many of these functions – of taking the product from design to manufacture – are increasingly being adopted by what are called contract manufacturers, such as those discussed in Chapter 2, in electronics or large-scale intermediaries in garments, such as Li and Fung. Often, the GVC lead firms may encourage such functional upgrading into full-package contract manufacturing, since it can reduce overall manufacturing costs. The lead firms, such as Apple, can then concentrate on the design, branding and marketing functions while the contract manufacturers take over all the intermediate steps of manufacturing after design, even taking on some detailed design functions, as described in Chapter 2.

Contract manufacturing can involve orders of large volumes; but does this result in the supplier getting a price advantage, in terms of being able to secure a higher price? It does not seem to be so as seen in the study by Applebaum (2006). The margins may also be very low, just 3 per cent or so for Apple's contract manufacturer Foxconn (Chan, Pun and Selden, 2016; Raj-Reichert, Chapter 2). Low margins can be compensated by high volumes, though, leading to larger profits, amount-wise.

Taking on more functions is a reduction of vertical specialization in value chains. This reduction of vertical specialization is a feature of development policy in LICs as they try to move towards middle-income status. This increases domestic value added in production. Furthermore, it is something for which developing economy firms could get support from lead firms, which would like to reduce costs by shedding functions, other than their core functions. Of course, the core functions of branding and marketing remain barriers to entry into the ranks of lead firms.

Another strategy is that of product upgrading – where the supplier moves on from low-value products with a low profit margin to higher-value products with a higher margin. There can be a number of strategies for increasing value capture in the low-income country. As Coe and Yeung (2015) as well as Pickles and Smith (2016) argue, following earlier work by Gibbon and Ponte (2005), increasing value captured by the supplier does not necessarily have to follow the route of product upgrading. Value capture could be increased by remaining or even shifting into low-value products that have a larger market, thus providing a higher total profit. This is the analysis of Gibbon and Ponte in the case of some South African wine growers, who deliberately moved down to low-price but high-volume market segments. High volumes can provide the scale that increases output and income per worker.

What makes process and functional upgrading possible? Firms that do better than others in production processes use more or less the same technology but organize its utilization better. The better organization involves both management and labour, the former in improving the organization of production and the latter in acquiring the necessary skill set. On both sides there is a development of capabilities in utilizing technology. This is in line with the capability based theory of the firm (Amit and Schoemaker, 1993), where the firm is not just a collection of resources but also includes the capability to utilize those resources. Firms that do better in utilizing available technology or resources will be able to secure process rents, compared to firms that do not develop such managerial and labour capabilities to better utilize the technologies.

Carrying out functional upgrading is a matter of acquiring the capabilities for various functions. Moving from cut-make-trim to full-package supply requires firms to acquire the capabilities to manage the supply chains of various inputs, being able to turn design drawings into products, carrying out detailed engineering processes, and so on. A lot of this functional upgrading involves reverse engineering, as discussed in the chapters on China's telecom equipment manufacturing (Chapter 7) and India's automobile industry (Chapter 8).

Introducing reverse engineering into the capabilities that are developed brings out an important factor in GVC functioning. Lead firms may support their suppliers in developing various functional capabilities that deal with manufacturing but are unlikely to support reverse engineering capabilities. Reverse-engineering a product, for instance a pharmaceutical drug, will enable the supplier to emerge as a competitor either with an own-brand product or a generic product. However, developing such reverse engineering capabilities first requires a firm strategy to shift from being a contracted supplier to becoming an own-brand, generic seller in the market; this change might not happen all at once, and firms may continue both manufacturing on contract and making their own branded products. It may also require the supplier firm to be ready to decouple from GVCs, as the Indian pharmaceutical firms or the Chinese telecom equipment manufacturers did.

Most important, reverse engineering requires a close link between the supplier firm and research and development (R&D). This R&D is required to investigate various possibilities and processes. It could be done within the supplier firm itself, but often involves links with national R&D organizations. In China the state-owned telecom equipment R&D units were handed over to the private producers Huawei and ZTE. Even in a relatively low-tech sector such as garment manufacture, the development of design facilities and related engineering capabilities requires the setting up of meso-level organizations, such as fashion and design institutes, along with R&D work by supplier firms.

Process and functional upgradation thus requires the development of various capabilities at both firm and national level. These capabilities can be broken down into management and labour competences at the firm level; R&D within and outside the firm, at the national level; and the development of workforces with the necessary education and skill sets.

Market growth and Prebisch-Singer-Kaplinsky effects

We now turn to a discussion of the Prebisch-Singer thesis as applied by Raphael Kaplinsky (2005) to include manufacturing in GVCs. The principal argument is that in a monopsonistic market the gains of productivity increases will tend to be captured by a few buyers or lead firms and will not accrue to the many suppliers. While Prebisch-Singer carried out this analysis on exports of primary products, Kaplinsky extended this to easy-to-enter manufacturing segments in GVCs. What happens when we introduce growth into the analysis? Producer firms and countries earning wages and profits are not only producers, they are also income-earners and consumers, minus any uninvested savings. Looking only at the production side leads to disregarding of the effects of growing income in the supplier economies and worldwide. Thus, an often neglected feature of GVC-based growth is that it involves the growth of income – even of per capita income – in the supplier economies. This growth of per capita income, when weighed by population, has led to the phenomenon of convergence in incomes (Baldwin, 2016). After the great divergence brought about by the Industrial Revolution, the post-1970 growth in developing countries has turned the divergence around and moved towards a convergence.

Some of the key data on divergence and convergence from Deepak Nayyar's *Catch Up* (2013) is summarized here. Table 15.1 shows the divergence between Asia and west Europe after the Industrial Revolution onwards. From a GDP per capita that was around half of that in west Europe in 1820, China and India slipped to around 10 per cent in 1950, at the time of decolonization. With subsequent catching-up the group Nayyar labels the 'Next 14', which include China, India, Turkey and some other Asian economies, the per capita GDP of this group went up from US$202 in 1970 to US$4,313 in 2013.

Table 15.1 Comparison of GDP per capita, 1820–1950

	1820	1900	1940	1950
West Europe	100	100	100	100
Japan	56	37	54	31
China	50	17	11	7
India	45	19	13	10

Source: Nayyar (2015).

Table 15.2 GDP per capita in developing and developed countries (US$ in current prices and current exchange rates)

		1970	1990	2000	2013
1	Next 14	202	981	1,648	4,313
2	Industrialized	2,873	19,303	25,711	39,723
3	World	892	4,201	5,286	9,275
4	1 as % of 2	7%	5%	6%	11%

Source: Nayyar (2015).

When per capita incomes are weighed by population, the Gini coefficient of global inter-country inequality declined from 58 in 1952 to 50 in 2000 (Milanovic, 2016). After the 2008 recession, which brought growth in the developed world almost to a standstill, the inter-country inequality would have declined even further. Simultaneously, however, the intra-country Ginis have increased for China by 6 per cent, India by 16 per cent and South Africa by 4.5 per cent. Only for Brazil has the intra-country Gini declined by 9 per cent in the 2000s.

The important point for our analysis at this juncture is the growth of the markets of the developing economies or 'emerging economies' (the 'Next 14' in Table 15.2) in particular. Their per capita GDP increased from US$202 in 1970 to US$4,313 in 2013, which is a massive increase, unprecedented in history. Of course, the growth of income in China, and to a lesser extent in India, is a major part of that story.

Moreover, no matter how such growth took place, these types of growth, which made China the second largest economy in the world and India the fifth largest, make a big difference to world demand. Such an increase in global demand mitigates, to some extent, the effect of the monopsony market-effect in GVCs. While developing economy firms may not be able to capture the benefits of their productivity increases, the growth in the scale of the market, along with the increase in the number of functions they perform, would together increase developing economy incomes from GVCs. This could moderate the effect of the Prebisch-Singer-Kaplinsky effect of stagnant or declining prices for developing country exports.

So far, it has been argued that (*a*) there are benefits in terms of domestic value added (wages, profits, and taxes) in entering GVCs, even at the low end, where only competitive profits are earned, (*b*) GVCs enable low-income countries to produce on scale for demanding international markets without having to undertake the difficult tasks of design, branding and marketing, (*c*) firms at the low end can undertake incremental improvements in production process to earn process rents and (*d*) they can also take up functional upgrading by taking on more functions to increase domestic value added in production.

However, in advancing to catch up in production capabilities, they need to develop specific production capabilities. What, though, is the meaning of a GVC-specific industrial policy? One of the early attempts at formulating such a GVC-specific industrial policy is that of Gereffi and Sturgeon (2013).

GVC-specific industrial policy as vertically specialized industrialization

GVC-specific industrial policy is one that involves not supporting all the segments of a product's development but focusing on key segments for in-house development while outsourcing other tasks to specialist suppliers. As put by Gereffi and Sturgeon, it is necessary to 'target special niches in GVCs' (Gereffi and Sturgeon, 2013, 354). How this would function in practice can be illustrated with the example of Brazil's development of the Embraer mid-size passenger jet aircraft (Nathan and Sarkar, 2014). Initially, Brazil tried to develop every component of the aircraft, from fuselage to engines and avionics. However, when this all-round effort failed, the company shifted to vertically specialized manufacture. It kept for itself the overall design, the manufacture of the fuselage and final assembly, and outsourced engine manufacture to the specialists in jet engine manufacture – Pratt and Whitney, and Rolls Royce. By using the services of specialized service providers, it was able to come up with a reliable and commercially successful product. The Embraer is a classic example of vertically specialized industrialization.

What this policy does is to extend the GVC division of production by tasks (conception – design, manufacture, branding – marketing) between firms depending on the level of the economy. Thus, economies are identified as basically being specialized as suppliers, non-specialized as full-package producers, and further specialized as conception-design-brand-marketing or headquarter economies.

While recognizing that economies and their firms can be distributed along these lines (this is discussed later on with national-level data, as analyed in Milberg and Winkler, 2013) the important point of policy is to identify ways of moving beyond the phase in which its firms exist. Thus, it is important for firms to develop capabilities for undertaking different functions in moving from simple assembly to full package supply and to undertake reverse engineering to move from reproducing products to making incremental changes.

Reverse engineering and the production of generic drugs are all ways of catching up in manufacturing. GVC analysis, however, points to capabilities not of whole sectors but of production segments. Using the notion of production capabilities, Hausmann *et al.* (2013) look at development as the move from an existing set of capabilities to a somewhat adjoining set, where the capabilities are not too different from the existing set. This would need to be modified in a GVC framework – the adjacent capabilities would be those of production segments and not of whole products. For instance, those who have set up factories to assemble garments could easily move into setting up factories for assembling shoes. The managerial and labour capabilities in these two tasks – assembling garments and assembling shoes – are not too dissimilar. Similarly, the capabilities needed to design garments could be extended to designing shoes, with some additional knowledge – in this case, the technical and ergonomic requirements for making shoes.

At the same time, one should recognize the importance of going beyond comparative advantages. The comparative advantage analysis is based on existing factor endowments, utilizing the presence of the more abundant factor (labour in this case) to build trade competencies. However, it is also necessary to go beyond static trade advantages based on cheap labour to build up competence in advanced technology production segments.

There are two reasons for such an advance. First, the advanced production segments or high-tech areas usually provide higher returns to scale. This surplus is needed for the accumulation of capital to increase growth. Second, participating in advanced production segments provides more opportunities for learning, and also for the spillover of these learning benefits to other economic sectors and segments. For instance, increased competence in the use of information technology (IT) would not just provide higher returns where it is used, but also allow people with IT competence to make a difference to production in other sectors. IT is a general purpose technology with high spillover benefits.

Consequently, development policy, while using the principle of comparative advantage based on existing factor endowments, must also seek to build new capabilities. Of course the problem of trying to go 'beyond feasible reach' could arise (Morris, Kaplinsky and Kaplan, 2012). It is often difficult to decide what is feasible, however, and mistakes may be made in the process.

For example, would the emergence of Kenya as an innovation centre in the development of mobile phone systems for transferring money have been considered to be feasible? However, it has happened. Though the initial software for the mobile payment and money transfer system, M-Pesa, was developed at the University of Cambridge, it was in Kenya that the adaptation and development of the mobile money platform occurred (Maree *et al.*, 2013). Since then, the Kenya-developed mobile payment system has been exported to many other countries, including India.

Deciding on beyond-the-horizon areas in which to develop capabilities could be based on two factors. One is that of the existence of a possible domestic market for the service or product to be developed. The domestic market is important because systems can be tried out in relative isolation in a low-price market. The second factor is that of the existence of an educational base for the development of required capabilities. For instance, a good system of tertiary education is clearly necessary for developing IT-based services.

In the manner that Africa has leapfrogged to mobile telephones, developing countries could also take steps for digitization. Digitization would be counter-intuitive for a labour-surplus economy. But international competition forces firms even in labour-surplus economies to adopt various measures of automation, if not to reduce costs to improve quality and reliability and meet new service requirements of clients. As discussed in Chapter 10, the Indian IT majors are facing a difficult challenge in moving from a business model based on low labour costs to one suited to clients' needs for digitization services. It should be noted that China's digital economy is already a force to reckon with in the world economy, and it has five companies (Baidu, Huawei, Tencent, Didi Chuxing and Alibaba) that are listed by the *MIT Technology Review* as being among the fifty smartest companies in the world, a list which does not feature even one Indian company (*MIT Technology Review*, 2017).

However, building the digital infrastructure would be of benefit both directly for economic activities, such as production segments in GVCs, and also for administrative processes, such as the provision of services by governments. Digitization could help increase the reach of educational and health services. In sum, a deliberate degree of digitization, building the capabilities required at various stages, would be of benefit in enabling developing countries to advance on a broad front.

Thus, policy based on comparative advantage, targeting labour-abundant production segments, should be combined with beyond-the-horizon thinking including digitization.

Reorganization of labour

A somewhat under-analysed aspect of upgrading is that of the role of labour. In GVC analysis, labour is usually relegated to being the dependent variable and given a separate term – 'social upgrading'. Economic upgrading, that is, of the firm, comes first, though it may not result in the social upgrading of labour (Barrientos, Gereffi and Rossi, 2011). However, what if an upgradation of labour was in fact a requirement for the upgrading of the firm? This is not a matter of meeting labour standards as a condition of getting orders through the value chains, but of better employment conditions or labour practice being a necessity for improving firm performance.

One of the few analyses of labour upgrading in the context of GVCs is that of Marion Werner (2012). She points out that the movement from CMT to full-package supply involved labour moving from being uni-skilled to becoming multi-skilled, with the ability to move between tasks in the newly set up sample rooms. Did this require a change from the usual precarious employment of sewers on the assembly line to more secure employment as owners tried to retain the multi-skilled 'utilities', namely the workers who could perform all the tasks connected with stitching a garment? The upgraded factory also required employees who could engage in detailed industrial engineering. Werner discusses the change in the gender composition of the workforce – from mainly women in CMT factories to mainly men in the 'full-package' factories, along with women in the industrial engineering section. However, there is no mention of whether there was a change in the employment system in terms of moving from precarious to more secure employment.

In the case of the apparel industry, it is generally accepted that Sri Lanka has been able to achieve higher productivity and quality and operate under the slogan 'Garments Without Guilt'. Many studies (for example, Goger, 2014, 2016; Ruwanpura, 2016a, 2016b) have documented some of the better labour and management practices in Sri Lankan garment factories and their benefits in terms of reputation and production (Perry, Wood and Fernie, 2014). Again, a study of the Mumbai textile industry showed that the adoption of better management practices (including operations, quality, inventory, human resource practices and the management of sales and orders) led to increases in productivity and profitability (Bloom et al., 2013). A study of Cambodia has shown that improved human resource policies increased profitability and provided stable orders (Robertson et al., 2016). There is substantial international literature that shows that improved human resources or labour practices can increase firm-level productivity as shown in the literature review by Ichinowski and Shaw (2003).

Earlier, a connection was made between the knowledge intensity of the GVC task and the quality of employment – the more the knowledge intensity, the higher the quality of employment (Nathan, 2016). However, that too was an analysis of employment quality as a dependent variable or outcome of the knowledge-intensity of the GVC task. In this book, Dev Nathan and Harsh (Chapter 3) take up the other side of the connection between employment systems or labour practices and the upgrading of firm performance. This moves the analysis away from a linear causality to a more evolutionary pattern.

Reverse engineering is a key factor in catching up in production capabilities, as demonstrated in the chapters on Chinese telecom equipment manufacture (Chapter 7) and Indian generic drug manufacture (Chapter 12). With these manufacturing capabilities the developing economies are able to set up their own lead firms, with their own value chains.

Emerging lead firms

Lead firms from developing countries have come up with a marketing strategy that does not involve immediate competition with existing developed-country lead firms. Indian pharmaceutical exporters began their journey into generic drugs by moving into less stringently regulated developing-country markets. They became the 'pharmacy of the developing world', supplying low-cost generic drugs. Subsequently, they moved into the lucrative but more regulated developed-country generics markets (Chapter 12). In similar fashion, Chinese telecom equipment manufacturers first marketed their equipment in small and developing-country markets, such as in Africa. After they had established themselves as competent suppliers they moved into the developed-country markets of the EU.

However, making the transition to developed-country markets is often not easy, as the difficulties of Indian pharmaceutical units in securing and maintaining US Food and Drug Administration (USFDA) registration show (Chapter 12). India does have the largest number of USFDA-recognized drug manufacturing facilities outside the USA, but some of them have faced difficulties in sustaining their FDA clearances.

One traditional way of moving from less stringent to more stringent markets has been though the use of export subsidies. In the pre-WTO (World Trade Organization) period, Korea was able to support exports to developed countries through a system of subsidies conditional on successful exports. Such an export-supporting subsidy cannot be carried out any more under WTO rules. What can be done, however, is to have subsidies conditional on producers meeting certain performance standards. Meeting these standards would then enhance the producers' ability to export to developed-country markets. In addition, these standards need not be set very high from the outset, but ratcheted up in step-by-step fashion.[3] Such a system is WTO-compliant.

There are some factors that are important in the development mentioned here. One is that supplier firms have a strategic goal of developing beyond their existing market strategies. They need to set themselves the goal to develop dynamic capabilities to be able to move into areas where they are not currently functioning, whether it is in developing functional capabilities or in targeting different markets (Teese, Pisano and Schuen, 1997). Two, firms cannot remain stuck with a strategy that merely lets them stay within their existing value chains; they need to consider when to remain within and when to step outside these value chains, as argued by Horner (2014) and Coe and Heung (2015). Emerging lead firms need to develop reverse engineering, something that remaining within a GVC would inhibit. After having acquired the technology, they could then themselves set up competing value chains.

Third, the development of functional and manufacturing capabilities is not only a function of firm strategies and activities but also requires substantial state support through GVC-appropriate industrial policy. By 'GVC-appropriate' we refer to an industrial policy that targets not sectors but segments and devises methods to support different forms of functional upgrading, whether within manufacturing segments themselves or from catch-up manufacturing to knowledge creation.

Such state and policy support is important even in the catch-up phase. As Gary Gereffi (2009) points out, China followed an active industrial policy of supporting the development of the functional capabilities of supplier firms, while Mexico was faithful to the Washington Consensus policy, allowing market forces to take care of development. The Chinese state actively fostered the development of what are known as *supply chain* cities – massive industrial zones concentrated on the unbundled manufacture of a product. The specialization, the large scale and the benefits of clustering together combined to produce highly flexible and low-cost manufacturing zones. The different results were clear to see. China has moved from being a subordinate manufacturer and emerged as a competitor in a number of industrial segments and developed its own lead firms – something Mexico has not been able to achieve on an international scale.

Even picking up 'low hanging fruit' would require public support of capability building. Botswana, Africa, for instance, is attempting to move from being a supplier of raw diamonds to processing (cutting and polishing) these

---

3   Thanks to Meenu Tewari and Partha Dasgupta for discussions on these issues.

diamonds. However, even basic techniques like cut-and-polish would require some training. In order to challenge India's current monopoly of the cut-polish process in small and lower-value diamonds, it is necessary for Botswana to set up a training institute for this purpose. Given the difficulty of retaining skilled workers, private employers will inevitably under-invest in training. Then, in order to move from diamond mining to diamond processing, it is necessary for a public organization or public–private partnership organization to develop the requisite training facilities.

Training for the development of higher knowledge-based capabilities has to be added to infrastructure investment as an essential function of government and public investment in utilizing GVCs for development. This training, however, has to be related to the demand for skills from enterprises involved in the value chain activities (Bamber, Guinn and Gereffi, 2014). This is often a challenge.

Higher knowledge-based capabilities are not merely a matter of explicit or codifiable knowledge. They often contain a large component of tacit knowledge – something that requires deep domain experience. Overall, as has been emphasized in the national innovation systems literature and is referred to in this book by Smita Srinivas (Chapter 14), there is need to build complementary organizations at various levels – research, training, coordination, and so on. In addition, a factor not much emphasized in the literature, the need to develop critical attitudes and methods of thinking, should also be considered (Mokyr, 2004).

The differences in results depending on the differences in state policy show that participation in GVCs does not have one invariant result. State and firm policy can either lead to moving up the value chain, or lack of appropriate state policy can lead to a country's firms stagnating in low-value segments of the value chain.

State policy is needed not only in the case of market failures, where individual firms may fail to invest sufficiently in R&D. It is also needed in the case of coordination failures, where there may be cooperation failures among numerous small firms. An example of the first case is Taiwan's electronics industry. Small units make up most of the industry. They obviously do not have the means with which to set up scale-sensitive testing and research laboratories. That market/collective action failure was offset by the Taiwanese state setting up the required facilities for R&D, which acquired, adapted and diffused technology, and coordinated related investments.

An example of state action to overcome coordination failures is the case of Indian leather products exporters (Tewari and Pillai, 2005). When they faced problems in eliminating dangerous chemicals banned in the EU, the state stepped in to bring about coordinated action. The chemical suppliers, tanners and manufacturers were all brought together, along with the Leather Research Institute, to clean up the value chain, right from the tanneries up to the final product for supply to the brands.

Rather than any form of market fundamentalism, what is needed is to supplement firm efforts to upgrade through appropriate state interventions and investments in overcoming market or coordination failures. Whether it is through the development of global supply of IT services (India) or high quality manufacturing (China) combined with various forms of upgrading and productivity increases, many low-income countries have made the transition to middle-income status or at least low-middle income status. Of course, this is not all due to GVC participation, but given the extent to which GVC-based exports have been important to growth in these countries, GVC participation has been a factor in this transition to middle-income status. However, what happens after the catch-up process is complete?

The middle-income trap

The World Bank's China report (2013) notes that some thirty countries have achieved middle-income status but have subsequently failed to advance to high-income status. They include Brazil and Argentina, which reached middle-income status in the 1980s and 1990s, but have since stalled. Four important economies that have gone beyond middle-income status are South Korea, Taiwan, Singapore and Costa Rica. The last two mentioned are often ignored in discussions because they are small, island economies. However, even their experience of shifting to high-value services is important in learning how to break out of the middle-income trap. South Korea and Taiwan are additionally important for their successes in manufacturing.

The difficulty of moving from middle-income to high-income status is often referred to as the middle-income trap. The problem of the middle-income trap can be phrased as follows: what happens after catch-up? What happens after low-income countries have been able to learn the methods of production of goods and services in and for the international market, and been able to carry out incremental process innovations and build functional capabilities to move from assembly to full-package supply in order to become middle-income economies?

In value chain analysis, the problem of development can be put in terms of advancing from low-knowledge segments to high-knowledge segments of production. As noted in the 'Introduction' to this volume, high-knowledge segments are also those that earn high rents. The rents earned have been linked in earlier writings to wages (Nathan and Sarkar, 2011) and the quality of employment (Nathan and Kumar, 2016). In this chapter, this relationship is further extended between knowledge and development outcomes as a whole, with development outcomes being summarized in terms of income levels. Thus, what is being argued is that there is a connection between the knowledge bases of production segments, rents earned and employment quality – including wages and overall development outcomes. Of course, this chapter does not present much evidence to support the relationship between knowledge, rents, wages and development outcomes. However, the structure presented in Table 15.3 is something that could be empirically investigated.

Table 15.3 Knowledge, rents and development

Knowledge bases of production segments	Rents and development		
	Low	Medium	High
Low	**Assembly**		Very little assembly in HICs – Brexit and Trump
Medium		**Full-package process rent**	
High	Unlikely – design and new products in LICs		**Innovation/Design**

Source: Author.

Table 15.3 is based on a micro-economic firm-based analysis of GVC production segments. At the micro-economic or firm level, the argument is that the knowledge base of production is related to the rents earned – they are non-existent or just competitive profits are earned when the knowledge base is relatively low, as in assembly (whether of garments or electronic products); there are limited process rents earned by firms that carry out process innovations of the incremental variety or functional upgrading to full-package supply with a medium knowledge base; finally, rents are high where major innovations in products are carried out with a high-knowledge base. The last would be the situation of Schumpetarian rents.

From the firm level, one needs to proceed to that of the economy as a whole. This can be done by aggregating different kinds of firms at the economy level, or as done by Coe and Yeung (2015), at the regional level. Here the hypothesis is that a low-income economy is vertically specialized in having a predominance of assembly-level firms; a middle-income economy is less-specialized in having a dominance of firms carrying out multiple functions as full-package suppliers and involved in incremental process improvements; and a high-income economy is again vertically specialized in having a preponderance of firms involved in major product and process innovations of the Schumpeterian type and correspondingly earning high rents. Preponderance is in terms of the contributions of different types of firms to national income.

This is the structure of what is known as the Smiley curve first formulated by former Acer CEO, Stan Shih, to illustrate the point that Acer needed to shift from low value-capturing production to high value-capturing design and branding (Shih, 2010). Milberg and Winkler (2013) find some evidence for the Smiley curve in a cross-country comparison. They plot vertical specialization against GDP per capita and find that LICs are specialized, as are HICs. It is the MICs that are the least specialized:

> … low-income countries seek to upgrade by reducing the overall level of vertical specialization (raising domestic value added in exports) and then reach a point where rising incomes involves increasing vertical specialization while focusing on the highest value added components of the GVC. (Milberg and Winkler, 2013, 308–09)

Vertical specialization can also be related to the nature of tasks performed in different GVC segments. Tasks can be divided on the basis of their routineness – routine tasks are accomplished following a set of specific and well-defined rules, while non-routine tasks such as creative problem solving and decision-making entail more complicated activities (Acemoglu and Autor, 2010; Autor, 2013). One would expect LICs to be specialized in routine intensive tasks, while HICs are specialized in non-routine tasks, and MICs somewhere in between, combining both.

An interesting study compared OECD (Organisation for Economic Cooperation and Development) countries for what is called the *routine intensity* of tasks (Marcolin, Mirodout and Squicciarini, 2016; following

Oldenski, 2012). Non-routine tasks are not all skill- or knowledge-intensive; some non-routine manual tasks such as personal care, which require a high level of interaction with the user, may not require high levels of knowledge. The outsourcing of routine tasks is possible because ICTs allow a firm to specify in great detail the tasks to be performed or the intermediate products to be manufactured. However, one can reasonably expect that non-routine tasks are those that require decision-making and cannot be outsourced, while routine tasks are those that can be outsourced.

Oldenski (2012), in a study of US service firms, found that firms were more likely to offshore a stage of production that contained more routine tasks and fewer non-routine or communication tasks. As non-routine tasks are correlated with higher wages and educational levels, this also translates into the offshoring of less skilled, low-paying jobs, while higher skilled and more paying jobs remain in the USA.

At a macro-economic level, with this broad division between routine and non-routine tasks, Marcolin *et al.* (2016) find that within OECD countries the percentage of routine employment varies between what they call the 'transition countries', the former Soviet bloc countries, and the USA. The percentage of routine employment in transition economies was about 73 per cent in 2011, having risen over the decade, while the same was 66 per cent in the USA, having fallen over the decade. One would well expect that if the comparison were between the USA and China or India, the difference in the percentage of routine employment between the two sets of countries would be much higher.

The comparison of routine and non-routine employment earlier covers the two ends of the economic spectrum. One can conjecture, though, that the proportion of these two follows the same distribution as that of vertical specialization – there is more routine employment at the low-income end and more non-routine employment at the high-income end, while the middle-income portion falls in between the two.

What does this mean for development policy? For increasing per capita income, a country needs to target the development of non-routine tasks in the sectors in which they are already performing primarily routine tasks. The movement from assembly to full-package supply depends on the development of capabilities for carrying out non-routine tasks, whether of design, branding or marketing. In the GVC terminology, it is lead firms that perform these tasks, which means that supplier economies need to develop lead firms.

The South Korean success in developing lead firms in electronics (Samsung, Hyundai and LG, for example) and automobiles is well known and is discussed in Chapter 13 of this book. Taiwan has developed its own lead firms too, with brands such as Acer and Asus in computers and other electronic equipment. The Chinese telecom equipment manufacturers Huawei and ZTE have been discussed in Chapter 7. Other brands such as Haier (consumer goods) have spread across international markets. From India, there are multinationals such as Tata and Mahindra, which have formed their own value chains across some world markets, including in developing economies in Africa. The major Sri Lankan women's inner wear manufacturers, MAS and Bendix, have developed their own branded lines, though on a much smaller scale than the examples given above, and are beginning to establish themselves in South Asia. Some Indian garment manufacturers have also set up their own brands or bought up established brands in order to set up their own value chains across India and South Asia.

A prominent area in which supplier economies have developed lead firms is that of the digital economy. China's Alibaba, an online retail platform, Baidu, a search service, and Tencent, a payments service, are among the biggest in the world in their categories. The US online taxi service aggregator, Uber, dropped out of the Chinese market and sold its stake to its rival, Didi Chuxing. In India, on the other hand, though there are vibrant digital economy companies, such as Flipkart the online retailer and Ola the taxi service aggregator, these companies face competition from US companies with much deeper pockets.

By upgrading from being suppliers to developing their own brands, there are a number of benefits. For one, the firms take on more functions and thus their overall revenues increase. Their profit margins also go up. It is not necessary to cite the examples of Apple or Samsung in order to highlight the high rents secured by lead firms with their own brands and GVCs on a global scale. Even on a more limited scale, there are newly emerged lead firms that prove this point. Discussions with an Indian women's inner wear producer, Gokuldas Exports, which has set up its own brand for the Indian market, showed that the rate of return from its own brand was more than three times than what it earned as a supplier to other brands. In Mumbai, garment exporters mentioned that because the returns of Indian brands are higher, even if they are really small brands, they are able to pay higher wages and thus attract more skilled workers than dedicated export suppliers.

From reverse to frugal engineering

A factor in catch-up is reverse engineering in developing economies (discussed in Chapters 7 on telecom equipment manufacture in China and in Chapter 8 on automobile production in India). The process of upgrading does not end with manufacturing what was already being made. The next step is in making something new, which does not need to be entirely new, but is an improved version of an existing product. Such a shift to making something new would result in the development of lead firms, which is crucial for earning high rents and moving out of the middle-income trap.

In developing lead firms, the large emerging economies, China and India in particular, can utilize their market structures, with large markets for low-value products – what Prahalad called the 'bottom of the pyramid', but can also be referred to as the 'base of the pyramid' (Prahalad, 2006). Products can be specifically developed for this large-volume, low-price market, such as low-cost smartphones or the Indian Tata Nano car.

The difference between these low-cost and conventional products is that the former are frugal in their use of materials. Not only are frills of various types removed, but there is also a reduction in the use of materials. For instance, for the Nano car, the electronic control unit (ECU) was completely redesigned. The need for redesigning was explained by the chairman of Bosch's automotive division.

> Normally we would adapt the products we use on premium European cars for use in the Indian market. And if our goal is to take 10 per cent out of the cost, we can do that with 'value engineering'. But if your goal is to take 60 or 70 per cent of the cost out, you have to start from scratch. (Quoted in Freiberg, Freiberg and Dunston, 2011, 154)

The former CEO of Renault, the Brazilian Carlos Ghosn, used the term 'frugal engineering' to describe this engineering based on economizing the use of materials and energy (Gomes, 2011). Frugal engineering does not create a low-tech version, but a high-tech one that reduces both material and energy costs. As analysed by Brynjolfsson and McAfee (2014) there is a substitution of knowledge, embedded in software, for materials and energy.

Thus, frugal engineering is not just about removing some features or functions in a product, but redesigning the product itself to reduce the overall cost. GE's China unit developed a PC-based ultrasound system that cost a mere 15 per cent of the high-end ultrasound machine. However, it was not just a question of removing some functions; rather, the low-cost unit used sophisticated software to take over some of the earlier functions carried out by expensive hardware (Immelt, Govindarajan and Trimble, 2009).

Similarly, India's IIT-Madras designed a low-cost automated teller machine (ATM) suitable for use in low business volume rural areas. Instead of the spring-loading mechanism of the conventional ATM, it used a gravity system. The result was an ATM that reduced the power needed by 90 per cent and eliminated the need for air-conditioning (see TENET, 2012; Vortex Engineering, 2012).

With the world as a whole having to move to more sustainable systems of production and consumption, frugal engineering will become more important in the global market place. This will lead to further emphasis on innovation for relatively low-income markets.

However, as the examples mentioned here show, frugal engineering for low-income markets is carried out not only by firms from the emerging economies but also by OECD firms. These HIC firms are not only looking to develop these products for the low-value developing economy markets, but also to take them back to their own home economies. Thus, GE is marketing both the low-cost electrocardiogram (ECG) and ultrasound machines developed in India and China respectively in the USA. Tata's Ace sold an electric version of the small truck to the US Postal Department (Freiberg et al., 2011). The introduction of versions developed in MICs to HIC markets led to the now-retired CEO of GE, Jeff Immelt, to support the use of the term 'reverse innovation' to describe this phenomenon (Immelt et al., 2009).

As Immelt put it, 'To be honest, the company is also embracing reverse innovation for defensive reasons. If GE doesn't come up with innovations in poor countries and take them global, new competitors from the developing world – like Mindray, Suzlon, Goldwind and Haier – will' (Immelt et al., 2009, 5). Through low-cost devices, China has captured the world market for low-cost smartphones and a whole host of household equipment, while India has become a centre for small-car production.

Frugal engineering can also be disruptive in high-income OECD economies. With the realization of the need to reduce the human impact on the environment, frugal engineering can be the way forward all over the world. Will the affinity of the middle-income economies (such as China and India) for frugal methods give them an advantage in developing environment-friendly new products?

Currently, the advances due to frugal engineering are based on technology that already exists. Frugal engineering leading to reverse innovation has so far been restricted to reshaping existing products in such a way that there is economy in the use of both materials and energy. It has not as yet been applied to the development of entirely new products. However, in this contemporary development of new products, an important GVC factor should be noticed – the separation of manufacture from conception and design, largely concentrated in lead firms in developed countries, while manufacture is outsourced to developing economies, largely in Asia.

This unbundling of the overall production process reduces the sunk costs that an integrated design-cum-manufacturing firm would incur in moving from innovation to products. The sunk costs are borne by the supplier in Asia, while the lead firm in the developed countries does not have to incur the sunk costs. This promotes what has been called 'fast innovation' (George, Works and Watson-Hemphill, 2005) Fast innovation is usually attributed to rapid technological development, as in computer chips. In consumer and other products, though, the factor of not having to bear sunk costs must have an effect in promoting this fast innovation. The lead firm no longer needs to be inhibited in coming out with ever newer products.

Apple is cited as an example of an innovator willing to cannibalize its own products. 'The most successful [innovators] aren't afraid to cannibalize their big revenue generators to generate new business' (Ante, 2012). Would Apple have been as quick to move from the iPod to the iPod Touch and then the iPad if it had to take account of sunk costs? With competition among Asian suppliers, manufacturing costs are pared down to the minimum – even Foxconn earns just about a 3 to 4 per cent margin on its revenues (Chan *et al.*, 2016; Gale, Chapter 2). The costs of changing production lines are borne by the Asian manufacturers, while the design-cum-marketing lead firms earn high margins through high-speed innovation of products, or, even for that matter, through fast fashion.

Limits to reverse innovation

Making new products does not necessarily involve the application of new knowledge. The set of all feasible technologies with existing knowledge is generally accepted to be larger than the set of existing technologies (Kaufmann, 2000; Mokyr, 2000). However, moving from knowledge to new technologies is a long and costly process. Much of the costs of this process are actually borne not by private sector firms but by the public sector. Further, as strongly argued in Mazzucato (2014), the public sector is involved not only in the creation of technology, but also in developing its commercialization. The uncertainty related to unused technologies reduces the incentive of firms to invest in their commercialization. For instance, in the development of new chemical entities in the form of anti-retro viral AIDS drugs, the US Government's National Institutes of Health did all the discovery and product development, before handing them over to private companies for commercial use (Light, 2006). Mazzucato notes that the key technologies of the iPhone, such as the touch screen and the digital assistant, were developed by the US Department of Defense and were ready for Apple to incorporate them into the iPhone. Apple's innovation was not in the development of those technologies, but in their application to the smartphone.

Thus, in the movement from incremental changes, such as in reverse frugal engineering, to creating new products, there is a big role to be played by non-commercial actors from the public sector. This should be part of a policy that is not specific to GVCs in developing new products and thus breaking out of the middle-income trap. As noted in Chapter 14 by Smita Srinivas, there is more to promoting innovation than GVC policy. However, it should be added, a policy to assist GVCs can help concentrate innovation efforts on segments of the value chain that relate to the core competencies related to a product.

Furthermore, it is necessary to consider that making breakthroughs in developing new products is not just a matter of public sector spending. It is not the deployment of simple economic power that results in the creation of new technology and, even more so, of new knowledge. There is the necessary development of sufficiently large scientific and technical manpower, and of a scientific establishment that is willing to experiment and be critical; both can be affected by the deployment of economic power.

However, such a scientific establishment itself cannot be developed in isolation from the rest of society. The movement from catching-up in manufacture or from the middle-income trap to catching-up or even leapfrogging in the creation of technology and knowledge requires a culture that is willing to critique existing thought to develop knowledge. The importance of critical attitudes in developing technology and knowledge is stressed by Joel Mokyr in both *Gifts of Athena* (2004) and the *Culture of Growth* (2015). One can argue that the gifts of Athena do not accrue to societies that do not encourage critical thinking, or, as it was put in a jointly authored paper (Kelkar and Nathan, 2002), there can be a cultural ceiling that comes into operation impeding the creation of new knowledge and technology.

It was the unevenness in the creation of knowledge and technology that led to the great divergence starting with the Industrial Revolution. The spread of knowledge has moderated the divergence and led to a form of convergence. Completing the convergence will, however, require overcoming the still existing unevenness in the creation of technology and knowledge.

In the economy, however, knowledge has to be manifested in technology and then in production. Thus, one can note the weakness of the pre-modern Chinese economy, which had knowledge and even the technology of paper, printing, gunpowder and the compass (Needham, 1954) but had not deployed them in an effective manner in production. The world's 'middle kingdom' is not necessarily the largest economy in the world but the economy that is the centre of technology and knowledge creation.

Conclusion

There are a number of ways in which one can categorize the states and transitions, whether of firms or economies, that have been analysed in this chapter. These are summarized here.

At the firm level, there is entry-level participation in a GVC, where the firm earns no rent. Firms that carry out process improvements or innovations can then earn some process rent. The next level is that of earning product rents; which itself can be differentiated between lower rents from incremental changes in products and higher rents from altogether new products.

At the level of functions this is the movement from being a basic supplier, such as of assembly in electronics or cut-make-trim in garments, to becoming a full-package supplier, and then going on to becoming a lead firm with its own GVC.

This is congruent with the movement at the level of tasks performed by most workers in a firm – from routine tasks in manufacture or services functionally upgrading to non-routine tasks, such as design and other forms of decision-making, and going on to conceive of new products and services. In terms of vertical specialization, it is a move from being specialized in low-return activities in low-income countries, to being less specialized in middle-income countries, and again to becoming specialized in high-return activities.

In the domain of knowledge, there is a progression from low- to medium- and finally high-knowledge bases of production. This can also be seen in the economy-level changes, depending on the preponderance of different types of firms in the economy – the first step is that of catch-up in production, then the making of incremental improvements, whether in process or products, and finally the creation of new products – a basic shift from knowledge utilization to knowledge creation. This is also the transition from low-income to middle-income and then high-income status. The most difficult change (leading to the difficulty of negotiating the middle-income trap) is from incremental changes to new products and to the creation of new technology and even knowledge creation.

While the sequences have been presented in a somewhat linear fashion, there can well be leapfrogging and advances in both technology and knowledge creation. However, the importance of making the transition from utilization of knowledge to creation of knowledge and technology remains undiminished in order for complete catch-up or complete convergence.

References

Acemoglu, Daron and David Autor. 2010. 'Skills, Tasks and Technologies: Implications for Employment and Earnings.' NBER Working Paper 16082. Accessed 10 September 2015. Available at nber.org/papers/w16082.

Amsden, Alice. 2001. *The Rise of 'The Rest': Challenges to the West from Late Industrializing Economies.* Oxford: Oxford University Press.

Ante, S. 2012. 'Avoiding Innovation's Terrible Toll.' *Wall Street Journal*, 7–8 January.

Applebaum, Richard 2006. 'Giant Retailers and Giant Contractors in China: Emergent Trends in Global Supply Chains.' Accessed 22 June 2017. Available at http://www.princeton.edu/~ina/gkg/confs/appelbaum.pdf.

Amit, Raphael and Paul Schoemaker. 1993. 'Strategic Assets and Organizational Rent.' *Strategic Management Journal* 14 (1): 33–46.

Autor, David. 2013. 'The Task Approach to Labor Markets: An Overview.' NBER Working Paper 18711. Accessed 1 September 2015. Available at nber.org/papers/w187aa.

Baldwin, Richard. 2016. *The Great Convergence: Information Technology and the New Globalization.* Cambridge, MA: Harvard at the Belknap Press.

Bamber, Penny, Andrew Guinn and Gary Gereffi. 2014. *Skills in Private Sector Development: Burundi in the Agribusiness, Coffee and Energy Global Value Chains.* CGGC, Duke University. Accessed 20 January 2016. Available at www.cggc.com.

Barrientos, Stephanie, Gary Gereffi and Arianna Rossi. 2011. 'Economic and Social Upgrading in Global Production Networks: A New Paradigm for a Changing World.' *International Labour Review* 150 (3–4): 319–40.

Bloom, Nicholas, Benn Eifert, David McKenzie, Aprajit Mahajan and John Roberts. 2013. 'Does Management Matter? A Study of the Textile Industry in India.' *Quarterly Journal of Economics* 128 (1): 1–51.

Brynjolfsson, Erik and Andrew McAfee. 2014. *The Second Machine Age: Work, Progress and Prosperity in an Age of Brilliant Technologies*. Boston: W. W. Norton and Company.

Chan, Jenny, Ngai Pun and Mark Selden. 2016. 'The Politics of Global Production: Apple, Foxconn and China's New Working Class.' In *Labour in Global Value Chains in Asia*, edited by Dev Nathan, Meenu Tewari and Sandip Sarkar, 353–76. Cambridge: Cambridge University Press.

Chang, Ha Joon. 2003. *Kicking Away the Ladder: Development Strategy in Historical Perspective*. London: Anthem Press.

Coe, Neil and Henry Wai-chung Yeung. 2015. *Global Production Networks: Theorizing Economic Development in an Inter-Connected World*. Oxford: Oxford University Press.

Damodaran, Sumangala. 2016. 'New Strategies of Industrial Organization and Labour in the Mobile Telecom Sector in India.' In *Labour in Global Value Chains in Asia*, edited by Dev Nathan, Meenu Tewari and Sandip Sarkar, 377–97. Cambridge: Cambridge University Press.

Davis, Dennis, Raphael Kaplinsky and Mike Morris. 2017. 'Rents, Power and Governance in Global Value Chains.' PRISM Working Papers, No. 2. Cape Town: School of Economics, University of Cape Town. Accessed 26 June 2017. Available at http://www.prism.uct.ac.za/.

Fang, Cai and W. Wang. 2010. 'Growth and Structural Changes in Employment in Transition China.' *Journal of Development Economics* 38: 71–81.

Freiberg, K., J. Freiberg and D. Dunston. 2011. *Nanovation: How A Little Car Can Teach the World to Think Big and Act Bold*. Nashville, TN: Thomas Nelson.

George, Michael, James Works and Kimberly Wawatsontson-Hemphill. 2005. *Fast Innovation*. New York: McGraw Hill.

Gereffi, Gary. 1994. 'Organization of Buyer-driven Commodity Chains.' In *Commodity Chains and Global Capitalism*, edited by G. Gereffi and M. Korzeniewicz, 95–122. Westport: Praeger

———. 2009. 'Development Models and Industrial Upgrading in China and Mexico.' *European Sociological Review* 25 (1): 37–51.

Gereffi, Gary and Tim Sturgeon. 2013. 'Global Value Chains and Development Policy: The Role of Emerging Economies.' In *Global Value Chains in a Changing World*, edited by Deborah Elms and Patrick Low, 329–60. Geneva: WTO, Fung Global Institute and Temasek Centre for Trade and Negotiations.

Ghose, Ajit. 2016. *India Employment Report*. New Delhi: IHD and Oxford University Press.

Gibbon, P. and S. Ponte. 2005. *Trading Down: Africa, Value Chains and the Global Economy*. Philadelphia: Temple University Press.

Goger, Annelies. 2014. 'Ethical Branding in Sri Lanka: A Case Study of Garments Without Guilt.' In *Workers' Rights and Labour Compliance in Global Supply Chains:*

Is a Social Label the Answer? edited by Jennifer Bair, Marsha Dickinson and Dough Miller, 47–68. New York: Routledge.

———. 2016. 'From Disposable to Empowered: Rearticulating Labour in Sri Lankan Apparel Factories.' In *Labour in Global Value Chains in Asia*, edited by Dev Nathan, Meenu Tewari and Sandip Sarkar, 239–64. Cambridge: Cambridge University Press.

Gomes, I. 2011. *Frugal Engineering*. Accessed 2 October 2011. Available at www. kmmg.com.

Hausmann, R., C. A. Hidalgo, S. Bustos, M. Coscia and Md. A. Yildirim. 2013. *The Atlas of Economic Complexity: Mapping Paths to Prosperity*. Cambridge, MA: The MIT Press.

Horner, Rory. 2014. 'Strategic Decoupling, Recoupling and Global Production Networks.' *Journal of Economic Geography* 14 (6): 1117–40.

Humphrey, John and Hubert Schmitz. 2000. 'Governance and Upgrading: Linking Industrial Cluster and Global Value Chain Research.' IDS Working Paper 120. Accessed 26 June 2017. Available at https://www.ids.ac.uk/files/Wp120.pdf.

Ichinowski, C. and K. Shaw. 2003. 'Beyond Incentive Pay: Insiders' Estimates of the Value of Complementary Resource Management Practices.' *Journal of Economic Perspectives* 17 (1): 155–80.

Immelt, J., V. Govindrajan, and C. Trimble. 2009. 'How GE Is Disrupting Itself.' *Harvard Business Review* 87 (10) (October): 56–65.

Kaufmann, Stuart. 2000. *Investigations*. Oxford: Oxford University Press.

Kaplinsky, Raphael. 2005. *Globalization, Poverty and Inequality*. Cambridge: Polity Press.

Kelkar, Govind and Dev Nathan. 2002. 'Gender Relations and Technological Change in Asia.' *Current Sociology* 50 (3): 427–41.

Light, Donald W. 2006. 'Basic Research to Discover Important New Drugs: Who Contributes How Much?' Accessed 21 September 2013. Available at kms1.isn. ethz.ch/serviceengine/Files/ISN/.../en/mff.05_chap3.pdf⊠.

Marcolin, Luca, Sebastien Mirodout and Mariagrazia Squicciarini. 2016. 'Routine Jobs, Employment and Technological Innovation in Global Value Chains.' OECD Science, Technology and Industry Working Papers 2016/01. Paris: OECD Publishing.

Maree, Johann, Rachel Piontak, Tommy Omwansa, Isaac Shinyekwa and Kamotho Njenga. 203. 'Developmental Uses of Mobile Phones in Kenya and Uganda.' Capturing the Gains Working Paper 2013/35. Accessed 30 June 2016. Available at www.capturingthegains.org.

Mazzucato, Mariana. 2014. *The Entrepreneurial State*. London: Anthem Press.

Milanovic, Branko. 2016. *Global Inequality: A New Approach for the Age of Globalization*. Cambridge, MA: Harvard University Press.

Milberg, William and Deborah Winkler. 2013. *Outsourcing Economics: Global Value Chains in Capitalist Development*. Cambridge: Cambridge University Press.

MIT Technology Review. 2017. '50 Smartest Companies.' Accessed 4 September 2017. Available at https://www.technologyreview.com/lists/companies/2016/.

Mokyr, Joel. 2000. 'Evolutionary Phenomena in Technological Change.' In *Technological Innovation as an Evolutionary Process*, edited by J. Ziman, 52–65. Cambridge: Cambridge University Press.

———. 2004. *The Gifts of Athena: Historical Origins of the Knowledge Economy*. Princeton: Princeton University Press.

———. 2015. *A Culture of Growth: Origins of the Modern Economy*. Princeton: Princeton University Press.

Morris, Mike, Raphael Kaplinsky and David Kaplan. 2012. *One Thing Leads to Another: Promoting Industrialisation by Making the Most of the Commodity Boom in Sub-Saharan Africa*. Cape Town: PRISM, The University of Cape Town. Accessed June 30, 2016. Available at www.prism.uct.ac.za/Downloads/MMCP%20Book.pdf.

Nathan, Dev. 2016. 'Governance Types and Employment Systems.' In *Labour in Global Value Chains in Asia*, edited by Dev Nathan, Meenu Tewari and Sandip Sarkar, 479–502. Cambridge: Cambridge University Press.

Nathan, Dev and Abhishek Kumar. 2016. 'Knowledge, Education and Labour Practices in India.' *Economic and Political Weekly* 51 (36): 37–45.

Nathan, Dev and Sandip Sarkar. 2011. 'Profits, Rents and Wages in Global Production Networks.' *Economic and Political Weekly* 46 (36): 53–57.

———. 2014. 'From Reverse Engineering to Reverse Innovation: GPNs and The Emerging Powers.' In *Globalization and Standards: Issues and Challenges in Indian Business*, edited by Keshab Das, 181–92. Berlin: Springer.

Nathan, Dev, Meenu Tewari and Sandip Sarkar. 2016. 'Introduction.' In *Labour in Global Value Chains in Asia*, edited by Dev Nathan, Meenu Tewari and Sandip Sarkar, 3–30. Cambridge: Cambridge University Press.

Nayyar, Deepak. 2013. *Catch Up: Developing Countries in the World Economy*. Oxford: Oxford University Press.

Needham, Joseph. 1964. *Science and Civilization in China: Introductory Orientations*, Vol.1. Cambridge: Cambridge University Press.

Oldenski, L. 2012. 'The Task Composition of Offshoring by US Multinationals.' Accessed 20 June 2017. Available at http://faculty.georgetown.edu/lo36/Oldenski_Task_Offshoring_Sept2012.pdf.

Perry, Patsy, Steve Wood and John Fernie. 2014. 'Corporate Social Responsibility in Garment Sourcing: Factory Management Perspectives on Ethical Trade in Sri Lanka.' Accessed 23 June 2017. Available at https://www.research.manchester.ac.uk/portal/en/publications/corporate-social-responsibility-in-garment-sourcing-networks-factory-management-perspectives-on-ethical-trade-in-sri-lanka(5565fcd9-a98e-45b0-bee0-e5ebe1b60818).html.

Pickles, J. and A. Smith. 2016. 'Delocalization and Persistence in the European Clothing Industry: The Reconfiguration of Trade and Production.' *Regional Studies* 45 (2): 167–85.

Prahalad, C. K. 2004 *The Fortune at the Bottom of the Pyramid: Eradicating Poverty Through Profits.* Upper Saddle River, NJ: Wharton School Publishing.

Prahalad, C. K. and G. Hamel. 1990. 'The Core Competence of the Corporation.' *Harvard Business Review* 68 (3): 79–91.

Robertson, Raymond, Hongyang Di, Drusilla Brown and Rajeev Dehejia. 2016. 'Working Conditions, Work Outcomes, and Policy in Asian Developing Countries.' Paper presented at ADB Workshop, January. Manila: ADB (mimeo).

Rodgers, Gerry, Amrita Datta, Janine Rodgers, Sunil Mishra and Alakh Sharma. 2013. *The Challenge of Inclusive Development in Rural Bihar.* New Delhi: MANAK Publications.

Ruwanpura, Kanchana. 2016a. 'Scripted Performances? Local Readings of "Global" Health and Safety Standards in the Apparel Sector in Sri Lanka.' In *Labour in Global Value Chains in Asia,* edited by Dev Nathan, Meenu Tewari and Sandip Sarkar, 265–86. Cambridge: Cambridge University Press.

———. 2016b. 'Living Wages: The Achilles Heel of the Sri Lankan Garment Industry?' Fashionrevolution.org. Accessed March 30, 2017. Available at http://fashionrevolution.org/living-wages-the-achilles-heel-of-the-sri-lankan-garment-industry/.

Shih, Stan. 2010. *Millennium Transformation: Change Management for New Acer.* Translated by Eugene Hwang. Aspire Academy Series. Accessed 4 July 2017. Available at http://www.stanshares.com.tw/StanShares/upload/tbBook/1_20100817144639.pdf.

Teese, David J., Gary Pisano and Amy Schuen. 1997. 'Dynamic Capabiliteis and Strategic Management.' *Strategic Management Journal* 18 (7): 509–33.

TENET. 2012. 'Products – Rural ATM.' Accessed 22 August 2012. Available at www.tenet.res.in/Activities/Products/doc/ruralATM.php.

Tewari, Meenu and P. Pillai. 2005. 'Global Standards and the Dynamics of Environmental Compliance in India's Leather Industry.' *Oxford Development Studies.* 33 (2): 245–67.

UNCTAD. 2013. *Trade and Investment Development: Global Value Chains: Investment for Trade and Development.* Geneva: UNCTAD.

Vortex Engineering. 2012. 'World's Lowest Power Consuming ATMs.' Accessed 22 August 2012. Available at http://vortex.co.in.

Werner, Marion. 2012. 'Beyond Upgrading: Gendered Labour and the Restructuring of Firms in the Dominican Republic.' *Economic Geography* 88 (4): 403–22.

World Bank and the Development Research Centre of the State Council, PRC. 2013. *China 2030: Building a Modern, Harmonious, and Creative Society.* Washington, DC: The World Bank.

Contributors

Dinesh Abrol is Professor at the Institute of Studies in Industrial Development, India. He was chief scientist at the National Institute of Science, Technology and Development Studies, New Delhi. His research interests are the pharmaceutical industry, intellectual property, technology assessment and science, technology and innovation policy.

Neetu Ahmed has over fourteen years of experience in research and teaching of management courses. She is currently pursuing PhD in International Economics at the Indira Gandhi National Open University (IGNOU), New Delhi. Her research interests include international trade and knowledge economy.

Prema-chandra Athukorala is Professor of Economics at the Crawford School of Public Policy, Australian National University, Canberra, and Fellow of the Academy of the Social Sciences in Australia, Canberra. He has published books and articles on trade and development and consulted, at various times, for the World Bank, Asian Development Bank and various UN organisations.

Penny Bamber is Senior Researcher at the Duke University Global Value Chains Center (GVCC), Durham. Her research focuses on economic development, trade competitiveness and social upgrading issues in developed and developing countries. Her work covers a wide range of industries, from manufacturing to natural resources and services sectors, and regions.

Jack Daly is Research Analyst at the Duke GVCC, Durham. His research there has examined manufacturing, agribusiness and service value chains in a variety of geographic locations. His experience in the Philippines led to analysis of the automotive, paper, rubber and coffee sectors.

Peilei Fan is Associate Professor of Urban and Regional Planning at Michigan State University, East Lansing. She has a PhD in Economic Development and an MS in Electrical Engineering and Computer Science, both from the Massachusetts Institute of Technology, Cambridge, USA. Her research focuses on innovation and economic development, and sustainability.

Stacey Frederick is Research Scientist at the Duke GVCC, Durham. Her research involves using global value chain analysis to identify upgrading opportunities for countries and firms in a variety of industries. She received her BS in Textile Management and her PhD in Textile Technology Management from North Carolina State University, Raleigh.

Gary Gereffi is the Founding Director of the Global Value Chains Center at Duke University, Durham. He has published numerous books and articles on globalization, industrial upgrading, and social and economic development, and is one of the originators of the global commodity chain and global value chain frameworks.

Harsh is a research scholar in Management (Industrial Relations and Human Resource Management, NET) at Birla Institute of Technology, Mesra. She has worked with various social, workers' and employers' organizations.

Qingcan He is a teacher of geography in Tsinghua University High School, Beijing. He majored in Human Geography at Beijing Normal University.

Joonkoo Lee is Assistant Professor in the School of Business at Hanyang University, Seoul. His research interests include global value chains, and economic and social upgrading, focusing on Asia. His work has appeared in *Proceedings of the National Academy of Sciences*, *Journal of Business Ethics*, and *Journal of Contemporary Asia*.

Sang-Hoon Lee is a doctoral student in the School of Labor and Employment Relations at the University of Illinois at Urbana-Champaign. His research interests are micro organizational behaviour topics such as team processes and effectiveness, employee work motivation and stress, and work–family balance.

Dev Nathan is Visiting Professor at the Institute for Human Development, India; Research Coordinator of Global Production Network Studies, New Delhi, India; and Visiting Research Fellow at the Duke University GVC Center, Durham, USA. His research interests include global production, labour, gender relations and indigenous peoples.

Gwanho Park is a construction supervisor at Korea Land and Housing Corporation, Jinju. He majored in architecture and business administration at Hanyang University, Seoul. His interests include economic geography, housing supply and policy and urban issues.

Gale Raj-Reichert is Lecturer in Economic Geography in the School of Geography at Queen Mary University of London. Her research interests are on labour governance in the electronics industry global value chain/global production networks. Gale's research has focused on the US, EU, Malaysia, Singapore, China, Vietnam and Hong Kong. Her current research interest is how socially responsible public procurement and labour standards in trade agreements affect labour conditions in global value chains/global production networks.

Sandip Sarkar is Professor at the Institute for Human Development, New Delhi. His research interests are industry, poverty, value chain, labour and employment.

Nidhi Singh is a scientist in the Department of Health Research, Ministry of Health and Family Welfare, Government of India, New Delhi. She is pursuing PhD at the Centre for Studies in Science Policy at Jawaharlal Nehru University, New Delhi, on molecular diagnostics innovation.

Meenu Tewari is Associate Professor of Economic and International Development at the University of North Carolina at Chapel Hill. She studies the political economy of development. Her current research is on production networks, institutional reform in the urban sector and the challenges of urbanization in an era of climate change.

Nasir Tyabji is an economic historian interested in the processes of industrialisation, technological development and innovation. He was Director and Professor at the Centre for Jawaharlal Nehru Studies, Jamia Millia Islamia, New Delhi. Earlier, he had taught at Jawaharlal Nehru University, New Delhi, and had been a Professorial Fellow at the Nehru Memorial Museum and Library, New Delhi.

Fan Xu engages in transportation planning and management in Rizhao Transportation Bureau, Shangdong Province, China.

Huasheng Zhu is Associate Professor at the Faculty of Geograpical Science, Beijing Normal University. His academic interests focus on industrial geography, and local entrepreneurial activity, innovation and industrial upgrading.

Shengjun Zhu is Assistant Professor at the College of Urban and Environmental Sciences at Peking University, Beijing. His major interests are globalization, regional development, global production networks, global value chains, industrial relocation and delocalization and industrial, social and environmental upgrading/downgrading. He has published in the *Journal of Economic Geography*, *Journal of Contemporary Asia*, *Urban Studies*, *Cambridge Journal of Regions, Economy, and Society* and *Environment and Planning C*.

Index

Subject index

absenteeism, 74, 77, 81, 144

Accenture, 10, 229–230, 234, 237–238, 242–243

acquired knowledge, 3

active pharmaceutical ingredients (APIs), 282, 283n2, 286, 311

Aerospace, 21, 28, 31–32, 44–47, 51–52, 59–60, 107–109, 111, 118–128, 178, 242

Allied Nippon, 137–138

animation, 317, 321, 332–341

antibiotics, 360

anti-retroviral, 16

apparel export, 194–195, 200, 204, 205n8, 207–210, 211n17, 212, 214, 216–217, 221–222, 322

Apparel Export Promotion Corporation (AEPC), 64, 64n1

apparel firms, 66, 97, 198, 201–203, 207–208, 211, 322, 326n3

apparel industry, 63–83, 97, 193–194, 196, 198n3, 199–209, 211–214, 222–224, 322, 390

Apple, 8, 12, 24, 26, 31, 36, 39, 43, 248–249, 251–252, 256–258, 261, 382, 398, 401–402

Artificial intelligence (AI), 230, 232–233, 238–239, 299

Asian Tigers, 319, 377

assembly-line, 34, 73–75, 390

ASUS, 24, 398

attrition, 71, 76–77, 79–80, 127

audit, 139–140, 206

automobile, 1–4, 8, 10, 14, 28, 52, 114–115, 135, 147, 180–182, 184–185, 266, 317, 320–321, 323, 327–332, 338–339, 364, 378, 383, 397–399

automotive industry, 45–47, 60, 114–115, 123, 128, 132, 134, 143, 145, 147, 181, 327–328, 339

backward linkages, 15, 113, 122, 161, 196, 204–205

Bangladesh, 70–71, 202n7, 203, 205n11, 208, 208n16, 211–212, 217–220, 222n23, 379–380

Beijing, 9, 33, 48–49, 261, 267–269, 271

BenQ, 24

brand name customer firms, 24

Brexit, 231, 395

British Telecom, 158, 164

Cambodia, 64, 66–68, 71, 82, 211–212, 217–220, 222n23, 379–380, 390

capital expenditure, 73

cash hoard, 235

Celestica, 20–22, 32, 34–47, 50, 59–60, 62

cellular manufacturing, 177

certification, 46, 122, 124, 136n3, 138–140, 147, 207, 295, 350

chaebol, 320–321, 324, 335–336, 340

child labour, 206

China, 1–2, 14–15, 21, 31, 33, 35, 47–51, 59, 71–72, 80, 86–100, 111,

113–115, 125–127, 151, 157–161,
163–164, 167–172, 205, 211–212,
217–220, 222n23, 230, 234, 248–260,
264–270, 272–273, 282, 300, 309n8,
322, 325–326, 330–331, 335, 341,
380–381, 383–386, 389, 392, 394,
397–400

Cisco, 22, 28–29, 44, 163

Citi FinTech, 231

Compaq, 22, 35

compliance, 21, 68, 139, 146–147,
186–187, 206, 213, 223

computer numerically controlled
(CNC), 124, 182

concurrent engineering, 178–179, 185

configuration technologies, 161, 172

consumer technologies, 44

contract labourers, 69, 76

contract manufacturing, 16, 20, 22–34,
36, 51–52, 59, 201, 293–294, 382

Coordinating Committee for
Multilateral Export Control
(COCOM), 171

core competencies, 7, 22, 26, 36, 91, 97,
263, 270, 273, 374–375, 402

core technologies, 43, 98, 161, 231, 264,
269

customer firms, 23–27, 29, 35–36, 40,
52

cut-make-trim (CMT), 6, 9, 196, 201–
202, 324, 378, 383, 390, 403

Daimler-Benz, 179–180

Datang, 157–158, 160, 170

decentralization, 97–99

Dell, 24, 26, 28, 35, 36, 36n2, 39, 43–44

design, 4, 6–7, 9–11, 14–16, 20–36,
40–45, 47–52, 59–60, 91, 98, 114,
117–120, 124, 145, 150, 161–163,
176–181, 183–184, 186–189, 196,
201–203, 208, 213, 220, 223–224,
229, 237–238, 241–243, 248, 253,

257, 259–261, 264, 266, 268–272,
283, 290, 304, 317, 319, 326, 326n3,
327–330, 341, 353–354, 356, 360–
361, 364, 366–367, 369, 378, 382–
384, 386–388, 395–397, 399–401, 403

developing countries, 8, 11, 33, 66,
111, 115, 120, 153, 162, 164, 176,
195–196, 200, 206, 207n13, 213n20,
230, 247–249, 265, 285, 297, 309,
309n8, 312, 321, 323, 325n2, 327,
338, 358–359, 373–374, 376–381,
385–386, 389, 391

development policy, 16, 373–404

digital innovation, 231, 243

diversification, 20–21, 23–26, 30–31, 34,
36, 44–46, 112–113, 138

domestic apparel producers, 195

domestic firm, 97, 113, 158, 161–162,
169–172, 280–297, 301–302, 306–
312

domestic market, 48, 87, 92, 98–100,
126–127, 135n1, 145, 151, 157–158,
164, 168, 185, 196, 248–249, 252,
257, 262–263, 265, 270–272, 287,
290, 293, 300, 302–303, 309–310,
312, 326, 329, 350, 357, 365–366,
379, 381, 389

domestic pharmaceutical firm, 280–281,
283, 283n2, 284–285, 287, 290–291,
294, 300, 309–310

domestic producers, 161, 170, 172, 325

drug discovery, 279–312

drug price control, 280

East Asia, 33, 169, 198, 200–204, 211,
224, 248, 318–320, 323, 325, 333

e-commerce, 232, 242, 263

electronics, 1, 3–4, 7, 14, 20–52, 59–60,
97, 107–109, 111–121, 123, 126, 128,
159–160, 316, 323, 327, 331, 340n8,
350, 364, 382, 393, 397, 403

emerging economies, 20, 51, 151, 158,
386, 399–400

end markets, 26, 32–33, 43–44, 47, 62, 98, 113, 128, 184, 223, 251, 257–258
end-users, 149
engineering, 7–8, 14–16, 20–21, 23, 25, 31, 33–34, 36, 40, 42, 44–49, 51, 59–60, 115, 117, 124, 139, 158, 176–189, 241–242, 374, 383–384, 387, 390–392, 398–402
evolutionary economic geography (EEG), 95–96, 100
exogenous rents, 12
export processing zones (EPZs), 48, 87, 108–109, 113–114, 127, 198–200
export-oriented industrialization (EOI), 17, 86, 88, 195, 377–378

fashion-basic, 213, 213n20, 214, 216–217, 222–224
Fiat, 45, 143–144, 328
first-tier suppliers, 20, 22, 24, 52, 118, 133, 144, 153, 330
flex, 14, 20–21, 25, 28, 32, 34–49, 59–61
foreign invested enterprises (FIEs), 200–201
foreign investment, 107, 115, 118, 127, 197–199, 266, 273, 316, 318, 324
forward linkages, 15, 353–354
Foxconn, 2, 14, 20, 25, 28, 30–31, 34, 42, 47, 59–60, 249, 263, 382, 401
frugal engineering, 15, 176–189, 374, 398–402
full-package supply, 6, 9, 13, 194, 382–383, 387, 390, 394–397

gaige kaifang, 86
garment, 1, 3–6, 9, 13–14, 64, 66–77, 80–82, 200n5, 202, 202n7, 213, 320, 322–326, 350, 353, 364, 377–382, 384, 388, 390, 395, 398, 403
GE, 231, 400
generic capabilities, 21, 23, 30

global buyer, 97, 135, 151, 195n1, 317–318, 320–321
global delivery model (GDM), 9–10, 15, 229–230, 232, 234
global innovation network (GIN), 33
global inter-linkages, 360, 386
global value chain (GVC), 1–5, 7–9, 11–12, 14, 16, 20–52, 63, 92–93, 95–96, 100, 107–128, 132–133, 142, 161, 163, 195–196, 224, 236, 247–248, 316–341, 350–351, 353, 359, 364–365, 368–370, 373–404
globalization, 32, 50, 86–87, 89, 92–95, 97, 99, 120, 159, 162n2, 164–169, 172, 330–332, 340
Go Out/regionalization, 91–92, 97
Go Up, 91–92, 97
Go West/delocalization, 91–92, 97
Great Dragon Technology (GDT), 157–158, 160, 170
Greater Colombo Economic Commission (GCEC), 198–200
GVC framework, 9, 195–196, 224, 387–388
GVC literature, 1, 3, 9, 14, 20–21, 23, 25, 319, 381
GVC policies, 7, 402
GVC structures, 2, 8–9, 380

Hangzhou, 266–269
headquarter economies, 2, 375
Hewlett-Packard, 22, 24, 26, 28–29, 35–36
high-income country (HIC), 5, 8–9, 230, 373, 395–396, 400
high-skill tasks, 15
high-skilled workers, 33
Hong Kong, 48–49, 91–92, 96, 163, 198n3, 200–201, 202n7, 204–205, 208–209, 263, 268, 323, 377–378
Huawei, 8, 15, 48, 157–165, 167–168, 170–172, 238, 249, 252, 256, 261, 265, 384, 389, 398

human capital, 14, 32, 91, 107–108, 123, 126, 128, 207–209, 213, 223, 273

human resource, 21, 66, 72, 390

human rights legislation, 70

human–computer interaction technology (HCIT), 256

Hyundai, 16, 136, 136n3, 138–140, 143, 153, 327–332, 341, 397

IBM, 10, 22, 26, 35, 44, 229–230, 232–234, 238, 374–375

ILO–IFC Better Work Programme, 64, 66–68, 71

import-substituting industrialization (ISI), 16–17, 376–378

incentive, 34, 69–70, 77–78, 82, 108, 109n3, 122, 148, 198–199, 296, 309–310, 328, 360, 366, 401

Indian Patent Act, 311

industrial catch-up, 1–2, 10, 374

industrial clustering, 89, 93, 100

Infosys, 9, 229, 233–242

integrated circuit (IC) design, 253

intellectual property rights, 8, 12, 283, 307, 311

intermediaries, 6, 141, 197, 202, 224, 382

International Data Corporation (IDC), 232

International Labour Organization (ILO), 64, 66–68, 70–71, 206

Internet of Things (IoT), 30, 40, 45, 230, 232–233

Intra-ASEAN trade, 114

IT Enabled Services (ITES), 230, 244

IT firm, 10, 231–237, 239–241, 243–244, 332

Jabil Circuit, 20–22, 25, 29, 32, 34–47, 49–50, 59–61

Japan, 7, 42, 59, 91, 108, 113–117, 121, 124, 126, 128, 137, 141, 163, 169,

177, 182, 185, 188, 237, 259–260, 288n5, 289, 296, 302, 316, 323–326, 328–330, 332–334, 339, 375, 385

Joint Apparel Association Forum (JAAF), 194, 205n10, 207–208

Kia, 327–328, 330–332, 341

labour law, 68–69

labour market, 3, 9, 14, 72, 90, 92, 197, 198n3, 199–200, 206, 224, 380–381

labour-intensive, 31, 47, 81, 87, 89–92, 94, 97, 99, 108, 112, 126, 206, 319, 322–324, 332–333, 373, 377–381

latecomer advantage, 159–160

latecomer disadvantage, 159

Latin America, 6, 127, 212, 353, 355, 377

lead firms, 2, 5–8, 11, 14–16, 21, 23–24, 64, 83, 89, 92–93, 96, 118, 121–122, 194–197, 201, 205, 225, 360, 364, 373–375, 379, 382–384, 391–394, 397–399, 401, 403

lead firm-supplier relationship, 23

Lenovo, 24, 48, 251–252, 256, 260–262, 267, 271, 273

LG, 252, 256, 269, 340n8, 397

liberalization, 100, 143, 198–200, 204, 208, 223–224, 283–284

light commercial vehicle (LCV), 182, 184

local firms, 98, 114, 122–123, 125, 169, 201, 203, 296, 317–319, 322, 329, 338–339, 357

lock-stitch garment, 75

low- or middle-income country (LMIC), 5, 9, 230

low quality trap, 148–150

lower/lowest tier suppliers, 133, 139, 152

low-wage labour, 86, 91, 142n6
Lucent, 59–60, 157, 160

marketization, 86–87, 89–90, 97, 99
Maruti-Suzuki, 138, 153
Mazda, 328–329
Mercedes Benz, 8, 15, 180
mergers and acquisitions (M&As), 21,
    32, 34–36, 42, 47, 51, 59–60, 241,
    311, 368
middle-income trap, 1, 374, 394–399,
    402, 404
middle-skill tasks/codifiable manual/
    office tasks, 3–4
Mitsubishi, 125, 143, 271, 328–329
MNC, 15, 33, 121, 124, 162, 249,
    288n5, 289
mobile phone, 42–43, 247–273, 388
mobile phone market, 248–253,
    256–272
Motorola, 36, 59–60, 160, 250–252,
    261–262, 265–271
Multi-Fibre Arrangement (MFA), 67,
    69, 193–195, 197, 198n3, 199–200,
    202–204, 209, 211, 212n19, 213–214,
    217, 221–224, 322–323, 325, 325n2,
    326

Nanjing, 259, 261, 267–269
Nano project, 185–189, 399
neoliberal, 310, 317, 320, 377
new product introduction (NPI), 42,
    177
newly industrialized economies (NIEs),
    169
Nicholas Piramal, 289, 294, 296, 300
Nokia, 157, 160, 244, 249, 251–252,
    265, 267–269, 271
North Atlantic Treaty Organization
    (NATO), 171

offshore manufacturing, 32, 35, 264–
    265, 318

operating system (OS), 31, 254, 262,
    271, 332
original brand manufacturer (OBM),
    196, 202, 247–273, 320, 326
original equipment manufacturer
    (OEM), 7, 10, 27, 42–43, 117, 133,
    136–139, 140n5, 150, 153, 196, 201,
    247–273, 322, 326, 334, 383
out-license, 300
own brand manufacture (OBM), 10, 16,
    24–25
own design manufacture (ODM),
    10, 196, 202, 248–249, 254–255,
    270–271, 326

patent, 8, 10, 15, 46, 158, 205, 230, 249,
    255–256, 259, 261, 263–264, 267,
    279n1, 280, 284–288, 292, 294–296,
    309, 311, 360
Patent Cooperation Treaty (PCT), 158,
    259
patent law, 16, 284
pharmaceutical, 1, 8, 16, 28, 90, 176n2,
    279–312, 363–364, 384, 391
phased manufacturing programme
    (PMP), 176–189
Philippines, The, 1, 14, 48, 107–128,
    208, 212, 230, 333
price-makers, 63
price-takers, 63, 82
problem-solving tasks, 3
process innovation/process
    improvements, 9–11, 13–14, 63–64,
    69–70, 74, 80, 82–83, 183, 230, 279,
    357, 364, 382, 394–396, 403
producer firms, 63
product development (PD), 4, 8, 16,
    22, 28, 32–34, 42–43, 50, 176–177,
    233, 262, 268, 282, 284, 288–291,
    296–297, 300, 319, 402
product innovation/productivity
    improvements, 1, 9, 11, 14, 63, 67, 69,
    144, 241, 284, 295, 357, 362

product upgrading, 10, 114, 124, 247, 319–320, 330, 338–339, 383

production segment, 2–3, 6, 13, 387–389, 395

productivity, 63–69, 71–72, 74, 79, 81, 96, 139, 141, 142n6, 144, 149, 182, 232, 292, 329, 331, 352, 354, 357–358, 373, 376, 382, 384, 386, 390, 394

profitability, 68, 203, 231, 234, 237, 390

public-sector research laboratories, 301

Ranbaxy, 288, 288n5, 289–291, 293–294, 296, 299–300, 302, 307

recession, 26, 36, 51, 151, 270, 386

relational knowledge, 3

rent, 1, 8–9, 11–15, 69–70, 72, 75–83, 364, 373–374, 379, 383, 386, 395–396, 398–399, 403

retailers, 63, 99, 193, 196–197, 201–203, 213, 225, 263, 326, 398

return on equity (RoE), 235

reverse engineering, 7–8, 15–16, 158, 176, 187, 374, 383–384, 387, 391–392, 398–399

Samsung, 7, 16, 119, 249, 251–252, 256–257, 261, 263, 268–269, 330, 340n8, 397–398

Sanmina-SCI, 20, 34, 119

Schumpetarian rents, 13, 396

semi-skilled/unskilled, 86

semiconductors, 28, 42, 47, 60, 111–113, 119, 128, 171, 331

set-based design, 178

sexual harassment, 64, 70–71, 77, 79

Shanghai, 48–50, 259, 261

Shanghai Bell, 158

Shenzhen, 158, 259, 264–265, 272

Siemens, 31, 119, 157, 271

Silicon Valley, 22, 30, 34, 158, 165, 167–168, 266

Singapore, 21, 34–35, 48, 50, 59, 91, 377, 394

sketch to scale, 14, 40, 382

smartphone, 7, 26, 31, 43, 47, 254–256, 258, 260–264, 266, 271, 399–400, 402

South Asia, 165, 167, 203, 222n23, 355, 398

South Korea, 1, 16, 91–92, 138, 158, 169, 171, 260, 270, 316–341, 377–378, 394, 397

Sri Lanka, 1, 15, 64, 66, 68–70, 72, 193–225, 390, 398

start-up, 41, 231, 237–241, 243–244

supplier firm, 6–10, 20, 22, 64, 121, 124–125, 148, 373, 382, 384, 392

supply chain, 10, 21, 29, 41, 44–45, 47, 73, 80, 93–95, 120, 136–137, 139, 141–142, 147, 150, 183, 194, 204, 264, 326n3, 327, 330–331, 378, 383, 392

supply chain management, 14, 22, 40, 42, 47, 51, 72, 237, 327

sustainable development, 12

Sustaining Competitive and Responsible Enterprises (SCORE)/ILO SCORE, 66

sweatshop, 14, 78

Taiwan, 7, 20, 24, 31, 33–34, 42–43, 48–49, 59, 91–92, 96, 169, 270, 318–320, 323–324, 333, 335, 377–378, 393–394, 398

Tata Engineering and Locomotive Company (TELCO), 179–185, 188–189

Tata Motors, 183–189

Tata-Benz collaboration, 8

TCS, 9, 229, 233–235, 237–242

telecom equipment manufacturers, 8, 15, 257–260, 384, 391, 398

telecom equipment, 1, 8, 15, 157–172, 257–260, 267, 383–384, 391, 398–399

territoriality, 2–3
Toshiba, 24, 42, 119
Toyota, 2, 115, 140n5, 143–145, 177–178, 328–330
Toyota Production System (TPS), 143, 177
trade union, 82, 199–200, 206
TRIPS, 16, 279–281, 283–284, 286, 293–294, 303, 309, 311

underdevelopment, 305, 308, 355
United States Securities and Exchange Commission, 21
upgrading, 1, 7, 9–15, 20–21, 24–25, 28, 30–31, 34, 36, 51–52, 90–93, 95–100, 107–128, 132–136, 138, 142, 144–150, 152–153, 162, 182, 193–225, 243, 247–273, 280, 295, 298, 308, 310, 316–341, 370, 373, 381–384, 386, 389–392, 394–396, 398–399, 403

value-added operation, 20
vertically specialized industrialization (VSI), 17, 373–404
Vietnam, 35, 64, 66, 68, 71, 111–113, 126–127, 151, 203, 211–212, 217–220, 222n23, 335

wage-cutting, 69
Washington Consensus, 373, 377, 392
Wipro, 229, 234, 237–242
wire harnesses, 45, 60, 108, 113–119, 126–128
Wockhardt, 289, 291, 296, 299–300
workers' union, 70, 82
workforce management/Labour practices, 64, 66, 75–80
work-in-progress (WIP), 178
World Bank, 72, 127n11, 318, 377, 394
world factory, 87

ZTE, 8, 15, 157–168, 170–172, 249, 251–252, 256–261, 265, 269, 273, 384, 398

Name index

Abernathy, F. H., 94, 193, 205
Abrol, Dinesh, 16, 249, 284
Acemoglu, Daron, 3, 396
Ackerhans, Sophia, 296
Adhikari, R., 209
Ahmed, Neetu, 15
Ahuja, Simone, 176
Albaladejo, M., 283
Albuquerque, E. M., 352–354, 358
Almeida, S., 206–207
Amin, A., 93
Amit, Raphael, 383
Amsden, Alice H., 161, 317, 319, 351–352, 377–378
Anand, Bharat N., 135, 186, 188
Ante, S., 401
Arocena, R., 352–353, 358
Arond, E., 249
Arrighi, Giovanni, 2, 12
Athukorala, P., 135, 197, 199, 202–203, 207–208
Austin, James E., 162
Autor, David, 3, 396
Avnimelech, G., 363
Azmeh, S., 91, 94

Babbitt, Laura, 71
Baggonkar, Swaraj, 189
Bai, C.E., 90
Baines, T., 178–179
Bair, Jennifer, 8, 132, 195, 197
Bakker, Sjoerd, 332
Baldwin, Richard, 2, 375, 385
Bamber, Penny, 14, 108–110, 114, 120–126, 393
Banda, G., 352–353

Bandler, J., 26
Barnes, 133, 135
Barrientos, Stephanie, 247–248, 389
Barrows, G., 193, 221–222
Basalla, 1988, 367
Bathelt, H., 92, 94
Bazan, Luiza, 248, 337
Bazan and Navas-Aleman, 2001, 248
Bedi, N., 286
Bedi, P. M. S., 286
Bhattacharya, S., 144
Bhide, Amar, 9
Biesebroeack, J. V., 132
Birch, K., 96
Bloom, Nicholas, 66–67, 390
Borcard, S., 47
Boserup, Ester, 80
Bound, Kirsten, 189
Bowonder, B., 179–180, 182, 184–185
Boyd, D., 22
Brown, Drusilla, 68, 71, 390
Brown, Jacob, 330
Bruche, Gert, 182, 184–185
Buciuni, G., 50
Buckley, P. J., 169
Burke, D ., 26
Bustos, S., 387
Butollo, F., 91–92, 94, 98
Byun, Jin-kyung, 327

Cammett, M., 93
Cantrell, A., 26
Cantwell, Johnand, 164
Caro, Felipe, 327
Carré, F., 132
Cassiolato, J. E., 355
Caulfield, B., 40
Chae, Soohwan, 331
Chan, Jenny, 382, 401
Chan, R. K., 87–88, 91

Chandran, Pradeesh, 231
Chang, Ha-Joon, 317–319
Chang, W., 89
Chataway, J., 352
Chaudhuri, S., 284, 309, 311
Chen, J., 262
Chen, L., 92–93
Chen, Martha Alter, 350
Chen, S., 259
Chen, W., 92
Chen, Y. C., 88
Chen, Zhao, 1, 34
Cheng, J., 271
Cho, D. S., 159
Ch'oe, Chong-il, 336
Christensen, Clayton M., 32
Chu, W., 249
Chu, Wan-wen, 319
Chu, Yin-wah, 317, 319, 321
Clegg, L. J., 169
Coe, Neil, 8, 13, 93, 383
Coe and Heung (2015), 392
Collett, T., 330
Corredoira, R. A., 135
Coscia, M., 387
Courvisanos, J., 357
Cross, A. R., 169
Cui, X., 267
Cumbers, A., 96

Daly, Jack, 14, 35, 47, 108–110, 114, 126
Damodaran, Sumangala, 375
Datta, Amrita, 380
Davis, Dennis, 11, 80, 375
Dehejia, Rajeev, 68, 390
Delporte, C., 49
De Paolis, F., 88
Dhanjal, Swaraj Singh, 238
Dhar, B., 284
Di, Hongyang, 68, 390

Dias, R., 249
Dicken, P., 93, 96
Dicken, Peter, 327
Differding, E., 289, 292
Ding, C., 260
Ding, R., 263
Dissanayake, J., 209
Dolan, C. S., 24, 52
Dong, L., 262
Dong, Q., 260
Drangel, Jessica, 2
Du, Y., 90
Duffy, J., 28
Dunlop, J. T., 193, 205
Dunning, J. H., 168
Dunston, D., 400
Dutrénit, G., 353, 355
Dyck, R., 35

Eadicicco, L., 46
Eifert, Benn, 66, 390
Einhorn, B., 24, 28–29, 33, 43
Ekanayake, R., 202–203, 207
Ely, A., 249
Engardio, P., 24, 28–29, 33, 43
Ernst, Dieter, 2, 6, 28, 32, 51, 158
Estoque, Willy, 124–125
Evans, C. L., 193
Evans, Peter B., 317–319
Evans, Y., 91

Fan, C. C., 87
Fan, Peilei, 15, 157–158, 160, 162, 164,
    169, 248, 267
Fang, Cai, 381
Fang, N., 249
Fan Xu, 16
Federica, A., 296
Feenstra, Robert C., 197, 204, 318
Fernandez-Stark, Karina, 194, 317

Fernando, M., 206–207
Fernie, John, 66, 390
Finger, J. M., 220
Finotto, V., 50
Fluery, A., 135
Foley, F., 204
Fontana and Guerzoni, 2008, 357
Foy, Henry, 321, 331
Frederick, Stacey, 14, 108–112, 114,
    118–126, 195–196
Frederick, T. B., 35, 42
Freiberg, J., 400
Freiberg, K., 400
Fressoli, M., 249
Frey. E., 22
Fröbel, Folker, 323
Fuentes, A., 132
Fujita, M., 87, 89, 94
Fung, V., 193
Fung, W. K., 193
Furukawa (2012), 116

Gallien, Jérémie, 327
Gao, Xudongand, 170
George, Michael, 401
Gereffi, Gary, 2–3, 10, 14, 21–24, 52,
    80, 86–87, 89, 92, 111–112, 114, 118–
    126, 132, 194–197, 201, 247–249,
    316–320, 323, 326, 378, 386–387,
    389, 392–393
Ghose, Ajit, 380
Gibbon, P., 383
Giuliani, Elisa, 319
Goger, Anneliese, 66, 69, 390
Gomes, I., 399
Gopakumar, K. M., 284, 309
Gopinathan, Rajesh, 238
Goto, A., 161
Govindrajan, V., 399
Grabher, G., 95

Granovetter, M., 93
Granville, B., 283
Gregory, M., 31–32
Guinn, Andrew, 393
Gulati, R., 135
Gunawardana, Samanthi, 70, 200
Guo, Q., 95–96

Hale and Wills, 2007, 206
Halpern, N., 35
Hamel, G., 374
Hamilton, Gary G., 22–23, 197, 204,
    317–318
Hammond, J. H., 193, 205
Hanson, G., 88
Harrigan, J., 193, 221–222
Harsh, 14, 381, 391
Hassink, R., 95
Hausmann, R., 387
He, C., 86–89, 91–98
He, T., 262
Head, K., 89
Heilman, W., 49
Heinrichs, Jurgen, 323
Henderson, J., 86, 91
Henning, M., 95
Henry Wai-chung Yeung, 13
Hess, M., 93
Hidalgo, C. A., 387
Hirschman, A. O., 351, 354
Hirschman, Albert, 79
Hŏ, In-uk, 335
Hobday, Michael, 162, 247
Holstein, William J., 330
Horner, Rory, 8, 392
Hou, X., 260
Hou, Y., 261
Hsieh, Michelle F., 320
Hsing, Y. T., 87
Hsueh, R., 87

Hu, D., 87, 89, 94
Hu, G. Z., 163
Huang, Y., 249
Huasheng Zhu, 16
Hubka, David, 337
Hughes, T. P., 358, 363
Humphrey, John, 3, 9, 21, 24, 52, 92,
    132–133, 135, 137, 195, 247–248,
    319, 381

Ichinowski, C., 390
Immelt, J., 399–400
Inagaki, K., 42

Jacob, R., 209
Janne, Odille, 164
Jefferson, G. H., 163
Jeong, Gi-su, 331
Jiasu, L., 279
Jin, J., 248
Jin, X., 248
Johanson, J., 168
John, Sujit, 242
Jones, Daniel T., 178
Jordan, L.S., 72

Kalecki, Michał, 357
Kalinowski, Thomas, 317, 320
Kalyanaram, G., 159
Kamphuis, B., 72
Kanellos, M., 42
Kang, Man-sŏk, 336
Kang, Sandul, 332
Kaplan, David, 388
Kaplinsky, Raphael, 8–9, 11, 63, 80, 133,
    135, 365, 373, 375, 379, 384, 388
Kar, Sayantani, 176, 189
Kardes, F. R., 159
Katz, J., 353, 355
Kaufmann, Stuart, 401
Kawakami, M., 24, 36

Keely, L. C., 283
Kelegama, S., 204
Kelkar, Govind, 402
Kenney, Martin, 1
Khanna, T., 135
Kim, D. J., 159
Kim, Dal, 330
Kim, Dongeun, 331
Kim, Jong-Cheol, 320
Kim, Linsu, 162, 171, 319
Kim, Seungyong, 332
Knorringa, Peter, 137, 318, 338
Kong, L., 248
Kowalski, Przemyslaw, 110
Kreinin, M. E., 220
Kreye, Otto, 323
Krishna and Tan, 2001, 221
Kuang, D., 262
Kuemmerle, W., 164–165
Kumar, Abhishek, 13, 395
Kumaraswamy, A., 135
Kurup, R., 241
Kwon, Seung-Ho, 329
Kýzýlgün, O., 204

Lakenan, B., 22
Lal, D., 197
Lall, S., 283, 351
Lan, T., 87
Lansbury, Russell D., 329
Lashinsky, A., 40
Lastres, H. M. M., 355
Lee, Im-ja, 326
Lee, Jae-Duk, 323, 326
Lee, Joonkoo, 16, 319–321, 334–337
Lee, P. K., 90
Lee, Sang-Hoon, 16
Lei, B., 249
Lemoine and Ünal-Kesenci, 2004, 86

Lent, John A., 332–333
Leonard, C. S., 283
Leonard-Barton, Dorothy, 162, 247
Lewin, Ariel, 1, 32–33
Lewis, Arthur, 349
Li, G., 98
Li, H. Y., 93
Li, L., 249, 270
Li, M., 264
Li, P. F., 92, 94–96, 98
Li, P. P., 169
Li, Y., 258, 264
Liao, H., 87–88, 91
Lieberman, M. B., 159
Light, Donald W., 402
Lim, Chaisung, 186–187
Lim, Jinho, 320
Lin, B., 279
Lin, G. C. S., 98
Lin, H. L., 93, 98
Lin, J. Y., 89
Lin, Xirong, 71
Lipton, J., 36
Liu, C., 258
Liu, Jianxin, 170
Liu, S., 262, 265
Liu, W., 96
Liu, X., 169
Liu, Y., 91–92
Lohr, Steve, 113
Lopez-Acevedo, G., 208
Lu, J., 265
Lu, Ming, 1
Lu, Y., 92
Luethje, B., 23–24, 33, 47
Luk, L., 31
Lundin, N., 32
Lundvall, 1992, 352
Luo, Y., 169

Ma, L.J.C., 88
Ma, Y., 261
Maat, Kees, 332
MacKinnon, D., 96
Mackintosh, M., 352–353
MacMillan, I. C., 89
Mahajan, Aprajit, 66, 390
Malerba, F, 351
Malik, V., 147
Marcolin, Luca, 396–397
Maree, Johann, 388
Markoff, J., 45
Marks, Michael, 43
Marquis, D. G., 357
Marshall, A., 93
Martin, R., 95
Massini, S., 32
Mathews, J. A., 163
Mazzucato, Mariana, 401
McClearn, M., 47
McDermott, G. A., 135
McIntyre, 2008, 206
McKenzie, David, 66–67, 390
McMaster, R., 96
McMillan, J., 86, 88
McNamara, Michael, 45
Mehta, Balwant, 80
Mei, L., 87, 90
Memedovic, O., 135
Metcalfe, J. S., 352–354
Metraux, N., 47
Mi, Y., 259
Milanovic, Branko, 386
Milberg, William, 14, 374–375, 387, 396
Minter, Steve, 29
Mirodout, Sebastien, 396
Mishra, D. D., 237
Mishra, Sunil, 380
Mo, Sejun, 331–332

Mokyr, Joel, 393, 401–402
Montgomery, D. B., 159
Moolgaokar, Sumant, 180
Moon, Nam-Cheol, 325
Morgan, T. P., 41, 43
Morris, Mike, 11, 80, 375, 388
Mudambi, Ram, 135, 319
Murgia, M., 26
Murmann, Johann Peter, 1
Myers, S., 357

Nadhe, Shivani Shinde, 238
Nadvi, K., 86, 91, 137
Nathan, Dev, 1–2, 8, 13–14, 16, 80, 374, 379, 381, 387, 390–391, 395, 402
Natrajan, Ganesh, 231
Naughton, B., 86, 88–89
Navas-Alemán, Lizbeth, 318, 337
Nayyar, Deepak, 2, 374, 385
Neidik and Gereffi, 2006, 195–196
Nelson, R., 351–352
Nie, X., 249
Niosi, Jorge, 121, 164, 169
Nirmal, Rajalakshmi, 241
Njenga, Kamotho, 388
Nohria, N., 135
Nordås, H. K., 209
North, D. C., 88
Nubler, Irmgaard, 5, 65

Oldenski, L., 397
Omwansa, Tommy, 388

Palepu, Krishna G., 186, 188–189
Pang, R., 260
Papaioannou, T., 249, 353, 356
Park, Byung-il, 330
Park, C., 309
Park, Gwanho, 16
Park, Jaewoo, 331–332

Park, Soojin, 331
Pasinetti, L. L., 352–353
Peeters, C., 32
Perez, B., 48
Perez, C., 353
Perry, Patsy, 66, 206, 390
Peters, E. D., 195, 197
Phadnis, Shilpa, 242
Pickles, J., 87–88, 90–95, 98, 383
Pickles and Smith (2016), 383
Pietrobelli, Carlo, 318–319
Pike, A., 96
Pillai, P., 394
Pink, Daniel H., 28
Piontak, Rachel, 388
Piore, Michael, 69
Pipkin, S., 132
Pirie, Iain, 317
Pisano, G., 236–237
Pisano, Gary, 392
Poncet, S., 90
Ponte, S., 383
Post, S., 362
Prabhu, Jaideep, 176
Prahalad, C. K., 374, 399
Pun, Ngai, 382, 401
Punit, Itika Sharma, 243

Qian, J., 163
Qingcan He, 16
Quinn, J.B., 28

Rabellotti, Roberta, 319
Radjou, Navi, 176
Rajapatirana, S., 197, 208
Raj-Reichert, Gale, 14, 23, 52, 382
Ramani, 2015, 364
Ratnam, Venkata, 82
Raugust, Karen, 333, 337
Reddy, A. K. N., 358, 363, 369

Reddy, P., 164
Reddy, Sanjay, 133
Rhee, D. -K., 159
Ries, J., 89
Roberts, John, 66, 390
Robertson, Raymond, 68, 390
Rodgers, Gerry, 380
Rodgers, Janine, 380
Rosa, J. A., 248
Rossi, A., 247–248
Rossi, Arianna, 389
Rothbert, 1942, 357
Ruwanpura, Kanchana, 66, 69–70, 207, 390

Sabel, Charles, 69, 133
Sachs, Jeffrey, 1
Saliola, Federica, 318
Samii, R., 144
Saranga, H., 135
Sarkar, Sandip, 1–2, 8, 13, 80, 374, 379, 381, 387, 395
Savchenko, Y., 208
Schamp, E. W., 95
Schmitz, G., 195
Schmitz, Hubert, 9, 24, 132, 137, 247–248, 318–319, 338, 381
Schmookler (1966), 357
Schoemaker, Paul, 383
Schuen, Amy, 392
Schumpeter, Joseph, 11, 351
Scott, A. J., 87, 91, 93
Selden, Mark, 382, 401
Serger, S. S., 32
Setia, S., 72
Sha, S., 279
Shambaugh, David, 1
Sharma, Alakh, 308, 380
Shaw, K., 390
Shen, L., 266
Shen, Xiaobai, 158, 161

Shi, N., 261
Shi, Y., 31–32
Shih, Stan, 14, 396
Shim, Doobo, 332
Shin, Dong-yun, 95, 332
Shinyekwa, Isaac, 388
Shuen, A., 236–237
Sierzchula, William, 332
Simhan, T. E. Raja, 189
Singh, Ajit, 169
Singh, Nidhi, 16
Singh, Shelly, 231
Sito, Tom, 333
Sjöberg, Ö., 88
Sjöholm, F., 88
Smith, A., 91, 94, 249
Smith, J., 352
Smith-Gillespie, Aleyn, 161
Soni, Pavan, 236–237
Squicciarini, Mariagrazia, 396
Srinivas, Smita, 16, 350–354, 356,
    358–362, 364–368, 393, 402
Srinivasan, Vishnu, 189
Stam, E., 95
Staritz, C., 205, 209, 222
Steinman, C., 36
Storper, M., 88, 92–93
Strover, Sharon, 337
Sturgeon, Timothy, 3, 7, 21–22, 24, 35–
    36, 92, 114, 126, 132, 378, 386–387
Suh, Chung-Sok, 329
Sun, H., 89
Sun, Y., 258
Sunley, P., 95
Sutton, J., 135
Sutz, J., 352–353, 358–359, 364–366,
    368
Szapiro, M. H., 355

Taglioni, Daria, 110
Tahilyani, Rachna, 186, 188

Tan, Z. A., 171
Tao, Z., 90
Teece, D. J., 236–237
Teese, David J., 392
Tendler, J., 133
Teubal, M., 363
Tewari, Meenu, 1, 8, 15, 94, 135, 137,
    151, 204, 374, 394
Thornton, Ian, 189
Thrift, N., 93
Tian, C., 248, 270
Tibandebage, P., 352–353
Tokatli, N., 94, 204, 249
Tong, S. Y., 90
Trimble, C., 399
Tschang, F. T., 164, 169
Tschang, T., 161
Tse, P., 31–32
Tung, R. L., 169
Tyabji, Nasir, 15

Vahlne, J. E., 168
Vallas, Milt, 334
van Liemt, Gijsbert, 35, 42, 46
Veeramani, C., 135, 151
Viswanathan, M., 248
Volpe, A., 94
Von Hippel, E., 357
Voss, H., 169

Wai-chung Yeung, Henry, 383
Wallack, T., 36
Wamae, W., 352–353
Wang, C., 98
Wang, J., 87, 90, 93–94, 260, 266
Wang, Jenn-Hwan, 319, 321
Wang, L., 260
Wang, P., 258–259
Wang, S., 264
Wang, W., 381

Wang, X., 262
Wang, Y., 89
Wang, Z., 257
Wassenhove, L. N. V., 144
Wawatsontson-Hemphill, Kimberly, 401
Wee, Bert van, 332
Weeratunge, C., 209
Wei, Y., 88, 263
Wei, Y. H. D., 86–89, 92–97
Weidner, K. L., 248
Weil, D., 94, 193, 205
Weinswig, D., 40
Wen, H., 248
Wen, M., 87, 94
Wenting, R., 95
Werner, Marion, 6, 8, 390
Wijesiri, J., 209
Williams, Robin, 161
Wilson, P., 362
Wind, Y., 193
Winkler, Deborah, 14, 110, 374–375, 387, 396
Womack, James P., 178
Wong, Joseph, 319
Woo, Meredith Jung-En, 320
Woo, Wing Thye, 1
Woo-Cumings, 1999, 318
Wood, Steve, 66, 390
Woodruff, C., 66–67
Works, James, 401
Wrigley, N., 207

Wu, D., 264
Wyman, Donald L., 319

Xie, Rui, 249
Xie, X., 86–89, 94

Yang, C., 87–88, 90–91, 93–96, 98
Yang, C. H., 91–93
Yang, H., 258
Yang, Q., 248
Yi, Byŏng-uk, 333
Yi, D., 265
Yi, F., 271
Yildirim, Md. A., 387
Yim, Haksoon, 337
Yip, A., 31–32
Young, 1928, 354
Yu, Kie-Un, 332–333

Zaheer, A., 135
Zedtwitz, M. von, 248
Zhai, E ., 22, 25, 28, 31–32
Zhang, L., 90, 263
Zhang, Q., 157
Zhang, Y., 261
Zhao, X. B., 90
Zhegu, Majlinda, 121
Zheng, P., 169
Zhou, L., 262
Zhou, S., 248
Zhu, 381
Zhu, Shengun, 14, 86–88, 90–98, 251